Fishers of Men or Founders of Empire?

The Wycliffe Bible Translators in Latin America

David Stoll

Zed Press, 57 Caledonian Road, London N1 9DN

Cultural Survival Inc., 11 Divinity Avenue, Cambridge, Mass 02138

Fishers of Men or Founders or Empire? was
first published by Zed Press, 57 Caledonian
Road, London N1 9DN, with the financial
assistance of Cultural Survival Inc., 11 Divinity
Avenue, Cambridge, Mass 02138, U.S.A., in
1982.

Copyright © David Stoll, 1982

Copyedited by Anna Gourlay
Proofread by Mark Gourlay
Typeset by Lyn Caldwell
Cover design by Jan Brown
Printed by Krips Repro, Meppel, Holland.

U.S. Distributor
Lawrence Hill and Co., 520 Riverside
Avenue, Westport, Conn. 06880, U.S.A.

**British Library Cataloguing in Publication
Data**

Stoll, David
    Fishers or men or founders of empire?
    1.   Summer Institute of Linguistics
    2.   Underdeveloped areas — Missions
    I.   Title
    266'.009172'2   BV2750

    ISBN 0-86232-111-5
    ISBN 0-86232-112-3 Pbk

Contents

Preface   vii

1. **Death of a Bible Translator**   1
   The Power of the Word   3
   The Evangelical Advance in Latin America   7
   Pax Americana and the Patronage Battle   9
   All Things to All Men   11
   Popular Views of Bible Translation   14

2. **The Founder in Guatemala**   19
   Thy Kingdom Come   22
   The Great Tribulation   25
   Progress, *Cargo* and Protestantism   30
   The Linguistic Approach   36
   We Are Christians Now, Sir   39
   Bible as Weapon   42
   The Rapture of the Saints   45
   Today There Is Liberty in Guatemala!   47
   Spiritual Revolution: Let God Fight Our Battles   51
   Spiritual Revolution: We Are An Exploited People   53
   Judgement Day in the Zone of the Generals   55

3. **From Mexico to Vietnam**   62
   The Miracle of Tetelcingo   65
   The Lord Himself Didn't Tell the Whole Story   71
   Mr. Townsend Goes to Washington   80
   The Good Neighbours Go To Vietnam   86
   Looking the Other Way in the Philippines   92

4. **The Summer Institute in Peru**   98
   Principal Backers   102

The Mysterious Wicleffe   109
The Founder Adjusts His Halo   111
The Bilingual Schools   114
Indian Apostles   120
Culture and Faith   125
Spiritual Warfare   129

5.   **The Summer Institute in Peru: Part 2**   138
Spiritual Guides for the Settlers   143
Cushillococha   146
Who Preaches God's Word Down Here?   150
The Conscience of the Bureaucracy   155
In Search of a New Rationale   157

6.   **The Summer Institute in Colombia**   165
Opening the Door   166
Planas and CRIC   169
The Vaupes   173
The Appeal to the State   178
They Divide Us Among Institutes   179
Occult Power   181
Satan's Kingdom   185
The Sierra Nevada   188
A Leftist Terrorist Bullet   191

7.   **Conspiracy Theory and State Expansion**   198
God Intervenes in Peru   201
SIL-Peru's Thirty-Fifth Anniversary   207
Ecuador   211
Colonels for Christ: Bolivia   217
Brazil   219
Panama   222
Mexico   223
Sundered Forever   230

8.   **International Linguistic Center**   237
To Every Nation   241
India and Nepal   242
Africa   243
Papua New Guinea   244
Indonesia   245

Post-Vietnam Asia 246
Latin America and the World 248
SIL Linguistics and Literacy Work 249
Faith Finance 259
The Bases and the Members 263
Charismatic Renewal 268

9. The Huaorani Go To Market 278
The Palm Beach Martyrs 281
The Conversion of Dayuma 285
The Foundation of Tigueno 288
The Removal 291
Protectorate and Pursuit of Liberty 298
SIL Sends an Anthropologist 302
Nampa 305
Rachel Saint Removed 307
The Palm Beach Shrine 309
Authentic and Ruined Aucas 312

Bibliography 323

Index 337

Tables

1. Summer Institute Branches, Field Areas and Advances, 1981 319
2. Wycliffe Home Divisions and Other Sending Countries, 1981 322

Maps

1. Southern Mexico, Guatemala, and El Salvador 20
2. The Western Guatemalan Highlands 21
3. The Peruvian Amazon 105
4. Language Groups of the Peruvian Amazon 106
5. Colombia 139
6. Huaorani Territory in Eastern Ecuador: Auca Zone of Protection 280

Cultural Survival Inc.

Cultural Survival Inc., a non-profit organization founded in 1972, is dedicated to the physical and cultural survival of indigenous peoples. Many cultures have vanished already and with them their irreplaceable knowledge and wisdom.

In the name of civilization and development, indigenous peoples are often deprived of their belief systems and their lands. Contact with industrial societies often causes social destruction through disease, destitution and despair. Cultural survival for indigenous peoples means the possibility of adapting in their own way, at their own pace, to the outside world.

Through research, publications and projects on five continents, Cultural Survival works with indigenous peoples to help them retain control over their own destinies. Indigenous peoples design and implement many of their own projects, while Cultural Survival supports and records them. Project evaluations serve as models for other indigenous peoples in similar circumstances.

Cultural Survival's activities are based on the premise that culture is a set of mechanisms which permit a group to have a sense of itself, to comprehend its situation, and to adapt to changing circumstances. Indigenous peoples do not want to be kept in 'human zoos'. Cultural Survival therefore does not work to preserve 'traditional' societies, but rather to maintain those mechanisms which permit a group to successfully adapt to change. Central among these is a positive self-image — respect for one's history and pride in one's self.

It is in this spirit that we support David Stoll's critique of the Summer Institute of Linguistics. SIL has become the world's largest international organization working with indigenous peoples, in part by cultivating a non-sectarian, scientific image. Its primary purpose, however, is to propagate evangelical Christianity in each community it enters. Unfortunately, salvation, as SIL understands it, requires the destruction of critical features of indigenous belief systems.

The group's practice of obtaining government backing for evangelism has multiplied questionable relationships with colonizing forces. Backed by ample resources, fellow 'believers' are elevated in every indigenous group leading to the promotion, and in many cases the imposition, of SIL's convictions. The resulting internal conflicts have prompted a vigorous reaction from Indian organizations and their allies. The fundamental issue, we believe, is that SIL's programme can undermine the cohesion of native communities — a cohesion essential for their defence against further colonization. We think that this book will contribute to the debate not just over SIL and other religious missions but all groups involved in the issues of cultural survival.

Preface

As this book went to press, its leading figure died peacefully near his home in North Carolina. William Cameron Townsend was eighty·five. The struggles over the organization he founded, known variously as the Summer Institute of Linguistics (SIL) and the Wycliffe Bible Translators (WBT), will surely continue. The first chapter introduces the central preoccupation of this work, the controversies over the group in Latin America. Chapters 2-4 explore SIL/WBT's formative years in Guatemala, Mexico and Peru. The group's wellspring in North American millennialism, its political alliances (with an excursion to South East Asia), its programme in the Central American highlands and in the Amazon jungle all come into play. The next three chapters describe the last decade of conflict in Peru, Colombia, Ecuador, Brazil and Mexico. Chapter 8 surveys SIL/WBT's activities in Africa and Asia, its technical competence, home financial base, membership, and response to the Latin American crisis. The last chapter traces the rise and fall of Wycliffe's most famous mission, to the Aucas or Huaorani of Ecuador.

What follows is indebted to the work of numerous people, among them Cameron Townsend, Ethel Emily Wallis, James and Marti Hefley, James Yost, Matthew Huxley, Laurie Hart, Scott Robinson, Stefano Varese, Robert Wasserstrom, Jan Rus, Peter Aaby, Soren Hvalkof, Thomas Moore, Richard Chase Smith, Stephen Corry, Douglas Brintnall, Marcel D'Ans, Jon Landabaru, Sheldon Annis and Robin Wright. I wish to thank SIL/WBT members, a number of other missionaries, and the native communities I visited for their kind hospitality. A special thanks is also due to the Louis M. Rabinowitz Foundation, and to the friends and family members who made this book possible.

David Stoll
August 1982

1. Death of a Bible Translator

The Lord, Chester Bitterman's friends realized after he was dead, had been preparing him for this moment all along. Two days before he was kidnapped, had he not mentioned that someone might have to die to take God's Word to the Indians of Colombia? 'I know this was God's ministry for Chet,' his widow declared. 'He was chosen!'[1] Bitterman had been chosen for martyrdom. When kidnappers shot him through the heart on 7 March 1981, they bestowed an honour previously reserved for Catholic missionaries, whom governments had killed for protesting against official terror. North American evangelical Protestants have rarely committed that offence: while advising converts to avoid politics, many have felt obliged to disclose the mystical unity between protest movements and the Devil. Now, for the first time, Latin American guerrillas were said to have murdered a missionary for having belonged to an alleged CIA front.

Bitterman's organization, the Wycliffe Bible Translators, is one of the largest of hundreds of North American-based enterprises dedicated to evangelizing the world. At the present rate, evangelical Protestant missionaries from the United States will double to 80,000 over the next decade.[2] Wycliffe's part in this expedition is translating the New Testament for the last unreached peoples. That has made it the most extensive linguistic operation in the world: recently its 4,300 missionaries were at work in more than 700 languages and entering a new one every eight days.[3] They hope to complete the Great Commission – 'go and make disciples of all nations' – by the end of this century.[4] When churches have emerged among all peoples, many evangelicals believe, Jesus Christ will return to reign over the earth for a thousand years.

While the Lord tarries, his emissaries are caught up in the great social upheavals of our time. With their ties from the local to the international level, Christian missions meet needs which governments do not. Even where missions no longer rule kingdoms of God on earth, they wield spiritual authority in contended terrain. At a time when religion is once again proving a great mobilizer of the poor, they have their fingers on the pulse of social revolution. Like few other outsiders in the Third World, missionaries have the power to support or hinder, bless or interdict the struggle for a better world here and now.

The question of which took the life of Chester Bitterman. The languages Wycliffe studies are spoken by indigenous hunters and farmers. Not only are their lands just as coveted as their souls: they are organizing to defend themselves nad, in the view of the powers of this world, are ripe for subversion. In the wind-swept, rolling grasslands of Eastern Colombia where Wycliffe buried its translator, guerrillas, drug mafias and government troops dicker for profits and supremacy. As cattle ranchers invade native land and North American corporations discover oil, missionaries of hostile ideological stripe vie for influence over Indians organizing into co-operatives, congregations and councils.

Here and elsewhere on the Latin American frontiers, Wycliffe has fielded linguistic missionaries in more than 300 languages, supported by air and radio networks and sponsored by governments. Although it has started to lose government contracts which it may not regain, and saved others thanks only to what it considers divine intervention, in the mid-1970s Wycliffe was an official arm of the governments of Mexico, Guatemala, Honduras, Panama, Surinam, Colombia, Ecuador, Peru, Bolivia and Brazil. Unless all the mission orders of the Roman Catholic Church were counted as one, no other transnational organization surpassed Wycliffe's influence among Indians. None matched its command of Indian languages and loyalties, its logistical system and official connections. Nor did any collide so spectacularly with Indian civil rights organizing and Latin American nationalism. The ties binding together this interior empire, to native people and to governments, started to snap.

For professional friends of the Indian, the 1970s was a competitive decade. Having broken ground for much of the civil rights organizing, missionaries, indigenist scholars and bureaucrats found themselves trapped between Indian militants and frightened, frequently brutal governments. Wycliffe's government contracts and fundamentalist theology left it in a particularly embarrassing position. With eternity uppermost in mind — would their charges go to heaven or hell? — translators continued to use the languages of native people to campaign against their religious traditions. Not only were many Indians rallying round those traditions: while they were trying to overcome their differences, Wycliffe insisted on separating out the saved from the lost. To defend themselves Indians defied governments: Wycliffe, to the contrary, believed that its official sponsors should be obeyed because they were divinely ordained. Bible translators began to appear on the agenda of Indian congresses as a threat to unity, land, culture and liberation.

As Indian followings passed into open rebellion, wavered or simply seemed ripe for the picking, patronage battles — power struggles between competitors for Indian loyalty and official backing — took on new overtones. While some like Wycliffe continued to proclaim their loyalty to the old regime, others started to support traditional Indian values and the militant defence of land. A new generation of evangelizers, protectionists, revolutionaries and government agents flooded into native communities, all determined to enlist Indians in contradictory plans for their future. The presumed beneficiaries tried to drive the best possible bargain with their benefactors, hedge their bets if not play rivals against each other, and expel those who caused more trouble than they were worth. In the Andes Indian nationalists proclaimed the return of the Inca Empire. In Guatemala, Christian farmers took up arms against government by murder. New alliances between Indians and wings of the colonizing society contended with older ones.

Patronage battles ignited the nationalist wrath which began to drive Wycliffe from official favour. Conflicts between translators and Indians became entangled with power struggles between Wycliffe and rival friends of the Indian, which were taken up by university committees, journalists and politicians who alerted the nation to its peril. Wycliffe's ambiguity, its divisive influence in native communities and defence of its contracts at high levels of state fuelled CIA suspicion. In country after country anti-imperialists accused it of destroying Indian culture, prospecting for minerals, and operating as an early warning system against political protest. To Wycliffe the controversies were the work of anthropologists and Marxists, probably masterminded from Havana and certainly by Satan, to drive the Lord's work from Indian territory and foment subversion.

At immediate stake in this war between left- and right-wing conspiracy theory is influence over native people and the direction they take in defending themselves. But there is another contest in the innuendo, one symbolized by the official assassinations of Catholic clergy and the, to date, unusual death of Chester Bitterman. It is for the loyalty of millions of Latin American evangelicals, who are caught between the fear of Godless Communism inculcated by their missionaries and their fear of the leading terrorist groups in Latin America, the U.S. -supported military forces of their own governments.

The Power of the Word

Like his colleagues, Chester Bitterman left the United States as a missionary of the Wycliffe Bible Translators (WBT) but arrived in the field as something else, a scientific investigator of the Summer Institute of Linguistics (SIL). While the memberships and boards of directors of the two entities are identical, the transformation is all-important to SIL/WBT's conception of the Lord's work. Its premises began to take shape early in this century, when Protestants who still believed that Reason and Revelation added up to Truth — the Fundamentalists — tried to purge evolutionary views of the Bible from the mainline denominations. Repulsed and ridiculed, many withdrew to start their own enterprises. In the 1940s, the less sectarian began to call themselves evangelicals: rather than excommunicate each other in doctrinal squabbles, they agreed to offer salvation to whoever would listen. By appealing to imperilled Gospel truth, fundamentalist entrepreneurs marshalled the followings which now seem the dominant force in North American Protestantism.

SIL/WBT's founder, William Cameron Townsend (1896-1982), began his career as a Bible salesman in Guatemala. Revered among the membership as Uncle Cam, he made his life's work overcoming linguistic and political resistance to

3

his product. From the start, Townsend recognized the value of evangelizing in native languages and translating the New Testament. Burdened by hundreds of tribes without the Bible, in 1934 he started a summer camp in Arkansas to equip missionaries with descriptive linguistics. It was named after John Wycliffe, the 14th Century 'Morning Star of the Reformation', who is honoured as the first translator of the Bible into English.

To get his latter-day Wycliffes into all those languages, Townsend knew that he would have to overcome a second barrier, the 'closed door' or 'political exclusion'.[5] To open these doors he conceived another policy, the gradual disclosure of his plans to those who might oppose them. In 1936 he and his first Camp Wycliffe alumni chartered themselves as the Summer Institute of Linguistics. Then, to reassure North American church-goers that this strange procedure was an evangelical mission, in 1942 they also incorporated as the Wycliffe Bible Translators. By going into the field as Summer Institute linguists rather than Wycliffe missionaries, they obtained long-term contracts from anti-clerical and Roman Catholic governments alike. In exchange for language studies, literacy work, and other services such as the 'moral improvement' of Indians, governments allowed a linguistic institute to operate wherever it please.[6]

Where church and state were one, or where the state had turned against the church, or just to maintain appearances, evangelical missionaries therefore joined the state. To avoid misunderstandings with official sponsors, Townsend instructed his followers to 'obey the government, for God is the one who has put it there,' a practice which SIL/WBT considers apolitical Christian service.[7] Nor were members ever to criticize their adopted governments in public, a policy they have maintained faithfully to the present. Meanwhile, Townsend was hitching the Lord's work to larger causes which might advance it, at home in churches and Washington, D.C., as well as in foreign capitals. Fundamentalist Red scares, Latin American nationalism, the defence of the Free World, the conquest of the Amazon, the Alliance for Progress and even Soviet-American detente all took God's Word into more languages. 'Bible translation' came to include anything from teaching native people to count money, to maintaining the short take-off and landing aircraft of the Peruvian Army. By the time a supposedly non-sectarian, non-ecclesiastical and non-missionary language institute began to produce the conflict, even bloodshed associated with evangelical church-planting, it had proved its value to the government. The regime supported SIL against its enemies: evangelical missionaries, who still insisted that they were no such thing, continued to foster congregations under state and scientific charter. 'That's our goal,' declared Cam. 'Two thousand tongues to go!'[8]

To protect these state contracts, the Summer Institute and Wycliffe insist that they are two organizations. Once identified as one and the same organization, it becomes apparent that a linguistic institute is a faith mission, whose every activity is intended to serve evangelism. Yet to most SIL/WBT members, the evasion is simply how the Lord goes about his work. They can cite Scripture to prove it. For decades some North American brethren were not impressed: they felt that SIL/WBT was violating the separation of church and state, entering into unholy alliances for the sake of expediency, and generally being dishonest. Gradually its success in penetrating closed fields and making converts demonstrated that it was a worthy cause. To this day SIL can prove, to its own satisfaction if no one else's, that it is not really a religious mission.

Wycliffe is the fund-raising and recruiting arm in the SIL/WBT division of labour, the guarantee that its linguists really are missionaries whose Bibles inspire new congregations. Headquartered in Huntington Beach, California, Wycliffe consists of national 'home divisions'. The U.S. division dwarfs the others, accounting for 71% of Wycliffe personnel around the world and 86% in Latin America. Another 20% come from Canada, Australia and Britain, with most of the rest from North-western Europe and New Zealand.[9]

Like many evangelical groups, Wycliffe is non-denominational. That is, its mandatory statement of doctrine is broad enough to include most evangelical Protestants.* The Bible is no vague inspiration for most members: it does things, on a battleground in which God and Satan contend for each soul. When members pray, perhaps by 'claiming' a Bible verse which promises what they seek, they expect answers and even miracles whether to cure a cancer or save a contract. Wycliffe does attempt to be more flexible than many evangelical groups: some translators even seem uncomfortable with their doctrinal provision for eternal punishment of the lost. Yet all but renegades believe that happiness in this life and the next is predicated on beliefs rather like their own.

As faith missionaries, each member 'looks to the Lord' to provide churches or individuals to supply financial needs, usually starting in the congregation where they grew up.[11] The Wycliffe publicity apparatus (about 50 books to date, dozens of movies and filmstrips, rallies, 200 dinner meetings a year, church nights, a monthly newspaper, a radio programme, branch and personal bulletins requesting prayer) provides the halo, by explaining how the Bible works miracles among native people oppressed by evil spirits and therefore in need of what they have never heard of. According to Wycliffe, this combination of home town intimacy and far-off glory provided most of its $26.5 million income in 1980.[12]

As SIL/WBT's training and operational arm, the Summer Institute does not consider itself a mission because its Bible translations, not its members, are responsible for any spiritual results. It is organized into field branches and

---

* Every six years, or before returning to the field from furlough, each member must reaffirm his/her belief in the Wycliffe Statement of Doctrine. Should their views on these fundamental truths change, applicants are informed, they must be prepared to resign. The statement consists of: '1) The doctrine of the Trinity; 2) The fall of man, his consequent moral depravity and his need of regeneration; 3) The atonement through the substitutionary death of Christ; 4) The doctrine of justification by faith; 5) The resurrection of the body, both in the case of the just and of the unjust; 6) The eternal life of the saved and the eternal punishment of the lost; 7) The divine inspiration the consequent authority of the whole canonical Scriptures' — the membership having instructed the board of directors' to interpret the last point as implying Scriptual inerrancy.'[10]

area offices which operate in more than 40 countries, chiefly in Latin America, Africa and along the Asian rim of the Pacific. Translators work unannounced where the government is ill-disposed; elsewhere their welcome includes offices in government ministries. Headquarters are in Dallas at SIL's International Linguistic Centre, which is affiliated with the University of Texas at Arlington. The Universities of Oklahoma, North Dakota and Washington have also lent their credentials to SIL, through its summer schools which, here and elsewhere, have trained more than 18,000 people most of them would-be evangelical missionaries, in descriptive linguistics.[13]

In the field SIL is a spectacle of dedication and technology which invites endless speculation. At its 'bases', now being renamed 'centres' to avoid the military connotation, as many as several hundred language technicians, support personnel and children live, work and pray together. The result tends to resemble a North American suburb, administered like a collective farm, in a vacation resort setting. Even after years in Spanish-speaking countries, a large fraction of the membership cannot carry on a conversation in this language. Thirteen branches enjoy the services of their own bush airline, the Jungle Aviation and Radio Service (JAARS). Headquartered near Charlotte, North Carolina, JAARS maintains 69 aircraft: light airplanes, small helicopters and DC-3 transports – along with SIL's radio networks and computers.[14]

To produce New Testaments and reading publics, translation teams – usually a married couple or two single women – shuttle between the base and native communities for several decades. By dispensing medicine, trade goods and wages in exchange for language help, airstrip construction and so forth, many teams have drawn native people into new political economies revolving around themselves. Each year they invite a few language informants to the base for intensive linguistic study, extraction of closely held beliefs, training in skills such as teaching, sometimes major medical care and – although SIL denies that it evangelizes – conversion to evangelical Christianity. Conveniently enough, Bible translation is an intensive form of Bible study. By removing paid assistants from their homes to the base, translators bring them 'face to face with the truth' – the power of the Word which, in Wycliffe's view, effects conversion.[15] Back home, the converted informants are expected to organize congregations under translator supervision. Where possible, SIL has trained its first converts as government bilingual teachers, turning state schools into evangelical pulpits and, in some cases, extending the religious campaign to dozens of communities and thousands of people.

Operating as SIL does, on mutual obligations with governments and native people, 'service' is an important word in its vocabulary. Whether educational, medical or air transport and radio, its services are often the best or the only ones available. Against much opposition SIL has championed bilingual education, a point on which more and more native people are insisting. Vaccination campaigns and emergency medical care have undoubtedly saved thousands of lives. For governments, 'service' is a function SIL shares with other philanthropists: socializing native people to accept state control and an expanding market economy.

The Evangelical Advance in Latin America

Except for a two-fifths contribution from other countries, chiefly in North-western Europe and the British Commonwealth, evangelical world mission is a U.S. enterprise.[16] This is especially so in Latin America, where most Protestant missionaries are North Americans. At one time the majority were commissioned by the mainline denominations affiliated to the World Council of Churches (WCC). But as the WCC became preoccupied with social justice, many of its missionaries left the field to national churches. Their withdrawal was more than compensated for by the evangelicals, for whom social justice has been less important than extending the only ladder of escape from eternal perdition.

Together with smaller numbers of ecumenical WCC Protestants, Roman Catholics and Mormons, evangelical missionaries are the most dedicated U.S. presence among the lower classes of the Third World. This fact has not been lost on their government, which subsidizes mission relief and technical aid through the U.S. Agency for International Development (USAID). Nor has it been lost on the Central Intelligence Agency (CIA).[17] Following exposure and church protest, in 1976 the CIA said that it would stop recruiting missionary collaborators.[18] A proposed CIA charter would prohibit paid use of U.S. missionaries but permit 'voluntary contacts or voluntary exchange of information.'[19]

Since the Vietnam War, more evangelicals have tried to distinguish between Christian duty and U.S. empire. But if only evangelicals read the Bible correctly, then the United States happens to the world capital of true religion. If Soviet imperialism, social revolution and rejection of the Gospel have a common origin in Satan, then foreign crisis reinforces the equation between true religion and the United States. And if salvation centres on transformation of the human heart, then Christians must not prejudice their mission by challenging the social order, that is, they must be 'non-political'. Thanks to this deeply embedded logic, most mission reformers are reduced to calling for 'social concern' and trying to overcome 'cultural distortion' of the Gospel, when the outstanding problem, as the crisis of the socially concerned and culturally conscious Wycliffe now demonstrates, is political.

North American convictions have had a clear impact on Latin American evangelicals. Converts may explain that the power and the glory of the United States is due to its Biblical (Protestant) foundation, and that the lack of one is the reason for Latin America's misfortune. Or mistranslate Romans 13:1 to prove that all existing governments, more precisely those sympathetic to North American evangelicals, must be obeyed because they are divinely ordained ('Every Christian ought to obey the civil authorities', the verse more properly reads, 'for all legitimate authority is derived from God's authority').[20] Or while warning against 'communists' in broad diabolical terms, explain that Christians refrain from political activity.

Much of this teaching apparently dates only to the Cold War when Christian missions adopted McCarthyism as staple fare. Far from a sworn enemy of revolutionary movements, Protestantism had originally been a natural ally. Carried to Latin America by British and North American merchants, it inevitably offended the Catholic clergy and landed oligarchy. Both dissenting religion and secular radicalism drew on the same aspiring, frustrated constituency, which saw little contradiction between the two. As late as the 1950s Catholic reactionaries in Colombia considered *protestantes* and *comunistas* synonymous, producing numerous Protestant martyrs. Thanks to the appeal of sectarian religion as an avenue of protest and advancement, a vigorous, influential 5% or so of the Latin American population is thought to be *evangelico*, a generic term for non-Catholic Christians. Tens of thousands of chapels dot the cities and hinterlands: inside workers, small farmers and petty traders pray and sing into the night.

In the mid-1960s the pro-Washington missionary consensus began to crack. With its Alliance for Progress, the United States tried to forestall revolution by stimulating hopes for reform and equipping military establishments for counter-insurgency. When civilian regimes jeopardized vested interests U S. embassies encouraged their military proteges to seize power. Right-wing dictatorships multiplied and the politics of religion shifted dramatically. Official violence forced wide reaches of the Catholic clergy to become a refuge for dissent; church sanctuary was violated; and many priests and nuns swung into opposition to the *status quo*. From 1968 to 1979 more than 800 were arrested, tortured, murdered or expelled.[21] In Central America guerrilla movements owed much of their success to clerical mobilization of the poor, for purposes such as co-operatives, and the hellish response this met from government forces.

The division between Catholic and Protestant was superseded by a new one over the theology of liberation identifying Christianity with social justice. In contrast to their Catholic and ecumenical Protestant countrymen most North American evangelical missionaries still seemed to identify Christianity with the latest military junta. While improving one's position, the reborn individual was to refrain from displeasing the government and the interests it represented; which included the U.S. Government and the interests it represented; the good life enjoyed by the Christians who financed the missions.

To many Latin Americans it seemed remarkable that such doctrines should come from the same nation which had the power of life and death over their economies; trained their soldiers; and, when differences arose, used its former pupils to overthrow their elected governments. The military and phallic metaphors used by the missions — the thrust for Christ, penetration, strategy, advance, occupation, conquest and so forth — were interpreted as evidence of yet another imperialist plot. From a survey of SIL religious material for native people, Mexican anthropologists reported that oppression and poverty were being attributed to ignorance of Scripture, prosperity to knowledge of same. SIL's ideology, the anthropologists concluded, 'seeks political domestication through . . . the personal relation with God, expressed in individual success.'[22]

But even if this was the message, how well was it being received? Thanks to right-wing mobilization of evangelical churches in the United States, more Latin American brethren seemed to be recognizing the double standard of missionary bans on political activity.[23] The tension between missionary fears, convert aspirations and the claim to be non-political is illustrated by the Sandinista revolution in Nicaragua. As the Somoza regime tottered in 1979, the U.S. evangelical journal *Christianity Today* reported that brethren were 'caught in the middle' between the National Guard and the revolutionaries. Yet, 'many evangelicals, particularly the young, sympathized with the rebels, although there was uneasiness over the Communist influence in the Sandinista camp.' A month later the correspondent clarified the meaning of 'sympathy' and 'uneasiness'. 'There was, and still is, tension in the churches. . . . Some pastors supported the Somoza regime on the basis of Romans 13, while many young people from Christian homes joined with the Sandinistas.'[24]

Despite evangelical support for the new government, to some North Americans it was obvious that Communists were using the church to destroy it. 'SATAN'S LATEST STRATEGY IS TO CONVINCE CHRISTIANS THAT GOD SUPPORTS THE REVOLUTION,' a fund-raising letter declares. 'Booklets like these are . . . leading Christians to believe that political activity will solve Latin America's problems. The result: division among Christians . . . some even training to fight with the revolutionaries. Open Door's response is to conduct VICTORY SEMINARS. . . . Changing the heart of man is the only way to change the environment.'[25] Thanks partly to a Full Gospel Business Men's Fellowship, the Sandinista interior minister approved the mass distribution of Bibles.[26]

The Pax Americana and Patronage Battles

The Summer Institute has taken up an extremely sensitive position in Latin American affairs. Across most of the political spectrum, Latin Americans hope that natural resources in Indian territory will rescue their dependent economies from huge foreign debts. Conscious of the role Indians could play in changing the *status quo,* governments and opposition political groups compete for their allegiance. Whether the spoils have to be divided with the transnational corporations which made the investments, or political activity threatens 'hemispheric security', the United States is part of every equation.

SIL members would like to believe that, if such a thing as U.S. imperialism exists, their organization has had no part in it. But when their founder, Cameron Townsend, needed diplomatic help, he went to Washington. The Bible translators would so like to disavow their support in this quarter that in 1977, following a crisis from which only the Lord's hand was said to have delivered SIL-Peru, its government liaison man told me that his branch maintained no contact with the U.S. Embassy. Two years later Wycliffe's President made a similar claim. When trouble arises, according to George Cowan, 'We have refused to fight back or appeal to our embassies as

9

foreigners.'[27] According to State Department cables, however, the Peruvian branch conferred with the embassy on repeated occasions in 1975-76.
SIL's support for the U.S. expedition in Vietnam seemed a sign of what could lie in store for Latin America. The translators had worked among ethnic minorities in more or less open revolt against the Saigon Government, the Montagnards. To prevent still more tribes-people from joining the National Liberation Front, the U.S. Special Forces hired tens of thousands to fight it. In Burma and Laos a three generation non-SIL mission family moved from inspiring mass religious movements to organizing intelligence forays into China and raising Hmong (Meo) armies for the CIA, that is, until American B-52 raids bombed their people into refugee camps.[28] The Americans were manipulating the longstanding distrust between ethnic groups to block a revolutionary movement and prop up the regime of their choice.

In Latin America, SIL has thrived on a similar pattern of U.S. power and internal colonialism. It took advantage of Inter-American protocol to obtain government contracts, then intervened in the conflict between colonizing societies and native people on an epic scale. The source of SIL's influence is 'dependency', the unequal exchanges endemic to world market expansion. In exchange for their labour, their land and conformity to a new order, native people come to depend on colonizers for trade goods, and sometimes even physical survival. The classic expression is the *patron,* a power broker who uses control over goods and services to exploit or manipulate his clients. In meeting native demands for tools, Western medicine and literacy, missionaries try to offer better terms of trade than other brokers. This attracts clients, generates patronage power and, against mutual adversaries, builds alliances between missionaries and native people. It nurtures strong bonds between the two, laying the groundwork for evangelism and making missionaries very useful to governments.

The Summer Institute and its rivals have long hurled nationalist propaganda at each other. If the North Americans were always accused of dividing the nation, they just as surely claimed to be unifying it. And if SIL was branded as an agent of imperialist penetration, who would make such a charge except left-wing subversives? Until the 1970s SIL's most consistent foe was its unacknowledged model, the Roman Catholic Church. Townsend only revived the written word in the language to which he supposedly gave it: centuries before, the Catholic missions had reduced Cakchiquel Maya to script.[29]
With his contracts, the founder tried to match and undercut earlier Catholic treaties with governments. In the ensuing competition for official favour, SIL was the clear winner. Indigenists organizing Indian Affairs bureaucracies welcomed its services, as did military officers and investors. Catholics suspected a U.S. embassy thumb in the balance, but governments considered the airborne linguists a more efficient agent for their plans.

Around 1970 SIL began to face alliances between Indians and new kinds of rivals. While Catholic priests and SIL teams had mobilized Indians against each other, clerical and nationalist objections had little to do with Indian grievances against translators, who usually paid more attention to Indian wishes than the competition did. But just as SIL's linguistic approach and logistical system had eclipsed the traditional, hacienda-style Catholic mission, now the translators were being threatened by an attempt to bridge the tensions of internal colonialism on which they had operated. Despite inferior resources and much inexperience, a new generation of rivals was offering Indians more tolerance for their traditions and more support for their land claims.

Growing corps of national linguists and anthropologists were one source of competition. They found themselves marginalized from the conduct of Indian affairs, not least because governments preferred to rely on conformist, U.S.-subsidized foreigners rather than citizens who criticized official plans and cost more money. Reforming Catholic missionaries also challenged SIL's position: having inherited the management of decrepit fiefdoms, they hoped to rally clients against evangelical inroads.

The first major anti-imperialist campaigns against SIL, in Colombia and Peru in 1975, followed lengthy, unsuccessful attempts to phase out the branches through bureaucratic channels. In Colombia, the President promised nationalization, which never materialized. In Peru the Prime Minister ordered SIL to vacate its premises; soon the branch was on its way to a new ten-year contract. These and other governments were not about to sacrifice loyal, self-financed North Americans to wild assemblies of nationalists and Marxists, social scientists and Indians who demanded larger subsidies. SIL's alliances with Indians were a check on civil rights organizing and leftist alliances with Indians; perhaps the North Americans were a government's only claim to a humane policy.

Like clockwork, it seemed, SIL's military and politician friends could be counted upon to block any curtailment of its activities, which would provoke nationalist vendettas, which would be used to accuse SIL's opponents of communist subversion, which would prompt nervous governments to continue supporting the North Americans. Yet the translators' victories heightened their sinister reputation and appeal as a nationalist sacrifice. Whether to give the U.S. Government a warning, court the opposition to their Indian policy or take a national security precaution, SIL's sponsors started to revoke its contracts. By 1981 130 translation teams wandered an official wilderness in Brazil, Panama, Mexico and Ecuador.

All Things to All Men

> *'If all members of a family are students, this does not mean that their home is a school. Even though in SIL all members base their convictions on the Bible, this does not make them an organized church or a religious group. . . . SIL refuses to accept the connotation of "missionary" in the confessional and institutional sense in which the press . . . uses the term.'*
> John Alsop, SIL-Mexico Director, 1979.

> *'We do not consider our members' work in a language complete*
> *until some of the local group are capable of reading the printed*
> *Word and there is a nucleus of believers to carry on themselves*
> *or with another evangelical group. . . .*
>
> George Cowan, WBT President, 1979.[30]

The Summer Institute has never explained that a nucleus of believers will arise in each language it studies, but after 45 years the results are obvious. Thanks to statements like John Alsop's, many Latin Americans refuse to believe a word the Summer Institute says: if it can deny being a religious group, then it must be composed of outrageous liars. The fact which the Summer Institute cannot admit, but which justifies all, is that it is a faith mission – to all intents and purposes, an expeditionary religious sect. Like any such group SIL/WBT rejects the label: how can it be sectarian to spread the single, true revelation? According to a sociologist, sects regard themselves as an elite with a well-defined boundary, apply rigorous standards to volunteers seeking admission, demand an overriding allegiance to a higher truth, and expel the wayward.[31] So do faith missions like the Summer Institute, which expelled a member scientist for heresy in 1968. In view of the animosity faith missions generate, it is no coincidence that the largest in the world is a supposedly non-sectarian institute which, for those times when Christian witness fails, has entrenched itself in the bureaucracies of foreign governments.

The dual identity is a versatile fiction. Time and again it has rescued non-sectarian linguists and non-ecclesiastical Bible translators as they foster evangelical churches. SIL/WBT believes that the 'two organizations' merely reflect its scientific and Christian roles, yet they have rationalized a sanctified system of plausible denial. Presentations shift between a SIL and a WBT 'side', 'context', 'role', or 'emphasis'. By 'waiting for the Lord's time in witnessing' – the semantic devices of crucial omission and strategic ambiguity – SIL/WBT withholds information which might displease its sundry audiences.[32] The distinction between the 'two organizations' permits retraction: when I said that, I was speaking in the context of our sister organization. . . .

In South America two phases have emerged in SIL's use of scientific credentials to protect its state contracts. During the 'closet' phase, Cameron Townsend went so far as to deny that SIL had a religious mission and was related to WBT. Even after admitting that his University of Oklahoma linguists hoped to translate the Bible, he maintained that they were not missionaries. Until this point WBT had described SIL as its subsidiary to home supporters; now they became 'affiliated' organizations with different purposes. The 'two organizations' phase has prevailed ever since. As Richard Chase Smith reported from Peru, the two identities are 'kept very separate, each reserved for its own audience, each revealed according to the image needed for the situation.'[33]

The man who improvised the dual identity always claimed to rely heavily on the Lord. 'Their main defense,' Townsend wrote of his methods in 1948, 'is that they have worked.' Yet the credit belonged to the Lord, as evinced by the many miracles – strokes of political or financial good fortune – which

Townsend advertised as the Lord's provision, even though he usually had arranged them himself. Since Wycliffe takes its 'inner urges to God in prayer,' he explained ten years later, success means that the Lord opened the door.[34] In this way Townsend sanctified his intrigues as the Lord's leading, institutionalized them in the dual identity, and initiated his followers into a sacred system of misinformation.

In keeping with the founder's basic principles, Wycliffe's can be summarized as reliance on the Lord and what serves to accomplish His work. Thanks to this combination of the prayerful and the expedient, what serves Wycliffe's ends has become the divine will. In George Cowan's *The Word that Kindles* (1979), one is impressed by the powerful rationality of the organization and its ability to find Scriptural precedent for everything it does. Dedicated to Bible translation, linguistics and non-sectarian Christian service, the programme would appear to be a fine one indeed. But while the premises underpinning it begin with standard evangelical beliefs, SIL/WBT has had to reinterpret them slightly to sanctify its state contracts and dual identity. From his reading of the New Testament, for example, Cowan concludes that Christ 'never advocated revolt in attitude or act against imperial or local authorities.' The dual identity, he suggests, conforms to the Apostle Paul's policy of being 'all things to all men', which is 'a legitimate expression of . . . freedom in Christ' [35] Finally, unlike most brethren, SIL has used its belief in the power of God's Word, the Holy Spirit and free will to avoid responsibility for making converts. It was the Lord who produced all those congregations, not us, and therefore we are not a religious mission.

Since evangelical metaphysics do not impress non-believers, scientific credentials remain SIL's first line of defence. When that fails, it is taking refuge in a metaphysics with a far wider appeal, a free enterprise view of native people as a market-place of ideas in which the individual is free to choose or reject an 'alternative'.[36] Bible translation merely offers native people a choice between their old religious beliefs and Christianity, according to this logic. It follows that SIL gives priority to the individual over the state; that politics is a lamentable interference in its humanitarian labours; and that the opposition to its work is an assault on religious freedom.[37] This is notwithstanding SIL's government contracts for the moral improvement of other people; the patronage power it wields; and the determination to see a 'nucleus of believers' around each New Testament. Regardless of whether native communities wish to accept SIL's presentation of alternatives, it or their brethren will persist until some have been won to the Lord. Reassured by their Lord and Milton Friedman, members find it hard to believe that moral, well-informed people could oppose their plans. If their own intentions are good, those of their opponents must be bad. It is easy to believe that Satan is responsible for the trouble they have brought on themselves.

Popular Views of Bible Translation

The Central Intelligence Agency became the popular explanation for the Summer Institute's staying power in government ministries. Like a spymaster's dream come true, here was a network of airplanes, radios and mostly North American linguists in remote but, sooner or later, 'strategic' areas all over the world. They had strong ties to discontented ethnic minorities and were deeply appreciated by local military officers. They knew the people, languages, customs and resources of their areas like perhaps no one else; their very presence served as a warning system against trouble; they propagated a Gospel of patience; and, voluntarily or under pressure from local officials they might well be available in an emergency.

There was no proof, but CIA resources did not wear badges. After decades of watching North Americans brand any objection to their hegemony as Moscow-inspired, many Latin Americans had lost patience. They no longer cared to distinguish between the objectives of different North Americans; the varying functions they performed; or what North Americans had considered doing, what they had done elsewhere, what they were in a position to do in one's own country, and what they had actually done.

The espionage accusations were accompanied by many others, often based on illegal activities by *gringos* (fair-skinned foreigners, especially North Americans) presumed to belong to SIL or folk interpretations of members' behaviour. A translator sinking a water-well could become a ransacker of the nation's mineral wealth. Since SIL had tried to hide the fact that it was an evangelical mission, perhaps there was a second level of duplicity concealing much more. Behind the academic facade was a religious sect, and behind that were geo-political objectives such as detecting minerals and creating zones of influence to control them.

Inspired by SIL's very broad definition of Bible translation, conspiracy theorists interpreted its activities in terms of transnational corporations, drug mafias and the espionage section of U.S. embassies. All were condensed into a single, mysterious and ominously powerful organization which operated in virtual independence from host governments, and contrary to their aims. In the press and in the popular imagination, a group of Bible translators became a Green Beret auxiliary with special brainwashing and sterilizing facilities, not to mention a complete inventory of the nation's mineral and botanical resources, which was turning native languages into military codes and cutting off the oil fields by preparing Indians to welcome the U.S. Marines. For the anthropologically minded, there were schedules of destruction which followed in SIL's wake. First it isolated Indians from the nation, then knocked the props from under their culture and imposed North American values. Finally, it scattered its disoriented converts through the nearest bordellos and haciendas as U.S. corporations seized their land.

The implication was that expelling a few hundred remarkably versatile imperialists would resolve most conflicts between Indians and their other colonizers. Nor was there any need to worry about the medicine and schools

SIL provided some groups who, for the present, could get them nowhere else. An observer for Survival International, a group with little sympathy for evangelical missions, called the campaign against the Peruvian branch 'primarily nationalistic rather than considering the real effects the SIL has on the Indians' (many of the anti-SIL arguments were exaggerated and even false). That the SIL "is an organ of *gringo* imperialism and teaches Indians to be *gringos* rather than Peruvians" summarises much of the anti-SIL lobbying. . . . If the SIL were to leave Peru at short notice, a number of services which have become necessary to the Indians would be stopped (especially in the health field). Critics of the SIL appeared to be little concerned with how these would be replaced. The issue is a very complex one.'[38]

When governments accepted SIL's offer to integrate, instruct or otherwise improve their native population, North Americans set up alliances with native people against local exploiters, by implication entire, racist colonizing societies. However salutary from the official point of view, wealthy foreign sectarians came to flourish in native communities where citizens were unwelcome. If this maddening spectacle was a divisive tactic of U.S. imperialism, then defence of the nation required SIL's expulsion. And if SIL had so exploited, alienated and deluded the natives that they supported imperialism, perhaps they were in need of forceful liberation. Anti-imperialists acting on this logic advanced the translators' cause, not their own. Faced with a choice between clumsy, unpredictable, perhaps lethal new paternalists and more reliable old ones, Indians chose the latter. Perhaps SIL inhibited army sergeants from raping their women. Internal colonialism provided the translators with a permanent rationale. It was reinforced as they drew native people into greater dependency and created new needs, which further justified their presence until that distant time when they had 'studied' (propagated a church in) each native language.

By accusing SIL of every conceivable offence, nationalists made it a scapegoat for internal colonialism. While they felt that Indian culture was to be protected, it was probably not to be protected at the cost of all that lumber and oil which would reduce the balance of payments deficit; therefore, Indians had to be integrated into the nation. Whipsawed with protectionist and integrationist arguments, SIL was accused of 1) assaulting Indian culture, thereby undermining resistance to colonialism, and 2) dividing native people from the nation, thereby hindering integration into the same destructive, colonizing society.[39] SIL could do both, but this was due to its alliances with Indians against Latin American colonizers. So long as it was blamed for internal colonialism and these alliances were ignored, so was the basis of the problem. The 'nation' was to triumph over 'imperialism' at a time when, in reaction to chronic racism, Indians were increasingly demanding recognition as nationalities in their own right.

Indian militancy was the real worry for governments: having regarded SIL as prophylaxis against unrest, they might well try to use campaigns against it to establish more effective control over native people, thereby discouraging further challenges from this quarter. SIL's rivals were in a most ambiguous position: while they generally supported civil rights organizing, more than a few hoped to replace SIL with a larger state apparatus administered by themselves, which meant expansion of a regime which they themselves had criticized for corruption, inefficiency and racism. As they tried to bridge the contradiction between indigenous self-determination and state expansion, Indians a and themselves, official initiatives ranged from the possibly salutary through the problematic to the definitely unpleasant. Whether the controversies were ultimately attributed to Washington or Moscow, left- and right-wing conspiracy theory led to the same conclusion: only the strong arm of the state could deal with a shadowy but monstrous threat. Cursing matches between jealous supplicants to this supreme being could easily lead to more repressive measures against native people.

Indian protest is at the root of the controversies: it is forcing competitors for Indian loyalty to reformulate their plans whether these are understood in terms of study, salvation, liberation or integration. Needless to say, nearly everyone, from bureaucratic empire-builders and tourist promoters to SIL and the New Tribes Mission, now claims to be a champion of indigenous culture and self-determination. What Indians want and what their cultures consist of are bitterly disputed, with Indian spokesmen produced to back up every position.

SIL's logic begins with the popular image of tradition as something hopelessly inflexible, backward and inadequate to face the modern world. Under pressure to abandon old ways, in George Cowan's words, native people 'need a moral and spiritual base upon which to discern which elements of the national culture are for their good and which are not. . . . The Bible provides a basis for moral judgement.'[40] Since SIL refrains from all coercion by simply offering an alternative, it respects the right of native people to choose their own future. And since it wants to reinforce the language and conceivably the 'ties in action' that define an ethnic group, it not only helps native people adjust to change; by supplying a new belief system, it reinforces their identification with their culture.

Obviously SIL's solicitude does not extend to religious tradition, the value systems which it considers Satanic but most native people consider the basis of their way of life. It is true, of course, that missions may deflect as well as multiply the pressures which disintegrate a culture. The most popular rejoinder to missionary work — 'leave the Indians alone' — delights the Summer Institute. For decades it has made the no-lose argument that civilization, now culture change, is 'inevitable'. The happy savage meets the same fate: he died in a contact epidemic. Offering their own bromide, translators customarily indict anthropologists for wanting to preserve Indians as cultural specimens, like animals in a zoo, rather than helping them adjust to change as SIL says it does. But while translators may believe that isolationism is the basic anthropological grievance against their work, they are in far more difficult terrain.

To construct the dual identity, SIL/WBT learned from supposedly value-free scholars who mocked fundamentalist beliefs. Just as they did, it could present itself as value-free (an impartial institute with a vague commitment to Christianity) when it was actually value-laden. Disapproving anthropologists could be kept at bay with the argument that, since anthropology is value-free like other sciences, its practitioners have no right to use their authority to make value judgements against Christian missions. With its nation-building claims SIL made itself congenial to Latin American indigenists.

The eclipse of supposedly value-free science, the rise of academic anti-imp· erialism and support for civil rights organizing unsettled SIL on several scores. First, the dual identity was a blatant use of the value-free claim to pursue disguised ends. Second, Latin American indigenists were rejecting the idea that North American brokers could unify their countries when the principal enemy was U.S. imperialism. Finally, the issue was not simply that SIL was changing Indians: it was *how* SIL was shaping change, and the attempts of native people to defend themselves. Even if some form of contact with the world market was inevitable, SIL's hidden church-planting agenda, with its sweeping disrespect for religious tradition and subservient attitude toward bad government, was not.

References

1. Richardson 1981:4.
2. Calculated from *Christianity Today* (Carol Stream, Illinois) 27 March 1981, pp.60-61.
3. *In Other Words* (Huntington Beach, California) Summer 1981, p.13; *Wycliffe Associates Newsletter* (Orange, California) January 1980, p.1.
4. Matthew 28:19.
5. Townsend 1948:67; *Translation* (official organ of the WBT, Santa Ana, California) 1944, p.13.
6. *Mejoramiento moral:* see the Colombian (University of Antioquia 1976: 10) and Ecuadorian (*Registro Official* (Quito) No. 227 19 May 1971, pp.4-5 (contracts).
7. Townsend and Pittman 1975:103.
8. Hall 1959:109.
9. Calculated from WBT 1981.
10. 'Statement of Doctrine, WBT Inc.,' flier distributed in early 1970s.
11. *In Other Words* November 1981, p.7.
12. Ibid., Summer 1981, p.32.
13. Ibid., p.12.
14. Hefley 1978:107.
15. Cowan 1979:250-52.
16. According to the standard reference (Wilson 1980:24), in 1979 60-65% of the world's Protestant missionary force came from the U.S. (42,304) and Canada (1,887).
17. Lernoux 1980:281-92.
18. *New York Times* 29 January and 12 February 1976.
19. *Guardian* (New York) 20 February 1980.
20. J. B. Phillips version.

21. Lernoux 1980:13, 464-65.
22. College of Ethnologists and Social Anthropologists 1979:9-11
23. *Christianity Today* 8 May 1981 p.39.
24. Ibid., 17 August 1979 p.41; and 21 September 1979 p.44.
25. 'Satan's strategy for Latin America,' circular, Open Doors with Brother Andrew (Orange, California), 20 May 1981.
26. *Christianity Today* 29 May 1981, p.34.
27. Cowan 1979:169.
28. McCoy 1972-265-7, 291, 297-309.
29. According to Cowan (1979:69), prior to Townsend 'Cakchiquel had never been written or systematically studied.' But Kenneth Pike (in Elson 1960:6) notes the probable influence on Townsend of Daniel G. Brinton (1884:7-17), who lists dozens of Catholic grammars, dictionaries, annals and religious works in Cakchiquel from 1550 to 1862.
30. Alsop 1979:7; Cowan 1979:253.
31. Wilson 1970:26-35.
32. Townsend and Pittman 1975:82.
33. Draft version of Smith 1981.
34. Townsend 1948:87; Hall 1959:154.
35. Cowan 1979:132, 215 (I Corinthians 9:22).
36. Judith Shapiro (1981:143) contrasts this view to that of Catholic missionaries attempting to 'decolonialize' their work.
37. The implications are presented in Merrifield 1977and the February 1980 issue of *In Other Words*.
38. Corry 1977a.
39. Aaby and Hvalkof (1981:176-77) note the contradiction between 'developmentalist' and 'traditionalist' critiques in their analysis of the debate between SIL and opponents.
40. Cowan 1979:146.

2. The Founder in Guatemala

To the plantation owners of Western El Salvador, it must have seemed like the end of the world. With volcanos in eruption, on a January night in 1932, Pipil Indian peasants rose up against their masters. In the town of Juayua, the Rev. A. Roy MacNaught of the Central American Mission awoke to a great banging noise. Down the street a mob was battering down the door of the telegraph office. After killing a policeman, the rebels burned the property of the richest man in town, shot him and sacked all the stores and houses of the wealthy. 'In the morning when I looked out,' wrote Rev. MacNaught, 'I saw the red flag flying from the town hall; we were under communistic rule for the first time.'[1]

One of Cameron Townsend's colleagues was witnessing the first Communist-led insurrection in the Western hemisphere. It followed an electoral fraud by a military dictatorship, which had allowed the Communist Party to participate and then declined to recognize its victories. The revolt was nipped in the bud except among the Pipil, who were soon mowed down by the army's machine guns. United States and Canadian warships hovered off the coast but never landed their Marines. In the reprisals which followed, estimated conservatively at one hundred to one, Rev. MacNaught saw many of his converts murdered as suspected communists. Four years later his ex-supervisor, Cameron Townsend, played upon their memory in 'A Tale of Indians and Upheaval in Central America'. The serial novel appeared in *Revelation* magazine of Philadelphia, and it tells us what was on Townsend's mind as he organized the Summer Institute of Linguistics.

Tolo, the Volcano's Son extols a Mayan Bible translation helper as the liberator of his people from plantation oppression. It is, for the most part, a thinly fictionalized portrait of Townsend's own work in neighbouring Guatemala, from 1917 to 1932 with the Central American Mission. But it seems to end in fantasy: the missionary's faithful evangelist and translation assistant, Bartolome 'Tolo' Timanit, makes the supreme sacrifice to stop a Mayan revolution led by a Russian Bolshevik. While the martyrdom is timed to coincide with the 1932 Pipil revolt in El Salvador, it takes place south of Townsend's own mission stations in the Western Guatemalan highlands. You will have land, schools, freedom if you follow God's Word and obey the government, Tolo tells his fellow Indians. The evil Russian shoots the

19

Map 1
Mexico, Guatemala and El Salvador

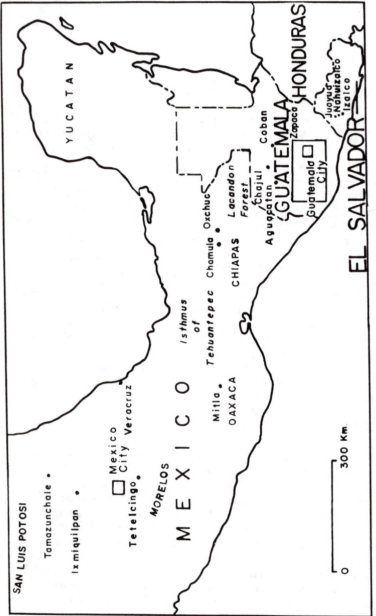

Map 2
The Western Guatemalan Highlands

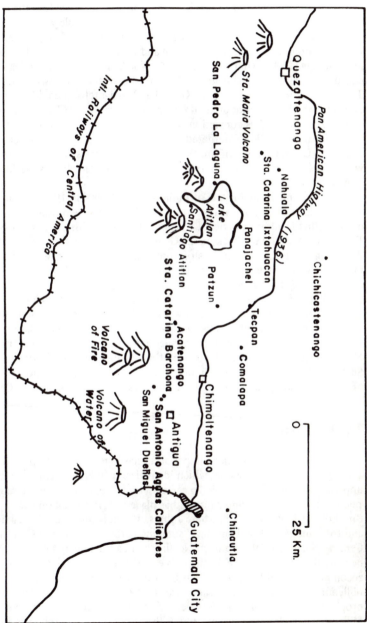

infiltrator and a volcano erupts, driving the superstitious rebels to their knees. Guatemala is saved from a bloodbath like the one across the border in El Salvador.

In the very conception of the Summer Institute, then, we find the spectre of Communism in the Americas and the hope that the Bible will exorcise it. Townsend's 15 years with Mayan farmers in Guatemala had acquainted him with the boondock capitalism of coffee and banana republics. He blamed the local ruling class for what he saw, not the North American companies and proconsuls who also profited from it. The suffering of the poor was such, Townsend believed, that only the Gospel and social reform could avert the upheaval which the Salvadorian *Matanza* (massacre) of 1932 augured for his own mission field. This conviction was so strong that he transformed the 'communist' evangelicals murdered in El Salvador into a probably fictional martyr to Godless Communism. 'Marshall[s] of progress', like his martyr Tolo, would frustrate extremists and lead the Maya of Guatemala to salvation, freedom and prosperity.[2]

As Townsend wrote his tale of Indians and upheaval in 1934-35, he was already taking Bible translation to Mexico, the site of the most openly sustained class conflict in Latin America. By looking forward to his place in the Mexican Revolution and looking back on his Guatemalan career with the Central American Mission, Townsend's story prefigures the Summer Institute's performance. Together with earlier, equally engaging reports on his work for the *Central American Bulletin,* it provides a fine opportunity to explore the meaning of Bible translation as he and the Summer Institute have understood it. These historical and semi-historical writings also raise basic questions about the North American evangelical missions. What has brought them to Latin America? How have they won followings among Catholic peasants? Have Mayan Protestants fulfilled the expectations of their North American shepherds? Such questions come together in one of the founder's more memorable images, of Mayan revolutionaries falling to their knees before a dying Indian Christ.

Thy Kingdom Come

European and North American imperialism has long been accompanied by an apocalyptic Christian mission, which identifies the march of empire with the approaching end of the world. To certain visionaries contact with strange peoples in Asia, Africa and America has placed Christendom on the threshold of Revelation 7:9, where John saw a multitude from 'every nation and tribe and people and language' standing before the Lamb of God. In 16th Century Spain and 19th Century North America the imperial nation has become the Chosen People destined to evangelize the world. As the crowning accomplishment of history, this has been thought to pave the way for the Millennial Kingdom, the thousand-year reign of Christ on earth. The Biblical prophecies of a terrible time of woe, the Second Coming of Christ and the Millennial Kingdom (not necessarily in this order) are to be followed by the

Last Judgement, a new heaven and a new earth. Thriving on the conviction that the world as they know it is in its last days, apocalyptic missions have identi-fied the rewards and trials of empire with the millennium and the tribulations which accompany it.[3]

With the last unreached peoples as their objective, Cameron Townsend and the Wycliffe Bible Translators are part of this tradition. Wycliffe usually leaves the implications to be drawn by those who will, however: no particular interpretation is said to be required. Not only would overt eagerness for the end of the world disturb many well-wishers, not to mention governments; millennial expectations must be kept under control to build a broad member-ship and evangelize properly. Nor does Wycliffe claim to represent the Chosen People, an honour which poses theological and recruiting difficulties. But the task has fallen largely to one nation, and Wycliffe in particular is driven by its urgency. Perhaps the Lord will return at any time and doom the unreached, which calls for an immediate effort to rescue them. Or perhaps the Lord is waiting for the completion of universal Bible translation in fulfill-ment of Matthew 24:14, a position espoused by Townsend and even the Wycliffe journal in a careless moment: 'Good news of the Kingdom will be proclaimed to men all over the world . . . and then the end will come.'[4] According to this view, Bible translation will hasten the Second Coming. For those of us who have not believed, it is not expected to be very jolly.

Strangely, there is never more reason for haste, nor a clearer sign of the approaching end, than social revolution. The early Christianity which evangel-icals believe they uphold was, after all, a religion of the downtrodden: the Kingdom was imminent and did not bode well for the rich and powerful. Visions of a new heaven and earth have always sprung from groups that would clearly benefit, not those enjoying the present. So many ragged prophets have promised that history is marching toward divine justice that, beyond the Christian sense, 'millennialism' refers to any scheme which offers an end to this evil world or age in the ambiguous terrain of a new one. Reported from most parts of the world, faith in such traditions erupts and subsides over time, carrying hopes for this world wrapped in the mystical language of the next.[5]

In South America Quechua peasants believe that the Inca, the god-king dismembered by the Spaniards, is growing back together under the ground and some day will return to liberate his people. So will King Tecun Uman in Guatemala. Just as the first Christians did not try to defeat the Roman legions, millennialists usually have not taken up arms; they are too weak. But invariably they mobilize against social disruption by restoring tradition, reinterpreting or even rejecting it in favour of a new religion which inherits something from the old. As the opportunity presents itself, a mystical project may turn into a struggle to make the better world here and now.

Like secular protest ideology, millennialism is a fickle beast. While it repudiates the social order, it must either shape a new one or come to some accommodation with the old so that, over time, it not only protests but conforms to, not only damns but sanctifies, the social order with the mystical promise. The political implications are shaped by the social fortunes of the faithful. The Quechua, who in some places act out the death and rebirth of the Inca in their ritual, have made the dead god-king a symbol for the present dark age and the suffering they must endure. The reborn Inca will change all that.[6] But among North American evangelicals, who have found their promised land without overturning the social order, millennial expectation has become associated with the prosperity and privilege of empire. Hope for the end of this evil age readily translates into support for militarism and counter-revolution.

The frequent clashes between missionary and indigenous millennialism also suggest an ability to communicate, through the shared belief in spiritual power. Townsend's 1936 novel illustrates this in a roundabout way: while the conflict between communist atheism (Destroy the temples! Hurrah for the Devil!) and Mayan respect for religion helps the martyr Tolo abort the uprising, in the historical Salvadorian revolt of 1932 communist ideas in fact reached the Pipil through their saint societies.[7] Actually most Indian rebellions in Mesoamerica since the Spanish Conquest have been associated with 'talking saints', images imbued with supernatural power who preach peasant revolution through interpreters.[8] If Townsend had not been engaged in polemics, a Mayan saint and his interpreter would have taken the place of the novel's improbable Russian instigator. In the rebels falling to their knees before a dying evangelist we have a contest between rival millennial schemes, in which the evangelical path to liberation gains the upper hand. Instead of facing the army's machine guns, some of the rebels surrender to Christ.

Townsend's novel dramatized the flourishing evangelical movement he left behind in Guatemala. Were it to be taken at face value, he had diverted the devout revolutionism of peasant farmers into a North American pacification scheme. But in the early 1950s the real-life Mayan Protestant heirs of the novel's anti-Communist martyr were organizing to seize landed estates. Soon they owed their real-life fugitives, prisoners and martyrs, not to communist persecution but to a counter-revolution organized by the U.S. Government. Simultaneously some Mayan Protestants were fulfilling Townsend's expectations as marshalls of progress by becoming the wealthiest men in their towns. In 1970, a Presbyterian missionary described the Indian and non-Indian Protestant churches of Guatemala as 'clearly anti-Communist'. They were so reluctant to discuss social issues that young Protestants trying to raise them were being expelled as subversives.[9] A decade later the Western Guatemalan highlands heaved against its bonds. Was Townsend's vision of Bible counter-insurgency being vindicated? In the words of an evangelical observer, in Catholic and to some extent Protestant communities 'the Bible, and not *Das Kapital,* is the motivating force behind the popular resistance to government repression.'[10] Keeping in mind the conflict between missionary and convert aspirations, let us turn to the religious heritage Cameron Townsend brought to Guatemala.

The Great Tribulation

> *'Capitalism has been weighed in the balance and found
> wanting. As sure as God reigns, Babylon is falling to rise no
> more. The international socialist commonwealth – God's
> Kingdom – shall rise on the wreck and ruin of the world's
> present ruling powers.'*
>
> Texan railroad worker, 1914[11]

The leading casualty of Biblical foundations in North America were the
original inhabitants, 10 to 12 million according to recent estimates. When the
Puritans seized a thickly populated and arguably more civilized domain,
Francis Jennings concludes, they 'made preparations of two sorts: guns and
munitions to overpower Indian resistance and quantities of propaganda to
overpower their own countrymen's scruples.' The propaganda became the
dominant North American view of native people, a conquest ideology which
took on philanthropic airs but continued to diabolize their way of life.[12] Only
in the 19th Century did many Protestants awaken to the possibility that they
might convert Indians instead of exterminate them.

The driving ambition of the frontier missions was persuading white settlers
to go to church. When Alexis de Tocqueville toured the United States in 1832,
he was surprised to hear frontier preachers 'speak so often of the goods of this
world, and to meet a politician where you expected to find a priest.'[13] In
evangelical revivals these men imbued frontier nationalism, the despair of the
backlands and the hope for a better life, with millennial aspiration. But as the
western frontier closed in the late 1800s, their promises of a glorious age had
to be reinterpreted. A new millennialism reflected the social disruption of
industrialization, reshaped the expectations of many people and spurred the
evangelical mission to North American frontiers around the world.

At mid-19th Century the United States had been celebrated as the 'coming
Kingdom' promised in the Bible. The small farmer's paradise seemed in sight
and Protestant churches championed the anti-slavery movement. The rampant
Christian utopianism of the time was based upon the *post*-millennial view of
the Bible, dominant in Protestantism since the 17th Century: Christ would
return to earth in physical form only *after* the thousand years of blessing if He
came at all. Under the progressive influence of Christianity, mankind was on
the threshold of the Millennial Kingdom. The world, and in particular the
United States, was marching into unprecedented enlightenment and
freedom.[14]

The Civil War (1861-65) shattered this dream of peace and glory in the
South. As middle-class churches rested 'at ease in Zion', land speculation and
bank foreclosures, agricultural depression and railroad monopolies drove
millions of farmers into debt, bankruptcy or tenancy. Agrarian protest
gathered in the Populist and Socialist movements, from whose platforms evangelical preachers thundered against the ungodly. 'I am a Socialist from the
Bible standpoint and also the political standpoint,' declared a tenant farmer

in Texas in 1914. 'And I fully believe that the Socialist movement is the fore-runner of the second coming of Jesus Christ.'[15]

This courtship was frustrated by a more vengeful millennialism, which despaired of human progress and prayed for an overwhelming divine interven-tion. According to the *pre*-millennial view, that favoured by the first Christians, the Second Coming would precede the Kingdom. Far from scaling new heights of virtue, an ever more sinful age was rushing headlong to destruction. The end was near: only the Lord's return, riding on the clouds in glory. would strike down the wicked and save the righteous. While some pre-millennialists identi-fied the impending cataclysm with banks and railroads, landlords and mer-chants, a contrary equation soon prevailed. The gathering evil became, not industrial capitalism, but the protests against it. This opinion swept the pre-millennial field and produced the most active evangelizers in contemporary Latin America: the Mormons, Seventh Day Adventists and Jehovah's Witnesses, the Pentecostals and the Fundamentalists, the last the precursors of today's evangelicals.[16]

In the proto-Fundamentalist camp were the founders of the Central Ameri-can Mission, organized in Dallas, Texas, in 1890. Three were businessmen dealing chiefly in land titles and mortgages.[17] The fourth was their preacher, Cyrus Ingerson Scofield (1843-1921), who became one of the intellectual fathers of Fundamentalism and the contemporary evangelical movement. Through Scofield's career we have a window on the social and ideological basis of, not just Cameron Townend's missionary apprenticeship, but evangel-ical world mission.

After fighting for slavery in the Civil War, Scofield moved west, joined the Bar and pressed a lawsuit against squatters occupying the 'large land interests' of his wealthy brother-in-law in Kansas. To homesteader attorneys who quoted John Greenleaf Whittier:

> They crossed the prairies as of old
> The Pilgrims crossed the Sea
> To make the West as they the East
> The homestead of the free,

Scofield responded:

> They crossed the prairies in a band
> To try to steal some railroad land.[18]

From making the West safe for corporations, it was a short step to the Kansas state legislature and appointment as District Attorney for the Grant Adminis-tration, where his duties included removing Indians to reservations and keeping them away from liquor.[19]

Saved from drink and politics in 1879, the born-again Scofield joined the genteel, inter-denominational movement which championed the new fashion in pre-millennial thinking, Millenarianism.[20] Preoccupied with Biblical prophecy, the Millenarians looked to an early Lord's return and knew, in Scofield's words, that 'this age ends in catastrophe; this age ends in judgement; this age ends in woe.'[21] He called it the Great Tribulation. Since the world was doomed, social reform would have to wait until Christ himself could supervise.

Since the churches were apostate, the Millenarians struggled to save those who could be saved before the end.

Scofield became a protege of Dwight L. Moody (1837-99), the most famous of the late 19th Century revivalists and the first identified by socialists as a class enemy. 'I say to the rich men of Chicago, their money will not be worth much if communism and infidelity sweep the land,' Moody told the men who financed his Moody Bible Institute. 'There can be no better investment for the capitalists of Chicago than to put the saving salt of the Gospel into these dark homes and desperate centers.'[22] Just as such men hoped to turn their workers 'to higher thoughts than labor agitation', Moody tried to manufacture the old frontier revivalism in the cities to save European immigrants from vice, poverty and Roman Catholicism.[23] In this he failed. But the evangelical religion he and the Millenarians reshaped did appeal to Protestants leaving the land for urban centres. Moody and Scofield translated social crisis into eternal terms for these people, defining loyalties in ways which persist a century later.

Evolutionary views of Christianity were undermining the philosophical basis of 19th Century Protestantism, a 'common sense realism' which held that every man who used his head would apprehend the same absolute truth. According to this conception, Scripture was as self-evidently trustworthy as the laws of science.[24] Now, however, historical analysis not only contradicted some of the common man's interpretations of the Good Book: it challenged the Millenarians' formidable faith in Biblical prophecy. They therefore undertook their own reinterpretation, a Biblical literalism which was only literal where convenient. According to Scofield's system, for example, the Sermon on the Mount — 'How happy are you who own nothing, for the Kingdom of God is yours. . . . But how miserable for you who are rich, for you have had all your comforts' — applied only in the future epoch of the Millennial Kingdom, not now.[25] So convinced was Scofield that the Word and only the Word counted, that he composed his elaborately footnoted Reference Bible. As intended, the faithful took his interpretations to be the infallible original; the Scofield Bible became the Fundamentalist chapter and verse. While some evangelicals including Townsend learned to question Scofield's extraordinary heresies, they remain orthodoxy for many and help define the permissible for others.[26]

Guided by their vision of light beyond the abyss, after 1886 the Millenarians championed the Student Volunteer Movement and its campaign for 'the evangelization of the world in this generation'. Scofield's interest in the mushrooming foreign missions was sparked off by the Englishman Hudson Taylor, whose huge China Inland Mission would suffer heavily in the Boxer Rebellion. A lecture by the U.S. Government's trade commissioner for Latin America, William Eleroy Curtis, drew Scofield's attention to Central America and particularly Costa Rica, where two Canadian families owning coffee plantations welcomed his first missionaries in 1891.

Pity for the spiritually destitute of Romanist lands followed anxiety over the poor and disorderly at home. According to his friend Charles Gallaudet Trumbull, Scofield organized the Central American Mission following his encounter with the Holiness Testimony of the 1880s. This proto-Pentecostal movement was sweeping indebted yeoman and tenant farmers afflicted by Scofield's own lawyer and speculator class. In 1910, an organizer thought that 'holiness people make good Socialists,' as some had made good Populists.[27] With their emotional worship and dream of an imminent promised land, the Holiness sects had more in common with the old frontier revivalism than Scofield. But he was not about to concede the gift of the Holy Spirit to poor, unlettered farmers. Scofield was 'anxious', the Southwest 'seethed' with Holiness Testimony but 'not so spoke the Word'. Instead, he took up Keswick sanctification, a genteel version of Holiness doctrine. To thrill with the indwelling Holy Spirit required 'the presentation or yielding of the body . . . the acceptance of the Christ life plan as one of sacrifice.' Scofield triumphed over despair and went on to found the Central American Mission.[28]

The story suggests that, in his theology and mission venture, Scofield was reacting to the millennial fervour of the poor. During the same period he denounced Socialism as 'bloody anarchy – the overthrow of all settled government; that upheaval of the lowest strata of society' pushing the age towards doom.'[29] Not coincidentally, the theology of the Great Tribulation replaced Christianity's social claims with an urgent message of salvation in another world.

As always, however, the North American millennial sword was cutting two ways, between fear of divine wrath and confidence in a prosperous future. In step with the revivalism of Dwight Moody, whose social message was that capitalism rewarded virtue with prosperity, the Great Tribulation proved to mean conformity and self-advancement as a client middle class. For people whose independence as small farmers and merchants was being destroyed, the fathers of Fundamentalism identified a new opportunity in the old language of sin and Christ's redeeming blood. Alarmed by the pace of social and intellectual change, bending this way and that to keep up with the times, the Fundamentalists stood firm on what they considered the Bible, organized new institutions around it and fortified their own sub-culture. A crisis of faith, George Marsden observes, froze their social and political views in the middle-class Protestant consensus which had prevailed around 1890. While they now felt like strangers in their own country, they continued to identify with an idealized older America. And while they believed that the United States had strayed from the path of righteousness, many remained convinced that it was the supreme embodiment of Christian virtue.[30] Out of the doomsday thunder emerged, once again and unmistakably, the old 'coming Kingdom' in terms suitable to a new epoch. For pre-millennialists, the old coming Kingdom was only going into hiding to re-emerge as America's world destiny. As the United States began to export its capital and contradictions, despair on the closed home frontier became hope, in countries like Guatemala, through an apocalyptic Christian mission.

One victim of the Great Tribulation was Cameron Townsend's father, a poor but Presbyterian tenant farmer pushed west, by debt, drought and falling agricultural prices, to Southern California, where William Cameron was born in 1896. As Asians and Latinos worked in the citrus groves, the Southern California boom proved a godsend for hard-luck Anglos like the Townsends. Cameron won a minister's scholarship to Occidental College, founded by the region's Presbyterian, citrus-owning gentry. On the verge of being inducted into World War I he dropped out of college, to sell Bibles in Guatemala under the supervision of the Central American Mission.[31]

Just as Townsend's family was saddled with all too tangible debts, an evangelical mission is based upon the belief that human beings owe a debt to God. Conviction of debt, obligation, guilt or sin is so integral to evangelical Christianity that its expansion can be visualized as a chain of sacrifices and surrenders from the homeland to the mission field. As evangelicals see it, to be saved (and born again) entails a personal relationship with Jesus Christ. But first one must be convicted of sin and surrender to Christ, an act in which the sinner acknowledges guilt for the very fact of being human (original sin) as well as the conduct of one's own life, and secondly, one's immeasurable debt to Jesus Christ, who sacrificed Himself on the cross to save sinful humanity from its just reward, eternal punishment.

Surrender to Christ assures the believer of salvation, but one remains a sinful human being in debt to God. Therefore, one must obey God's call, an obedience to divine command which manifests itself in a life of faith, discipline and sacrifice. Perhaps the highest calling is that of the foreign missionary: following the example of the Lord, to sacrifice oneself for a damned, yet to be reborn humanity. Since people at home have already heard that Christ died for their sins, surrendering to or rejecting Him as they will, the missionary is called to the frontiers of the faith, where people have not heard the redeeming message. To lead them to salvation the missionary must convince them of their debt to God, or convict them of sin.

Thanks to the vision of men like C.I. Scofield, others like Cameron Townsend took the chain of sacrifice and surrender to Latin America. But while Scofield planned to alert the heathen to the Great Tribulation, the impending destruction of an age so evil that it could not be reformed, three decades later his missionary Townsend was marshalling the Maya for progress. Recognizing their hopes for this world, Townsend decided that they were in an onerous state of debt to their masters because they had not acknowledged their spiritual debt to God. A small farmer's son hoped that the Maya could follow his own example of self-advancement.

What then, did the debt Townsend ask them to recognize as their own entail? In his novel *Tolo, the Volcano's Son,* Townsend explains in language that he may well have used with the Maya.

'[The preacher] said that bad things are like a mean *patron* and enslave us,' a Mayan boy tells his father, 'but that we can be free if we get Jesus to be our new *patron*. He said that we had been in debt to the old *patron* but Jesus paid the debt and there's no use working for the old *patron* any more.'

Tragedy befalls the family, and a man of God offers solace: 'Yes, Tata Felipe, "the wages of sin is death." We have to die because we are all sinners. After we die we must be judged, and God will be the judge. When He looks on the books and finds that we are in debt, He is obliged to put us in jail. However, His heart is so very big toward us that He sent His Son to pay our debts. . . . His blood fell onto the account book where our debt was written down and washed out all record of it. "The Blood of Jesus Christ . . . cleanseth us from all sin." Now all we have to do is accept Him as our new *Patron.*'[32]

For the Maya, *patrones* and account books, jail and peonage were facts of life. The preacher is using debt peonage to explain sin, debt payment to explain a wash in the Blood of the Lamb. Two tendencies are at work in this projection of social relations into the heavens. First, unlike *patrones* who falsify accounts to keep the Maya in debt, God wipes out the debt; he can free the Maya from bondage. But second, the suffering Jesus who went to the cross because he angered the *patrones* of His day has been identified with the class which daily crucifies the Maya: God has been presented as the great coffee baron in the sky. In Townsend's view, Christianity would rid Indians of their most grievous burden, vice and superstition. Once Indians accepted their new *Patron* Jesus Christ, they would work willingly for their old *patrones* to advance themselves. Once Indians no longer had to be forced to work with chain and whip, plantation owners would replace debt peonage with wages. Indians would become free, and Guatemala enjoy the fruits of progress.

With this illustration of how political economy infiltrates Christian mission, we can open the door to the Kingdom which North American pre-millennialists have offered Latin Americans. As the United States expanded, a doomsday Gospel to the heathen turned hopeful. But while aspiring to improve the world, pre-millenialists only postponed the date of their world cataclysm. They also came to identify the Great Tribulation with peasant and socialist revolution. At the climactic, counter-revolutionary moment in Townsend's *Tolo* novel, a repentant rebel groans: 'The judgement day has come. Help me, God, oh, help me, a sinner.'[33] Were the established order overthrown, according to this conception of the divine plan, it would be tantamount to the end of the world. To Latin America, pre-millennialists like Townsend have carried a Gospel of progress under capitalism and, when business as usual is interrupted, of imminent doom and other-worldly salvation.

Progress, Cargo and Protestantism

Carleton Beals has left a memoir of progress in *Banana Gold*. After interviewing the U.S. Minister to Guatemala, who confides that he helped improve the national labour law prior to its passage, Beals proceeds to President Jose Orellana (1921-26), who

> received me at once — a most likeable unpretentious personality . . . .
> Time and again he started to tell me about guarantees for American
> capital, the development of roads and railroads, the concessions that
> had been granted; the possibility of exploiting petroleum, but I switched
> him back to those Quiches of the highlands that had so fired my

imagination. A bit irked, he remarked, 'Yes, they are very docile, which is a great advantage; they are not rebellious as in other parts of Latin America.[34]

Still, the President took enough interest in the Maya to visit Cameron Townsend's mission with the U.S. Minister. 'Why don't more missionaries come now that we want them,' Orellana exclaimed, 'as I would like to see one in every town.'[35]

North American plutocrats and preachers were harvesting the Liberal Revolution of 1871. The old regime, that of the Roman Catholic clergy and the Spanish-descended *criollo* aristocracy, had excluded the non-Indian or *ladino* (literally 'crafty one') middle strata from the land. Behind that issue lurked another: who would control Guatemala's scarce, predominantly Mayan labour force? Although Indians were drafted for the plantations, their land was protected to ensure the cheap, stable reproduction of labour. But when the European markets for Guatemala's vegetable dye exports collapsed, plantation owners switched to coffee. Coffee demanded more land, labour and capital, which were provided after the *ladino*-led Liberal Party triumphed over the clerical regime in 1871.

As the Liberals recruited foreign investors, they seized fallow Indian land and divided community holdings into private plots, which could be forced onto the market and into *ladino* hands. New laws strengthened the mass conscription of Indians for plantations, highway and railroad building. The Liberals also abolished clerical dry laws and declared debt hereditary, making it easier for *Ladinos* to lure Indians into debt with liquor, seize their land and bind them over to the plantations in the lowlands.[36] Still, Protestant missionaries remembered the Liberal Revolution as a great victory for their cause. Its man on horseback, Justo Rufino Barrios (1871-85), enjoyed expelling Catholic clergy and declared religious liberty. Since North American Protestants had not yet awakened to their duties in Guatemala, he invited them to come.[37] Missionaries gradually realized that their Liberal sponsors were to blame for the increasing exploitation of Indians, but this insight was eclipsed by the abomination of Mayan folk Catholicism.

'Conditions are as dark as in Africa,' Townsend informed the *Christian Herald* of New York in 1922:

> Drunkenness is almost universal and is considered a virtue, especially on one's saint's day. Oppression has almost reached the stage of slavery through the forced labour system. The Indian's religion is a strange mixture of the worst forms of Romanism, nature worship and spiritism. Witch doctors are ten times more numerous than priests and both combine to take away the Indian's money, giving him nothing in return. What between oppression, vices and false religion, which only sinks him deeper in the throes of his sins, the Indian is without hope. But praise God! no! ...[38]

By indicting vice and superstition, as personified in the diabolical trinity of witch-doctor, Catholic priest and saloon-keeper which so appealed to home supporters, moralists like Townsend blamed the exploitation of Mesoamerican Indians on their political economy: the *cargo* system, its saints, folk healers and ritual alcoholism. Unlike proper capitalists, the Maya did not believe tht that each man's selfishness was to the greater good of all. Yet more than a few were ready to revolt against just this ritual order.

Cargo systems revolve around the worship of idols named after Christian saints. They can be visualized as ladders of community obligations which men climb as they grow older. The offices or *cargos* ('burdens') require so much time and money that men sometimes have to be forced to accept them. The cost of alcohol, Catholic rites and other items to honour the saints imposes a ritualized tax on Indians, by channelling their surplus to the clergy and *ladino* merchants. But the most expensive *cargos* accrue to the wealthy: at the very least the tax falls on those most able to pay it, and possibly wealth differences are kept in check, promoting unity against *ladino* encroachments. In effect, Townsend was attacking both a method of exploitation and a defence against the gross inequalities of the *ladino*-dominated economy. The solution to the contradiction between exploitation and group solidarity, Paul Diener suggests, is the saint who preaches revolution.[39]

During the hard, final years of the Manuel Estrada Cabrera dictatorship (1898-1920) it was an unusual saint whose blessings led to the first Protestant congregations in Mayan towns. Missionaries rejoiced at this sign of Scripture's power to save: busy among *Ladinos,* they had merely hired a handful of men, including a few Maya converted in *ladino* towns, to sell Spanish Bibles, which most Indians could not even read. As always, however, the Maya tried to incorporate a new idol and its holy men into their traditions. Like the more vocal saints, the Spanish Bible 'talked' through its interpreter.

One of Townsend's best Mayan evangelists began his career with the Bible by making a Spanish edition his household saint and becoming a folk healer with a book of occult magic. In 1921 the founder came up against 'a false prophet of considerable calibre', a man from Chimaltenango who had seen the heart of Christ, talked with an angel and called for a return to the saints to avoid a drought. Townsend's claims suffered when people informed him that a 'god' was over in the next town, but his work prospered on the same kind of welcome.[40] Often, he reported three years later, the first evangelist in an unreached district was received as a 'saint.'[41] The rupture with heathenism began when the audience grasped the implications of the Bible. One did not burn candles to this new idol nor get drunk in its honour, and its worship demanded repudiation of other saints. At this point the evangelist was probably chased out of town, but perhaps not before his message had fallen on sympathetic ears.

One of the first groups of Cakchiquel Maya Protestants emerged near the old colonial capital of Antigua, in the relatively bilingual, literate, independent and market-oriented towns of Santa Catarina Barahona and San Antonio Aguas Calientes. According to Townsend's earliest account, six months before his arrival in October 1917 a few men from Santa Catarina appeared at the door of the Central American Mission's *ladino* pastor in Antigua. They wanted to be converted. According to Townsend's later accounts, their leader Silverio Lopez had become disgusted with the futility and expense of 'witch doctor' remedies for his sick and dying children. Burdened by new debts, the man picked up a scrap of paper in the road about Jesus turning the mercenaries out of the Temple, which inspired him to buy medicine in a drug store and look up the pastor. He soon converted 40 kin and neighbours and, at his apogee in the mid-1920s, pastored five congregations.

Fifty years later the man's son could not recall Townsend's story of swindle and woe. He did describe his father's drinking problem, which together with his weakness for women forced him to leave the Protestant church. Another of Townsend's lapsed evangelists makes the customary distinction between conversions 'from the heart' and conversions 'for money' to suggest that the Santa Catarina pastor had been motivated by avarice. The accounts indeed stress the man's 'scanty earnings' lost in candles, pilgrimages, rum and witch-doctors, who 'had repeatedly taken his money and given him nothing in return.'[42]

Economy is a central theme in Townsend's conversion stories, whether they entail repudiating saints, liquor or folk healers. In poverty-stricken, *ladino*-dominated Patzun, where he found another spontaneous congregation, the first convert was an old man named Miguel Ajpop. The owner of an idol house, Don Miguel was revered as 'lord of the *cofradia* [saint society]' for his section of town. 'All [his] savings' went for candles, fire-crackers and alcohol to keep the saints happy. He gave away all the images and turned his idol house into an evangelical temple.[43]

In the more prosperous Comalapa, the Bible salesman Cixto Guajan had stumbled upon yet another group of unmissionized believers. Cixto himself had been about to borrow money to celebrate his birthday saint when he heard about the Gospel. He was so impressed that he decided not to celebrate his saint, to the dismay of family and neighbours. But now Cixto knew that he could worship God 'in his own home, in the field, anywhere' and forswear the expense of community religion.[44]

The Comalapa pastor, Felix Chicol, was a literate carpenter and tailor. Owing to his wealth he had become 'popular' and been made a *cofradia* secretary, the same responsibility that had dissipated the savings of Miguel Ajpop. Indeed, Felix '[drank] up all the property inherited from his father' and had to borrow money from a plantation agent. In peonage he converted to Protestantism, abandoned liquor and worked his way to freedom. To his former boon companions Felix declared: 'My father left me lands and an education. You made me secretary of your religious organization and I became a drunkard. I went in with you with money, good clothing, in my right mind, decent, and came out a hog.'[45]

When the 'wealthiest chief in San Antonio' died in 1920, his sons were obliged to throw a lavish funeral. The drinking lasted for more than a month, during which the sons occasionally begged the mission for medicine so that they could sober up and halt the festivities. According to Townsend, there 'was the desire to reform in time to save a little of their inheritance from being lost.' One son died a debtor in the lowlands, but his son became a prosperous Christian. Six years later the elder's other son, former principal of the San Antonio government school, was reduced to rags, bare feet and a hoe by his enemy drink. In total disrepute he accepted Christ, said he no longer had any desire for liquor, and was offered the principalship again.[46] 'As a by-product of salvation comes a train of material blessings,' Townsend reported. 'When drink and superstition have gone, health and happiness enter the door.'[47]

The unabashed dollar Christianity of these stories supports a common view of peasant Protestantism: that it consists of a rising petty bourgeoisie avoiding community obligations. Since group well-being was thought to hinge upon the humour of the saints, traditionalists considered the abandonment of *cargos* by Protestant minorities, particularly the men of means who tended to lead them, 'bewitched'.[48] Protestant elders remember the early years in San Antonio, Patzun and Comalapa as 'stick and stone'. Time and again missionaries and Mayan evangelists set off public disturbances. 'We had a regular riot before the evening service,' Townsend wrote after a Lake Atitlan expedition, 'but God kept the angry crowd from doing us injury and we had a great time giving out the old, old story.'[49]

The turmoil seems the very picture of the cultural penetration team, splitting apart harmonious Indian communities for the world market. But the impressive ritual orders of the Western Guatemalan highlands concealed unpleasant changes since the Liberal Revolution. While *cargo* systems had tolerated disparities of wealth, they protected each family's access to enough land to feed itself. Now that the Liberals had abolished protectionist legislation, *Ladinos* were manipulating debt and alcoholism to extract Indian land as well as larger number of peons than before.[50] Judging from Townsend's stories, even prosperous men could quickly find themselves marched off to the plantations. And if the wages of traditional morality could be peonage, new entrepreneurial possibilities called for individual appropriation of surplus previously available for community duties. As competition for ever scarcer land increased, it was concentrated in fewer hands. Some men were forced to become petty traders, hire themselves out as day labourers or look for work on the plantations. Last but not least, by increasing social conflict in Mayan towns, the Liberal Revolution seems to have spurred a definite increase in fear of witchcraft and folk healers to deal with it.[51] Where one man's gain tended to be another's loss, successful entrepreneurs were especially subject to *envidia* or envy, an affliction which might well be resolved by dissipating their good fortune on folk healers.[52] No wonder that some Maya felt the traditional order exploited rather than protected them.

Unlike modern-day translators, who seem quite conscious of the shaman's power, Townsend dismissed the 'witch-doctors' as charlatans, just as he dismissed the saints as dumb idols of wood. But the Maya could not, even if they were sceptical of the benefits: to break with the folk healers and saints they needed a more powerful spiritual agency, one which would protect them against powers in which they still believed. Ricardo Falla has traced the connection between economic advantage, spiritual protection and religious protest in his study of a Quiche Maya town. He found an emerging class of merchants who traced both their conversion and accumulation of capital to a non-empirical power (God, destiny, the world market) beyond the traditional community. Illness in the family, fear of witchcraft, and frustration with folk healers were common portals to the new religion.[53]

In San Antonio Aguas Calientes, Protestantism seems to have been associated with increasing production for the market — especially coffee — and the commercialization of local weaving for tourism. When Sheldon Annis surveyed the town in the late 1970s, some 20% of the 5,000 population was Protestant, as were 20 out of the 27 men owning at least one business, one motor vehicle and more than ten acres of land. He found a very rough correspondence between religion and economy: a more individualistic, commodity production 'Protestant' mode consisting of the landless on the one hand and the well-off on the other had emerged out of the more traditional, communal and subsistence-oriented 'Catholic' mode. Successful Protestants told *de suelo al cielo* (from dirt poor to heaven) stories: like Townsend's tales, they begin with a fallen spiritual state, typically of vice, ruin and illness. Thanks to a radio sermon or evangelist, the disillusioned sinner realizes that folk Catholic tradition is responsible for his problems. But repentance and surrender to Christ are only the beginning. There follows a long uphill struggle of 'trial, temptation, backsliding and rededication' which is just as much an economic process as theological: non-productive investments, such as traditional ritual, are realized to be 'sinful waste'. One man's story includes 'a twenty year struggle with drink, accidents, temptations of the flesh, bus route licensing difficulties, thrown rods and blown head gaskets, loss of faith and family, and seemingly endless confrontations with police and bureaucracy. . . ."But through rectification of our ignorance," ' he stoically recalls an oil leak which cost him three years of savings, 'we are redeemed'.[54]

By 1926 Townsend counted 2,000 Indian Protestants, chiefly Cakchiquel.[55] 50 years later, 19 evangelical denominations claimed 19,500 Cakchiquel speakers, 5% of an estimated 375,000 people.[56] Their significance lies in a far wider repudiation of the traditional order: in the 1940s Catholic missionaries began to counter Protestantism by organizing their own anti-*cargo* reform movements. The defections crippled the hierarchies for others, who might abandon their duties without joining a new religion. Faith-driven missionaries taught the Maya scepticism: according to a member of the Central American Mission, the Indian churches are 'content with numerous professions of faith and numerous backsliders, who drift in and out of church life as children driven by every wind of doctrine and experience.'[57]

Until the fall of the Liberal dictatorship in 1944, Robert Wasserstrom suggests, emerging class differences in Indian towns were expressed in the only form of expression permitted the Maya: religion. Social conflict ascended to the world of the gods, in whose terms it returned to earth in the form of Bible, saint and loudspeaker wars. After 1944 these conflicts took on an

overtly political form, demonstrating that Mayan Protestants had transformed
a pietistic exercise promoted by missionaries and politicians into a protest,
not just against vice and superstition, but against the social order itself.[58] Like
earlier saints and their interpreters, the Bible blessed submission to *ladino*
power, solidarity with other Indians and, at an opportune moment, political
mobilization. Since then a heavily Protestant and reformed Catholic petty
bourgeoisie has emerged in the highland towns, but its path of advancement
soon closes for other Maya. The new Indian merchants, labour contractors, bus
owners and commercial farmers have only displaced *Ladinos* or other Indians
from a declining highland economy. Land, the basis for wider prosperity,
remains monopolized by wealthy *Ladinos*.[59]

The Linguistic Approach

Cameron Townsend launched his career peddling Spanish Bibles on foot and
mule through Guatemala, El Salvador, Honduras and Nicaragua for the Bible
House of Los Angeles. With a guide from the new congregation in San
Antonio/Santa Catarina, which was his first assignment, he started on the path
which led to Wycliffe's linguistic approach. In the coastal plantations he
watched *ladino* overseers abuse their Indian peons; he also saw that the peons
listened to his assistant because he evangelized in Cakchiquel. 'The Indian is
the object of the greatest hatred on the part of the *ladinos* or Spanish-speaking
race,' Townsend wrote in 1920. 'The common expression is that he is no better
than an animal. . . . The result of this oppression is abject poverty and extreme
submissiveness. But likewise, deep in his heart runs a long stream of bitter
resentment.'[60]

If the Indian was to *Ladino* as Black was to White in the Southern United
States, then each would have to come to the Lord in his own way.[61] But while
the missionaries considered God's Word essential to salvation, Mayan congregations were springing up around poorly apprehended Spanish Bibles. Even in
the unusually bilingual San Antonio where Townsend started a school, he
discovered that his pupils did not understand much of what they read.[62] Worse.
as they turned into 'interpreters' for other converts, they incorporated tradition into the Gospel with embarrassing results.[63] To explain and supervise,
Townsend decided, he would have to learn their language himself. Catholic
missionaries had learned this lesson four centuries earlier, producing a considerable literature in Cakchiquel and other languages. They had refrained from
written Bible translation, however: native exegesis would have sown the
theological and ecclesiastical chaos which contemporary missionaries so
deplore. But Townsend's Cakchiquel Scripture, the Central American Mission
dutifully explained in 1925, would bring an end to 'attempted, off-hand
translation by ignorant men.'[64] As myth enveloped history, a belated, not
entirely intelligible or even much read New Testament was held responsible
for building Mayan Protestantism. It was used to sanctify a linguistic, separa-
tist approach to evangelism and argue that every other indigenous group needed

the same.

First in the language of pragmatism, then revelation, Townsend and a few other North Americans were identifying ethnic boundaries as the rock upon which they would build their church. Instead of placing Mayan Protestants under the pastoral care of *ladino* converts, they took advantage of *ladino* racism against Indians to interpose themselves between the two groups. The Indian churches would shelter their members against discrimination, help them advance more rapidly and, of course, keep them under the missionary wing. Other missionaries opposed this strategy: they felt that 'the Indian work was divisive and would only drive a deeper wedge' between Indians and *Ladinos*.[65] In rejoinder, Townsend decried the pride and ambition of *ladino* converts, blaming them for obstructing the work of Mayan evangelists in Chimaltenango, Tecpan and Acatenango.[66] But while inveighing against 'old ideas of race superiority' and 'failure to understand Indian ways', he also learned to appeal to a higher objective: in the *Tolo* novel the missionary is said to be using the Cakchiquel language 'as a means of destroying itself'. 'It ought to be destroyed,' adds a model convert. 'We Indians are divided by the many languages we speak. Spanish will unite us together with one another and with the *Ladinos*.'[67]

Townsend felt that a Cakchiquel-Spanish edition of the Bible would help Indians acquire the more prestigious, advantageous tongue, whereupon parents would raise their children as Spanish speakers.* In a generation or two they might be indistinguishable from *Ladinos,* a cultural rather than biological category which includes Indians who put on a successful *ladino* performance. The first Mayan Protestants were trying to do just that: they 'thought that when they put away their idols, it also meant putting away the language in which they worshipped the idols,' recalled a Presbyterian working in Quiche Maya, Paul Burgess. Some converts hoped 'to better their social position by winning recognition as "brother" among . . . *ladinos*.'[69]

To pass as a *Ladino* did not make for a successful evangelist to Indians, however. To place the Indian work on a proper footing, some Mayan evangelists would have to pretend to be more Indian than they felt. At the request of his superior A.E. Bishop, Townsend wrote, the Patzun preacher Antonio Bac 'was willing to put off the clothes of the Spanish race. . . . It was a hard step but a necessary one and Antonio took great joy in it as he does in every sacrifice he feels God has called him to make. Now he would not think of going out to evangelize without his Indian costume, for its usefulness is second only to his Bible. He revels in his ability to slip up on other Indians unawares.'[70]

---

* For politic reasons which may well be borne out by experience, the Summer Institute now maintains that its bilingual education programmes supplement rather than replace the mother tongue with the trade language. At the site of the founder's first mission, however, Spanish has replaced Cakchiquel as the most widely used language. To avoid 'embarrassment' at school, parents teach their children Spanish first.[68] Townsend cannot be held responsible, and San Antonio remains an Indian town.

The missionaries were helping converts put on *ladino* airs at the same time that they were persuading them to step back into their 'Indian costume'. The result was an ambiguous but flexible middle ground between Mayan tradit-ionalism and the attempt to pass oneself off as a *Ladino*. [71] It freed Protestants from the *ladino* demands expressed through the *cargo* system but, because of an ethnic church, kept alive their ties with at least a fraction of the commun-ity. For those unwilling or unable to meet their traditional duties, Ricardo Falla notes, a new religion might be the only way to affirm their identity as Indians.[72] More bilingual, literate and open to outside influence than other Indians, Protestants learned how to deal with *Ladinos* on less unequal terms by manipulating both Indian and *ladino* signals. They were among the first to negotiate ties with *ladino* political groups. [73]

But when Townsend joined the Central American Mission in 1919 to work in San Antonio/Santa Catarina, his superiors disapproved of the language-learning plan. Nor was it easy for him and his bride, Elvira Malmstrom of the Moody Memorial Church in Chicago, to come to live in San Antonio. When they moved out from Antigua in early 1920, 'the town and even the Christian Chief were opposed as it would break all precedents for a foreigner to live in their midst.'[74] Despite resentment at missionary interference, the Townsends quickly became the centre of a hive of activity. They supervised a day school for children and a night school for adults; attracted 'orphan girls' whose board they paid; received, instructed and dispatched eager Mayan evangelists who went on the mission payroll. Western medicine, including chenopodium for hookworm, cemented their welcome. 'This has been a week of great blessing,' Townsend wrote after they had given 114 people quinine for malaria. 'Through the sickness on all sides many homes continue to be opened to us.'[75]

Within a few years the San Antonio station consisted of the *Escuela Nimayja*, its boarding facilities and a clinic financed by a wealthy woman in Southern California, an electric generator, a store selling new agricultural requisites, and a coffee processing plant donated by a St. Louis merchant, A.E. Forbes. The mission bought coffee beans from local men, sold the product to the Forbes Company and used the profits to support the school.[76] To learn Cakchiquel the Townsends spent time in the more monolingual Patzun, then moved to the resort town of Panajachel, on Lake Atitlan, where they helped organize the Robinson Bible Institute. Named after the founder who drowned in the lake, the Robinson trained Cakchiquel, Tzutujil, Quiche and Mam evangelists, who worked the lakeshore towns in the mission launch. Other missionaries followed, including Townsend's brother Paul and a brother-in-law, and Cameron became superintendent of the Central American Mission's central district. His winning portrayals of the Cakchiquel attracted the attention of the American Bible Society, so that by his late 20s Townsend was known as the man who had gospelled a heathen people with spectacular results.[77]

All those North Americans caused problems, of course. According to Townsend's biographers James and Marti Hefley, some 'thought it unseemly to bring Indians into their homes'.[78] The mission bulletins mention the resent-ment of Mayan evangelists over doctrine, salary and supervision. With the *independientista* movement around 1930, Mayan Protestants united with their *ladino* brethren against the North Americans in the Central American and other missions. At stake were salary scales, missionary control of church finances and property, and 'the relation of foreign to native workers'.[79] It was at this point that the San Antonio station fell apart. When Townsend returned from California around January 1931 with the Cakchiquel New Testament, he found that his missionaries had lost control of their charges. Most had defected from the mission to set up their own church.

The Hefleys do not mention that the San Antonio converts were revolting against Townsend's brother Paul, whom a Protestant elder describes as a 'businessman' rather than a missionary like the fondly remembered Cameron. According to the elder, the people 'wanted their own organization' which required 'taking over the church because the mission had everything'. But when a spokesman discussed the matter with Paul, he became angry, saying 'this is not yours, it belongs to the mission.' According to the elder's version of events, Paul cut off the electric current lighting the chapel during a service of worship which displeased him. The next day Paul and a few supporters blocked up the chapel door from the inside. The crowd outside tried to take the nails out of the frame, the two sides 'nearly came to blows' and 'nearly everyone joined the *independientistas*.'

The North Americans ultimately recaptured most of the churches, apparently by convincing Mayan independents that their *ladino* allies would only turn on them after seizing control. This, anyway, is how a mission loyalist explained the conflict: *Ladinos* intended to grab the churches and oppress the Indians. According to the Hefleys, 'anti-American propagandists' were to blame but, when Cameron returned, 'the old men poured out their grievances' to him. He overcame the crisis by telling the elders that they could do better working with the mission than against it.[80] Like Townsend's widely imitated work in the Western Guatemalan highlands, the history of evangelical missions to Latin American Indians has been engraved in a triangular struggle between Indians, missionaries and *Ladinos*.

We Are Christians Now, Sir

Mayan traditionalists were not the only ones offended by Protestantism: it threatened an entire superstructure of colonial control. Cameron Townsend and his colleagues regularly blamed Roman Catholic priests for sowing diabolical rumours and inciting mobs.[81] What little clergy remained after the Liberal purges might indeed live well on the fees for ritual services; their displeasure was certainly matched by that of *ladino* 'slave-catchers'.[82] In 1924, Townsend reported that, according to the Antigua tax collector, liquor sales in San Antonio had dropped 25% since entrance of the Gospel.[83] *Finca* (plantation) owners around Patzun and Acatenango opposed Protestantism: they feared that it would help their peons work out of debt and leave.[84] Nevertheless, many more *finca* owners welcomed Townsend's Gospel,

39

and a critical factor in many confrontations in the Indian towns was that imperfect but divinely ordained instrument of justice, the Government. When Mayan traditionalists took umbrage at Protestant disruption — anything from refusing to help repair the Catholic church to blasphemy against the saints — the mission appealed to *ladino* authorities, who intervened in the name of religious freedom.

After Paul Townsend and his evangelists 'had a hard time getting an entrance' in the very Catholic San Miguel Duenas, 'we had to take the matter up with the President [of Guatemala] before it was straightened out.' Conceding that 'it always causes hard feelings to go to a higher authority,' Paul arranged matters through a local *finca* owner the next time San Miguel put up a fight.[85] In Nahuala and Santa Catarina Ixtahuacan, Quiche towns with a long history of foiling land-thieving *finqueros* and politicians, Townsend and others were told: 'Maybe the government gives you license to preach that religion in the rest of the Republic but our two towns are different. You had better clear out and stay out or we will kill you.' When the Nahuala elders brought Protestants before the Department Governor with the charge that they were 'upsetting the order of things in the towns, the Governor turned upon the chiefs with the question, "What are you?" In railing terms he answered his own question. "You are nothing but pagans, worshippers of nature. I wish that you would be civilized like these men." '[86] The Nahuala story suggests one reason why Liberal politicians were fond of Protestant missionaries: they promised to splinter the more 'fanatical' Indian towns into religious factions. Far from promoting the Lord's work out of piety, Paul Burgess wrote, the Liberals hoped to break 'the power of the Catholic Clergy over the masses.'[87]

Townsend's journeys through the *fincas* could be a chain of welcomes from owners and their administrators, often Europeans. The record of one such trip in 1925 mentions the hospitality of a Swedish *finquero*, a Belgian manager, a German owner and a German manager, plus three other *finca* welcomes, typically leading to a service from the porch of the manor house.[88] Since Protestant abstinence, literacy and thrift could conceivably cost a *finca* its previously drunken, illiterate and indebted labour force, Townsend stressed that his message was sound business. Among his testimonials was the story of a *finquero* who in 1922:

> purchased a large plantation in the district of Zacapa. Much of the land was covered with jungle but he determined to bring it under cultivation. . . . What was his surprise upon arriving to find that the labourers had practically taken possession of the property. Being far away from towns in a wild and lawless section, they had become a law unto themselves, lived, planted, and harvested on the owner's land but refused to help him with his work. . . . Finding himself in such a predicament with even his life imperiled, [he] abandoned his property.

After indebted *colonos* were sent into the jungle to carve out a new *finca*, they not infrequently claimed it as their own:

A year later, with fear and trembling, [the owner] determined to make another visit to his land. A cordial welcome awaited him. . . . In a body [the labourers] presented themselves and asked his forgiveness . . . and offered gladly to work for him in the future. He could not understand what had changed them from semi-savages to perfect gentlemen. Then the spokesman explained: 'We are Christians now, sir. . . . We have surrendered our lives to Him and would serve you too. The only request we would make is that you give us liberty to worship God as we believe.'

The labourers had chosen a less risky, non-alcoholic path to freedom. 'No wonder,' commented Townsend endorsing his product, 'that many unbelieving planters call our workers to preach the Gospel to their laborers. The believer no longer drinks nor engages in brawls. He is a faithful and more intelligent workman. His honesty can be depended upon.'[89]

To play down the threat posed by Protestant virtue, Townsend was offering *finca* owners a higher form of labour discipline. Actually, only compulsion could bring large numbers of Indians from the highlands to work on the hot, unhealthy coast. But even the growing pool of 'voluntary' labour created by land shortage in the highlands was superior to conscripts. As a wishful *finca* manager tells a convert in the *Tolo* novel: 'I wish that all our help were voluntary rather than compulsory. We would be able to pay more and there would be more of an incentive. . . to do well, providing, of course, that something would change them so that they would not spend all their wages on rum. Of course, it is useless to pay decent wages to drunkards. They would work less and drink more. Tell the bookkeeper to assign one of the better huts to you.'[90]

The founder's political trajectory, not to mention apotheosis in the Summer Institute, can be traced to his early appreciation of the wisdom recorded by Ruth Bunzel; there was no point in not being friends with the military governor.[91] As an itinerant Bible salesman, he had learned to seek the protection of town officials before the riot instead of during it. Surprised by the ease with which he impressed men in authority, dreaming of all the good he could do, this idealistic young man elevated a tactical necessity to God-given principle. Henceforth he would identify his purposes with military officers/ *finca* owners/politicians who were not only fighting for freedom from the death grip of Rome, as a mission director put it, but amassing landed estates as fast as their access to the public treasury would permit.[92] By 1921, Townsend had advanced from governors and diplomats to President Carlos Herrera himself, who supplied a letter of introduction to 'his numerous large *fincas* in Mr. Townsend's bailiwick'.[93] It was probably either Herrera or his successor Jose Orellana who 'found that his best workers were those who had been converted to the gospel' and 'showed no little kindness' to him.[94]

Townsend's culminating glory in Guatemala was General Jorge Ubico (1931-44), the strongman who steered the coffee planters through the Great Depression. When the Cakchiquel New Testament was ready in May 1931, Townsend presented the first copy not to the Cakchiquel but to their Caesar, who asked him to repeat his good work among the Kekchi Maya.[95] Just 25 years before, the Kekchi had revolted against the encroaching *fincas;* since Ubico had served as their governor soon after, it may well have been at their expense that he acquired some of the estates which made him the third largest landowner in the country. 'We have overlooked a gold mine in [the Indians],' states the President in the corresponding episode of *Tolo, the Volcano's Son,* 'extracting, as it were, only lead, when all along the ore has contained . . . a high percentage of gold.'[96]

The founder spent the rest of 1931 promoting the Cakchiquel New Testament in literacy campaigns, all the while dreaming of Bible translation in more Mayan languages, more literacy campaigns and a chain reaction of evangelism through the *finca* labour pool. On 21 January, 1932, the chain of volcanos facing the Pacific began to erupt, especially the Volcano of Fire above San Antonio. Disturbing news began to filter across the border from El Salvador. Pipil Indians had cut telegraph wires, captured entire towns and hoisted red flags. They were burning haciendas. From the Patzun literacy campaign during these unsettled days, novelist Townsend places the departure of his Bible translation helper for martyrdom and glory in the coffee *fincas* south of Quezaltenango.

Bible as Weapon

Tolo, the Volcano's Son (1936) arrays a Russian Bolshevik, duped Indians and the Devil against a missionary, his enlightened helper Tolo, the Ubico regime and God. During the 1920s the German star over Guatemala had been eclipsed by the North american. By the early 1930s the Central American oligarchies were reeling from the collapse of their foreign markets, laying off workers and slashing wages, The novel's port of entry for the communist virus is revolutionary Mexico, which planters blamed for the militancy of their workers and where Townsend was about to constuct the Summer Institute.

The Bolshevik martyrs Tolo on 21 January 1932, widely mistaken for the following day when thousands of Pipil Indians in neighbouring El Salvador revolted against a dictator known as 'the Witch' because of his interest in the occult. A few weeks before, in Guatemala, President Ubico had rounded up communist organizers there, including Juan Pablo Wainwright, to whose execution Townsend's novel refers. No Russians were brought to light in either country. But according to the Hefleys, 'with a few facts changed and names disguised' the novel's 'people and events were straight from the Townsends' experiences.'[97]

Tolo is named after Bartolome de Las Casas, the 16th Century missionary 'Protector of the Indians' and pioneer of the linguistic approach, in whose steps Townsend saw himself following. Born in peonage on a *finca,* Tolo returns with his family to Patzun where they turn Protestant. A missionary couple who are clearly the Townsends take him to their boarding school in San Antonio. Tolo becomes their best Bible translation assistant, moves with them to Panajachel and then to the United States (as two of Townsend's assistants did) to finish the New Testament. But a cloud passes across this bright dawn for Tolo's race. A young Quiche returns from an education with an atheistic Red governor in Mexico. A plot is afoot. Before the burden-bearer's strap can be traded off for books, saloons give way to dairies, superstition be dispelled by knowledge, idol huts turned into schools, witches replaced by doctors, vultures by sewers, filth by cleanliness, and Indian towns transformed into prosperous and enlightened communities under the light of the Gospel, scheming instigators may turn the cowed and ignorant masses into a desperate mob, bathing Guatemala in blood.

When the Quiche communist argues that land is the first step toward improvement, Tolo replies that 'we need enlightenment more than we need land.' In fact, the Bible is the missionary's 'most trusted weapon' against a 'spark of radicalism' from Mexico. 'The missionary had labored feverishly to avoid this danger, his most trusted weapon being the Bible. Invariably he had found that this Book would put darkness to flight if its teachings were allowed to penetrate. Through its influence he hoped to see nuclei of new-born men and women formed in all the towns to labor in behalf of progress. These counteract extremists, should such arrive.'

The trusting communists enlist Tolo in their plot. On 16 January 1932, a courier informs him of the final conclave. Led by a Russian, Indians throughout the *fincas* will unite with urban artisans to smite the oppressor with revolver and bomb. Tolo is with the missionary in Patzun, where a government-supported literacy campaign is in full swing. Taking care not to inform his mentor, Tolo goes to the capital to reveal the conspiracy to the President. Having received the Cakchiquel New Testament from Tolo's hand the previous year, the President hopefully will 'proffer . . . some promise of reform to dissuade the rebels from their plans.

At the palace Tolo collides with a colonel, who is surprised to hear about the conspiracy. Only his declaration that the rebels will be shot like Juan Pablo Wainwright stops Tolo from telling all. Instead, Tolo offers to return with the details if he fails to undo the conspiracy himself. The colonel claps him in jail, then frees him to be followed by the President's notorious secret police. On 20 January Tolo shakes the police off his trail and reaches the Pacific Coast rendezvous on the railroad.

> Fellow Indians, [Tolo declares to the Mam, Cakchiquel, Tzutujil and Quiche rebels the next day] it is vice and ignorance that hold us underneath the heel of oppression. Superstition is our Master. . . . The despoilers you decry, merely have capitalized our vice, our superstition, and our ignorance. Quite naturally they have come to look upon us as dumb animals. . . . I know of a dynamite which will blow these things out of the human heart. It also carries with it the seed of new life. . . . When this takes place with our race, then we shall be free. Our

government will grant us schools. We shall secure land honestly.

As a rapt assembly absorbs Tolo's message, the Satanic Russian ('the hard lines of [his] face lighted up with fiendish delight') shoots him. The Santa Maria Volcano erupts and the earth quakes, driving most of the rebels to their knees and the Russian into flight toward Mexico. From El Salvador arrives word of the great machine-gun massacres of the Pipil; the Quiche communist surrenders to Christ.[98]

In 1978 I outlined this scenario to three of Townsend's proteges in Guatemala. They told me that I must be mistaken as to the date, since nothing like it could have happened until after 1944, the year Ubico was overthrown. A brief newspaper search on the embryonic underground uncovered by the Ubico Government in January 1932 disclosed a few suggestive items: the capture of a man organizing *finca* workers in Izabal, plans to organize peasant women, alleged ramifications of the communist plot in the western highlands and especially Quezaltenango.[99]

Even if the conspiracy south of Quezaltenango was a millenarian fantasy, it was the Wycliffe founder's version of the historical revolt in El Salvador. Townsend had surveyed the Pipil for the Central American Mission in 1926-27. He thought they were more bilingual, less alcoholic and less given to nature worship than the Maya of Western Guatemala, also better off economically since wages had replaced conscription.[100] At the time of the Pipil uprising five years later, the Townsends were in Guatemala at the San Antonio station. Judging from their letters, they were preoccupied by the volcanic activity and their literacy campaign.[101]

The Pipil of El Salvador were the province of the Central American Mission's Rev. and Mrs. A. Roy MacNaught, formerly of the Robinson Bible Institute. In the months preceding the January 1932 insurrection, they had little to report except an increase in Sunday School attendance.[102] MacNaught's list of communist atrocities in the town of Juayua totalled two dead and three wounded. Generally the rebels were more interested in violating the property of the wealthy than killing them.

After the uprising was crushed, MacNaught believed that the guilty had received their just deserts. 'We cannot say that the government was too severe,' he wrote of what followed liberation from communist rule. 'A man who embraces red doctrines, who rebels against his government, who pillages and burns is worthy of death.' Still, the missionary was shaken by the massive, indiscriminate reprisals:

> The government determined (they should have so determined long ago) to exterminate completely the common enemy, communism. The soldiers searched the houses of Juayua first and wherever stolen goods were found, the man of the house was taken out and shot. After finishing with Juayua they went out into the country and began bringing in the poor folks. . . . They had in their possession a list of those who were communists. The men were brought up before these officers and,

if their names were on that list, they were waved off to the place of execution. . . . All day long (and this lasted for several days) we could hear the shots in the plaza as the work of execution went on.

In the town of Nahuizalco, MacNaught reported, 300 men ordered into the plaza to 'get . . . their identification cards' were machine-gunned when they tried to escape; 400 boys were lined up and shot on a single day. A month later he received word that 2,500 men had been executed in this town alone.

What was most difficult for MacNaught to explain was that he owed his numerous dead converts not to the communists but to the government. Perhaps for this reason he was somewhat hesitant to call them martyrs. On the second day of liberation, a convert gave him the deed to her shack 'because she feared that the soldiers were going to take it away from her.' The woman's husband had been shot in the road after being ordered to appear in town. MacNaught's beloved Pipil preacher, Pedro Bonito, was executed after being denounced as a Red. Soon MacNaught learned that the *ladino* defence league of Nahuizalco had rounded up all the male Protestants they could find and had them shot; raided the chapel; burned all the Bibles; and stolen the furnishings. If that were not enough, the defence league let MacNaught know that, if he returned, they would kill him too.* [103]

This is quite a different picture from the one Townsend painted in his novel. The Salvadorian rebels had not touched Catholic churches, Catholic priests, Rev. MacNaught or his temples. Since the Communist International had neglected its affiliates in Central America (revolutionary conditions were supposed to be absent), the only foreigners spending large sums to promote their ideology were missionaries. Most importantly, Townsend reversed the probable loyalties of Indian Protestants in an uprising. As a Salvadorian *finca* owner wrote, in self-fulfilling prophecy if nothing else, 'there was not an Indian who was not afflicted with devastating communism.'[105] Of the deadly post-liberation rumours that New Testaments were 'communistic propaganda' and that Protestants had been the ringleaders, MacNaught allowed that, 'as a few of the believers were mixed up in the affair, it lends color to their statement.'[106] In the town of Izalco two *ladino* evangelicals led the revolt along with the Pipil elders.[107]

The Rapture of the Saints

Instead of memorializing the Central American Mission's martyrs, Townsend tried to bridge the gulf between Protestant peasants and plantation owners

---

*Thomas Anderson estimates that the rebels killed no more than 100 people, including police and soldiers. (He could document only 43 deaths, however) Estimates of government reprisals ranged as high as 40,000, but Anderson questions these, suggesting only 8-10,000 for logistical reasons such as the government's ammunition supply.[104]

with an anti-communist martyr, probably a pure fiction. The need for recon-
ciliation, to say nothing of Townsend's deep faith in it, is underlined by
returning to his native Southern California, where the congregations who financed
his work included oilmen and plantation owners. Here, as in other places where
Townsend found likeminded backers, Fundamentalism was being promoted by
wealthy Millenarians with an abiding interest in domestic evangelism and
foreign missions.

The Fuller family of Southern California is a case in point. In the 1920s
Henry Fuller directed profits from his orange groves to 54 missionaries around
the world, including Townsend. During the same years, his son Charles Fuller
was a rising radio evangelist, supporting his ministry through speculation in
orange groves and the oil beneath them. After his paper estate collapsed in the
early 1930s, Charles Fuller went national with his listener-supported 'Old-
Fashioned Revival Hour'.[108] He was one of several leading Christians to bless
Townsend's plans for Mexico, and by the time he joined the SIL/WBT board
of directors, in 1945, he was the most popular radio preacher in the United
States.[109]

The same class of Millenarian financed the Bible institutes. The first and
most famous was Chicago's Moody Bible Institute, which recently has been
credited with producing 'about ten percent of the world's missionary force'.[110]
Here Townsend connected with a Quaker Oats Company heir in the 1940s.
Two decades earlier he had improved his theological credentials and field budget by joining the Church of the Open Door in Los Angeles.[111] The major
backer of Open Door's Bible Institute of Los Angeles was Lyman Stewart, a
founder of the Union Oil Company and financier of the *Fundamentals* books
which gave Fundamentalism its name.[112] Through the Bible institutes, wealthy
Millenarians trained many of the leaders of the contemporary evangelical movement. Through the Bible institutes they taught less fortunate Protestants the
prophecies and pieties which, with the post-Second World War boom, produced a much larger, broader-based mission movement.

Townsend's novel took advantage of the great Fundamentalist comeback of
the 1930s: to accuse opponents of complicity in a world communist conspiracy to destroy Christianity and the United States. At the time, the peril to
Millenarian fortunes seemed very real. For several years before Townsend wrote
his novel, the highly capitalized fields and groves of Southern California had
been wracked by labour strife. The field hands were being organized by the
U.S. Communist Party, a fraternal party of the group which had planned the
Salvadorian uprising. In Townsend's own Orange County, in the reaction of
the Protestant gentry to a 1936 strike by 2,500 citrus workers, Carey McWilliams thought he had witnessed a portent of American Fascism.

'I well remember,' McWilliams wrote, '. . . my own astonishment in discovering
how quickly social power could crystallize into an expression of arrogant
brutality in these lovely, seemingly placid, outwardly Christian communities.'
Since wages had been cut at the beginning of the Depression, the farmworkers
were demanding a wage increase from 25 to 40 cents an hour. The county
sheriff called up 400 men. Workers were beaten up, shot at, jailed by the

hundred and herded around courtrooms with revolvers and clubs 'as though they were prisoners in a Nazi concentration camp'. In Santa Ana, where Townsend used to spend furloughs with his family and later established Wycliffe headquarters, 115 workers were confined in a stockade erected just prior to the strike. Food supplies for the strikers were hijacked off the highways. A camp filled with women and children was tear-gassed by vigilantes, who were applauded in the local press. The Christian conscience of Orange County was conspicuous by its absence, because the churchgoers who financed Townsend's rise from tenant farmer's son to mission builder owned the citrus groves.

'As a sharply defined segment of social life,' McWilliams explained, the citrus belt in and around Orange County had 'three dominant symbols: the church, the orange, and the "no trespass" signs that mark all approaches to the groves.' To help oneself to the fruit of this American Garden of Eden was to risk retaliation from a usually God-fearing proprietor or his armed guardian angel. Unlike the hinterlands crossed by the Townsend family half a century before, there were no dilapidated or abandoned churches in these towns. Expensive, well-kept temples graced the district in abundance.

'Throughout the citrus belt the workers are Spanish-speaking, Catholic and dark-skinned, the owners are white, Protestant and English-speaking,' McWilliams reported. The segregation between the two was all pervasive. Thanks to the growers' association, owners might never have to cross their workers' path, let alone visit the 'jim-towns' where, not unlike the shanty towns which now ring Latin American cities, their workers lived. The intermediate class of townspeople – small businessmen, professionals, clergy – 'invariably adopts the grower-exchange point of view on all controversial issues and, during periods of social tension, is quickly neutralized or goes over, en masse, to the growers.'[113]

Since Townsend enjoyed the support of the same social class at home and in Guatemala, it seems fitting that the God of his novel should resemble an enlightened plantation owner. This God is a businessman, supervising the circulation of commodities and the distribution of grace from the homeland to the mission field. Townsend's novel looked ahead to revolutionary Mexico, where his Bible translators would presumably labour feverishly against challenges to this deity. The founder's stirring portrait of upheaval in the Central American plantations may have opened guarded purses to finance a new mission, which would not only open the pearly gates to the lost but help the benefactors. For C.I. Scofield had warned it was no longer possible, in a world rushing toward doom, to 'go on with our buying and selling, confident that our accumulations will represent some fleeting value for yet a few transitory years.'[114]

Today There Is Liberty in Guatemala!

Without gospelled Indians and social reform, Townsend predicted, 'oppression would inevitably react with bitter interest upon the oppressors.'[115] He had considerable faith in reform. It was in the self-interest of Guatemala's rulers to make the Maya more productive, after all, and what benefitted *finca* owners would benefit Indians. He had appealed to Indian resentment of *Ladinos* as well as to *ladino* authorities against Indian traditionalists, encouraged Indians to take off and then put on their Indian costume; evangelized them in their own language while claiming to undermine it; and promised workers liber ation while offering their *patrones* more disciplined employees. If Mayan Protestants were advancing themselves peacefully thanks to these devices, then surely the Gospel would save not only the Maya but their masters, in the short term by frustrating extremists and in the long term by demonstrating that prospering Maya prospered everyone.

After Jorge Ubico was deposed in 1944, Townsend's successors had to deal with the disparity between their own and their converts' version of the millen nium. It is appropriate that, 20 years after Townsend's departure, his own Summer Institute inherited the evangelical burden for the Bibleless tribes of Guatemala. By this time, many Indians and poor *Ladinos* had reason to believe that their day was arriving. Under Presidents Juan Jose Arevalo (1945-51) and Jacobo Arbenz (1951-54), Townsend's hopes for reform began to be realized. Labour conscription was abolished, civil liberties guaranteed, and unions allowed to organize. Quick to take advantage of the most democratic regime Guatemala had ever known, *ladino* and Mayan Protestants became known as strong supporters of the two governments.[116] In 1952, the Arbenz Government embarked upon a long-awaited land reform. While the elders of the *cargo* hierarchies tended to oppose it in the fear that their own holdings would be jeopardized, Mayan Protestants figured prominently in the new agrarian committees and peasant leagues.[117]

To the misfortune of the Arbenz Government and its supporters, they construed land reform to include dislodging the United Fruit Company from its powerful position in national affairs. Just as Townsend had playfully injected a Russian Bolshevik into a local uprising two decades earlier, the U.S. Government now accused a government promoting small and medium-scale capitalist farming of being a pawn of Moscow. And just as the converts of North American evangelical missionaries had been classified as 'communists' in the Salvadorian *Matanza,* they fared rather poorly in the 1954 counter-revolution organized by the U.S. Government.

In the Pocomam Maya community of Chinautla the Protestant leaders of the peasant union were sent to the capital for trial, their followers chased into the hills or jailed.[118] In the Lake Atitlan towns of San Pedro La Laguna and Santiago Atitlan, trade-prosperous Protestants were jailed as communists.[119] A former ward of the Townsends, whom they had helped to become Guatemala's first woman medical doctor, was forced to leave the country after a North American friend appeared on the U.S. Embassy's list of subversives and her husband was jailed for his association with Arbenz. As the embassy-installed and inaptly designated National Liberation Movement returned expropriated land to *finca* owners, Protestants withdrew from politics.

In San Pedro La Laguna, notes Ricardo Falla, 'the religious battle of the loudspeakers returned with a vengeance.'[120]

The political loyalties of the Central American Mission can be inferred from its post-liberation statements. No matter that a democratically elected government supported by many Protestants had been destroyed. Or that one of the rebel fighter planes (piloted by employees of the U.S. Central Intelli-gence Agency) had strafed the mission's radio station and nearly killed Mr. Van Broekhoven.[121] Or that 'no liberties [had] been curtailed in the work' under Arbenz.[122]

> Since 1952 [the mission informed U.S. supporters] four intercessors have prayed daily that: 'The door of Guatemala and other Central American Republics . . . remain open in spite of Communistic agitation . . . that Satanic opposition in the form of Communism be broken . . . that leaders overstep themselves, bringing disrepute upon their cause . . . that souls seek peace in Christ. . . . '
>
> And God has answered in detail! Today there is liberty in Guatemala! Communistic power has been dramatically broken, their plans were bungled; leaders overstepped themselves, and through the unsettled conditions many have turned to Christ. . . .
>
> In spite of a serious setback, the relentless efforts of the Reds have not ceased in the Isthmus. *Pray* therefore, for the defeat of the Commun-istic agitation especially in Honduras.

Just as the collapse of the Arbenz Government was engineered by the CIA, what the Central American Mission described as 'the mighty part prayer played in the dramatic defeat of Communism' probably refers to more than long hours spent on knees.[123]

The mission's problem was that many, if not most, Mayan Protestants did not understand repossessing their land or 'communism' to be the 'common enemy,' as Rev. MacNaught had put it. In Patzun some of the men demon-strating for land were members of the mission congregation. In 1954, a new pastor arrived, one who had long worked under North American supervision at the Robinson Bible Institute. Under his leadership the elders tried to discipline or expel 19 members whose offence, the pastor explained to me, was 'carrying two cards' — apparently meaning that good Christians could not be 'involved in communism'. With the fall of the Arbenz Government, accor-ding to the pastor, these men 'suffered the judgement of God' although some once again became good church members. As for the missionaries' role in this important affair, the pastor's memory failed. All he could remember was that the communists were 'just waiting for the moment' to expel the mission-aries, whose only advice was to keep on praying.[124]

The Summer Institute had come to Guatemala just two years before, invited by the Protestant missions and under contract to the National Indigen-ist Institute. As translators moved into a dozen languages during the 1950s, at home two ceremonies for SIL aircraft destined for Peru and the Philippines included the founder's fellow Orange Countian, Richard Nixon, who as Vice-President had supervised the 1954 CIA invasion.[125] At a ceremony sponsored by the Santa Ana Chamber of Commerce two years later, Nixon stated that his government was a staunch supporter of 'people to people' programmes like the Summer Institute. He hoped the airplane would 'break down barriers of misunderstanding' and blessed it in the name of 'the message which draws us all together'.[126]

Four years later, in November 1960, popular opposition in Guatemala to the regime of Miguel Ydigoras was so strong that part of the army revolted. In the capital, SIL translators were within earshot of the fighting. As James Hefley and SIL-Guatemala director John Beekman phrase it in their 1968 account, 'Communist agitation and terrorist attacks' threatened civil war and President Ydigoras became 'very concerned about helping the Indians'. The President was so concerned that he met with Beekman and Juan Rosales of the National Indigenist Institute:

> The three men moved into earnest talk about ways to help the Indians. All knew that the Indians, who comprised 60% of Guatemala's population, were for the most part desperately poor and ripe for Communist agitation. Communism would lose its appeal only when their standard of living and literacy could be raised. Dr. Rosales told the president about immediate plans to print primers for the Quiche Indians in their own language. . . . 'We are working for a spiritual revolution among the Indians,' John [Beekman] declared. 'We believe that knowledge of the Christian Scriptures will set the Indians free from vice and superstition and put them on the road to first class citizenship.'

Ydigoras reiterated his support for the Summer Institute. Beekman declared that he would have SIL's prayers during the crisis.[127]

Although Ydigoras proved too corrupt, even by post-liberation standards, he and his successors also had the backing of the U.S. Government. By 1967, when the Mendez Government awarded Townsend the Order of the Quetzal on the 50th anniversary of his arrival in Guatemala, thousands of small farmers had been killed in Vietnam-style counter-insurgency by the Guatemalan military and U.S. Special Forces.[128] One casualty was Emilio Roman Lopez, a former Cakchiquel Protestant pastor who had worked in the Arbenz land reform programme only to see it destroyed and his associates killed; he had then organized a local electoral victory which the government refused to recognize. He died leading a Cakchiquel contingent of the *Fuerzas Armadas Rebeldes.*[129] But as another case showed, pacifism was no protection against the army. A Chorti Maya Protestant taught that savings should be diverted from traditional ritual to feeding the hungry and buying land. In 1972 he was denounced as a communist guerrilla and, along with five colleagues, shot through the head. Six years earlier, after traditionalists in the same municipality joined *ladino* guerrillas, the army executed over 300 men.[130]

Twenty-five years of this kind of liberation have had a certain impact on

North American evangelical missionaries. For tactical reasons, as well as misgivings about government terror, they now stress their neutrality. An elder in Patzun reiterated the public missionary position when, in the midst of his fearful accounts of communist iniquity, he stated: 'The evangelical people should not be political. We Christians are in between, supporting neither one nor the other but with God.'[131]

Spiritual Revolution: Let God Fight Our Battles

For the benefit of the Maya and his plantation owner backers, Cameron Townsend hoped to divert the Mayan potential for social upheaval to the heavens, from which it would return to earth in the form of material blessings for all. John Beekman called the transaction 'spiritual revolution' in his meeting with President Ydigoras: the Summer Institute has continued to pursue the same stabilizing goal its founder envisioned in the 1930s. But even spiritual revolution is a possible contribution to social revolution. To start Protestant movements the translators must harness peasant aspirations to the cause of salvation. Just as the Protestant revolution in Europe collided with the powers of this world, the same is to be expected in modern peasant communities whose margin of survival – in land per capita, in purchasing power – is diminishing. Spiritually liberated converts still burdened by old shackles can easily overstep the bounds of patience and decorum desired by their missionaries.

In view of evangelical religion as a stabilizer which may backfire, let us consider two latter-day triumphs in the Mayan highlands which Wycliffe has publicized at home in books and movies. One is among the Aguacatec Maya in Guatemala, to be taken up in the next section. The other, to which we now turn, is across the border in Chiapas, Mexico, where Jan Rus and Robert Wasserstrom have analyzed SIL as an agent of political control.

The Summer Institute began moving into the mountains and forests of Chiapas around 1940. Land reform in Mexico was drawing to a close and the government re-dedicating itself to agribusiness and export to the United States. As cattle ranchers and coffee planters redoubled their encroachments on Mayan peasants, the translators demonstrated the superiority of their religion through a policy which Rus and Wasserstrom call Antibiotics and the Word. In the 1950s, some witnessed miracles surpassing their founder's in Guatemala, and by 1960 Wycliffe had produced 25,000 Chol and Tzeltal Mayan converts.[132]

Gospel advance was bloodier in Chiapas than in Western Guatemala, but translators persevered in the conviction that persecution and martyrdom built stronger churches. As SIL's Marion Cowan quoted John Warneck concerning the first converts: 'The whole odium of the violated tradition will of course fall first on them, and they will seldom escape a martyr's death. But that only strengthens their own faith, and increases their power to draw others after them.'[133] According to Rus and Wasserstrom, the translators were stumbling into feuds related to the loss of land to cattle ranchers and coffee growers. The translators accepted at face value local explanations that witch-craft was responsible for the chronic house-burnings and homicides; it confir-med their view of indigenous culture. They found their readiest hearing among the weakest faction, whose adoption of Protestantism could lead to a new round of killing.

The debt-free, prospering Tzeltal Protestants of Oxchuc became a showcase. Despite the murder of various Protestant leaders on suspicion of witchcraft — a function of their accumulation of wealth — about half the municipality chose Protestantism and took control of the town government from *Ladinos* and Catholics. The translators saw alcoholism, illiteracy, disease, fear of witchcraft and homicide plummet. But by the late 1950s the Oxchuc Tzeltal faced famine. And as *ladino* bosses threatened SIL members for upsetting their plans, the social basis of agrarian conflict emerged with greater clarity. The translators turned to development schemes which posed a minimal threat to vested interests.

To avert famine, a SIL agronomist encouraged the Oxchuc Tzeltal to ter-race their hillsides, reportedly with good results.[134] Here, and among the Chol Maya, SIL chose to remedy conflict over land like a number of other missions, by encouraging converts to move away. Instead of fighting for land reform, many Maya took advantage of a government programme to become coffee cultivators in the Lacandon Forest. This is a thinly soiled territory which settlers, lumbering and cattle concerns may soon turn into a wasteland. Recently, bloody clashes between ranchers and homesteaders of rival creeds have been on the rise. Buoyed by his success with the Chol, John Beekman went to Guate-mala and told the President that the Bible would set Indians free from vice and superstition.

The political implications of SIL's supposedly non-political programme have been striking in the Tzotzil Mayan municipality of Chamula. The town-ship is controlled by men who made their fortunes as government labour agents, bilingual teachers, liquor smugglers, usurers and so forth. By investing some of their profits in the *cargo* hierarchy, they made themselves the guardians of religious orthodoxy as well as the political bosses of Chamula. When they had four SIL converts murdered in the mid-1960s, SIL appealed to the Mexican Government, which threatened the elders with troops unless they respected Protestant religious freedom.

In 1968, SIL's Chamula congregation was still small when coffee workers, sharecroppers and petty traders revolted against a new tax imposed by the tyrannical elders:

> Thousands of Chamula people were easily organized under the leader-ship of a few federal teachers [wrote the translator] . . . . Not only were the bosses afraid of the strength of the large numbers against them, but of the possibility of the opposition taking armed action. . . . This is just the beginning of a unique tribal conflict whose outcome is still undetermined. . . . We feel . . . it is part of God's plan to at least begin

to crack the tribe for an entrance of His Word.[135]

During the ensuing years of confrontation, SIL's Chamula preachers instructed the faithful not to confront their persecutors. Instead, they were to pray that the bosses would open their hearts to Jesus:

> Let God fight our battles [preached the leading Bible translation helper and pastor].... If any of you are killed, it is the responsibility of those who remain to bury the dead. You are not to retaliate. God is the One who has set the elders in authority over us, therefore we must pray for them. They are part of God's plan.... God is in control and He always works for our good.... If we are killed by them, let us consider since God is over all, this is part of His will.[136]

SIL's church-building strategy was amply rewarded. After the federal government sent troops and jailed the rebel leadership in 1973-74, the Protestant flock multiplied, perhaps ten times, to 800 families, many of whom had taken part in the political protests. The Protestants had become a non-combatant third party between the bosses and the active opposition, conclude Rus and Wasserstrom. From the emergence of political protest in 1968 to its suppression in 1973-74, SIL's religion attracted restless Chamulans unwilling to confront the bosses directly. With federal intervention, Protestantism attracted many more people for whom the avenue of political protest was now closed. SIL had performed a definite service for the federal government: it provided an alternative channel, sectarian religion, into which the government could force militants.[137] Since then the elders have expelled the Protestants from their homes and the municipality.[138]

Spiritual Revolution: We Are An Exploited People

Another face of spiritual revolution appears in Douglas Brintnall's *Revolt Against the Dead,* a portrait of how Protestantism and missionary-reformed Catholicism have helped to erode *ladino* authority in the Guatemalan municipality of Aguacatan. The Aguacatec Maya live in Huehuetenango Department, northwest of the Cakchiquel, and were relatively isolated in Townsend's time. While they were forced to work on the *fincas* like other Maya, evangelical religion made no headway among them until after 1952, the year a SIL couple from Canada, and a Catholic priest of the U.S. Maryknoll Order, arrived on their separate missions.

Since the 1940s the Catholic clergy had been trying to contain Protestantism by undermining traditions that they, too, regarded as heretical. The conflicts between Mayan traditionalists and anti-*cargo* Catholics — called *catequistas* or catechists — were especially bitter because control of places and objects of worship was at stake. The usual result was a three-way split between traditionalists, Protestants and catechists, which left the *cargo* hierarchies a shadow of their former selves.

This was to be the case in Aguacatan, where Brintnall has called the collapse of the *cargo* system a revolt against the dead, because of the strong Aguacatec ancestor cult which underpinned it. The traditional order was so controlled by the elderly that they continued to supervise their progeny after they were dead. Indeed, the happiness of the deceased depended upon the behaviour of their descendants. When the living did right by their families and neighbours, the dead were content. When the living misbehaved, their ancestors suffered for it. Through a series of shaman-assisted transactions, the erring descendant was restored to righteousness.

Now, however, a new cash crop was creating a propitious atmosphere for missionary work. Thanks to new entrepreneurial opportunities, men with suitable land were switching from subsistence farming to the lucrative production of irrigated garlic. They even hired other Aguacatecs to work for them. But land shortages and hunger still forced others to continue migrating to the plantations every year. While some Aguacatecs prospered, the least fortunate were being pauperized. In other ways as well, garlic farming aggravated tension within the traditional order. It was so profitable that sons of wealthy men could afford to defy their fathers as soon as they received the first installment of their inheritance. Besides undermining gerontocracy, garlic farming challenged the wealthy *Ladinos* who ruled their neighbours with an iron hand. Some Aguacatec were no longer dependent on labour contractors; a few were even prospering more than most *Ladinos.*

Since the *ladino* elite had turned the Aguacatec *cargo* hierarchies into 'dependent and exploited structures', religious dissent had obvious political implications.[139] To cast aspersions on the power and virtue of the ancestors was to impugn *cargos* which benefited *Ladinos.* But for a decade, from 1954 to 1964, the Aguacatec remained absorbed in their internal religious struggles. Sons of wealthy elders with irrigated garlic fields led the break and joined the Catholic *catequista* movement. Protestantism also started in the irrigated zone, but its leaders were men who had quarreled with the wealthiest and most powerful families. The Catholics won more converts than the Protestants. They also clashed more frequently with the traditionalists, gradually wresting control of saints and shrines in riots and lawsuits financed by garlic profits. Protestantism only boomed after the early 1960s, perhaps because, now that their *cargo* hierarchies were doomed, embittered traditionalists preferred the less offensive of the two heresies.

After 1964, Catholics and Protestants became political activists with one overriding aim: to throw the *ladino* elite out of municipal government. Even though the new religions had split the Aguacatec three ways, new Indian leaders and ritual organizations under missionary protection did not depend on *Ladinos* like the elders of the hierarchies. The new religions also created ritual ties between Eastern and Western Aguacatecs, who had distrusted each other too much to work together. Maryknoll's campaign for an indigenous clergy, SIL's need for Bible readers and its Protestant bilingual *promotores*, the U.S. Peace Corps and the U.S. Agency for International Development

(USAID) all contributed to another important development: literacy.* Breaking the *ladino* monopoly on printed communication with the outside world, it helped Catholics and Protestants wrest control of two local political parties from *Ladinos.*

The first Indian mayor was a Protestant, elected in 1970 by a party which included Catholics and traditionalists. Since the *ladino* establishment defended its position by fair means or foul, even electoral politics was a rough affair. According to Brintnall, the SIL couple 'tried to remain neutral, but they were upset that leading Protestants were involved.' The soon-to-be Protestant mayor had been their protege, and they must have been disturbed by his campaign.

'We are an exploited people,' he told Aguacatec Christian Democrats. 'If we are to put one of our own people in the office of [mayor], then we must begin to plan now. This is what we must do. All the *Ladinos* in office, all the *ladino* appointees must be swept out of the [town hall] just as if they were garbage in the marketplace. Death to the dogs! Death to the dogs!' Not surprisingly, the first Aguacatec administration was frustrated by a national state of siege. Troops arrived; *Ladinos* accused most Indian leaders of holding an illegal meeting; and those who did not flee were arrested, some tortured.[141]

The anti-*ladino* cause has been the great unifier of Eastern and Western Aguacatec, Protestant, Catholic and traditionalist. The factions remain, however, not least the four congregations into which the original Central American Church has splintered. Class divisions are emerging: Aguacatec have even replaced *Ladinos* as labour contractors for the plantations. While the first converts to the new religions tended to be garlic farmers, and church leadership remains in their hands, later converts have not been so fortunate and Protestants tend to be poorer than Catholics. After the 1971 military occupation, poor Protestants and Catholics braved *ladino* threats to organize peasant leagues. Both traditionalists and poor rural *Ladinos* have joined, but the leagues are strongest in heavily Protestant hamlets.[142]

Judgement Day in the Zone of the Generals

Some missionaries have been cautious about equating spiritual rebirth and material betterment, but the Wycliffe founder never was. Since Townsend left Guatemala in 1932, the New Testament has been translated into the major language groups. Wage labour has made great inroads into peonage: the economy has boomed; and the government has remained in the hands of

* The bilingual promoters or teacher aides work for the Ministry of Education. Since the start of the programme in 1964, SIL has supplied primers and helped to select and train teachers. USAID began subsidizing expansion in 1969. Two years later, SIL acknowledged its help in publishing primers and paying a part-time salary to a SIL consultant. In 1977, the staff of 426 people had a budget of $411,000, supplied by the Guatemalan Government according to USAID, which for 1978-81 was to provide $840,000.[140]

Ubico and heirs, with the exception of the 1945-54 experiment in democracy and reform. Certainly, some Protestant converts have prospered but, in general, how have the Maya and poor *Ladinos* fared?

As for Townsend's hoped for enlightenment, an estimated 80-90% of the Mayan population is still illiterate. One obstacle to enlightenment is starvation: the Institute of Nutrition for Central America and Panama has estimated that 75% of Guatemalan children under five are malnourished. The quest for enlightenment therefore takes us back to a problem which Townsend deemed secondary — land tenure. According to the national census, the maldistribution of land increased between 1950 and 1964. In the western highlands during this period, the average size of the small farm dropped by nearly half.[143] The growth of free wage labour — in the late 1970s rural wages averaged $1.50 a day — reflects the growing inability of the small farm to sustain life. While large landowners monopolize the most fertile land for exports such as coffee, cotton and cattle, Guatemala is importing food staples such as corn and beans. Owing to the land tenure system, Guatemala does not produce enough food for its people and most farmers lack the land and income to eat properly. We may conclude that, while the Maya were impoverished when Townsend arrived in Guatemala, after 60 years of progress many are probably poorer, and that a better life for the masses is not just a change of heart away.

There is, none the less, an explanation for this in the fundamentalist canon, the pre-millennial conviction that an ever more evil age is rushing to its end in the Great Tribulation. To many evangelical missionaries, seduced for some time by visions of progress like Townsend's, the doomsday warnings of C.I. Scofield are being vindicated by the threat of social revolution. Among Mayan Protestants, the North American millennium has asserted itself in a preoccupation with eschatology, those signs and warnings of an age approaching its end. But ages are always coming to an end and there is always an impending day of judgement. The question is, for whom?

Generally oblivious to the contradiction between evangelical commitments and their wish to help hungry people, young North Americans continue to reinforce the foreign missions. At the 1979 convention of the Inter-Varsity Christian Fellowship in Urbana, Illinois, nearly 2,000 took the world evangelism pledge to go abroad. To the south, down the expressways and past the U.S. Border Patrol, in Mexico and Guatemala, Wycliffe translators find themselves trapped. As the basis for subsistence for hundreds of thousands of converts dwindles, the translators remain theologically and contractually mortgaged to the *status quo*. They are starting to discover that their converts are on the other side.

On the 50th anniversary of the Cakchiquel New Testament, Wycliffe published a new edition of *Tolo, the Volcano's Son*. Although all references to 'missionary' had been changed to 'translator', 'communist' to 'revolutionary' and 'Russian' to 'foreigner', the expurgated Tolo still narrowly escapes becoming an informer, dies a martyr to godless revolutionaries and saves Guatemala from a bloodbath.[144] Now, however, the Western Guatemalan highlands were already strewn with real corpses. In fact, the death squads were directed from an annexe to the same presidential palace where Tolo had hoped for a promise of reform.[145] In Comalapa, plainclothesmen calmy kidnapped persons from their homes after dark, tortured them to death, and dumped their twisted, mutilated bodies in the road.[146] In a typical clearing operation, troops arrived in a jeep, then by the truckload, machine-gunned some inhabitants, tortured others to death slowly, and allowed the rest to escape, spreading the word. Villages and fields emptied as Christian farmers fled before the Guatemalan Army. Some had been members of USAID-sponsored co-operatives. They were joining the boys in the hills.

Except for an occasional, confidential and vague prayer request, Wycliffe remained silent. It dared not tell supporters that official terror already was doing what no Bolshevik ever could — galvanizing the Maya into a revolutionary force. When open fighting erupted again in the late 1970s, it was in the 'zone of the generals' in the north. Here, the military landlord-entrepreneurs who rule Guatemala have used their soldiers as private armies to seize Indian land along a new highway where U.S. corporations have struck a mineral bonanza. Unlike the predominantly *ladino* guerrillas of the 1960s, the resurgence throughout the western highlands was Mayan: Indian fighters occupied their own villages to address their people in their own languages.

The government turned on the Catholic clergy and its lay catechists with special fury. Maya of every creed had discovered that co-operatives, education and leaving home to pass as a *Ladino* were no solution to land monopoly. But it was priests and nuns who confirmed what their catechists had read in their Bibles, that injustice was contrary to God's Word. The churches became a framework for popular organizing, and government death squads began to drag off their victims. Hundreds of lay catechists and, in little more than a year, nine priests were murdered. Not all Bibles were subversive literature, however. There were the sects which, in the words of a Mayan writer, 'preach that God made rich and poor, that hunger, misery, exploitation and massacres are the will of God, that the authorities, even if they are criminals and assassins, are to be obeyed.'[147]

As those same authorities knew, obedience to their divinely ordained governance included reporting subversive activity. They therefore attempted to enlist the evangelical churches in a new literacy crusade, which happened to be supervised by the national police. Pastors reported that they were 'trapped between right-wing and left-wing terrorists'.[148] By following missionary instructions to preach obedience to the government, they were presumed to be supervising the *oreja* ('ear' or informer) networks whose accusations are followed up by the death squads. But the government was so quick to kill that it seemed to be driving even theologically docile congregations into the opposition. Apparently for being respected men in suspect villages, conservative Protestant pastors began to die by divinely ordained hands.[149]

Like many Catholic clergy, at least half a dozen SIL teams had been forced to leave the field by the end of 1980. But they were escaping guerrillas rather than the government, which had entrusted them with preparing its official literacy plan. The SIL-Guatemala branch wishes to avoid further incidents like the one in the Uspanteco Maya village of Las Pacayas. Here, in July 1979, the Guerrilla Army of the Poor expelled a SIL family and burned its house, clinic and language data.[150] Some months before, Wycliffe had requested prayer for the safety and quietness of heart of its Ixil of Chajul translators, because the Guatemalan Army was moving in. How did this missionary couple get the chance to live Cameron Townsend's dream?

References

1. MacNaught 1932:8.
2. Townsend 1936:350.
3. See Phelan 1956 on 16th Century Spanish millennialism.
4. Wycliffe's usual millennial appeal is limited to Revelation 7:9 (e.g. Cowan 1979:203), but Townsend (*Translation* Summer 1955 p.5) and *Translation* (September/October 1974 p.11) have cited Matthew 24:14 as if they were speaking for the organization.
5. Wilson (1975) describes many examples.
6. Nathan Wachtel, in Ossio 1973:39, 45-9.
7. Anderson 1971:20.
8. Diener 1978:109.
9. Emery 1970:5/54.
10. *Christianity Today* 4 September 1981 p.58.
11. Green 1978:165.
12. Jennings 1975:vii, 15-31.
13. Cited in Geyer 1961:224.
14. Niebuhr 1936:150; Tuveson 1968:33-5.
15. Green 1978:165, 169.
16. Weber (1979) provides an overview of pre-millennialism while Anderson (1979) traces its political trajectory in the Pentecostal case.
17. Obituaries of two founders and early council member: *Central American Bulletin* (Paris, and Dallas, Texas) 15 November 1921 pp.2-4; 15 September 1925 pp.1-2; and July 1940 pp.1-2.
18. Ibid. 15 September 1921 pp.2-3.
19. Trumbull 1920:22-24.
20. Sandeen (1970) has traced the evolution of Millenarianism into Fundamentalism.
21. Scofield 1924: 15 May p.17.
22. McLoughlin 1959:269.
23. McLoughlin 1978:142.
24. Marsden 1980:14-17.
25. Hefleys 1974:60 (Luke 6:20-24).
26. Barr 1978:190-207.
27. Green 1978:172.
28. Trumbull 1920:66-69 and Spain 1954:4-9, 17-18.
29. Scofield 1924:15 January p.14.
30. Marsden 1980:93, 135, 204.

31. Hefleys 1974:11-27.
32. Townsend 1936:246, 274.
33. Ibid. p.438.
34. Beals 1932:76-78.
35. *Central American Bulletin* 15 September 1924 pp.4-5.
36. Jonas and Tobis 1974:18-19; Figueroa Ibarra 1976:28-61.
37. Burgess 1957:16-17.
38. Townsend 1922.
39. Diener 1978:109.
40. Letter, *Central American Bulletin* 15 July 1921 pp.11-14.
41. Townsend 1924-5:15 July p.12 and 15 September p.10.
42. Townsend 1920:9; Townsend 1921; Jordan 1926:14-16; Hefleys 1974: 32-3; and author's interview, San Antonio Aguas Calientes, 19 August 1978.
43. Townsend 1924-5:15 September pp.11-12.
44. Jordan 1926:27-31.
45. Ibid.1926:35-37.
46. *Central American Bulletin* 15 September 1926 pp.9-10.
47. Townsend 1924-5:15 September p.14.
48. Townsend 1921.
49. *Central American Bulletin* 15 January 1924 p.25.
50. Bunzel (1952:90, 258-9), who did fieldwork in a Quiche town in the early 1930s, describes the use of alcoholism and debt by plantation agents.
51. For a Quiche Maya case, see Falla 1978:286-9.
52. Warren (1978:75-83) describes the workings of *envidia* and folk healing in the Cakchiquel town of San Andres Semetabaj.
53. Falla 1978:185-7, 328.
54. Sheldon Annis, personal communication and draft version of Ph.D dissertation on San Antonio Aguas Calientes, University of Chicago.
55. Jordan 1926:16.
56. Lloret 1976:248.
57. Ibid. p.276.
58. Wasserstrom 1975:461-65, 478.
59. See Falla 1978:524-5; Warren 1978:156-8.
60. Townsend 1920:5.
61. Elvira Townsend, pp.16-18 *Central American Bulletin* 15 November 1920.
62. *Central American Bulletin* 15 July 1920 pp.9-10.
63. Townsend 1924-5: 15 September pp.9-10.
64. *Central American Bulletin* 15 January 1925 p.3.
65. Hefleys 1974:58-9.
66. Townsend 1924-5: 15 January pp.17-20; Townsend 1925:11.
67. Townsend 1924-5: 15 January p.17; Townsend 1936:311.
68. Sheldon Annis, op. cit.
69. Burgess 1957.
70. Townsend 1924-5: 15 January p.17.
71. Warren (1978:136-7) describes the importance of being able to pass as a *ladino*, a point made by Townsend (1936:350). Brintnall (1979b: 647-9) discusses the contradictory meanings attached to 'ladinoization'.

72. Falla 1978:546.
73. Falla 1972:38.
74. Townsend, *Central American Bulletin* 15 May 1923 pp.14-16.
75. Ibid. 15 January 1921 pp.12-14.
76. Hefleys 1974:56; Townsend 1936:276.
77. The most thorough ABS description of Townsend's work is Jordan 1926:13-44, 60-2.
78. Hefleys 1974:59.
79. *Central American Bulletin* 15 March 1929 pp.7-8.
80. Hefleys 1974:70 and author's interviews, San Antonio Aguas Calientes. and Patzun, August 1978.
81. E.g. Townsend 1928.
82. Bunzel 1952:10,86-8.
83. Townsend 1924-5: 15 September p.15.
84. Ibid. January 15 p.20; Jordan 1926:40.
85. *Central American Bulletin* 15 July 1926 p.18.
86. Ibid. 15 May 1927 pp.8-9.
87. Burgess 1926:215.
88. Townsend 1925:11, 14-15.
89. Townsend 1924-5: 15 September pp.13-14.
90. Townsend 1936:289, 310.
91. Bunzel 1952:173.
92. Lewis Sperry Chafer, *Central American Bulletin* 15 March 1923 p.7.
93. Ibid. 15 November 1921 pp.17, 20.
94. Wallis and Bennett 1966:25.
95. *Central American Bulletin* 15 July 1931 pp.3-6.
96. Townsend 1936:352.
97. Hefleys 1974:85.
98. Townsend 1936:350, 394, 434, 437.
99. Guatemala City: *Nuestro Diario* 30 January 1932 p.3; *El Liberal Progresista* 30 January 1932 p.1; *El Imparcial* 29 January 1932 pp.1, 6.
100. *Central American Bulletin* 15 January 1929 pp.3-5.
101. Ibid. 15 March 1932, pp.11, 16-17.
102. Ibid. 15 January 1932 p.13.
103. MacNaught 1932.
104. Anderson 1971:135-6.
105. Anderson 1971:17.
106. MacNaught 1932:26-7.
107. Anderson 1971:117.
108. Fuller 1972:87-97, 191.
109. Hefleys 1974:83 and *Translation* July/August 1968 p.11.
110. *Eternity* (Philadelphia) November 1981 p.19.
111. Hefleys 1974:52, 160.
112. Sandeen 1970:189-91.
113. McWilliams 1973:218-25.
114. Scofield 1924: 15 January p.15.
115. Townsend 1936:350.
116. Emery 1970:5/53-4.
117. Falla 1972:38.
118. Reina 1966:93.

119. Falla 1972:34; *Imparcial* 8 July 1954 p.2.
120. Falla 1972:34.
121. *Central American Bulletin* July 1954 p.3.
122. Spain 1954:210.
123. *Central American Bulletin* September 1955 p.3.
124. Author's interviews, Patzun 21-2 August 1978.
125. Hefleys 1974:194-5 (Peru); *Translation* Fall 1958 pp.10-11. (Philippines)
126. *Boletin Indigenista* (Mexico, D.F.) December 1956 pp.322-9.
127. Beekman and Hefley 1974:226-37.
128. *Translation* January-February 1968 p.13; Jonas and Tobis 1974:195-9.
129. Jonas and Tobis: 1974:36. 186; Melvilles 1977:289-90.
130. Diener 1978:107,110.
131. Author's interview, Patzun, 21 August 1978.
132. Beekman and Hefley 1974:23.
133. Cowan 1962:200.
134. Tzeltal: Siverts 1969:171-84; Slocum 1956:491-5; Turner 1979:254.
135. Rus and Wasserstrom 1981:170.
136. Steven 1976:147, 156.
137. Rus and Wasserstrom 1981:166-70.
138. While some estimates of the Chamula refugees run into the thousands *Uno Mas Uno* 2 July 1980 p.6), according to the translator (*In Other Words* December 1981pp.1-3) they number in the 'hundreds'.
139. Brintnall 1979a:173.
140. Academy for Educational Development 1978:109; SIL/WBT 1971:71; USAID 1978:699.
141. Brintnall 1979a:159-62.
142. For a Wycliffe account of the Aguacatec work, see Wallis 1956:61-8.
143. Jonas and Tobis 1974:16, 23, 27, 29.
144. Townsend 1981.
145. Amnesty International report, *New York Review of Books* 19 March 1981 pp.38-40.
146. *The New Republic* (Washington, D.C.) 11 April 1981 pp.23-5.
147. *Akwesasne Notes* (Rooseveltown, New York) August 1980 p.27.
148. *Christianity Today* 8 May 1981 p.43.
149. Ibid. 4 September 1981 p.58.
150. Ibid. 21 September 1979 pp.44-5.

3. From Mexico to Vietnam

The Summer Institute of Linguistics appeared during the anti-clerical years of the Mexican Revolution. By extending a Good Neighbour hand to teach Indians Spanish, a few linguists from the United States won the trust of officials and multiplied through the mountains and jungles south of the border. Gradually the linguists explained that they also hoped to translate the Bible. In *Two Thousand Tongues To Go,* the history of the Wycliffe Bible Translators by Ethel Wallis and Mary Bennett, divine providence unlocks Cameron Townsend's door to Mexico. At the time the book was published, in 1959, dual identity decorum precluded explaining exactly how the Summer Institute of Linguistics and the Wycliffe Bible Translators came to be. James and Marti Hefley make some headway in their 1974 biography of the founder, *Uncle Cam:* miraculous coincidences start to look like calculation and showmanship. Now that the Summer Institute has fallen from official favour in the land of its birth, we might well ask how it found its way into the cradle.[1]

The Lord himself seemed to have forsaken Mexico in the 1930s. In the uneasy calm following the great upheavals two decades before, Protestants had moved into public life and prospered like never before. Their enemy. the Catholic Church, found itself disestablished. Under the rule of General Plutarco Elias Calles (1924-34) and lesser revolutionary *caudillos,* Mexico became famous for clerical sedition and religious persecution. When the Catholic clergy went on strike in 1926, small farmers revolted against the Calles dictatorship with the cry 'Long live Christ the King!' During the Socialist Education Movement in the early 1930s, the campaign against religion became so furious that even Protestants were forced underground.

To explain its installation in Mexican affairs at this awkward moment, SIL has always invoked the friendship between its founder and President Lazaro Cardenas (1934-40), one of the great Latin Americans of this century. Supported by Communists and, in the opinion of some, a worthy precursor of the Antichrist, Cardenas brought fellow revolutionary generals to heel, sided with workers against industrialists, distributed more land than any other president, and upset North American investors by nationalizing their oil wells. Then, after harnessing popular discontent to the Institutional Revolutionary Party, which has ruled Mexico ever since, he watched it unravel his reforms for the rest of his life. Since political murders and religious persecution continued rampant under Cardenas, the Catholic novelist Graham Greene entitled his portrait of Mexico *The Lawless Roads.* Cameron Townsend motored these same roads with his friend the President and, in a full-scale biography, hailed him as the Mexican Democrat. Under the patronage of Cardenas, Townsend reopened a closed field to North American missionaries and fashioned a versatile instrument for evangelical expansion elsewhere. He made an agnostic anti-imperialist SIL's patron saint in Latin America and saw his handiwork prosper for more than 40 years.

Like a windvane, Townsend identified himself and his followers with larger causes which could be abandoned when they no longer served the cause of Bible translation. At home, he played to fundamentalist fears by offering to put Bolsheviks to flight with an uplifted Bible. In Mexico, he hitched Wycliffe's star to *indigenismo,* the ideology of the first Indian affairs bureacracies in Latin America. By publicizing the linguistic preliminaries of Bible translation, offering to teach Indians Spanish and integrate them into national life, he fashioned an institute after the very dreams of Mexican indigenists. When Cardenas reclaimed the oilfields in 1938 and North American reaction threatened to destroy his institute, Townsend defied the anti-communist furies by turning into a Good Neighbour crusader for Mexican rights.

These expedients were the political foundation of the Summer Institute. Cast in the image of *indigenismo,* Townsend's mission introduced descriptive linguistics to country after country, for the announced purpose of forging national unity. From anti-trust critic of North American investment in Mexico, Townsend proceeded to become its advocate in South America. Here, his indigenist institute also became a self-appointed representative of the U.S. Government's Point Four programme and pioneer of civilization in the Amazon jungle. When the United States launched its anti-communist crusade in the Far East in the 1950s, the Summer Institute was there too, in beleaguered Manila and besieged Saigon, just as it was all over Latin America when the trumpets sounded for the Alliance for Progress in the 1960s.

As Townsend charmed generals and politicians, communists and cold warriors, his most grievous affliction were his own, frequently horrified followers and backers. Sponsored by the Pioneer Mission Agency, the graduates of the first Camp Wycliffe (1934-) could scarcely reconcile themselves to Mexican laws barring foreign clerical activities, nor did they fancy working for what they regarded as a Bolshevist regime. As he always would, Townsend gave priority to field, over home politics, in the correct belief that regardless of the methods employed, spectacular field openings would reconcile brethren to his dance of the seven veils and draw many more. The founder insisted, not just that his followers work for friends in high places even if they were suspected of communistic tendencies, but that the immediate satisfactions of soul-winning be subordinated to the more fruitful, long-range goal of Bible translation.

These were the opening rounds of a battle, which Townsend fought into the 1970s, to overcome North American parochialisms that impeded Wycliffe expansion. The disputes between Townsend and his brethren, over how Fundamentalists were to adjust to their country's global prospects, gave rise to the 'two organizations' as we know them today. When, in 1936, Townsend persuaded his followers to charter themselves as the Summer Institute of Linguistics in Mexico, the move did not allay the anxieties of his backers in the United States. Townsend learned that he could no more afford to explain to home supporters than to Mexican friends what he was doing. The joint incorporation of the Summer Institute and the Wycliffe Bible Translators, in California in 1942, institutionalized a double pretence for consumption at home as well as in the field. The withholding of information became the pivotal feature of SIL/WBT practice, internally as well as externally, as Townsend and his lieutenants tried to keep the membership behind them for the next test of faith.

The ensuing anxiety and scepticism are responsible for SIL/WBT's remarkable elaboration of institutional myth and rationale, to say nothing of the awe in which it has held the founder. The cost of constant opportunism was the accumulation of pledges which could not be kept, confusion within Wycliffe, and distrust from others. But although SIL/WBT has posed as all things to all men, trusted to politics in the fore and faith in whatever is necessary, it has never deviated from the goals expressed by its founder in terms of translating God's Word. Fixity of purpose owes something to SIL/WBT's belief that, despite its unprecedented range of experience with native people, and many subterfuges, it cannot afford to risk offending home supporters and host governments. Master illusionist though he was, Townsend could not help but commit himself in ways which defined the enduring loyalties of his organization and led to its present crisis in Latin America.

If home supporters could not be told exactly how Wycliffe was going about the Great Commission, it was all the more important to assure them that, despite whispers of unethical conduct, their missionaries were harvesting a mighty spiritual crop. And if members had to be schooled in more subtle approaches to evangelism than setting off the street brawls in which the founder himself had once delighted, they still expected to see an authentic New Testament church spring forth from each Bible translation. In each language it entered, therefore, a non-sectarian institute was pledging itself to a sectarian programme. To abandon it would spell Wycliffe's destruction.

With his Hail Caesar policy, the founder proceeded to install a faith mission in foreign governments. By the time SIL's true nature began to emerge, it would be established in the eyes of man as well as God. And as its true goodness unfolded, Townsend seems to have felt, opposition would diminish. Any fundamentalist theologian could have predicted the opposite. State-sponsored North American evangelism produced endless ill-will and made protecting the contracts SIL's overriding imperative.

Obliged to pull whatever levers offered themselves, Townsend was soon taking advantage of what was politely termed the Inter-American system. Friendly chats with U.S. ambassadors led to calls in Washington, D.C., where he offered SIL's services in exchange for diplomatic endorsement. Meanwhile, to build the home support base and protect himself against suspicion of being a fellow traveller, Townsend sometimes exploited fear of the Red menace. An ex-SIL member suggests that Latin American leftists soon recognized Townsend as a pragmatist, not an ideologue, and therefore not a threat, whatever he told people back home. But if the founder was less interested in serving U.S. foreign policy than taking advantage of it, many of the people he brought into the organization were not as sophisticated. They took their right-wing ideology seriously, and eventually they faced flesh and blood communist devils. The group's enthusiasm for U.S. military intervention in South East Asia has been taken as a clear warning in Latin America.

The Miracle at Tetelcingo

In 1942, Cameron Townsend appeared under a pseudonym in a tract on Protestantism and the Mexican Revolution. Alberto Rembao was writing for the Committee on Co-operation in Latin America, a liberal, New York-based council of denominational missions. The identity of his hero had to remain veiled, explained Rembao, because he 'is in the midst of projects that one of these days may yet, God willing, result in brilliant achievements.' 'James Warren' is a missionary linguist from California and friend of the President of Mexico, a man not known for sympathy to religion or the United States. But the President is pleased that Warren is translating the Gospel for the Indians. The North American is in his preliminaries, 'going about among the folk of the valleys and mountains and hills, learning the language of the region, but scientifically so,' and the President hopes that his friend will reach the very heart of the Indian. The President also appreciates James Warren for another reason:

> The secretaries had orders to let [Warren] come in whenever he wanted to see the President. People wondered what business, what mysterious business, the American had with him. Could it be that it had to do with the oil controversy? It was interesting, and even astounding, that such an important person as the Minister Plenipotentiary of . . . had been made to wait when the missionary appeared in the antechamber.

But while Warren is a subject for speculation around the National Palace in the late 1930s, he is no enigma to the left-wing director of the Bureau of Indian Affairs. 'You know, Mr. Warren,' the official says, 'you are not deceiving me. In so far as I am concerned, I know the ultimate meaning of your activity. Your interest is not scientific *per se*. . . . I know what you mean by being "Evangelical". You are a Protestant propagandist, are you not? But have no fear. I like the Protestants.' Warren is quite a flexible man: in one of his heart-to-heart talks with the President, he upholds a new 'philosophy of

65

motives' as opposed to the 'philosophy of rules'. 'The spiritual content of the message is the real thing,' Warren proposes, and 'the point is that when you have the good motive, rules become secondary.'

The real James Warren, Cameron Townsend, always told the story of how he had met Lazaro Cardenas with an air of wonder. At the time he had no idea that the President of Mexico knew about his work. After two faith-testing years of failure, in 1935 the door to that unhappy country had opened a crack. But gangs of Socialist Red Shirts and Fascist Gold Shirts were still tearing each other apart in the streets, and all churches were closed in 13 states. Then, as Townsend worked in the Indian town of Tetelcingo in January 1936, the President of the Republic himself paid a surprise visit. Hearing the founder's hope of translating the Bible into Mexico's Indian languages, the grave, direct Cardenas asked only if the linguists would help Indians in practical ways as Townsend was. Assured they would, the President told the founder to bring all the helpers he could.[2]

Over the years, in homily after homily to the membership, Townsend never found more decisive confirmation that the Lord created Wycliffe. The chain of miracles leading to Tetelcingo had begun five years earlier, in a reportedly chance encounter next to the Robinson Bible Institute in Guatemala. The name of Moises Saenz has always hung about the origin of the Summer Institute: even the chronicler of James Warren launches into this figure as another illustration of his central theme, 'the infiltration of the Christian spirit into many enterprises that on the surface seem to be exclusively of lay character.'[3] A missionary-schooled Presbyterian, Moises Saenz had just ended a memorable tenure as Under-Secretary of Education; his younger brother, General Aaron Saenz, was a crony of the most powerful man in Mexico, *jefe maximo* of the revolution Plutarco Elias Calles. Providentially, Townsend had just dedicated the Cakchiquel New Testament when he stumbled into Moises in the town of Panajachel. The educator was so impressed by the founder's pedagogical experiments that he offered him official backing to do the same in Mexico.[4]

As a leading light of what would soon be called *indigenismo,* Saenz hoped to use anthropology to incorporate Indians into the nation. But by the early 1930s, he and his colleagues were becoming disillusioned with their results in teaching Indians to speak Spanish. Bilingual education seemed a promising solution. It was advocated by a 'strange assortment of bedfellows,' an authority remarks, including Townsend and admirers of the 'little nationalities' policy of the Soviet Union. In 1913, Joseph Stalin had proposed the bilingual policy initiated under Lenin: allow a minority to use its own language, Stalin argued, 'and the discontent will pass of itself.'[5] The discontent worrying Mexican indigenists was among small farmers looking to the Catholic Church as an ally against the land-grabbing Calles regime. Saenz himself had promoted rural schools and circuit-riding 'missionary teachers' as a weapon against folk Catholic superstition.[6] The Cristero insurgents had been put down only the year before he visited the Robinson Bible Institute. This was a fight Townsend would be more than happy to join.

Soon Moises Saenz was fighting another kind of battle, with his own colleagues in the Department of Education. The Red Shirts had demonstrated
that razing churches and hunting down Catholic priests did not mean that land
was being distributed. Yet under the Socialist Education Movement, Marxists
were turning Saenz's beloved schools into vehicles to organize peasants, now
against the Catholic clergy but in the future perhaps against rising families
like his own. When Narciso Bassols became Secretary of Education in
March 1932, he was less interested in idealist theories of Indian incorporation than in modifying 'the systems of production, distribution and consumption of wealth' which oppressed them.[7] Citing philosophical differences,
Saenz resigned from the department in January 1933.[8]

The next month, according to the Hefleys, Townsend decided to work in
Mexico. But by the time he reached the border in November 1933, the
government had learned of his plans in a magazine article.[9] Only the invitation
from Saenz enabled him to cross. Since his backer was out of favour and lec-
turing at the University of Chicago, Townsend met a cold reception in the
capital. Saenz's rival, Director of Rural Education, Rafael Ramirez, opposed
bilingual education and fancied evangelical schemes even less. But thanks to
Frank Tannenbaum, the Columbia University historian close to both Saenz
and Ramirez, the latter reluctantly permitted Townsend to study the rural
schools.

To expedite his next visit to Mexico City, on returning to the U.S. to organize the first Camp Wycliffe for mid-1934, the founder made several fateful
decisions. One, Wallis and Bennett mention, was to publish newspaper articles
demonstrating that he supported the Mexican Revolution. Two others, the
Hefleys add, were henceforth to present himself as a linguist rather than a
missionary, and secondly to explain that he was supported by 'individuals',
not the Pioneer Mission Agency.[10]

Religious persecution was approaching its zenith when, in late 1934, the
Calles machine inaugurated General Lazaro Cardenas as the country's next
President. Townsend passed two months in the home town of the Saenz
brothers, the Protestant stronghold of Monterrey, whose industrialists had
reason to fear the new chief executive. Here the founder began writing his
apology for counter-revolutionary conspiracy, the *Tolo* novel, which he finished early the next year in Dallas.[11] Of the Monterrey interlude, it was reported that 'the Lord used Mr. Townsend in a very real way.' The visit had been
a 'stepping stone' in the campaign to get into Mexico.[12]

The Lord now demonstrated his gift for irony. In June 1935, Cardenas
purged what a Camp Wycliffe observer termed 'the fanatical atheists': Calles
and those *caudillos* who would not recognize his supremacy as President.[13]
Aaron Saenz hung on, but soon resigned due to his close association with
Calles and an old feud with Cardenas. As the President consolidated support
for his reforms, he upheld the legal measures against religion but discouraged
anti-clerical agitation, in the belief that land reform and schools would undermine the Catholic clergy more effectively. He also adopted Moises Saenz's
proposal for a Department of Indian Affairs, welcoming indigenists into

government to plan a scientific approach to Indian education. Within two
months of the June 1935 purge, at the dawn of the heroic age of *indigenismo,*
a Professor Townsend had secured permits to bring half a dozen students into
the country for linguistic research.[14]

The scholars made their debut in September 1935 at the Inter-American
Scientific Congress in the capital. Professor Townsend introduced his followers
as 'linguistic investigators' and 'mention[ed] at every turn the praiseworthy
results of the Mexican Revolution'. He explained that his study of the rural
schools had revealed a need for linguists to study the Indian languages; his new
summer school of linguistics would be willing to supply them. To 'some' of
his new indigenist friends, the Hefleys add, he mentioned that his linguists also
hoped to translate the Bible. According to Wallis and Bennett, this gathering
was the birthplace of the *Instituto Linguistico de Verano.*[15]

To demonstrate what his linguists could do for Mexico, Townsend now
moved to Tetelcingo, an impoverished Aztec town a few hours from the
capital in Morelos. Here, less than a decade before, peasant guerrillas of the
1910-19 revolution had resumed their struggle for land during the Cristero
insurrection. And here Townsend once again demonstrated his skill in winning
presidential favour. As Wycliffe writers have explained: 'Aware that . . . revolutionary . . . leaders believed religion "to be the opiate of the masses, and
that religious workers were parasites", he had more than horticulture in mind
in expanding the Aztecs' diet.'[16] After a month of organizing Potemkin
improvements, Townsend began returning to Mexico City to report successes,
talk up the Revolution which made such progress possible, and solicit tree
seedlings and water pipes. Later he recalled that his famous vegetable garden
soon perished like the other achievements, 'but it was beautiful while it lasted,
and it had its effect.'[17]

On one of his forays back to the capital Townsend talked with the U.S.
Ambassador, Josephus Daniels who, according to Wycliffe, became one of
its 'strongest backers' during the first years.[18] Ambassador Daniels suggested
that Townsend write a report on his activities, something favourable to the
Revolution to send to Washington. 'Because he wanted to be open and above-
board with Mexican officials,' according to the Hefleys, Townsend sent a copy
to his new friend General Genaro Vasquez, the Secretary of Labour, who
showed it to President Cardenas.[19] And so we come to the 1936 miracle at
Tetelcingo, that Venus flytrap for the unwary anti-clerical, through a report
for the U.S. State Department which Townsend's friends brought to the
attention of Cardenas, who was known for his field inspections and special
interest in Indians.

'Our project fitted into their scheme beautifully,' Townsend wrote
following the President's visit.[20] He was introducing a novel institution to
Mexico, a team of linguists specializing in Indian languages. Moises Saenz and
other indigenists were fascinated by the possibility that descriptive linguistics
would rescue them from the problem of Indian monolingualism. First teach
Indians to read and write in their own languages, Townsend advised (thus
creating a public for his translated Bibles); then Indians could make an easy

transition to Spanish in the classroom.[21] His linguists would analyse the languages and produce scientific primers using the psychophonemic method he had developed in Guatemala.* Armed with their first investigations, the North Americans became esteemed participants in every seminar, conference and project devoted to Indian education, their services solicited by the National University, the National Polytechnic Institute, and the Departments of Education and Indian Affairs.

After making his own pilgrimage to Tetelcingo, an unnamed anti-clerical educator wrote the President that he was 'almost convinced that the power of spiritual faith is greater even than that of education, and that by means of it a more rapid transformation of the Indians can be brought about.'[23] Cardenas sent Townsend a note requesting more studies and praising his 'valuable teachings'.[24] To Townsend his teachings were synonymous with 'expulsion of the solid and united curse of Roman Catholicism from the lands to the South.'[25] This was a meeting of minds which had to be explained carefully. In 1940, for perhaps the first time in public, Townsend expounded his Institute's 'threefold program' — linguistic research, practical help and spiritual service. An orator from the National University responded that the group's message was 'far above Catholicism and far above Protestantism; it was the message of God's love in non-sectarian service.'[26]

Townsend was also to fit into the Mexican scheme in a way which he probably did not forsee. In the presidential diary a few months before the meeting at Tetelcingo, we find Cardenas brooding over Catholic propaganda against his government in the United States.[27] This was a problem that his predecessors also had faced. As Cardenas read Townsend's flattering report to Washington, it may well have occurred to him that Protestant missionary opinion had carried weight before. In the 1920s, President Calles had used the Committee on Co-operation in Latin America to defuse Catholic demands for U.S. military intervention. But when Calles allowed the Protestants to be fed into the anti-clerical mill too, this kind of assistance became hard to come by. If the new President Cardenas had seen Townsend's favourable articles in George Dealey's *Dallas Morning News,* it may have occurred to him that Townsend had access to opinion-makers and businessmen in the U.S. The thought may even have dawned that, back in 1914, as U.S. Navy Under-Secretary, Ambassador Daniels had ordered the occupation of Veracruz by U.S. Marines. While Daniels would oppose military intervention during the 1938 oil crisis, a president aiming to bring North American investors under control had to reckon with the possibility.

Townsend has averred that 'no one knows how Mexico might have gone had it not been that General Cardenas had a friend who was an evangelical.'[28] Another speculation is what Townsend's fate would have been if, at polite but firm presidential suggestion and considerable cost to his fundamentalist

---

* The psychophonemic method leaned heavily on descriptive linguistics. According to Heath, 'simple syllables composed of letters of marked contrast were introduced prior to complex syllables containing letters of slight contrast.'[22]

reputation, he had not lobbied New York and Washington in defence of his friend's nationalization of 17 oil companies. In *The Truth About Mexico's Oil,* a booklet distributed to Congressmen in 1940, Townsend chides the United States for its unfair business practices and failure to live up to President Roosevelt's Good Neighbour Policy. He lambasts the companies for raping Mexico's oil fields, exploiting workers and manipulating governments. Behind the scenes, he made himself available to Cardenas and Ambassador Daniels as a sounding board. The significance of these efforts is unclear: the Hefleys say that the New York and Washington lobbies were a failure. But according to Cardenas, Townsend had 'served my government in an important way' during the oil company campaign against him.[29]

In 1939, the First Assembly of Philologists and Linguists made the founder's psychophonemic method the standard for native language primers. The only available linguists were North Americans, most of them Summer Institute members. As Cardenas left office the next year, he helped his Indian experts to organize the Inter-American Indigenist Institute (III) at a hemispheric conference. Among the goals recommended for each country's Indian policy was bilingual education. Moises Saenz became the III's first director and, before his death in 1941, introduced the Summer Institute to Peruvian indigenists. Using his friendship with the much-admired Cardenas to dispel any suspicion of *gringo* treachery, Townsend made the III an official channel for his linguists in South America.

The subsequent administration stabilized Mexico for export production to the United States. Land reform slowed and indigenist projects were attacked as showcases of subversion. The anthropologists who would be entrusted with the task of organizing the post-war indigenist bureaucracy decided that the *Cardenista* reforms had been futile, because social and economic conflict only symptomized a more basic cultural division. Acculturation of Indians into Mexican society, not the ethnic pluralism and equality preached by the *Cardenistas,* was the only solution to the Indian problem, a formula which appealed to those in power.[30]

Townsend's *Lazaro Cardenas – Mexican Democrat,* published in 1952, carried a very different message from his broadside against U.S. oil companies 12 years before. It embalmed the accomplishments of the Cardenas era, and not incidentally the founder's own anti-trust Good Neighbour reputation,for Cold War consumption. In Townsend's hopeful view, *caudillismo,* as represented by the Calles millionaires, had been only a prelude to the Cardenas reforms,which laid the foundation for a happier Mexico free of poverty and class strife. To the grief of Cardenas, it did not work out that way. The 'Tata Cardenas' of the Indians became the weeping Cardenas as he saw his promises betrayed. After enthusiastically joining the Cold War, Townsend eventually had to reckon with statements like the following, from the man he admired so much, at a 1961 conference a month before the Bay of Pigs invasion of Cuba

> The fundamental force which blocks the development of Latin America, [declared the Mexican Democrat] is United States imperialism. Its close

alliance with national oligarchies, the ruinous effects of its economic and cultural penetration brand it as the main cause for the general stagnation which prevails on the Latin American scene. The defeat of imperialism is a fundamental condition for any development plan for our countries.[31]

As Cardenas slowly arrived at this conclusion, the Summer Institute was winning the endorsement of every Mexican president to the present. Three of these men, Philip Agee has revealed, were liaison contacts for the CIA in the 1960s.[32] With the help of Cardenas, SIL had forged an enduring alliance with one of the very national oligarchies which he finally condemned. To refute charges of imperialism, SIL still refers to Townsend's anti-trust tract and his Cardenas biography. A more recent work, undertaken at the founder's request and published the year Cardenas died, makes the two a trilogy. It is an admiring portrait of a long-time financial and political supporter, James Hefley's *Aaron Saenz — Mexico's Revolutionary Capitalist.* In 1970, Hefley reported the state-financed Saenz fortune to be well over $150 million dollars, calling him the 'sugar king' of Mexico.[33]

The Lord Himself Didn't Tell the Whole Story

'I used to tell the group in the early years in Mexico', Cameron Townsend has explained to a later generation, 'that we were at all times on the edge of a volcano: problems, difficulties, opposition.'[34] Yet it would have been hard to find better allies than Cardenas, the indigenists, an anti-interventionist U.S. ambassador, and the Saenz family. Townsend had his bets covered and, except for the President's request to lobby against the oil companies, his friends seem to have been most understanding. From the Hefley's biography it is clear that, after Townsend tied his knots with the indigenists and jumped into the arms of the great reformer, his most serious problem was his own brethren. They did not like walking along the edges of his volcano; he was scaring them with a little hell-fire. Out of the battle between the fundamentalist and the expedient emerged the SIL/WBT arrangement, a semantic muddle calculated to solve political problems at home no less than in the field.

By organizing his own mission, Townsend was bidding for a post of honour in a highly competitive industry, the faith missions movement. These independent, inter-denominational bodies had just one reason for existence which they never let themselves forget, the systematic evangelization of the world. During Townsend's years in Guatemala, they gained momentum in a burst of 'religious free enterprise': as the more liberal denominational missions repulsed Fundamentalist witch-hunters, the latter turned to faith missions such as the Central American, or started their own.[35] By demonstrating the purity of one's convictions, declaring war on apostasy, or announcing a campaign to spread that old-time religion, men like Cameron Townsend could

71

find the funds and recruits to launch their own spiritual empires.

As the first faith entrepreneurs broke with denominational funding, they had sanctified their departure with the watchword: 'reliance on the Lord'. Faith missionaries consider prayer to be the driving force behind their work, and they operate on faith that the Lord will move others to finance it. They communicate with the homeland through the prayer bulletin, a list of requests for petition (to deal with a problem) or praise (for having solved the problem) which is linked to presentation of the 'need', for further effort to reach the lost. As has become the custom, supporters respond not only with prayer but money. Besides tapping directly into the church public and wrapping solicitation in sanctity, faith fund-raising produces rapid growth when combined with the sophisticated advertising techniques Wycliffe has employed. Each recruit tends to draw money from his/her social network; the pool of potential recruits cuts across denominational boundaries; and the Wycliffe name assures supporters that the cause is a worthy one.

But since faith missions cannot rely upon denominational loyalty and bureaucracy, their cash flow depends upon pleasing a multitude of pastors, church committees and faithful. Once people have been moved to contribute they want to see the promised results: darkness breached, souls saved, new churches organized. Since faith entrepreneurs have encouraged and exploited unrealistic expectations, the interplay of faith and shoestring finance can easily lead to inaccurate reporting of what is actually happening in darkest Africa or the mysterious Amazon. If supporters learn that they themselves have been kept in darkness their faith abused, their hearts and purses snap shut.

Faith missions are the principal guardians of each other's morals, since only they know what is really going on. Owing to overlapping home constituencies, they have a strong common interest in maintaining the odour of sanctity. But the Lord's leading is a private experience and, especially during the depressed 1930s, established missions did not want new ones competing for finite quantities of recruitable youth and disposable income. In the field there are even more opportunities for disagreement, so it is no surprise that faith entrepreneurs have occasionally denounced each other as frauds. In fact, although the faith missions organized themselves into two associations to deal with this sort of problem, in the 1950s Wycliffe had a falling out with each. Yet now that Wycliffe has become a major evangelical institution, supreme caution reigns. 'Support' and 'losing support' preoccupy many a Wycliffe administrator, determining what information does and does not reach home supporters.

The Lord led Townsend to Mexico through the Victorious Life Testimony, a non-denominational medium for genteel Presbyterian businessmen in Philadelphia. Its leading apostle was C.I. Scofield's biographer Charles Gallaudet Trumbull, one of the last leaders of the Millenarian movement before it became indistinguishable from Fundamentalism. The 'victorious life' was Keswick sanctification doctrine, which had become the Fundamentalist answer to the claims to the Holy Spirit made by the Holiness and Pentecostal movements.[36] To anxious Millenarians absorbed in the prophecy of doom, the victorious life offered personal triumph: 'victory over sin, and power in service . . . God's call to all, as missionary Christians, to share this with others to the uttermost part of the earth.'[37] A mission organizer of the Victorious Life Testimony, Leonard Livingston Legters (? - 1940), helped Townsend plan the Mexican advance and provided the Testimony's faith apparatus to finance it.

The two had become acquainted in 1920, when the Townesnds invited the Rev. Howard Dinwiddie of the Victorious Life to the first Cakchiquel Bible conference. L.L. Legters came too: a former Presbyterian missionary on a Comanche and Sioux reservation in the United States, he had just shaken free of a pastorship in South Carolina. His wife was dying and he was restless. According to Wycliffe, Legters' vision for the unreached tribes dated from his tour of Townsend's work. According to Paul Burgess, the missions in Guatemala were close to schism over the Indian work when Dinwiddie and Legters made matters worse by proposing a new, separate Indian mission. Townsend mentioned only Dinwiddie in his dispatches, but in 1921 Legters became field secretary of the Victorious Life's new Pioneer Mission Agency.[38]

Pioneer was a reconnaissance and fund-raising operation, not a full-fledged field mission. Legters' duties included annual visits to unreached parts of Latin America, in what both he and Catholic missionaries regarded as a direct continuation of the Thirty Years War in Europe. After scouting Satan's strongholds, he would pound the church circuit to denounce the thousand tribes still in darkness and demand that they all be reached in this generation. Among those most impressed by Legters' reports of lost Amazonian tribes was Townsend, who had come to feel trapped in the narrow valleys of the Central American Mission. Yearning for distant jungles and weighing the risks, Townsend decided that he had the answer — aviation — and could find the money to pay for it. Finishing the Cakchiquel New Testament about the time the Wall Street stock market crashed in 1929, he began an unsuccessful search for backers.

Discrepancies in the Wycliffe accounts and the Central American Mission bulletins, suggest that Townsend's famous 1932 case of tuberculosis was more exculpatory than incapacitating, an excuse to leave Guatemala.[39] The Central American Mission considered his proposals too expensive, wanted him to stay with the Cakchiquel, and hoped that he would not start a new mission.[40] Despite the Saenz invitation, the Amazon reportedly captivated Townsend until February 1933, when Legters persuaded him to choose the more economical Mexico. At Townsend's suggestion, the two also agreed to train Bible translators for the country's 50 or so Indian languages. They did not agree to start a new mission, however, only to train translators for others.[41] The first Camp Wycliffes were apparently intended to supply recruits for another Pioneer-sponsored enterprise, whose objective Townsend seems to have appropriated as his own.

Legters had been making plans for Mexico for several years before the height of the Protestant crisis. In January 1930, he and a Presbyterian missionary, James Dale, claimed a hill for Christ outside Tamazunchale, Potosi. Dale and his wife, Dr. Katherine Neel Dale, planned to free the estimated 45 Indian tribes of Mexico from illiteracy, serfdom and the Catholic Church. In April 1934, the Pioneer Mission took them under its wing so that they could organize their own Mexican Indian Mission.[42]

Two months later, Townsend held the first Camp Wycliffe on a farm near Sulphur Springs, Arkansas, where brother Paul was working for the evangelist and educator John Brown. Camp Wycliffe also would be referred to as the Pioneer Missionary Camp, a point neglected in the Wycliffe accounts.[43] As the Pioneer-edited *Camp Wycliffe Chronicle* was pleased to announce in 1936, the problem was no longer getting into Mexico, but finding enough volunteers.[44] Soon there was another difficulty, however, not mentioned in the *Chronicle* or its parent bulletin the *Pioneer News:* opposition to Townsend's methods within Pioneer.

Townsend and Dale had similar ambitions for the tribes of Mexico, Dale first, judging from his own account. While the two helped each other in various ways, Townsend soon outpaced his senior colleague, who failed to organize his own mission board until 1944. Nor did Dale have any need for Townsend's subterfuges, because he had found his Mexican patronage elsewhere. While Townsend went to the capital, Dale stayed in San Luis Potosi protected by General Saturnino Cedillo, last of the revolutionary war-lords. Cedillo gave sanctuary to hundreds of Catholic priests, organized more bands of Gold Shirts after Cardenas disbanded the Red Shirts, and died in an abortive 1938 rebellion. As Townsend went 'Bolshevik', Dale went 'Fascist' and his Mexican Indian Mission never prospered like Wycliffe: in the mid-1960s it claimed 18 members to Wycliffe's 1,400.[45]

According to Townsend, just before the miracle at Tetelcingo in January 1936, he received a letter from a missionary. This man, like Dale, had been in Mexico for many years; his son, very much like Dale's son, had spent a great deal of money on a visa; he 'was in close touch with the agency which handled our funds in Philadelphia'; and he had intercepted information concerning Townsend's open door. The unnamed missionary felt that Townsend was deceiving Pioneer and wanted to know how he had obtained permission to operate. Soon Townsend replied that his invitation came from none other than President Cardenas. Judging from the Hefleys, the same missionary was not impressed. Believing that Townsend was in Mexico under false pretences and deceiving home supporters, he returned to the United States to denounce Townsend's 'fakery' and 'dishonesty'.[46]

If this was James Dale, what he may have intercepted was the first number of the *Camp Wycliffe Chronicle* in January 1936. While Pioneer was reserving the honour of organizing a new mission to Dale, he would have read that the Lord had so 'definitely blessed' Camp Wycliffe that the 'leaders of the movement' were overcoming their fear of further dividing the missionary force with the belief that 'the Lord would have us go on as a group.' Needless to say, the Camp Wycliffe expedition would always co-operate with others or 'even disband', if that was the Lord's leading.[47]

Townsend's problems with his own followers began later that year, as they incorporated in Mexico under the name of the Summer Institute of Linguistics and went on the government payroll. When President Cardenas salaried the group as rural schoolteachers, two left for Peru, in Townsend's words because 'we were assigned to work under a man . . . said to be a Communist.'[48] Those who remained objected to their leader's 'secular involvements' and his 'political alliance' with Cardenas, especially after he began defending oil nationalization. In one exchange Townsend even defended 'sincere' socialism, argued that he would do the same in Russia if he had the chance, and blasted 'the ones who went off half-cocked in their criticism'. Opposition to the government, he warned, could result in 'deadly opposition' to the work.

Townsend's linguists also were upset by his admonitions against overt proselytism. Since Mexican law barred foreigners from clerical functions, Camp Wycliffe alumni were to obey the law and confine themselves to Bible translation. They also were to refrain from distributing religious tracts, keep their distance from religious controversy and 'witness only on a personal level to friends'. To young missionaries on fire for the Lord, Townsend was demanding that the very offer of salvation be withheld in favour of political advantage and a more abundant harvest in the future. 'Most of the SILers went along with a minimum of grumbling,' conclude the Hefleys.[49]

The constraints required by the metamorphosis from faith mission to linguistic institute gave birth to basic SIL claims, which often fail to reflect practice but do protect its alliances with governments. Since 1935, Townsend had been claiming to be 'non-sectarian'. With his followers' revolt against Bolshevism, Townsend called for political neutrality. And in his response to the problem of practice — how to be non-sectarian faith missionaries — we see the beginning of SIL's claim to be 'non-ecclesiastical'. This will-o'-the-wisp is supposed to restrain zealous translators, distinguish SIL from other evangelical missions, and surmount the church-state objection to its contracts. Yet Wycliffe always has assured home supporters that it works with other evangelical missions and that Bible translation produces new evangelical congregations.*

---

* SIL is allegedly non-ecclesiastical because: 1) members confine themselves to Bible translation; 2) they are forbidden from exercising pastoral functions such as marriages, burying and preaching in a language other than their own, leaving these duties to local leaders; and 3) they do not establish denominational church systems. But while Townsend always admonished members to keep a low profile, they were expected to turn language informants into church leaders.

'Our purpose is to translate the Word as soon as possible,' the founder advised in 1948, 'and to accomplish this it is better not to get tied with responsibilities such as 'pastoring' a congregation of believers. This can be postponed at least, by

Wycliffe has provided just one account, and that only recently, of how the SIL/WBT arrangement came to be. According to the Hefleys, it was the result of two reformations in the Pioneer/Camp Wycliffe/linguists arrangement, in 1936 and 1941, triggered by ultimatums from Pioneer.

In late 1936, a letter from L. L. Legters caught up with Townsend in Mexico. His partner 'was having trouble with the Pioneer Mission Agency.' The Pioneer board of directors, which included Legters, wanted a measure of decorum so badly that it was threatening to strangle Gospel advance. It could not continue to forward funds from faith supporters unless the Camp Wycliffe expedition organized a committee, a group of elders in the U.S. who would oversee field activities. According to the Hefleys, Townsend felt that such a home committee 'might not understand' what his group was doing.

The Pioneer ultimatum forced Townsend to present his recruits who understood all too well what he was doing, with an accomplished fact, that they were now the Summer Institute of Linguistics. Appealing to the field governance tradition in faith mission, he urged his followers to 'run our own affairs from the field under the Lord's leading'. To incorporate in Mexico, they obviously would have to be a linguistic agency rather than a religious mission. The Summer Institute of Linguistics would be a suitable name because 'a suspicious country wouldn't consider it a threat.'[52] There were objections to this logic, but Townsend's recruits had little choice because already he was translating Camp Wycliffe as the *Instituto Linguistico de Verano* for Mexican ears.[53]

The principle that ultimate authority resides in the membership, rather than the board of directors, came out of this archetype of democratic SIL decision-making. While Townsend would continue to double-bind his members with accomplished facts, they were his only possible source of legitimacy apart from divine guidance, whose credibility was rather low at this point. The attitude of at least some recruits toward the SIL arrangement is suggested by

---

beginning where there is no congregation. . . . When several Indians have believed, it is well to meet with them regularly in . . . their homes to study the Word. Call it a "study," not a "service." Singing and praying should be in the Indian language with Indians leading, though the missionary may have to do some unobstrusive steering from his seat in the audience. Just as soon as possible, the missionary should teach an Indian privately how to give the message or lead the study. This develops native leaders and keeps the missionary out of the limelight.'[50]

'The policy of our group is first to begin translating the New Testament,' a 1944 Wycliffe publication stated. '. . . . Then, in propagating the translation . . . to establish a local church with a local . . . leadership.' Since local leadership is a standard evangelical goal, it does not distinguish SIL from other missions. While members do not teach ecclesiastical systems of any kind, according to a recent Wycliffe flier they do 'share a vision of church planting and church growth' with the native evangelists they have trained.[51] A few members are said to have been expelled when their proselytism has endangered branches. The preaching of many more has been beyond administrative control or excused, however, on grounds they were only 'sharing their faith' or 'assisting' at a service actually led by a native person.

L. L. Legters' son David. A leading rebel of these years, young Legters supervised a Pioneer-financed team of Mayan evangelists in the Yucatan, helped draw up the 1936 SIL constitution, and resigned in the early 1940s. 'Some of their ease of movement,' a friend explained decades later, 'came from the fact that Wycliffe had listed them as translators. Because of a new government drive to educate the masses, this title and its implication that the great illiterati would somehow be helped by trained foreign teachers helped to level official obstacles in the way of Protestant religionists.'[54]

The conservative businessmen of the Pioneer board continued to forward money, but they were not pleased by the SIL manoeuvre and what followed. 'We do not trouble about money,' Townsend explained to Ambassador Daniels. 'The Lord will provide. . . . When it is learned what we are doing, the money comes.'[55] Yet it did not come in sufficient quantity, the Hefleys suggest owing to Townsend's support for Cardenas. The founder remembers it as a lonely period: 'I am so glad that we were dependent at first on a fund-forwarding arrangement which was just a courtesy and not very efficient, and that we could not permit publicity to go out because some such had been used against us in Mexico. We were completely dependent on the Lord. We said, "Lord, you know we are down here. We cannot let others know. We cannot broadcast our situation." '[56]

Actually Pioneer continued to publicize the Mexican expedition as well as Camp Wycliffe, but it did not tub-thump and, like later Wycliffe publicity, its releases were not very informative. While SIL materialized on the masthead of the *Camp Wycliffe Chronicle,* there was no explanation of how or why this entity came into existence. Judging from the various Pioneer bulletins, supporters were not informed that their missionaries were salaried by the Cardenas Government or operating under the auspices of SIL: there was a Camp Wycliffe in Arkansas conducted by SIL, and then there were the alumni in Mexico under Pioneer sponsorship. After chief fund-raiser L. L. Legters died of a heart attack in 1940, privation ensued.

Two events in 1941 precipitated the second reformation – independence from the Pioneer Mission and the incorporation of Camp Wycliffe/SIL along today's lines. The first was another ultimatum from Pioneer: now that Townsend was doubling his force to 100 in a single year, it insisted that he open his own home office to handle contributions and advertise the work. The second event was an invitation to move Camp Wycliffe to the University of Oklahoma at Norman. As George Cowan has explained, state law barred the university from sponsoring a religious organization.[57]

To stimulate faith in the homeland and allay the reaction to Townsend's Mexican policies, the group would have to organize as its own faith mission. To secure university sponsorship, the faith mission would have to circumvent the law in the United States by incorporating itself as a non-religious organization. In late 1941 Townsend's conferees – Camp Wycliffe linguists Kenneth Pike and Eugene Nida, as well as the new fund-raiser William Nyman – therefore accepted his suggestion to form 'two organizations' whose membership and board of directors would be the same. While the Summer Institute would continue to be non-sectarian, the Wycliffe Bible Translators would have a statement of doctrine like every other faith mission. William Nyman, a retired lumber merchant and member of the Church of the Open Door in Los Angeles, incorporated the two entities in California in 1942. The same year, Camp Wycliffe moved to the University of Oklahoma, where as SIL its trainees could earn academic credit.[58]

The new arrangement shored up the dual identity at home, because now Townsend's board members would 'understand' his policies. Judging from WBT publications, however, home supporters did not understand that their missionaries were operating in the field under SIL auspices until the late 1950s, because WBT did not tell them. At home, SIL was presented as a dependency of WBT: except for the fine print stating that SIL 'maintains Branch Offices in Mexico and Peru' and co-operates closely with governments, it was merely an academic title for the Camp Wycliffe sessions.[59] Field operations are never referred to as anything except Wycliffe operations. While the SIL session at the University of Oklahoma attracted large numbers of other missionaries, until the 1950s it seems to have been open only to Protestants. In view of SIL's presentations to Latin Americans, they could rest assured that they were dealing with a dependency of a state-supported, secular institution.

The men who fathered SIL/WBT, sometimes against their own wishes — Townsend, Legters, Dale, Saenz, and much of the Pioneer board — were Presbyterians, but Wycliffe proved far more appealing to Baptists and independent fundamentalists from churches like Open Door. To dilute the sectarianism in his ranks, Townsend tried to broaden the home support base, a move facilitated by an important split in the Fundamentalist movement. In 1942, the more moderate Fundamentalist leaders, such as Charles Fuller, organized the National Association of Evangelicals (NAE). Resolving to give priority to evangelism rather than arcane fundamentalist disputes, the NAE became the nucleus of the contemporary born-again establishment. The evangelical leaders Townsend cultivated eventually gave him more manoeuvring room, but his die-hards fought back. While the first Camp Wycliffe/SIL session at the University of Oklahoma impressed mission publicist Martha Moennich as a 'united body', actually it was seething with sectarian passion. The independent fundamentalists among the 'Wycliffes' attacked Townsend for allowing a member of the Presbyterian Church, U.S.A. to take the course, and for inviting a woman with 'Pentecostal leanings' to speak in chapel. Pioneer threatened to cut off the funds it was still forwarding. Senior members were upset because some of the students and new members did not share their view on eternal security.[60]

To justify their presentation of this fanatical fraternity, Wycliffe spokesmen have appealed to expediency: while governments would not have accepted us as missionaries, they did accept us as linguists. 'If linking up too much with sectarian work at the start works against us to the extent that we lost the opportunity to live in the country,' Townsend reminded fieldworkers in 1948, 'then we cannot help our friends. If by being extremely cautious [for] the first few years we gain permanent permission to live with the Indian tribes and translate the Scriptures for them, we shall be making a great contribution to the work of our friends.'

This sort of reasoning does not satisfy many evangelicals, however: it does not sound Scriptural, a misapprehension the founder has always laboured to correct. 'The Lord Himself set the example of not telling His enemies the whole story,' Townsend maintained in 1948. 'Even His friends had to come to a realization of Who He was. . . . We don't have to tell everyone all we know in order to be honest. I Sam. 16:1-3.'* In *Remember All The Way,* a collection of talks to the membership published in 1975, he argues that: 1) it was God who led us to present ourselves as we do; 2) businessmen do the same sort of thing; 3) our host governments accept the policy; and 4) there is Biblical precedent for it. Namely, just as Jesus came out of Nazareth 'disguised very effectively' as a carpenter, Wycliffe missionaries go to the filed as linguists and literacy workers. 'Was it honest for the Son of God,' asks the founder, 'to come down to earth without revealing who He was?'[61]

Based upon this principle, in order to harness state power to an evangelical plan for native people, Townsend taught his followers to become a new kind of missionary, to some degree in practice but more in presentation. It used to be said of mission builders that they were men greatly used of God: in contrast, Cameron Townsend used God, and faith became his handmaiden. By self-definition recruits were servants of the Lord, Townsend derived his authority from the same Lord, and those who did not like his methods could leave. Many more flooded into Wycliffe in obedience to God's call.

For the membership, Townsend constructed a new and sanctified semantic universe, a cult of divine expediency derived from evangelical meanings, but essentially privy to Wycliffe itself. Within this privileged world, members could be non-sectarian, non-ecclesiastical Christians whose task was planting congregations of 'real' Christians. The business of moving from a SIL contract to WBT church-building became an 'outworking' of God's unfolding plan for salvation. Caught between the requirements of honesty and expansion, Wycliffe institutionalized the plausible denial as holy writ.

Since SIL/WBT's mission is divine, contradiction inadmissable to the larger world has become just as inadmissable within SIL/WBT itself. Obfuscation has become a many-layered self-deception: faith, Scripture and miracle allay the doubts. This is why, in 1975, Wycliffe could present the disguised Jesus to evangelicals in the U.S., as Summer Institute spokesmen in several countries denied that their organization ever had deceived anyone.

---

*What we do tell, of course,' Townsend added, 'must be true. This is why some recruits are reticent about saying that they are linguistic investigators. . . . they think that they don't qualify. This is one reason why Dr. Pike and others have been so insistent about everyone's working hard on linguistics.'

Mr. Townsend Goes to Washington

During the oil crisis, Cameron Townsend brought Lazaro Cardenas together with Southern California friends for a Good Neighbours picnic. Alberto Rembao called the founder's work 'linguistics as an Inter-American bond'.[62] By identifying his linguistic institute with the causes of Mexican nationalists, Townsend earned it an enviable reputation. But even before the Second World War, the founder's visions were encircling the globe. Camp Wycliffe would train translators for a thousand tribes without the Bible. From Mexico his missionaries would carry the Gospel to the farthest parts of the earth. As U.S. military alliances reached around the world, Wycliffe learned to confuse Christianity with an expanding North American domain, and checks on North American expansion with threats to Christ's Kingdom.

'Your job of prayer for us,' WBT's new *Translation* bulletin instructed home supporters in 1944, 'should be to weaken the enemy, enabling us to take his long-prepared and well-fortified positions. . . . [Like artillery fire] your praying for us should be so fervent and so concentrated and continuous that the enemy may be blasted out of the positions that we are preparing to take: in all the tribes of Mexico, in the continent of South America, and beyond.' As Wycliffe marshalled prayer for the next advances, it pointed to 15 million tribes-people in Western China. In Tibet, 'the particular problems to be faced are: living at the highest habitable altitudes of earth, combating Buddhism, contacting nomadic people.' The interior of French Indo-China harboured a million and a half aborigines: 'the word of the only two missionaries among them is: "the vast tribal empire of this great hinterland remains untouched." ' 'VICTORY MUST FIND MISSIONARY FORCES READY FOR FINAL ADVANCE,' Townsend alerted supporters. 'FORMERLY INACCESSIBLE REGIONS WILL LIE AT OUR DOORS. NOW IS THE TIME TO TRAIN PIONEERS.'

Some of these destinations were rhetorical for the time being, but there are several indications of preparation for the Soviet Union. Perhaps this was Alberto Rembao's idea of brilliant achievement, a friendship with Joseph Stalin which would make the Townsend-Cardenas drama look like a rehearsal. In 1944 *Translation* called for 'Christian Russian young people of the U.S. and Canada' to attend Camp Wycliffe, 'to meet the challenge of these 27 million people of Soviet Asia.' Townsend mentioned 'get[ting] ready for Siberia' in the same breath as starting in South America. If Soviet officials saw that Wycliffe translators were capable linguists, 'we might be invited' into the country.[63]

To consolidate the invitations into Peru as well as Mexico, Townsend sought the help of U.S. ambassadors. Josephus Daniels and the Cardenas lobby brought him to the attention of the State Department in Washington. The reason for looking forward to Siberia was the U.S.-Soviet alliance during the Second World War. Here and elsewhere, SIL's fortunes not only revolved around the relations between a foreign government and its own: as Bible translation came to resemble a paramilitary operation, no government would tolerate it without close ties with Washington, all of which raise the question of what SIL's relations with the U.S. Government have been. The available information could be far from complete because, as Townsend cast about for ways to take his linguistic institute to far-off lands, the U.S. Government organized a peace-time foreign espionage arm. Called the Office of Strategic Services during the Second World War and chartered as the Central Intelligence Agency in 1947, it would make extensive use of missionaries. But while the Summer Institute has taken advantage of U.S. power, it may also have tried to remain apart from clandestine activities for one compelling reason: fear.

At the level of the State-Department and the White House, in exchange for official endorsement, Townsend offered to serve U.S. foreign policy by promoting Inter-American friendship, spreading literacy and fighting Communism. His overtures took the form of grand schemes which, overtly, had nothing to do with evangelical religion but whose actual purpose was to win diplomatic advantage for Wycliffe. One such proposition dates to September 1950 when he visited the *charge d'affaires* at the U.S. Embassy in Lima. According to Willard Barber's memo, Townsend proposed 'a volunteer inter-American brigade' for the 'Korean military operations.' Twelve years before, to demonstrate his concern during the Mexican oil crisis, he had organized an Inter-American Brigade which consisted of half-a-dozen Camp Wycliffe alumni.[64] Now at least 100 volunteers were to be recruited in each Latin American capital. After training in the United States they would be dispatched to Korea, the 'official result. . . to show the world that the Latin American peoples want to take part in the struggle against communist imperialism.'[65]

In 1956, Townsend began appealing to the State Department and the White House for ceremonial assistance in a fund-raising and publicity scheme, the Inter-American Friendship Fleet. Since the Friendship Fleet illustrates the consensus between governments and investors which has sheltered SIL from enemies, let us consider the ideological implications of a scheme for financing the group's transportation. Less than a decade after starting the Jungle Aviation and Radio Service (JAARS) in Peru, Townsend had offended some of the wealthy fundamentalist businessmen who purchased the first airplanes. To expand JAARS he persuaded his board of directors to accept an unorthodox form of faith fund-raising which he had already used in Peru: solicitation of non-evangelical sources, specifically 'commercial firms and possibly foundations'.[66]

Local committees of businessmen, their wives, and city mayors raised the money, appealing to civic religion and Inter-American friendship rather than salvation of the lost. The airplanes were named after the localities where the money was raised, not the corporations which occasionally contributed a share: hence the 'Friendship of Miami' which the Celanese Corporation helped purchase in 1965 for Colombia, where, ten years later, a subsidiary was refusing to pay government-awarded pollution damages to an Indian community on grounds that the money would be used to arm guerrillas.[67] By persuading U.S. officials to participate in the many dedication ceremonies,

Townsend showed foreign governments that SIL had the backing of the U.S. Government and was a broadly based, non-sectarian organization. In the case of the 'Friendship of Miami', the White House turned down Townsend's request for a message to President Valencia of Colombia: according to the State Department, SIL's missionary activities had offended Catholic clergy.[68]

Financing airplanes became an excuse to stage diplomatic blitzes which, ideally, proceeded from donor cities to Washington to the capital of the host country, ritualizing SIL's association with the two governments, private enterprise and related causes. The $30,000 for the 'Spirit of Kansas City', sent to Ecuador in 1958, came from an unnamed New York philanthropist and the Women's Kansas City Commission for International Relations and Trade which, like other Friendship Fleet sponsors, hoped to foster commerce with SIL's host countries. Vice-President Richard Nixon declined an invitation, but the ceremonies did include ex-President Harry Truman; Ecuador's Ambassador to the U.S., Jose R. Chiriboga; and ex-President of Ecuador Galo Plaza. 'Friendship is our best defense' was Cameron Townsend's theme. Ambassador Chiriboga noted that Latin America was blessed with 70% of the products considered essential to U.S. national security, and that Russia and her satellites were doing their best to win the poor and ignorant Latin American masses. The airplane was part of the peace offensive which would save Latin America for democracy. Galo Plaza called the airplane another way to implement Truman's Point Four programme by means of the private sector, a method of fighting the communist aggression of doctrine and propaganda.[69]

John Kennedy's Alliance for Progress seemed a particularly fertile diplomatic opportunity. In early October 1961, Townsend and his Inter-American Coordinator, Robert Schneider, discussed 'hemispheric solidarity' with the Assistant Secretary of State for Inter-American Affairs, Robert Woodward. Having failed to recapture Cuba some months before, the United States was doing everything it could to solidify the Western Hemisphere against further setbacks. Since SIL's Washington office was only established some years later, Schneider worked from Philadelphia. The following week he sent the Assistant Secretary a proposal 'to secure the goodwill of the peoples of Latin America while aiding them culturally. These groups, often living in isolated areas, are special targets of Communism. This project, then, would discourage Communism by equipping the people to read and write and by supplying literature of the Free World.' To promote the effort, Jacqueline Kennedy could chair a committee of first ladies from all over the hemisphere. SIL would be happy to provide consultants.

Two coincidences seem worthy of note. First, that same month Townsend opened the door to Colombia, after a decade of failure and in a miraculous manner to be described in Chapter 6. Second, Schneider hoped to present the plan to Arthur Schlesinger Jr. at the White House 'through the courtesy of a mutual friend, Col. William R. Kintner'.[70] The same year, Colonel Kintner left his post as chief of long-range planning for the U.S. Army Chief of Staff. From 1950 to 1952 he had been a senior staff member of the CIA's Office of Policy Co-ordination, the covert action or 'dirty tricks' arm, as a planning specialist for paramilitary activities. From here he moved to the planning board of the National Security Council, then to the Eisenhower White House as an adviser to Nelson Rockefeller on Cold War operations, and then to the Army Chief of Staff from 1959 to 1961. *The Front Is Everywhere* (1950), one of Kintner's books on the Cold War, became required reading in his branch of the CIA.[71] In the *New Frontier of War: Political Warfare Present and Future* (1962), Kintner argues that private American organizations, including religious missions, should be enlisted in the cause.[72]

Contacted 20 years later, Kintner recalled discussing SIL with Arthur Schlesinger Jr., but not the outcome or his particular interest in SIL. Whatever that interest, sooner or later it must have occurred to military planners that the Bible translators might solve a chronic deficiency in readiness for psychological warfare. 'Psywar' required specialists in local languages and customs, specialists who were rare indeed in indigenous societies ripe for subversion, and here was a linguistic institute which not only tried to cultivate God-fearing, anti-communist followings: it had airplanes, radios, contracts with foreign governments and 2000 tongues to go.

The CIA had approached his mission hierarchy at the summer schools 'on many occasions', SIL's Washington representative, David Farah, explained in 1976, but it always refused to co-operate.[73] Clarence Church called accusations to the contrary 'probably one of the cleverest tricks to come out of the bag of the Evil One in recent years'.[74] The reason the Summer Institute may well have refused to co-operate with the CIA, or learned to refuse through hard experience, or at least tried to, is illustrated by consultations between a SIL official and the U.S. Embassy in Bogota in February 1979, two years before the Bitterman kidnapping. For some time SIL's contract with the Colombian Government had seemed to dangle by a thread. Just a few months before, three Cabinet Ministers had taken premature credit for SIL's expulsion. As if this were not enough, Bible translators found themselves in the midst of illegal marijuana plantations. The guards threatened their physical welfare. Worse, following a counter-guerrilla sweep by government troops, nine armed men had robbed two SIL women and forced them to leave their Coreguaje outpost on pain of death. The eastern plains of Colombia were so overrun by 'bandits, *marijuaneros* and guerrillas' that even the SIL base at Lomalinda might not be safe.

> If they remain silent and in place [reported Consul Irving Kanter] they are exposed to consequences of being foreigners in a hostile, lawless environment; without adequate police protection — defenseless. If they report what they know to Colombian authorities (inform) they could be targetted in reprisal. If they report to U.S. officials (not trusting Colombian authorities), they could open themselves to charges of being U.S. agents — brought by their political enemies. If they do nothing, with any happenstance contrary to criminal interests, the SIL could still get it in the neck.

The Bible translators were therefore trying to mind their own business: the

SIL official 'stated that to date the Institute's policy was not to volunteer information to Colombian authorities concerning illegal activities (either revolutionary or narcotics) in the area of their operations.'

Consul-General Richard Morefield was less sympathetic: a hear-no-evil, see-no-evil policy was likely to offend the Colombian authorities. While the SIL official believed that the government refrained from putting intelligence queries to organizations like his own, Morefield knew of no such policy. If the Colombian Government asked, he stated, SIL 'would have no alternative but to provide the information requested.' And if SIL felt that the government could not assure the safety of its members, 'they would have to reconsider their program of activities in Colombia.' 'Failure to co-operate,' Morefield warned, 'would only lead to great difficulty.'[75]

The risk of being considered strategic is underlined by the case of a SIL supplier, the Helio-Courier Aircraft Company. From this firm, JAARS obtained its Short Take-Off and Landing (STOL) airplanes, which could use short jungle or mountain airstrips and comprised most of the Friendship Fleet. In exchange for sale at cost, SIL helped the company sell others in new markets such as Peru.[76] Another leading Helio-Courier customer was the CIA which, like SIL, began buying the planes as they came on the market in the mid-1950s. As SIL introduced the plane to the Amazon, the CIA used it to supply its Montagnard armies in South East Asia. According to a 1977 Helio-Courier Company lawsuit, the CIA in 1962 demanded that the company turn over the blueprints and tools needed to manufacture the plane. When the company refused, its lawsuit charged, the CIA planted a 'secret agent' in Helio-Courier's Washington office and purloined what it wanted, then manufactured the plane illegally, sabotaged company sales, and destroyed the business by making Helio-Courier synonymous with 'illegal and immoral activities'. According to the company, it was being punished for refusing to become one of the CIA's many subsidiaries.[77]

For self-preservation if nothing else, SIL evidently has tried to keep its distance from intelligence gathering and official violence. Religious missions tend to be an early casualty of warfare: combatants suspect the mission of being in league with the adversary and move in for an easy kill. To survive long enough to produce all those New Testaments, SIL must maintain the appearance of neutrality. Since loyalties are uncertain and the consequences of supplying information may be felt quickly in someone's flesh — perhaps one's own — the best way to maintain that appearance is to behave as if one were neutral. Even in South Vietnam, where SIL members spent much of the war within the safety of U.S. fortifications, they seem to have tried. According to an anti-war Mennonite missionary, in 1966 an 'anthropologist' began staying with two SIL women posted to the Bru people near Khe Sanh. When branch headquarters found reason to investigate the anthropologist's movements, it was discovered that he also resided at the 'embassy house' (CIA centre) in Hue and ordered the translators to stop giving him lodging.[78]

The ease with which the 'anthropologist' won the confidence of the SIL women suggests that Clarence Church's claim to home supporters — 'no member of the organization in . . . more than 40 years . . . has ever participated in intelligence gathering for any purpose' — is implausible.[79] When a sponsoring government makes a national security demand, as the North American diplomat Morefield noted, SIL has no choice but to comply. If members count upon the Lord to rescue them from such dilemmas, how is a man like the first JAARS supervisor, Lawrence Montgomery, to define his obligations? Recruited from the U.S. military mission in Lima, Montgomery continued to serve as a U.S. Air Force reserve officer and, when Townsend arranged to have JAARS made a subsidiary of the Peruvian Air Force, he presumably acquired responsibilities to that institution as well. In 1961 he took leave of absence, which became permanent, to work for the Helio-Courier Company in various locales including South East Asia. As Montgomery's career suggests, the local institutional structures in which SIL has flourished are part of a larger one. Take, for example, a 1969 SIL-Philippines notice — 'A special literacy project is to be conducted by the Mindanao State University and the Presidential Assistance Committee for Community Development. The publication [a SIL primer in Maranao] was financed by the Asia Foundation.' Here two of the three co-operating institutions, the Asia Foundation and the Presidential Committee, had their respective origins as CIA fronts in the late 1940s and early 1950s.[80]

If Townsend asked the U.S. Government to help obtain and protect certain foreign contracts, he may well have tried to avoid long-term obligations which could restrict SIL's manoeuvring room, endanger field workers and, were they to be discovered, end their hoped for long-term bailiwick. But flaunting SIL's charms at governments guaranteed that, in emergencies, it would be asked to fulfil its contractual commitments to provide interpreters, air and radio services, and of course, information to national functionaries requesting it. When the founder sometimes overplayed his hand and lost control of a situation, it is possible that he repaired to his government for help, just as, recently, certain SIL officials have consulted with U.S. embassies to save their branches. In a large, autonomous membership, such expedients would probably become common knowledge only by mistake.

To use an unwilling SIL for its purposes, the CIA could take various routes. It might be able to find sympathetic members willing to deceive their associates. Or it could plant an evangelical officer or agent as a Wycliffe recruit with needed skills, which SIL would reward with rapid advancement to a supervisory position. Or it could take advantage of grants from the U.S. Agency for International Development. When the agency gives private organizations money, information — progress reports, problems — flows in the opposite direction. Philanthropists who wish to avoid recruitment into intelligence networks become accountable to inspectors and consultants. 'At one time, many AID field offices were infiltrated from top to bottom with CIA people,' the Agency's Director during the Carter Administration stated. 'The idea was to plant operatives in every kind of activity we had overseas, government, volunteer, religious, every kind.'[81]

Even if one does not care to accept SIL members' claims to innocence, they may be sincere. 'We don't even know what the CIA is,' a member despaired as her branch was driven from Mexico with a CIA reputation. The danger her organization poses is not primarily that of a 'front' for something else. While the Summer Institute was organized as an intrigue, it is clearly an evangelical intrigue with its own jealously guarded objectives. The deeper problem is the group's naivete, its capacity for looking the other way and serving dictatorships, if that will serve the Great Commission, its susceptibility to contractual extortion and right-wing propaganda, such that members can easily come to believe that the trap into which they have stepped is the Lord's plan. Of this there is no better illustration than Bible translation in Vietnam.

The Good Neighbours Go to Vietnam

In January 1953, Wycliffe's General Director announced that 'a major advance has begun into the Far East' led by Deputy Director Richard Pittman:

> Tribes without the Word in the Philippine Republic as well as in the Formosan domain of that stalwart Christian statesmen, Chiang Kai Shek, are the first objectives [Cameron Townsend wrote]. This will bring Wycliffe into rather close quarters with an advance of another nature. . . that has little regard for the Word of God. This Marxian advance has already engulfed two great nations and a big proportion of earth's population, has driven out missionaries before it and endeavoured to destroy the fruits of their labors. What chance has Wycliffe's seemingly puny advance in the face of such odds? . . . We count on your prayers for Wycliffe's counter-advance to translate the Bible for scores and scores of tribes almost under the nose of Communism; and someday on into tribal areas that exist behind the Iron Curtain . . . Let us call on God for recruits (scores of them during 1953), funds, official favor, open doors and protection until every language has been given God's Word.[82]

Welcome only in American dependencies, Wycliffe would march on these convictions in Asia for the next several decades. Formosa was soon forgotten, but in the Philippines and South Vietnam linguistic diplomacy quickly reached the highest level. Since the new fields were not closed to evangelical missionaries, Wycliffe would help friendly governments stop the 'Marxian advance' in exchange for protection against it. By contracting its divine mission to shake-down regimes whose chief prop was the United States, Wycliffe ranged itself against anti-colonial movements even before setting foot in the villages.

The Summer Institute's first man in Manila was Richard Pittman, whom the founder had groomed for leadership in Mexico. On the first visit, in April 1951, he conferred with Filipino officials, including Foreign Secretary Carlos Romulo, and reported that an invitation was likely. Unfortunately, an American lesson in democracy seemed to be collapsing under the weight of its own corruption. Led by the People's Liberation Army or Huks, small farmers and labourers were overcoming the private armies of the landlords who had fattened under American and Japanese occupation. As the government in Manila lost ground, the United States reintervened with a counter-insurgency programme which became a dress rehearsal for the early stages of the Vietnam expedition.

The man whom American advisers would publicize as the Cold War saviour of the Philippines, Ramon Magsaysay, became SIL's father figure in Asia. While he was still Secretary of Defence, Pittman sent him a copy of *Lazaro Cardenas — Mexican Democrat* along with congratulations for restoring order. Magsaysay responded with personal favours and, after capturing the presidency, saw that SIL received a contract in February 1953. According to Wallis and Bennett, his friendship with Pittman developed along Cardenas—Townsend lines.

The second advance on the East Asia rim was in a more stable jurisdiction, the Australian trust territory of Papua New Guinea. Local nerves apparently helped prompt the move: in 1955, the year after the Viet Minh forced a French army to surrender at Dien Bien Phu, an Australian mission director named Robert Story reminded Wycliffe of the many unreached languages in the East Indies, their strategic position during the recent World War when Americans and Australians had repelled the enemy shoulder to shoulder, and the present danger: 'countries now closed to missionaries'. Even closer to home, Indonesia — newly independent, Muslim and expansionist — was making ominous noises. Wycliffe was already running a linguistics course in Australia, as it was in Canada and England, and in 1956 Australian and Canadian members launched what is now SIL's largest branch.

Two subsequent initiatives underline the likely reason for good fortune in the Philippines. In South Vietnam, Richard Pittman again found official favour and protection at the highest level: when he arrived in early 1956 with a letter from Magsaysay to President Ngo Dinh Diem, the latter was 'very friendly'. But the same year Pittman's luck ran out in Indonesia. While the Secretary of Education was sympathetic, President Sukarno was not. Unlike Diem and Magsaysay, he was not advised by U.S. counter-insurgency experts, nor did he fancy giving Americans the run of his country.

At the time Pittman was introduced to Magsaysay (1952) and Diem (1956), each was under the tutelage of Colonel Edward Lansdale of the Central Intelligence Agency. In Manila, Lansdale was station chief of the CIA's Office of Policy Co-ordination, whose Washington staff at this time included our previous acquaintance Colonel William Kintner. The model psychological warrior, Lansdale masterminded the government terror against the Huks, supervised Magsaysay's rise to president, and planned his ill-fated reforms (Magsaysay to Pittman: 'Townsend's biography of Cardenas has given me a pattern for national reform.')[83] According to a CIA boast, Lansdale had 'invented' Magsaysay.

In South Vietnam Lansdale was supposed to create another. To bottle up the Viet Minh in the North as the defeated French withdrew, the arriving Americans installed Ngo Dinh Diem as President in Saigon. Richard Pittman was not alone in crossing the South China Sea during this period: the Freedom Company and Operation Brotherhood that Magsaysay sent his counterpart, Diem, were actually CIA operations set in motion by Colonel Lansdale.[84] Even if he and his associates were not directly responsible for answering Wycliffe's prayers, they designed the nation-building programmes of which Wycliffe became a part.

In Lansdale's new assignment he understood the importance of the 900,000 Montagnards, the ethnic minorities who lived in the forested highlands where much of the war would be fought. Accustomed to taking advantage of the ancient hostility between Vietnamese and Montagnard, the French had made the mistake of alienating the latter in the hills around Dien Bien Phu, turning that fortress into the trap whose fall forced their withdrawal. In mid-1955, about six months before Pittman came to Saigon, Lansdale began preparing to use the hill people as a 'trip wire' across revolutionary supply routes and sanctuaries.[85] But in keeping with the regime to whose Department of Education SIL contracted itself in 1957, the Montagnards found Diem far more oppressive than the French had been. He took away their administrative autonomy, resettled northern refugees in their 'wilderness' and uprooted them from their homes to bring them into the Saigon perimeter. As a Pentagon analyst recognized, his policies forced many Montagnards into the revolutionary camp.[86]

Lansdale says that he wanted to keep Americans from 'get[ting] between' the Montagnards and the Saigon Government, but precisely that was necessary.[87] Lansdale himself helped persuade President Kennedy to expand the U.S. Special Forces or Green Berets, who began organizing Montagnard irregulars in 1961. At peak strength these forces numbered 45,000 in South Vietnam alone, with more in the CIA's 'Secret Army' in Laos. But even under American patronage they considered themselves independent of the Saigon Government and occasionally revolted against it. Many others fought for the National Liberation Front.[88] As the struggle for Montagnard loyalty sharpened in the late 1950s, the first translators began moving into 19 language groups.

Evangelical missionaries were far more successful among the hill minorities than among the Vietnamese. They counted 45,000 Montagnard converts when, in the early 1970s, the American troop withdrawal and the mass desertion of Montagnard soldiers from their new Saigon officers coincided with a wave of feverish revivals.[89] Many converts had been found where the Green Berets recruited their troops, in the confusion and despair of fortified villages and then refugee camps to which they had fled or been removed by American or Saigon forces. The Christian and Missionary Alliance was the principal church-planting agency, with SIL in a support role. The translators produced the bulk of the Montagnard language material — grammars, dictionaries and primers — available to the Saigon Administration. In 1967 the SIL branch, the Department of Education and the U.S. Agency for International Development embarked upon bilingual education.[90] With USAID fund ($163,000 up to 1971), SIL eventually prepared 200 titles and helped train 800 teachers in

17 languages.[91] Translators also supplied ethnographic information to the U.S. forces, as is confirmed by their contribution to a handbook on Montagnard culture for the U.S. Marines.[92]

Most SIL teams consisted of single women or couples raising children, some virtually assigned to the Green Berets for protection.[93] In *Translation* and James Hefley's *By Life Or By Death* (1969), we read of early visits to Montagnard home areas which are already insecure. Sometimes the Bible translators can visit only under armed escort, sometimes the people are already sympathetic to the communists. Then we read of the Montagnard removals, either to the jungle and the communists, or to the Green Beret forts and the refugee camps. While the Montagnards are usually 'kidnapped' by the communists, they 'escape' to the Americans or, if there are too many 'infiltrators', they are 'resettled'. Sometimes the Montagnards just disappear. Those remaining under American control the SIL teams follow, setting up house near Green Beret bunkers or heavily garrisoned provincial capitals; visiting their language helpers during the day; and finally evacuating in American military transports under American covering fire.

The Wycliffe accounts for home supporters are littered with communist atrocities, but I found only one reference to an American mistake and none to American crimes. The American fire-power which cost so many Montagnards their homes and lives was simply the war. Although SIL might seem to have become part of the American war effort, like other evangelical missions it claimed to be non-political and neutral. The explanation for contradictory appearances was simple: if we do not reach the Montagnards with the Gospel now, they may never be reached, and the only way to reach them is through the American side. Humanitarian aid could be substituted for evangelism to make the same argument: 'there is no other way.'[94] If Bible translation had come to depend on American intervention, communist aggression was to blame. And if the communists opposed the Lord's work, they were the enemy. But since the Lord's provision – not the Cold War – was responsible for SIL's presence in Vietnam, its mission was spiritual rather than political. The politics of America versus Communism ascended to heaven and returned to earth as holy war, God against Satan, the ultimate stage in SIL neutrality. The Vietnam War had become a war for souls, Laurie Hart observed, each justifying the other and together constituting SIL's position.[95]

Was there any other way? A few Quakers and Mennonites resisted strong pressure from the U.S.-Saigon Administration, lived with people being bombed by the Americans and became acquainted with the National Liberation Front (NLF). Douglas Hostetter met a Vietnamese pastor with an NLF congregation.[96] But for the evangelical missions 14 missionary and many more convert martyrs, became the Lord's seal on their work.[97] In 1963, two SIL men and an infant were caught in a road-block and reportedly executed when Saigon forces came to the rescue.[98] During the 1968 Tet Offensive the branch's Hank Blood was captured in the overrun provincial capital of Banmethuot along with another missionary and a USAID technician. The two missionaries died in NLF hands, reportedly for lack of food and medicine, and have been memorialized in James and Marti Hefley's *No Time for Tombstones.* * At Kontum, during Tet, according to James Hefley, 960 North Vietnamese died in attacks on a Green Beret bunker in which SIL adults and children were sheltering. The only American casualties were a soldier who sprained his ankle and another who bruised himself on a gun.[100]

In private, the SIL branch was forthrightly in favour of the war.

> When you were in Vietnam [branch director David Blood wrote President Johnson in 1965] . . . you promised that America would stand by Vietnam. We are very grateful to God that you have had the courage to keep this promise and that your commitment in words has been matched by very appropriate actions.
>
> Those of us who have lived and worked in Vietnam for a few years have felt the treachery of the enemy and are convinced of the necessity of putting an end to his wicked works. On March 4, 1963, two adult members of our own organization and one 4-month-old baby were murdered, on the road from Saigon to Dalat. Just a matter of days ago, another acquaintance of ours, Peter Hunting, of International Voluntary Service, was assassinated on a road southwest of Saigon. These people who have been murdered without a cause (and the list is long) have been from the ranks of the real peacemakers and those who have been helping the people of Vietnam.
>
> Of course, we are all praying that peace will come to this land again, but we know it will not come automatically. And it will most certainly not be brought by those who are so illogical in their protests against the very essential military actions by our forces and the Vietnamese against this utterly diabolical enemy.
>
> Those who have been staging demonstrations in Washington and other places, calling for peace in Vietnam, should be informed that they have been demonstrating in the wrong cities. They should hold their demonstrations in Hanoi and Peking and other communist capitols, since these are the centers where wars are being fomented these days.
>
> I am sure the vast majority of Americans are behind you on your Vietnam policies. I am also convinced that, even if the majority were against you, you would still follow your own convictions as God has given you 'to see the right'.
>
> Please be assured of our continued prayers for you that God will give you His strength and His wisdom to fulfill all His will.[101]

---

* The NLF accused its prisoners of being CIA spies. The survivor, who became the Hefley's source of information, spoke Rade and had worked for the International Voluntary Service (IVS) before joining USAID. According to ex-CIA Director William Colby, an unnamed Rade-speaking IVS worker joined the CIA after helping it set up a local Green Beret and USAID programme.[99]

Two years before Hank Blood was captured, his brother, and the branch, believed that the war should be pressed at any cost because it was against an utterly diabolical enemy. Since American withdrawal might jeopardize converts and SIL could see the eternal meaning, it kept its heart for the war after most of the American expedition and public had lost theirs.

To supporters who doubted SIL's wisdom in persisting against all adversity, branch director Richard Watson wrote in 1971 about:

> watching the newspapers, troop withdrawals, etc. and feeling that all is lost and that we have little time left. We may not have much longer, but it would be far better to have our eyes on the Lord's soon return than on the changing political scene. God uses military troops, but He had other methods also.
>
> God turned the tables in Indonesia on the eve of a Marxist revolution, and the spiritual response of thousands turning to Christ has been tremendous.
>
> Cambodia put all missionaries out of their country in 1965, and it seemed God's work there was finished. Suddenly — a coup d'etat and a new responsiveness to mission work. . . .
>
> These would be terrible days in which to live if our only vision were the television. The earthly vision is doomed to become increasingly more terrible, but the heavenly vision more wonderful.[102]

The branch was lapsing into C.I. Scofield's doomsday millenarianism, in a mood of fear and despair which sanctified the bloodiest adventures. By keeping its eyes on the Lord's 'soon return', the branch could pray that its evangelical enclaves be protected by further violence. Martyrdom and the high-technology killing of communists had numbed the missionary troops into ceaseless grace.

The Wycliffe accounts dwell upon missionary sacrifice and Montagnard suffering, especially as inflicted by the other side. But except to assess the impact of enemy reprisals on surviving converts, there is no reflection on the physical cost of world mission to the Montagnards. Since evangelical converts were often regarded as agents of the Americans and treated in approximately the same way that the Americans dealt with presumed infiltrators, the cost could be high. Even now tens of thousands of Montagnards may be paying for world mission, aggravating as it probably did their conflicts with the new government. While the much-anticipated communist bloodbath never materialized, the mass flight of evangelical missionaries with other Americans confirmed the relation between their religion and U.S. power. In contrast to the survival of other churches, the stridently anti-communist Christian and Missionary Alliance reports that its Montagnard church organization 'has been almost totally destroyed.'[103]

Now, as the former SIL-Vietnam translators take the Gospel to other lands, they can reflect upon their work at a safe but frustrating distance. Bru translators John and Carolyn Miller had plenty of opportunity as prisoners of the

North Vietnamese for eight months. In her memoir of this difficult period, *Captured!*, Carolyn Miller treats her captors with commendable generosity. But world mission apparently has not been complicated by much reflection on SIL's support for the Vietnam War: it was, after all, non-political. In Miller's opinion, Christ's Kingdom is superior to Communism because the latter places little value on the individual, cannot transform the human heart, and is imposed by force.[104]

Looking the Other Way in the Philippines

The heavenly vision has the chance to become even more wonderful in the Philippines. Here the Summer Institute has fielded 64 teams, its largest branch after Papua New Guinea and Mexico. Christ's Kingdom has enjoyed the consistent favour of President Ferdinand Marcos (1965-): in 1978 he commended SIL for supporting his government 'to insure the sustained progress and prosperity of national minorities throughout the archipelago.'[105] less co-operative missionaries Marcos has jailed and deported: SIL's Jungle Aviation and Radio Service operates as a dependency of the Philippines Air Force and the Department of National Defence.[106]

The branch set up its southern base on the island of Mindanao. By continuing the American policy of colonizing Mindanao, the government hopes to relieve pressure on land monopoly in the north and take the island away from its Moro (Muslim) population, many of whom were forced into Manila's orbit only after 1900. Christian colonists are now in the majority, but they have not escaped landlords and usurers. One reason is that Ramon Magsaysay and his successors turned Mindanao into a playground for American agribusiness and lumbering corporations. According to the evangelical monthly *Sojourners*, for example, in 1978 the Del Monte Corporation was throwing hundreds of non-Muslim Bukidnon farmers off their land in order to grow pineapples. The Bukidnon owe their misfortune to government 'land reform'. In keeping with official policy since Magsaysay, a decree from Manila enabled local bosses to register Bukidnon land in their own names and rent it to Del Monte for nominal sums.[107]

The 29 SIL teams on Mindanao and the nearby Sulu Islands are based at Nasuli, in Bukidnon Province near Malaybalay. The local Catholic bishop, Francisco Claver, is a leader in the Christian resistance to the 'New Society' of Ferdinand Marcos. SIL also must reckon with an estimated 30,000 soldiers of the Moro National Liberation Front (MNLF), as well as the New People's Army whom non-Muslim minorities and Christians have joined. Hunting and bombing them, killing their supporters, 'resettling' others, and generally replaying Christ's Kingdom in Vietnam, are a large fraction of the Marcos armed forces. After the MNLF liberated the traditional Muslim capital of Jolo City in 1974, the Philippines Air Force destroyed it. According to a 1979 estimate, 60,000 civilians have been killed and one million turned into refugees.[108]

Another movement disturbing the New Society is taking place among the 500,000 Igorot of Northern Luzon, where about 20 SIL teams are based at Bagabag in Nueva Vizcaya Province. Here Magsaysay-initiated dams have displaced 30,000 Igorot, and Marcos-built dams promise to displace 90,000 more. American gold mining corporations need hydro-electric power; American agribusiness needs irrigation; and Igorot militia have allied themselves with the New People's Army.[109]

At home, Wycliffe has rarely mentioned the war between the Filipino Government and many of the people it serves. The main problem of indigenous people in the Philippines is clearly pagan religion, especially demons. But in 1976 the censorship began to crack with *Kidnapped!*, British translator Eunice Diment's account of her three-week abduction by the MNLF in the Sulu Islands the year before. And with Doris Fell's *The Lady of the Tboli* (1979), we have the story of a SIL team among the 40,000 Tboli of Southern Mindanao.

In the 1950s and 1960s the SIL women watched 'lowlanders' — Christian peasants and bosses — push the Tboli off their land and into the mountains. They ached at the injustice and the increasing difficulty of reaching the group with the Gospel. Their language informant/evangelists, young men whom the SIL women had raised and helped educate, insisted upon seeking legal redress for their people. Their efforts were fruitless. Then, in 1968, the branch solicited the help of the government in Manila. Despite threats from cattle ranchers and local authorities, the Bureau of Forestry surveyed a reservation with the help of SIL's evangelists. The proposed reservation never received the presidential approval of Ferdinand Marcos, and the Tboli continued to lose their land.

Still, the branch did succeed in introducing the Tboli to the Presidential Arm for National Minorities (PANAMIN) of Manuel Elizalde Jr. Some years later PANAMIN and Elizalde were notorious for corraling minorities into small areas and attacking dissenters with armed guards hired from other groups. Soon the SIL women had unanticipated difficulties with the same philanthropy: while Elizalde appreciated their medical and literacy work, he disapproved of Bible translation. Worse, PANAMIN recruited most of their Tboli evangelists to organize its show-case settlement at Kemotu, where they lost interest in evangelism and acquired numerous wives.

By the early 1970s, the long-suffering SIL women were shouldering yet another burden, the growing unrest on Mindanao. Muslim 'black shirts' were fighting the government. While the translators doubted that the black shirts had any grudge against the Tboli, judging from the Wycliffe account all they did was pillage, burn and kill. The possibility of government crimes, or that some Tboli regard the Muslims as allies, is not mentioned. In September 1974, Tboli were killed in nearby skirmishes and JAARS evacuated the SIL women.

Half a year later they found hundreds of Tboli men organized into government self-defence units, some of which were led by their former evangelists. The men brought their guns to worship service. When SIL-Vietnam members evacuated to the Philippines in April 1975, their stricken faces magnified the urgency of completing the Tboli New Testament. Evangelical Christianity was spreading in the mountains. By promoting literacy and solidarity beyond the family unit, it was giving the Tboli 'new courage to stand up for their rights against the lowlanders'. A believer refused to sign a petition demanding that the SIL women leave. Their former protege Mai Tuan, now a PANAMIN political boss with four wives, was beaten up in a Manila prison and returned to the Lord. A few others helped to finish the New Testament, which was welcomed by 1,000 people in 1979.

The SIL-Tboli team had questions. Had God 'allowed PANAMIN?' Why did the 'glitter of success' seduce so many of their young men? For the moment, the SIL women have found their answer in the young Tboli Church because 'the nature of God is to endure.' Hopefully that will not stop the Philippines branch from asking more questions.[110] By 1981 the war was forcing teams to leave the field in Northern Luzon as well as Mindanao.

References

1. For the next two sections I am indebted to Jan Rus and Robert Wasserstrom (1981) for their insights into Townsendian diplomacy.
2. Wallis and Bennett 1966:88-90.
3. Rembao 1942:5, 10, 15-16, 19, 31, 57.
4. Wallis and Bennett 1966:58-9; Hefleys 1974:72-73.
5. Heath 1972:107, 110.
6. Rembao 1942:30.
7. Raby 1974:36-37, 51.
8. Saenz 1936:126-7, 295-6; Novo 1933:55, 67-8.
9. *Wycliffe Associates Newsletter* November 1977 p.7.
10. Wallis and Bennett 1966:54-61; Heath 1972:102-3; Hefleys 1974: 75-83; Bravo 1977:97.
11. Wallis and Bennet 1966:68; Hefleys 1974:85.
12. *Annual Reports of the Pioneer Mission Agency* September 1934-August 1935 p.5.
13. *Camp Wycliffe Chronicle* January 1936 p.1.
14. *Pioneer News* November 1936 p.5.
15. Hefleys 1974:87-9; Wallis and Bennett 1966:76; Heath 1972:103, 112.
16. Hefley and Steven 1972:23.
17. Townsend and Pittman 1975:45.
18. Hefley and Steven 1972:26. Through Daniels the group obtained a favourable notice from the *American Foreign Service Journal* (1939).
19. Hefleys 1974:93.
20. *Camp Wycliffe Chronicle* June 1936 p.2.
21. Bravo 1977:97.
22. Heath 1972:117-8.
23. Wallis and Bennett 1966:113; Townsend and Pittman 1975:36.
24. *Camp Wycliffe Chronicle* June 1936 p.1.
25. Ibid. January 1936 p.2.

26. Wallis and Bennett 1966:114.
27. Cardenas 1973: Vol I:225.
28. Townsend and Pittman 1975:37.
29. Hefleys 1974:102-10; Cardenas 1973:Vol. II:201.
30. Rus n.d.
31. Aguilar 1968:166.
32. Agee 1975:606-7, 613.
33. Hefley 1970:14. 87. For a reference to family business methods, see Weyls 1939:259.
34. Townsend and Pittman 1975:12.
35. Marsden 1980:34, 194.
36. Anderson 1979:39-41; Marsden 1980:101.
37. Howard 1941:29.
38. Wallis and Bennett 1966:37-41, 47-8; Hefleys 1974:49-50; Burgess 1957. The biographer (Dame 1968:15) of Legters' son attributes 'the foundation of the Pioneer Mission' to the Townsend-Legters partnership.
39. Compare the vigour suggested by the *Central American Bulletin* (15 May 1932 p.21; 15 November 1932 p.4; and 15 January 1933 p.3), which does not specify the malady, with the dire picture painted by Wallis and Bennett (1966:53, 132) and the Hefleys' (1974:75) rather more active convalescent.
40. Hefleys 1974:69, 73-4, 76, 78.
41. Wallis and Bennett 1966:129.
42. *The Mexican Indian* (Philadelphia) January-February 1945 p.2; Floyd 1944:181; Dale 1943:112.
43   *Camp Wycliffe Chronicle* January 1936 p.4.
44. Ibid. June 1936 p.2.
45. Goddard 1967:425, 537, 712-14.
46. Townsend and Pittman 1975:15; Hefleys 1974:99.
47. *Camp Wycliffe Chronicle* January 1936 p.2.
48. Townsend and Pittman 1975:36.
49. Hefleys 1974:113-15; Wallis and Bennett 1966:99.
50. Townsend 1956.
51. McKinlay 1944:17 and 'Introduction to the Policies and Practices of WBT Inc.,' leaflet distributed 1977.
52. Hefleys 1974:95-6.
53. SIL-Mexico 1960:15.
54. Dame 1968:34. Compare the same author's (Dame 1941:152) SIL-style presentation of the Legters and Martha Moennich's (1944:104) evocation of their zeal.
55. Daniels 1947:167-71.
56. Hefleys 1974:103; Townsend and Pittman 1975:11.
57. Cowan 1979:214.
58. Hefleys 1974:117-19; Townsend and Pittman 1975:14.
59. Last page of *Translation* September 1950. A year after Townsend (*Translation* Winter 1957-58 p.3) mentioned the SIL field arrangement, Kenneth Pike (1959) explained more fully in *The Bible Translator*.
60. Moennich 1944:16, Hefleys 1974:121.
61. Townsend 1956 (originally 1948); Townsend and Pittman 1975:58-63, 125.

62. Rembao 1942:10.
63. *Translation* 1944 pp.8, 11. 13; Fall 1945 p.4.
64. Hefleys 1974:106-8.
65. Willard F. Barber, Memorandum of Conversation with Mr W.C. Townsend, 22 September 1950, released to author under Freedom of Information Act.
66. Hefleys 1974:192.
67. A 3 January 1966 letter from Bill Moyers to Townsend (Lyndon B. Johnson Library, Austin, Texas) mentions Celanese. Antonil 1978:256, 262.
68. C.F. ME 4-3/S*, 3 January 1966 letter with attachments from Moyers to Townsend, Johnson Library.
69. Hefleys 1974:196 and 33 pages from Series 320, Nixon Vice-Presidential Papers, Laguna Niguel Federal Archive, filed under SIL.
70. 10 October 1961 letter with proposal, 'An Idea for Inter-American Friendship', from Robert G. Schneider to Robert F. Woodward, released to author under Freedom of Information Act.
71. Smith 1976:87.
72. Kintner 1962:287.
73. Willoughby 1976.
74. *In Other Words* October 1976 p.8.
75. Memoranda, 'Limited Official Use', by Irving M. Kanter 9 March 1979 and Richard M. Morefield 12 March 1979, released to author under Freedom of Information Act.
76. Hefleys 1974:192.
77. *The Real Paper* (Boston) 14 January 1978 p.3; Robbins 1979:303-7.
78. Hostetter 1973:8.
79. *In Other Words* October 1976 p.8.
80. 'World News' *Translation* January-March 1969; Smith 1976:164, 252-3.
81. Cotter 1981:321.
82. 'The Director's Column' *Translation* January 1953.
83. SIL diplomacy: SIL/WBT 1972:46-7; Wallis and Bennett 1966:284-94, 307-12; Hefleys 1974:170-3.
84. Lansdale-Magsaysay-Diem: Smith 1976:94-5, 101, 179. 251-2.
85. Lansdale 1972:327; McCoy 1972:105, 264.
86. Chomsky and Zinn 1971:255.
87. Lansdale 1972:327.
88. Klare 1970:324-36; Fitzgerald 1972:239, 311,421. For a photographic account of a Montagnard revolt against the Saigon Government, see Sochurek 1965.
89. Hoke 1975:568-70.
90. Hart 1973:31.
91. Pike and Brend 1977:46-7, 50.
92. Mole 1970. The study was done for the U.S. Navy's Personal Response trans-cultural programme.
93. Hefleys 1969:94-102. For photos of one such situation, among the Jeh, see Sochurek 1968.
94. Hefleys 1969:94.
95. Hart 1973:21-2.
96. Hostetter 1973:5.

97. Hefleys 1969:12.
98. Pittman 1969; Brichoux 1970.
99. Hefleys 1976; Colby 1978:165-7.
100. Hefleys 1969:145-77.
101. 1 December 1965 letter from David L. Blood, branch letterhead, Lyndon B. Johnson Library.
102. *Translation* October-December 1971 pp.2-5.
103. *Christianity Today* 12 December 1980 p.71.
104. Miller 1977:197.
105. *In Other Words* Summer 1978 p.6. Presidential Merit Medals in 1973-4 to Kenneth Pike and John Kyle (Ibid. August 1975 p.5 and December 1978 p.6); President's mother christens Manila headquarters (Ibid. October 1977p 4.); Townsend receives Presidential Citation from Ambassador Romualdez 2 November 1978 (College of Ethnologists 1979:82-5); Government nominates branch for UNESCO award (*In Other Words* December 1979 p.6); branch one of the few non-governmental agencies to receive education ministry award for helping build the New Society (Ibid. September 1980 p.6).
106. *Philippines Herald* 3 May 1972.
107. *Sojourners* (Washington, D.C.) October 1978 pp.16-18.
108. Chomsky and Herman 1979:241.
109. Razon and Hensman 1976.
110. Fell 1979:170, 183, 201.

4. The Summer Institute in Peru

As we in the United States must have rubber-tired vehicles, men are again beginning to herd up the Indians to take them to the swampy rubber territory. May Jesus soon come to put a stop to the suffering that comes from the greed for money!

L. L. Legters from the interior of Brazil, 1926.

Who will open Tibet, or claim the last acre of the Amazon . . . the merchant or the missionary?

W.C. Townsend, 1942

Sooner or later, whether we like it or not, civilization is going to come to these tribes. Our concern is that it be *Christian* civilization.

W.C. Townsend, 1958.[1]

Jesus has not come to put a stop to suffering from the greed for money, but a hundred Bible translation teams have played their part in the political economy of the Amazon. Wherever the Summer Institute went in the world's largest tropical forest, it encountered a system of exploitation imposed during the rubber boom around the turn of the century. Many Indians survived the rubber era only in permanent debt to mestizo *patrones,* who exchanged trade goods for labour on the dearest terms. The *patrones* themselves were in debt to usurers in the towns, who passed on the product of Indian sweat, misery and annihilation to European and North American firms. If Indians were not under the control of the *patron,* it was because they had fought him off, fled to inaccesible regions or come under missionary patronage. Since then, the extension of missionary work, roads, colonization, state bureaucracy and corporate investment has reduced the number of Indians in less than permanent contact to a small fraction. As more native people come to live in fixed, often mission villages along the larger rivers, the forms of brokerage upon whi which they depend — trader, foreman, missionary, boss, bureaucrat — have multiplied, as has the opportunity for patronage battles and civil rights movements.

Missionaries have operated ahead and behind their rivals, by sedentarizing and concentrating small semi-nomadic bands and providing a sanctuary for

Indians rejecting more demanding outsiders. Owing to the *patrones* and the precarious state of refuge regions, Indians might be in a worse position without missionary medical work and schools. But the Christian cause has also been enormously useful to governments eager to strengthen frontiers with neighbouring countries; extend control over possible guerrilla sanctuaries; extract natural resources; and resettle small farmers displaced by land monopoly elsewhere. In so far as governments are concerned, the mission of the mission is political socialization: ameliorating oppression, teaching native people that they now belong to Ecuador or Peru, fostering new forms of leadership and economy which bind them to the national society, and minimizing resistance to colonization.

No other Christian mission in the Amazon matches SIL's network of language specialists, air and radio-linked bases and outposts, and frequently bilingual schools. Of its five Amazonian advances — first in Peru, then Ecuador, Bolivia, Brazil and Colombia — the one in Peru has shaped the lives of the most people.[2] Here the base-airplane-bilingual school evangelizing machine became a model for other branches as far away as the Philippines; SIL has combined state backing, longevity and authority in native communities like perhaps nowhere else except Mexico; and, after near expulsion in 1976, it managed to swing the government's Indian policy back to its own point of view. For the same reasons which made the Peruvian branch a laboratory and show-case for subsequent advances — an obliging government with large ambitions and jungle Indian communities upon whom SIL could have a rapid, obvious impact — it deserves our close attention.

Peru has been second only to Brazil in the sweep of its Amazonian projects, bordering as it does on four of the five other states sharing the basin. But when Cameron Townsend arrived in 1945, the government had few means to prepare jungle Indians for the coming wave of North American-financed national expansion. On the far side of the vast, subjugated Quechua peasantry in the Andes were speakers of dozens of indigenous languages, at all stages of contact from near assimilation to war. Beyond isolated towns and settlements, state authority faded into a few military outposts and an occasional Roman Catholic mission.

Townsend's offer to bridge the gap was rewarded with the first, precedent-setting government contract for his University of Oklahoma linguistic institute. To win official backing against the Catholic Church, he promised to accommodate Indians to colonization and actively promoted it. Bible translation became part of the infrastructure of state expansion: colonization schemes led to state and business subsidy of the Lord's work. A military dictatorship sponsored a SIL-administered bilingual school system, which the North Americans used to break the Catholic monopoly in the jungle, make themselves the nucleus of official integration programmes, and build their own formidable system of patronage.

The branch constructed its base at Yarinacocha, an ox-bow lake suitable for flying boats, near the town of Pucallpa, terminus of Peru's first trans-Andean road. Translators brought their language informants to the base;

converted and trained them there as bilingual teachers; then sent them home to draw dispersed, mobile populations together around schools, and turn classes into congregations. To deal with the many health, subsistence and social problems created by the new settlement pattern, the branch launched community development projects, which reinforced the tendency of its teacher/pastors to become entrepreneurs. Through its Indian teachers, the branch rolled school, church and trading-post into one — a new system of authority, exchange and production that it used to suck native people into the colonizing society and campaign against their religious traditions.

Townsend had curried official favour by claiming that his linguists would not only Peruvianize Indians, but speed the disappearance of their languages. Actually, SIL was organizing congregations in the various languages, which gave it a large stake in them. As conflicts spawned by the programme surfaced, spun out of control and endangered evangelical prospects, the rationale shifted away from the civilization of primitive tribespeople toward protecting them from its evils. Oil exploration, roads and settlers were inevitable, SIL decided: it was merely helping native people adjust to colonization by giving them a new faith. It tried to adopt a more 'cultural' approach which, in 1970, a member called the 'way of least resistance'.

When a young man teaches a translator his language, so the story goes, he may well realize that his old beliefs will not stand up to the modern world. Christianity fills the 'faith void' quite nicely. Trained as a bilingual teacher, he 'has an infinite advantage in introducing change' compared to an outsider, because he has his people's respect and knows their capacity for accepting new ideas. He teaches people to read and write, but at an appropriate pace and in their own language. He promotes the new hygiene necessary for living in larger, permanent settlements, in a way the people understand. Discouraging polygamy, he respects existing unions to avoid displacing women. But the most serious problem he faces is the 'faith vacuum', an 'emotional shock' which, like hopeless fear of evil spirits, Wycliffe invariably perceives among pre-literate peoples. Again, the teacher and other Bible-fed leaders work slowly. The aim is not to immediately replace the old religious beliefs — that is impossible, and Wycliffe recognizes the harm in trying — but to 'reach sound, culturally acceptable solutions' in the light of Scripture.[3]

To win over Indians and protect them from *patrones,* translators offered a more accessible trade good and tried to replace barter or labour/debt exchanges with cash. Teaching how to handle money helped Indians defend themselves against patronal fraud, but more consumption of trade goods meant more production for market to pay for them. Contradictory perceptions of the programme, as 'liberation' from debt peonage and 'enslavement' to the trade good, reflect its implications at different stages of contact.

On a main river, where native people were already dependent on the colonizing society, the introduction of teacher salaries, cheaper trade goods and a cash economy tended to loosen the control exercised by *patrones.* Two of the Peruvian branch's most publicized evangelical movements, among the Piro and Ticuna, emerged from this kind of situation. Generally a bilingual school community offered far more — in education, medicine, native leadership, and a degree of toleration for the culture — than a *patron*.

Up tributary streams, SIL found more independent native people: although they may occasionally have sought contact, obtained a few trade goods such as steel cutting tools, and suffered from epidemics, they still kept some distance from outsiders. In one such case, among the Campa at Quempiri in the early 1960s, the people were not only beyond the money economy but had a 'sour grapes' attitude towards trade goods. According to the Wycliffe account, the salary of teacher Jose Flores 'had a profound sweetening effect'. Ignoring the lessons taught by past patronal exploitation, kin and neighbours wanted the beautiful things the teacher was acquiring. They also wanted free medicine, which may well have been needed, since Quempiri was a concentrated, unhealthy village of 250 people. Traditionally, the Campa shared everything they had, but the teacher found his resources stretched because now he was dependent on the new money economy, not hunting and gardening like everyone else. The solution was 'extremely painful'. He pressured everyone but his closest kin to make their own money by producing commodities.[4]

Translators frequently recruited their first bilingual teachers from *patron*-dominated areas, then used them to bring more independent populations into SIL's patronage system. In the early 1950s, for example, the Machiguenga team arrived in the domain of the Pereira family along the Urubamba River and recruited teachers from among its Machiguenga clients. By the 1960s, the team was sending its teachers into remote mountain valleys, refuge regions where other Machiguenga had fled from the rubber boom, and SIL extended its chain of airstrip-school-trading centres.[5]

SIL's eagerness to bring all Indians into permanent contact did not mean that it could protect them from other outsiders for long. In the 1950s a translator joined a Cashinahua group after it had repeatedly dealt with traders for metal tools and then withdrawn. 'You wanted to learn our language and our ways,' a Cashinahua told the translator a decade later. 'You told the *patron* that his prices were too high, and that he should treat us with fairness. He feared you because you talked strongly . . . and because you came from the other side, from where his chief lives. Therefore, he treated us better, at least when you were living with us.'[6]

Once teams had learned the language and nursed Indians into new needs that could only be met by the colonizing society, they spent less and less time in the group and gradually left it to their native assistants. Seizing opportunities provided by the new order, the teacher might graduate from trader — selling industrial goods and buying food, hides and other items produced by the traditional economy — to employer of labour for the production of cash crops such as coffee. As others joined the market economy to emulate his consumption patterns, 'Bible translation' transformed tribespeople into peasants. This is ultimately the product of market expansion and development policies, not just their expression in the SIL programme, and it brings with it the depletion of soil and game, the impoverishment of traditional knowledge

75698

of the environment, and government-backed settler invasions.[7]

Eventually, the Peruvian branch counted converts in each of the 32 languages in which it had worked. In 24 there were 320 bilingual teachers and 12,000 pupils in 210 communities.[8] If 150,000 indigenous people live in the Peruvian Amazon according to SIL's conservative estimate, the schools would recruit from at least one-third of them.[9] As the branch recovers from its brief fall from official favour in 1976, it hopes to increase the proportion by pushing into other languages and propping up its bilingual school congregations as a basis for more evangelism, not to mention further expansion into the Quechua dialects of the Andes.

The branch's faith mission victories may prove hollow, however. Its government-sponsored evangelical campaigns have created so many enemies that it is completely dependent on official favour. Social disarray and ecological deterioration seem to be outlasting enthusiasm for North American religion. And as some members began to grasp the implications of their programme, the government extracted its part of the bargain by using their inroads to expropriate Indian land. All over the jungle, translators and their native teachers planted the Peruvian flag, brought people together around schools, taught them how to sing the national anthem, count money and pray, and now their anthems and prayers are being betrayed. From the Maranon to the Urubamba Valleys, indigent colonists backed by entrepreneurs and officials are spilling down the Andes, molesting Indian women and stealing Indian land.

What made the branch such an effective agent of colonization was, above all, its bilingual school system, the largest in the Amazon. Despite the uses to which it has been put, the system's superiority over previous ones is demonstrated by its popularity among Indians. As the schools enter their fourth decade and some graduates lead civil rights organizing, it is uncertain whether they would survive without SIL. Thanks to the nature of the regime which the branch has served with outstanding loyalty, expulsion could have serious consequences for more than a few of its Indian clients. But as the pace of colonization accelerates, SIL's standing as a friend of Indians is being tested where it counts most, among the branch's own huge Indian following. For it cannot afford to join the coalition of Indians and intermediaries challenging colonization plans.

Principal Backers

During the Second World War, the U.S. Rubber Development Corporation turned to the Amazon as a source of rubber and quinine, stimulating North American interest in the region. While strategists considered South America a bastion of essential raw materials, businessmen would end the War with quantities of surplus capital.[10] In Lima the *Peruvian Times,* organ of the Anglo-American business community, thought that two new influences promised rapid development of the Amazon. One was the airplane, the other the discovery of oil. It was impossible to travel through Eastern Peru, the

Times reported, without running into one oil company surveyor after another.[11] The source of the excitement was the Ganso Azul Petroleum Company, proprietor of the first commercial oilfield in the entire Amazon. The site had been discovered by a Los Angeles geologist in 1929, the same year that Cameron Townsend began looking for backers in Southern California to finance his own Amazonian plans. 'There is surely some Christian oil man who would give us a plane,' brother Paul wrote in a Presbyterian newsletter.[12] Sadly, there was not. But when Ganso Azul was finally brought into production by Southern Californian businessmen, chief among them was mining magnate Harvey Seeley Mudd, benefactor of the Congregationalist counterpart of Townsend's Alma mater.[13]

Missionary solicitation of interested investors was not considered irregular. In the 1920s, Protestant missions in Peru enjoyed the charity of the government's main financial props, the Morgan banks and the Rockefeller family's International Petroleum Company. By appealing to the U.S. Consul, they could usually win their disputes with the Roman Catholic Church.[14] But as Peruvian governments defaulted on their foreign debt in the 1930s, Protestants found themselves in financial straits and threatened by Catholic reaction. By the end of the decade, North Americans worried that, like much of the rest of Latin America, Peru was drifting into the arms of friendly Germans, Italians and Japanese.

During the Second World War the United States supplanted Britain as Peru's leading trade partner, and a flood of funds made for much Inter-American friendship. Along with new military missions arrived the *servicios,* technical teams to train Peruvians in U.S.-style agriculture, health care and education. The services were the brain-child of Nelson Rockefeller, who, before the War, had become concerned for the future of his family's holdings. As Co-ordinator of Inter-American Affairs in Washington, he also helped to dismantle Fascist enterprises. But while the frequently Italian and Spanish Catholic clergy were considered a stronghold of Fascist sympathies, the U.S. Government disavowed any interest in promoting Protestantism. As Catholic and Protestant partisans jockeyed for position in the State Department, in Peru, contracts were to be had for the asking.

Based on his war-time work in teaching English as a foreign language, Kenneth Pike obtained SIL's invitation from Minister of Education Enrique de la Rosa in late 1943. But when de la Rosa gave Townsend the green light a year and a half later, his exit visa from the United States had to be cleared from the U.S. Embassy in Mexico City. According to the Hefleys, 'an influential ultraconservative Catholic in the State Department had been sitting on [it].'[15] Like subsequent contracts, The Peruvian agreement stipulated technical functions but left a loophole for spiritual uplift. In exchange for an office in Lima, visa and import privileges, and the right to operate airplanes and radios, SIL would study each indigenous language, prepare primers, interpret for the authorities, organize linguistic courses, discourage 'vice by all means possible', and translate 'books of great moral and patriotic value'.[16]

The same year that President Manuel Prado (1939-45) approved SIL's

Ministry of Education contract, he banned Protestant propaganda on the gounds that it was divisive, unconstitutional and unpatriotic.[17] Although the decree was of little or no consequence, the Catholic rejoinder to ambition on the scale of Townsend's was likely to be loud. He therefore introduced his Wycliffes as the 'Linguistic Institute of the University of Oklahoma'.[18] Except for a few, conscience-salving asides, which only the initiated would understand, until 1954 frequent notices in the *Peruvian Times* omitted all reference to the Bible and Christianity.[19] According to a Catholic missionary who became the branch's first friend in this quarter, during the first years members 'hid their religious purpose, the fact that they were evangelical missionaries' but often led religious services among Indians.

As the University of Oklahoma linguists moved into the jungle, Townsend occupied himself in Lima making further agreements with government ministries and building alliances for the contest with the Catholic Church. The indigenists of Peru were easily won over: the usual complement of men said to be communists had lost their enthusiasm for revolution in favour of national integration. Luis 'Tempest in the Andes' Valcarcel, an associate of the Marxist theoretician Jose Mariategui and de la Rosa's successor as Education Minister, would defend SIL 30 years later. Dr. Hugo Pesce, another Mariategui associate, would have a building named after him at the SIL base. Townsend became a member of the Peruvian Indigenist Institute, apparently the only foreigner, and was so esteemed that he represented Peru at congresses of the Inter-American Indigenist Institute.[20]

The U.S. Embassy also brought the university linguists under its wing, permitting SIL to muddle the distinction between private and official U.S. sponsorship, its own 'linguistics school mission' and the U.S. Government's *servicios* or 'missions' expanded under the Point Four programme.[21] One of SIL's first tasks happened to be preparing primers for the Peruvian-North American Co-operative Educational Service.[22] Ambassador Prentice Cooper helped Townsend negotiate the purchase of a Grumman Duck amphibian from the U.S. Navy Mission, then delivered it to the government in a ceremony. According to Cooper, 'a scientific and cultural institution of the United States' would be using the airplane for 'health, cultural and scientific missions'.[23] When Townsend screened a film about SIL in 1951, the Peruvian Senate sent its thanks to the Ministry of Education, and the U.S. Embassy wrote letters of appreciation to two Senators.[24] With the help of indigenists and government ministries, the U.S. Embassy and Point Four services, Townsend brought Congressmen, the Lima businessmen they represented and, most importantly, Peruvian military officers, into his camp.

The Jungle Aviation and Radio Service, which Townsend organized in 1948 in the face of opposition from the SIL/WBT board, was his most valuable asset in the swapping of favours and winning of influence. The first pilot and JAARS supervisor, Larry Montgomery, was — as we noted in an earlier chapter — recruited from the U.S. military mission in Lima. When a military mission plane crashed in the jungle in 1947, only SIL's Grumman Duck was able to land a party near the wreckage and a SIL translator served as guide.[25] JAARS

Map 3
The Peruvian Amazon

Map 4
Language Groups of the Peruvian Amazon

performed errands for a number of government ministries, including supply and emergency flights to isolated garrisons and the transport of prisoners to the penal colony at Sepa.[26]

The Summer Institute won many of its gains under President Manuel Odria (1948-56), an air force general whom Townsend had charmed as Minister of Aeronautics before he seized power. Odria figured in the story of the flying boat, a Townsendian bluff which JAARS credits with a victory over an archbishop. Probably with that object in mind, Townsend had persuaded two Mexican Cabinet Ministers, leading indigenists and Aaron Saenz to buy a war surplus Catalina amphibian, in memory of brother Moises. Quaker Oats heir, Henry C. Crowell, threw in $5,000, with the comment that the 'project was so worthwhile as a diplomatic gesture that even if the plane were flown into the jungle, tied to a tree, and forgotten, his money would have been well spent.'

In Mexico City, President Miguel Aleman bestowed the craft upon the Peruvian Ambassador, Oscar Vasquez Benavides, with instructions to deliver it to his own President for SIL's work. But when the plane reached Peru, 'the archbishop of Lima was planning an all-out attack against the work of SIL, hoping to run them out of the country. The archbishop had personally advised President Manuel Odria against participating in the ceremonies to receive the plane.' Compelled by the involvement of his Mexican counterpart, ,, however, Odria accepted the plane at an April 1951 ceremony featuring U.S. Ambassador Harold Tittman. 'The move was of tremendous diplomatic value,' concludes JAARS. '. . . . The archbishop had to call of his attack for two years — and by that time SIL was so thoroughly accepted by the Perui Peruvian government . . . that the attack was scarcely noticed.'[27]

Unfortunately, JAARS was a terrible financial drain. Its first five airplanes were financed by two Christian businessmen in Southern California; the Bible Institute of Los Angeles; Henry Crowell of Quaker Oats and the Moody Bible Institute; and an unnamed party in Texas.[28] But with scandal still lingering from the founder's Mexican policies, soon reinforced by scandal over his Peruvian policies, not enough people back home believed that Wycliffe was the Lord's work. By 1952, therefore, the branch was making public appeals to wealthy Peruvians and foreign businessmen. In September, a Friends of SIL committee was organized. Five years before, SIL had disclosed to the *Peruvian Times* that it enjoyed only 'a limited constituency' and was 'dependent on contributions from people who feel inclined to help such work'.[29] Now the *Times* reported that SIL 'is faced with economic problems', and the Lima daily *El Commercio* that donations, 'whether of clothes, tools or money', would be accepted at the SIL office in Lima.[30]

Formation of the Friends committee was coincident with a rush for Amazonian oil. Having repealed protectionist legislation earlier that year, Odria reopened coast and jungle to foreign, chiefly North American, oil companies in October 1952. Since some companies lacked their own aviation, they appreciated even a small flight service like JAARS, which at its peak had a dozen planes. Commercial traffic, often for oil companies, subsidized translator flights to such an extent that the Hefleys call it JAARS' 'fiscal life-saver'.[31] Gospel advance depended upon it politically as well as financially, so that the contest between merchant and missionary for God's last acre was now a joint enterprise.*

Two events during the first bidding for oil leases — the inception of the bilingual schools and the arrival of Robert Le Tourneau — led to a showdown with the Catholic hierarchy. Le Tourneau was a manufacturer of heavy machinery and self-made fundamentalist millionaire from Longview, Texas. A major Pentagon contractor, he flew about in a converted B-26 bomber and ultimately produced bomb casings for the same war in which a favoured charity, the Christian and Missionary Alliance, endeavoured to save Montagnard souls.[34] Like other Christian businessmen, Le Tourneau relied closely on the Lord in the conduct of his business affairs. But he had extraordinary difficulty distinguishing the two. 'God,' he declared, 'is chairman of my board of directors.'[35] In Peru he became known as 'the partner of God' and identified evangelical religion with capitalism so thoroughly that SIL would now like to forget him.[36] At this stage of his career, Le Tourneau's chief delight was building huge machines to knock down trees.

The year before he came to Peru, Le Tourneau launched his own material and spiritual Point Four programme in Liberia by leasing 500,000 acres to clear jungle, log mahogany and grow cash crops. 'Hungry natives,' he explained, 'will listen to us about God if we can show them a field of grain with a combine harvesting more in a day than they can eat in a year.'[37] He felt that this kind of help would be 'a sure vaccination against the smallpox of Communism and a practical demonstration of the power of Christianity.'[38]

According to the first of many notices in the *Peruvian Times,* in April 1953, Le Tourneau was surveying the route of the proposed Tambo del Sol-Pucallpa railway, a scheme to connect Sierra and Amazon which had wrecked fortunes and hopes for half a century.[39] Among the persons in his party, the *Times* listed Townsend; ex-Ambassador Vasquez Benavides, now Le Tourneau's legal representative in Peru as well as head of SIL's Friends committee; Dr. V.R. Edman, President of Wheaton College, a distinguished evangelical institution near Chicago; and W.G. Nyman, 'Secretary-Treasurer of the Summer Institute of Linguistics, of which Mr. Le Tourneau is one of the principal backers.'

'Possibilities for large-scale colonization,' the *Times* added, had been brought to Le Tourneau's attention by Drs. Vasquez and Townsend.[40] Le Tourneau credited only Townsend, who had not only invited him to Peru but introduced him to President Odria and served as interpreter in their negotiations.[41] In the *Times,* the founder vouched for the many benefits to be expected from the

---

* In 1959 the Peruvian Times reported that SIL was opening a new airstrip for the Union Oil Company of Los Angeles between the Huallaga and Ucayali Rivers. A JAARS pilot flew in labourers by landing on floats in a nearby lake, then tested the new strip with a wheeled plane. A number of similar exercises were scheduled.[32] In 1964, oil traffic accounted for 12% of JAARS-Peru flights (with 50% for SIL, 20% for the Army and 11% for other evangelical missionaries). In 1969, oil traffic accounted for 16% and the military for 18%.[33]

proposed Le Tourneau concession: it would become 'a bustling center of agriculture, cattle raising and progress', halve the cost of hauling lumber to the coast and consume unmarketable Ganso Azul petroleum.[42]

Some months before, in November 1952, Townsend had persuaded the Minister of Education, General Juan Mendoza, and President Odria to sponsor a SIL-administered bilingual teacher training programme. General Mendoza's next assignment was in Washington, D.C., as chief of the Peruvian delegation to the Inter-American Defense Board.[43] In Mexico, SIL had never been able to rely upon government literacy programmes to induce Indians to read the Bible. Now, for the first time, SIL would control a government literacy programme. To members who argued that he was mixing tribute to Caesar with tribute to Christ — Catholic instruction was still mandatory in government schools — Townsend cited a precedent from the Book of Exodus (2:1-9): 'It's like Pharoah's daughter paying Moses' mother to nurse her own baby.'[44] In other words, a Catholic state will unknowingly subsidize Protestant missionaries to evangelize Indians.

The Mysterious Wicleffe

The first teacher training course was held at Yarinacocha, the SIL base near Pucallpa, in early 1953. Confronted by an obvious threat to their pedagogical monopoly, the Catholic missionary bishops protested to the new Minister of Education. In *El Comercio* a Jesuit priest, Jose Martin Cuesta, reasoned as follows: 'Dr. Martha Hildebrandt tells us . . . that the Summer Institute of Linguistics is . . . dedicated to . . . nothing but philanthropy and philology. The Director of the Summer Institute, Mr. Townsend, always has declared the same. . . .' But these claims did not explain certain facts: 1) Unlike other scientific bodies from the religiously diverse United States, a member had admitted in 1951 that the Linguistic Institute was composed exclusively of evangelical Protestants. 2) They had shown a remarkable affinity for Protestant mission stations, providing all kinds of services to them. 3) Contrary to SIL's public statements, its planes were noticeably less available to Catholic missionaries. 4) Nearly all the 20 students at the first SIL-Ministry of Education training course were Protestants or sympathizers. 5) As confirmed by Franciscan, Dominican, Passionist, Augustinian and Jesuit missionaries in contact with members of the Linguistic Institute, many of them were mounting sectarian campaigns against the Catholic religion. 'Aside from being a scientific and disinterested organization,' Martin Cuesta concluded, the Institute was also an evangelical Protestant mission.[45]

In government ministries, Townsend argued that his linguists were being confused with Seventh Day Adventists and Sylvester Dirks, an ex-member flourishing as a Protestant pastor. He also persuaded the air force to make JAARS a subsidiary of its *Transportes Aereos Militares.*[46] By introducing Le Tourneau to President Odria, Townsend fortified his position even more. But despite an attempt to be discrete, Le Tourneau's evangelical plans were soon public record. In July, the Archbishop of Lima protested to President Odria, but again without result.

On 8 August 1953, Monsignor Buenaventura Leon de Uriarte — the Spanish Franciscan Vicar of Ucayali, apostolic shepherd of the Linguistic Institute's central theatre of operation — threw down the gauntlet in the pages of the Lima daily *La Prensa.* Like his brethren, Uriarte accused SIL of 'making an active and tendentious campaign to convert the Indians of our Amazon to evangelical Protestantism.' He charged that SIL was 'hiding its true intentions behind a series of disguises.' But Uriarte went even further: he accused the linguists of being an arm of the 'Wicleffe Bible Translators'.

Le Prensa printed Townsend's reply beside the Bishop's accusations. 'How could a scientist who believes in our loving Jesus Christ,' he began, 'live among human beings who worship the boa [constrictor] and . . . not tell them anything about Christianity?' 'We do not carry out evangelist work,' the founder continued, 'because the Institute has a mission of scientific character and not a religious end.' 'On the other hand,' reported the interviewer, 'Dr. Townsend admitted that personally he is part of "Wicleffe Bible" but advised that the Institute had nothing to do with it.'

To prove his claims, Townsend flourished testimonials. He exhibited a letter from President George Cross of the University of Oklahoma and dropped the names of two prominent linguists, Drs. Charles Fries and Louis Luzbetak, at the Universities of Michigan and Chicago.[47] As *La Prensa* weighed the discrepancies between the statements of the venerable Bishop and the distinguished University of Oklahoma scientist, a *Peruvian Times* journalist stepped forward. 'The members of the Institute have not told the whole truth in this important affair,' explained Malcolm Burke, a North American Catholic. While Burke deplored the Bishop's unchristian statements and applauded SIL's work, he noted that 'the linguists, together with their scientific work, carry out an undeniable missionary campaign. This is so certain that it is not a matter for debate. The linguists are missionaries.'[48]

On 12 August, Bishop Uriarte produced a University of Oklahoma bulletin mentioning SIL's relation to Wycliffe. A few days later he raised the Le Tourneau issue, charging that SIL was conspiring with its 'millionaire friend and financial backer. . . . to Protestantize our jungle.' According to *La Prensa,* Townsend was now declining comment and asking where he could find Uriarte, 'to make a detailed exposition of the Linguistic Institute'.[49]

The Hefleys skip the founder's interview with *La Prensa,* the subsequent no-comment and anxiety to get his hands on Msgr. Uriarte. Instead, Townsend prepares his 'only reply,' In his second published reply, to *El Comercio* on 19 August, Townsend made no reference to his first, either to suggest that he had been misquoted or was retracting:

> We have, then a double aspect. Our work of dual nature brings us contacts
> of dual nature and for this reason I founded a second institution which
> is also non-sectarian, called Wycliffe Bible Translators. It consists of a small
> office in Glendale, California and another even smaller, in Chicago,

Illinois. It has absolutely no life apart from the Summer Institute of Linguistics and exists solely to obtain funds and recruits for our work. The two institutions are analogous in many respects.

As for the 'principal backer', Townsend explained that SIL was co-operating with everyone, even Mr. Le Tourneau, 'with whom we have no other connection than a recent friendship.' A few days earlier, Le Tourneau's son Roy told *La Prensa* the same, adding that SIL had been 'included once in the contributions made by the Le Tourneau Foundation to various organizations, but we do not have connections with [it].'[50]

The Summer Institute was non-sectarian, Townsend stated, because 'no sect contributes with donations to our work. Individuals and independent groups . . . sustain us.'[51] Not only did he forget to say anything about the Wycliffe Statement of Doctrine; he has since allowed his testament to be described as a 'classic in Christian diplomacy'. The archbishops were not impressed, and a few days later issued a declaration backing Uriarte.[52] In early September, President Odria convened a special meeting of his Cabinet to pass a resolution backing SIL, increased its subsidy and decorated Townsend for distinguished service.[53] The Le Tourneau contract was signed in December.

The Founder Adjusts His Halo

In his second published reply to Monsignor Uriarte, Townsend admitted that his linguists were motivated by a profound love of God; he confessed that they were connected to Wycliffe Bible Translators; he declared that they intended to translate the Bible; but he did not admit that they were missionaries, let alone evangelical missionaries. On the contrary:

> No pastor, whether Protestant or Catholic, can be a member . . . without abandoning his vocation to follow ours. . . . We do not call ourselves Protestants but simply believers in Christ. . . . Beyond the teachings of the Catholic Bible we do not go. . . . We are not responsible for the teaching of ecclesiastical rites and systems of any kind because we are not sectarian. The missionaries, be they Catholic or Protestant, will have to take charge of such religious teachings.

Yet until Wycliffe arrived in Peru it had been, as Townsend described the Mexican Government's feelings, 'nauseated with the evils of Rome.'[54] A 1944 Wycliffe publication exposed the Romanist Virgin Mary as a costume for Lucifer.[55] JAARS dates Townsend's 'service to all' policy to 1946, when he arranged to have four ministries subsidize the Grumman Duck, and, in his own words, 'gave the gas tank to the Air Force'.[56] But flights for Catholic missionaries were not frequent enough to be a major strain on the pilots until 1952-53, when Townsend apparently increased them as a politic measure.

The pilots had come to Peru to fly for Christ, not drop off newspapers and Mrs. Townsend's confections at Catholic stations, and this was like helping the enemy.[57]

Soon Townsend showed that a burdensome state requirement could be turned to advantage. As he pointed out in *El Comercio,* his Institute had contracts with two universities, five republics and four Peruvian ministries. And as he emphasized in *La Prensa,* while his linguists and Catholic missionaries were really great friends, Msgr. Uriarte's declarations were lamentably 'going to have repercussions' in the common task of civilizing the Indian. In particular, Catholic missionaries had enjoyed JAARS service.[58] To prove it Townsend exhibited their thank-you notes. After 1953, Catholic missionaries recall, service to all included taking their photographs as they stepped into the planes of a government airline. Later the photos would be shown to government ministries, bishops and the Papal Nuncio.

Yet Msgr. Uriarte had accomplished more than he could have imagined. By dragging Wycliffe out of the closet in Peru, he flushed the Summer Institute into the open in the United States. Since many home supporters would have been appalled by SIL's claims in Peru, they had never been told about them. Wycliffe tried to spare them Townsend's statements of August 1953: in the next two numbers of *Translation* we read only of the first government-backed teacher training course, each of whose graduates it was hoped would be a witness for the Lord; an unconnected but strong clerical opposition, followed by resounding government endorsement; 'refinement of several points of financial and administrative procedure'; the resignation of 1942 chartist Eugene Nida from the board of directors; his replacement by Benjamin E. Needham, a Southern California avocado grower and member of a Le Tourneau party in Peru; 'a marvelous spirit of harmony and faith to advance'; and assurance 'of continued co-operation' from the University of Oklahoma.[59]

One of Nida's reasons, however, for leaving Wycliffe was Townsend's way of presenting the work. The founder was suffering a second case of exposed duplicity, this one immune to decree by the Odria dictatorship, because it was at home in the faith support base. In the *New York Times,* some supporters must have read that, according to Dr. Townsend, the Linguistic Institute made its airplanes equally available to Catholic and Protestant missionaries.[60] In the *New York Herald Tribune* they learned that, according to Townsend, 'the main work of his organization is investigation, though it contributes also to the spiritual needs of the Indians.'[61] And in the *National Geographic,* many more discovered that, according to W. Cameron Townsend, 'we're not really a religious organization, but we do introduce the Indians to Christianity by translating part of the Bible;...'[62] Soon, mail from the homeland was full of anger, and Christian businessmen felt that they had been deceived. In 1949, contributions to JAARS averaged $3,500 a month, for one month around 1954 they totalled $21.67. By 1958-59 the scandal had proceeded from the Evangelical Foreign Missionary Association to the Interdenominational Foreign Missions Association (IFMA), which together comprised most of the faith mission industry. According to the Hefleys, one issue was co-operating with Catholics, the other that 'the primary purpose of Wycliffe's work was scientific and cultural, not spiritual.'[63]

The chain-reaction expose forced SIL/WBT thinkers to overhaul their system of plausible denial. In August 1953, Townsend had declared that Wycliffe 'has absolutely no life apart from the Summer Institute', but the two still had to be presented in very different ways. The 'closet' stage of the dual identity gave way to the 'two organizations'. In Peru, vague references to Christian civilization, spiritual work and even the Bible began to creep into SIL's presentations. They are exceeding scarce in the reports of *Peruvian Times* correspondents until the late 1950s; in the branch's own reports to the present, one might as well avoid a vase of eye strain. At home SIL graduated from dependency to affiliate of WBT by the late 1950s. *Translation* made its first reference to co-operation with Catholics in 1958, in the form of flights for 'missionaries — both evangelicals and others'. In the previous issue, Townsend even mentioned that Wycliffe operated in the field as the Summer Institute.[64]

Characteristically, Townsend considered this painful but rewarding adjustment a triumph of Christian virtue over his Fundamentalist and Catholic adversaries. In 1975, the year after the Hefleys presented the founder as a pioneer of inter-faith co-operation under the heading of 'the language of love', Wycliffe published a collection of talks in which he fondly recalls using the JAARS air service to play Catholic missionaries off against each other.[65] That same year, Wycliffe produced a revised edition of its 'Answers to Questions,' a source of the 'party line' for which SIL has become famous and prefaced 'not for public distribution since it is not intended to raise questions where none have existed'. Should members fail to satisfy interrogators with these answers, they are instructed to refer questions to headquarters. The six answers to questions about Catholics are chiefly denials that Wycliffe co-operates with them, including the following:

> *44. Is it true that WBT co-operates with the Catholic Church?*
> Some claim that we do, from Townsend's 1955 [sic] article for *El Comercio* in Peru. The fact that article had to be written indicates that we do not. Certainly the Catholics do not consider we cooperate and have forbidden priests to accept favors. Evidence that we have been kind has but incensed the hierarchy further, since it undermines their charges against us. . . .
> Mr Townsend's article made quite plain the evangelical faith of every Wycliffe member and quoted Scripture to that effect. The article was successful in quieting the public Catholic attacks against us and gave the leverage for the government officially to rebuke and show its displeasure with the Catholic attacks and express its appreciation of our Bible translation work.[66]

The reason the hierarchy was incensed by a non-ecclesiastical programme is suggested by another internal document, 'Strategy for the Conclusion of Our

Work in Peru', which apparently dates to the early 1970s. Under the heading 'Ecclesiastical Leadership and Organization', SIL's minimum goals include: 'to have at least one or two Christian groups formed and organized so the Church can choose its own leaders, establish its own sanctions, participate in the sacraments and relate itself with the believers of the rest of the tribe and the nation.'[67] Elsewhere, the Wycliffe literature refers to this task as 'church development'.[68]

Braving anticipated financial repercussions, Wycliffe withdrew from the IFMA in late 1959. But it only did so after procuring an endorsement, in the form of a 'Call . . . to Reach 2,000 Bibleless Tribes in this Generation' from leading evangelicals such as Charles Fuller, V.R. Edman of Wheaton College and Billy Graham, a SIL/WBT board member at the time and spiritual counsellor to President Eisenhower.[69] Divided and ineffectual, the IFMA ran a vague 'For Your Protection' notice.[70] As Townsend's critics feared, however, his promotions kept the recruits coming and Wycliffe mushrooming. About this time it became the world's largest faith mission.

Less than a decade later the evangelical opinion leader *Christianity Today* considered Wycliffe's success second only to that of Billy Graham. The journal was impressed by Townsend's penetration of Catholic states, calling the contracts 'the backbone of Wycliffe strategy', while other evangelical missionaries accused Wycliffe of 'implicit duplicity' and violating the U.S. principle of church-state separation, *Christianity Today* suggested that they were jealous because Wycliffe produced four times as many converts. Entering communist countries was the next big challenge.[71]

The Bilingual Schools

Since the 19th Century the Amazon has been available as a myth of national redemption. Tarnished by the sorry results of colonization schemes, the myth is periodically refurbished to justify yet another. In the 1950s, after some 100 years of experience along these lines, two of the most vocal apostles of progress in the Peruvian jungle were the North American evangelists Cameron Townsend and Robert Le Tourneau.*

---

*Le Tourneau financed an experiment in a number of trends — the company concession, clear-cut logging and cattle ranching — which may destroy the Amazon forest in a few decades. In exchange for 400,000 hectares around the Ganso Azul oilfield, Le Tourneau agreed to build a 50 kilometre road to railway specifications, settle colonists and, at least rhetorically, level the entire Amazon jungle with his big machines.[72] Although it emerged that profit was an objective, Le Tourneau said that the principal aim was the foundation of a Christian colony.

At Tournavista his technical missionaries established the Missionary Communications Service for the South American Indian Mission, a school for missionary children and an Indian Bible Institute. SIL's physician staffed the clinic on Thursdays and Le Tourneau equipment improved the Yarinacocha airstrip.[73] Eventually the company invested

Countering charges that the Linguistic Institute threatened national sovereignty, Townsend played on the imagination of Lima's upper crust to establish his North American pilots and investigators as Peru's staunchest heroes. They were pioneers of progress and fatherland in the untamed Amazon. Certainly there was superstition and exploitation to be dispelled, but the bilingual schools were planting the Peruvian flag where it never had waved before, creating new patriots and consumers. Eventually, the multitudes bound to earth on the Coast and Sierra would follow JAARS in 'beautiful clouds of metal birds, carrying passengers, products, doctors, teachers, everything necessary for modern life to all corners of the jungle.'

To the image of the Green Hell infested with savages Townsend contrasted the good will, intelligence and ambition of jungle Indians. But since his hosts were more likely to consider Indian languages a national disgrace than source of pride, he claimed that his linguists would help to destroy them in favour of *Peruanidad*. Through bilingual education, Townsend explained in 1950, 'languages that today mean isolation would become instruments with which their own extinction would be accelerated.' Encouraged by the success of the bilingual schools, five years later he could see the day when the beautiful languages his investigators were studying and preserving would disappear, replaced by Spanish as they ought to be, and the Summer Institute move on to new fields.[79]

Townsend understood that this day might be very far off indeed, but he needed to wring sympathy from extremely hard *criollo* hearts. The intellectual climate in which he launched the bilingual schools is suggested by one of the first friendly newspaper headlines: ' "Savages" . . . take special training course.'[80] Msgr. Uriarte for his part had no doubt that the new schools were 'patriotically and pedagogically a disgrace': the Protestants were trying to turn *Indios* who scarcely knew how to speak Spanish, add or subtract into schoolteachers in three months.[81] Jose Martin Cuesta had a higher opinion

perhaps $8 million, grazed 5,000 head of cattle and shipped lumber to the coast. But while Tournavista was to be a salesroom to demonstrate how Le Tourneau machines could demolish a hectare of forest in half an hour, they bogged down during the long rainy season and proved less economical than local labour. Construction of the road to railway specifications proved costly, leading to endless haggling with the government, halting the land transfer at 60,000 hectares, and contributing to company reluctance to grant Peruvian settlers land titles.[74]

According to the Peruvian Times, local workers were being raised from a low-level, self-sufficient economy to a 'cash-flow consumer group'.[75] Since nearly all the managers were North American, and since nearly all Peruvians were workers or squatters who could not obtain their own land titles, Tournavista looked less like a home-steading colony than a company ranch. Le Tourneau nevertheless claimed spiritual dividends, a reference to the expectation that everyone on the premises would become a brother in Christ.[76] In November 1964, the Lima daily El Expreso headlined that Tournavista 'has turned into a powderkeg which could explode from one moment to the next.' A weak S.O.S. signal had been received in Pucallpa: little was audible except 'they want to burn us' and a platoon of police hurried to the rescue. The Tournavista workers attributed mass layoffs to their attempt to organize a union.[77] Five years later the company asked the government to liquidate the holding.[78]

of SIL's Indian teachers — more than a few were products of Catholic schools, after all — but like other Catholic missionaries, he felt that bilingual education would only delay incorporation into the nation.[82] These were among the first of many arguments against it, which SIL would still be countering 25 years later.

To the indigenists, the bilingual schools made the Summer Institute perhaps their dearest cause. A compelling case was made by Efrain Morote Best, a leftist educator who supervised the training course and schools for the Ministry of Education from 1956 to 1958. The Catholic *internados* or boarding schools, Morote reported, were still trying to make their charges 'stop being Indians' through methodical pressure to suppress their language and culture. Students learned to be ashamed of their origin and to imitate alien behaviour. As Spanish was acquired, they lost fluency in their own language, were unable to resume life among their people, and drifted into the towns where they settled to the bottom of the social order. The government's *normal* schools were no better. But bilingual education was 'a revolutionary step from the educational and social point of view' because Indians could be taught basic subjects in their own languages, in their own communities and by other Indians.

Morote encouraged SIL translators and their Indian teachers to confront the *patrones* by emphasizing arithmetic — keeping accounts, replacing barter with cash and staying out of debt — and promoting the idea of co-operatives. As such lessons reached the adults, they learned just how badly they were being cheated. The *patrones* began to retaliate by withdrawing the hospitality they had extended translators, punishing Indians who were getting out of hand, and mounting nationalist propaganda. Soon Morote's campaign was having repercussions in Lima in the form of a second wave of opposition to SIL, which he attributed to an alliance of 'mistaken priests', *patrones* and politicians representing their interests.[83]

Of years of religious intrigue in the Ministry of Education the Hefleys mention one incident. In January 1959, not long after the Army had forced Morote to leave his post and an IFMA witch-hunter was due to investigate SIL's evangelical fibre, Townsend learned of a directive addressed to the new training course director. Father Robert Binet would be teaching religion during the coming term. The order was in clear conformity with the law: while it would only install Catholic religion at Yarinacocha, the next step was clearly catechism in each of the Ministry's bilingual schools run by SIL. Officially, the directive was none of Townsend's business, except to see that it was implemented. Were we to believe his previous statements, SIL had no objection because it was leaving religious instruction to Catholic and Protestant missionaries. But while a half-hearted catechism might have been an antidote to mission rivalry, for the most profound reasons many SIL teams could not have translated it, let alone permitted their teachers to propagate the damnable doctrine. Were the order to have been implemented, many translators might have found a more useful calling and stated their case back home in the plainest of terms, wrecking the founder's repuation and institute once and for all.

On the grounds that SIL was non-sectarian, Townsend therefore persuaded Minister of Education Jorge Basadre to revoke the order.[84] According to an internal Catholic document, SIL subsequently vetoed the reappointment of the course director who had received the order; its author only retained his post after the missionary bishops intervened with the President; and the pressure to remove him was later traced to SIL.

Morote had chosen the Maranon Valley as his principal theatre, employing bilingual teachers as his co-operative organizers. At Chicais, where a school drew Aguaruna around it so quickly that four teachers were assigned, a village council was organized, legal title to the land solicited, and a residence erected for children from other locales. The teachers tried to ban destructive hunting and fishing methods, introduced rubber and fruit seedlings, and set up a marketing co-operative for skins and wild rubber, which the Army helped them sell in Iquitos.[85] The reaction of the *patrones* has been memorialized in *La Casa Verde,* a novel by Mario Vargas Llosa. In 1958, he accompanied a Morote-led party into the Maranon by courtesy of JAARS. While Vargas Llosa keeps his friends offstage, we read about Morote-reported events: how the Catholic nuns at the Jesuit station in Santa Maria de Nieva were taking children from their parents with the help of soldiers, then naively releasing their wards to gentlemen who took them to the cities to be servants and prostitutes. We also read of the public whipping and torture of the mayor of Urakusa, one of Morote's Aguaruna organizers trained at Yarinacocha, by the civil authorities of Santa Maria de Nieva.

Another figure Vargas Llosa left out of his novel was Robert Le Tourneau who, several years before, had visited the Maranon after applying for one million acres of the Xingu Valley in Brazil.[86] His legal adviser was still Oscar Vasquez Benavides of the Friends of SIL Committee.[87] Le Tourneau proposed building a $20 million highway into the Maranon, which the Odria Government accepted pending receipt of a U.S. loan.[88] Oil companies, colonists, Lima industrialists and importers were excited about the plan: the *Peruvian Times* pointed out that it would 'open up a vast area for agriculture, lumber, cattle raising and minerals', maybe even massive hydro-electric projects.[89] Several years later, the same month the *patrones* tortured the mayor of Urakusa at Santa Maria, Jose Martin Cuesta asked for a larger subsidy from the Ministry of Education so that the Jesuit Mission could open its own bilingual schools. The Army proceeded to ban Morote from the region, the Aguaruna co-operative went the way of private enterprise and, when Vargas Llosa returned in 1964, he thought that nothing had changed except for the worse.[90] But the Maranon was changing more than he thought.

The translators were, for one, concentrating a large fraction of some 20,000 Aguaruna around 67 bilingual schools. In the quest for souls, they and the Jesuits were waging a struggle that one of the latter calls 'a bit of the 16th Century'. According to Cesar Sarazara Andia, an Aguaruna who calls the Catholic *internado* preferable to the *patrones* but seems just as ambivalent about the Jesuits as SIL, 'the world divided between following the Jesuits or the bilingual school missionaries. Families split. . . . This has

lasted until now. Beside a Jesuit school stands a school of the evangelists
with the name Bilingual School, up and down the Maranon River* [91]
Another big change was the new highway, commenced by the Morris-Knudsen
and Brown and Root Companies of New York and Houston, then extended
by the Army. By 1970, the road had reached the vicinity of SIL headquarters.
Five years later it was almost to Santa Maria de Nieva. In the wake of the road,
pushing toward a new oil-field being opened by Mobil of New York and Union
of Los Angeles, came the *Guardia Civil,* real estate speculators, government-
sponsored colonists and many more squatters. For allies, the Aguaruna had
their missionaries.

Morote believes that SIL was essential at the time he worked with it
because, without the linguistic studies which no one else was in a position to
do, there would have been no bilingual schools.[93] But as the Aguaruna experience demonstrates, more was involved than enlightened pedagogy or a
measure of independence from *patrones.* While SIL was thriving on anti-clerical
reactions to the Catholic clergy, its friends also considered it faster and surer in
the task at hand. To military officers, indigenists, politicians and businessmen,
as reiterated whenever possible by SIL, the schools were teaching jungle Indians
that they were citizens of Peru, strengthening the national frontiers and preparing the way for colonization.

Thanks to its teachers and airplanes, SIL earned a reputation as the government's most effective instrument among jungle Indians. By organizing the
schools and delivering military payrolls on time, it made itself indispensable.
As reiterated over the decades, here were unselfish North American experts
performing a noble service for Peru, a vacuum filled and an eminently national
result. To prove it there are reams of seldom interrupted, SIL-inspired nationalist propaganda. For a single airplane dedication in 1962 the branch counted
25 press reports.[94] 'I believe in you, Peru,' a journalist wrote after quitting the
SIL base.[95] Training course director Augusto Mateu Cueva was moved to
verse: 'I departed more Peruvian than ever/carrying you in my heart/ Oh!
Yarinacocha. . . .'[96]

To the genteel visitor from Lima, the rustic but comfortable houses of the
linguists, exotic flora and lake-shore, classrooms, airplanes, obliging North

---

* 'We had no idea of why they were fighting', an Aguaruna told a conference at the
University of Wisconsin in 1978. 'We were shocked by all this and began to criticize
both SIL and the Jesuits. If they are Catholic or Protestant, and have the same holy
Bible as the basis for their work, they should be able to work together more peacefully.
Despite the conflicts which they have amongst themselves, when a problem arises among
us, they say that it is sin and tell us to stop. But we, being their children, say, "But
Father, if you behave the way that you do, how do you expect us not to behave
similarly?" We simply get more confused. Now among the native people there are
divisions, not because we wanted it that way, but because of these institutions which
have entered our territory. We received the blame but we were not guilty. The missionaries should begin to ask themselves why these problems occurred and who is really to
blame.[92] Some of the competitively situated schools merged after the government
took control of both systems in the early 1970s.

Americans and respectful natives at one's disposal were the very picture of what national integration ought to be. Almost equally impressed Anglo-Saxons compared Yarinacocha to a resort: it was a more commodious, appealing version of the Tetelcingo garden. The teacher graduations Townsend turned into ceremonies of state, inviting politicians, military officers, bishops, newspaper editors and ambassadors. Many a heart swelled with pride to see the Peruvian flag run up and jungle Indians standing at attention, singing the national anthem, doing calisthenics, marching, and receiving diplomas and citizenship papers from appropriate officials imported for the occasion.

The patriotic displays were part of a larger system of circumlocution to disguise SIL's control of a Ministry of Education programme, the use to which it was putting that programme, and the perennial failure to transfer it into Peruvian hands. With a few exceptions such as Morote, Peruvians were limited to subsidizing the schools, protecting them and SIL from enemies, and relieving members of some of the work load. The Ministry-appointed training course director usually came out to Yarinacocha for the three-month duration, returned to Lima to be replaced by someone else the next year. Except for a few favours conceded to the more friendly Catholic missionaries, SIL selected the students and often subsidized the pre-salary stage of their training. While Peruvians taught many of the courses at the SIL base, the translators' command of the native languages meant that they did the tutoring and moral counselling. Although a Ministry co-ordinator was nominally in charge of the school system in 1956-58 and after 1964, he depended on SIL members to administer the far-flung teachers and deliver their pay. Student teachers depended upon translator evaluation to finish the six-year training cycle and win Ministry appointment.

Since SIL and the Ministry insisted that the schools were a Ministry programme, officially there was no need for a transfer. The North Americans were only partly responsible for their enclave. The government appreciated the low cost and reliability of its foreign experts. Few Peruvian indigenists were willing to endure a measure of physical discomfort at regular intervals and never achieved a comparable experience. They lacked the *esprit de corps,* airplanes and radios with which SIL members faced their fear of the jungle. When the Ministry asserted more control after 1970, the branch claimed to have always wanted that, but had been frustrated by a lack of Peruvian interest. The wish to be unburdened seems to have dated only to the late 1960s, however, when the branch found itself on the horns of a dilemma: the increasing demands of the schools were retarding Bible translation.[97] Until this time, friends of SIL calling for Peruvian responsibility — men like Morote and the journalist Hugo Neira whose purge in 1976 Wycliffe would hail as an act of God — were voices crying in the wilderness. SIL was far more interested in fostering the illusion of national control: as the founder's instructions have been summarized, 'whenever possible, Peru and Peruvians were to receive credit for the accomplishments of SIL.[98] Transfer never descended from the vaguest Townsendian rhetoric, because it could only be accepted on impossibly narrow, covertly faith mission terms, as demonstrated by the branch's practice of pulling all available wires to protect its arrangements from Catholics taking Townsend at his word.

To do otherwise would have contradicted SIL's only purpose in coming to Peru. It never mentioned evangelism, maintaining that religion in the bilingual schools was confined to a legally required Moral Education course, a short, daily and non-sectarian Bible reading. Townsend even banned missionary language from radio communications: terms like 'pray for' became 'please remember'. Thanks to their authority and command of the native language, translators could perform their spiritual responsibilities in the same defensive obscurity in which Indians conduct their affairs. According to an anthropologist, Amuesha teachers told him that they had been instructed not to discuss their new religion with outsiders. Only in reports for the homeland was it explained that bilingual teachers and spiritual leaders, schooling and evangelism were identical, with the possible distinction that classes were held during the day and worship services at night.[99]

In the 1950s, some translators wanted to dismiss teachers for failing to maintain their Christian witness, but except for polygamy, the civil code did not allow retaliation for breach of fundamentalist morals. Other translators argued that purges would mean fewer teachers, less subsidy and violation of the law. The disagreement reflected the difference between those members confining themselves largely to stated goals —Bible translation and literacy — and others (including members of the teams in most of the large groups) intent on propagating congregations. Since Morote, and several other course directors, made it clear that SIL could not impose its standards, the fundamentalists were forced to conform. But since they were along for the long term while the course directors were not, they could still make life miserable for their lapsed pastors and reportedly managed to purge a few, which the branch denies.

Indian Apostles

To Efrain Morote Best, the bilingual teacher was a frugal, temperate, abstinent man possessed by an apostolic Christian mission. At the annual exodus from Yarinacocha, he reported, the teachers returned to their people 'carrying pigs, chickens, turkeys, ducks, seeds and seedlings of fruit trees, outboard motors, shotguns, victrolas, flashlights, bicycles, clothes, medicines and, together with all this, a good pile of books, notebooks, pencils and primers. . . . From that time on, the bilingual teacher is an adviser to the group. He is looked upon as the symbol of advancing civilization.'[100]

The Bible translators were unleashing a trade goods bonanza. They descended from the sky in airplanes, unloaded bulky talking machines, offered gifts, set up North American households, hired informants to learn the language and took the most willing away in their airplanes to Yarinacocha. The businesslike atmosphere at the base saved time; it was easier to elicit closely held beliefs; and as *Peruvian Times* correspondent David St. Clair reported, informants were 'given a taste of "civilization".' (When I asked an informant why he liked Yarinacocha, he replied: 'There's a lot of lemonade there, sweets.' Since the answer embarrassed him, he laughed, 'Besides, it's better there than here.') As St. Clair also stated, the base was like 'another world' which made Indians 'want to improve their own primitive surroundings'.[101] Since informants were discouraged from leaving their primitive surroundings altogether, Yarinacocha was hello and goodbye to the power and the glory unless they were invited back.

To make Indian visitors feel at home, they had their own Indian-style village, which also owed something to racial segregation (originally fear of Indian germs) and sometimes deteriorated into a slum in striking contrast to members' quarters. Like any mission or indigenist project, the base was reproducing prevailing class relations, but manipulating them in certain ways, to bring about that better day ahead. Middle- and upper-class Peruvians were, for example, excluded from all but symbolic occasions such as civics class. But all year wage labourers residing off base (and on a temporary basis the language informants) kept the floors clean. For jungle Indian visitors the contrast between the creature comforts of the North Americans, the indigence of Pucallpa workers, and themselves made the base a concentrated lesson in stratified society. It emphasized their low position, stimulated material aspirations and promised rapid self-advancement.

Judging from Wycliffe accounts, the first converts were generally won here rather than at home among their people. A particular aura surrounds Bible translation: as George Cowan has explained, the native speaker must 'state to the satisfaction' of his Wycliffe translator 'the meaning of every book, chapter, verse and phrase' to be rendered, which not even a Bible institute requires.[102] Translators may deny that they are evangelizing: in their view it is the Word of God and the Holy Spirit at work in the heart of the informant, not any pressure or influence on their part, which leads to conversion. Sooner or later informants from virtually every language are likely to come to the Lord at the translation desk: without those converted native speakers, it is doubtful that SIL could produce vernacular New Testaments.

The informants whom translators chose to take the teacher training course, were usually men who had acquired some Spanish and a few years of primary school outside their group, in Catholic *internados* or the occasional Protestant mission, as army conscripts or foremen of *patrones*. The 700 *sole* a month teacher salary

> is indeed a large amount in a native village [St. Clair explained] but it is a definite inducement on the part of the Government to get the pick of . . . each tribe. The teachers themselves see this opportunity as a chance to better not only their village, but themselves as well. For here is their big opportunity to throw off the poverty and subjection that many of them endure. Here is their chance to be somebody, rather than just another native in another village.[103]

If teacher candidates had not already surrendered to Christ, receptivity to the idea was usually a criterion in their selection. Thanks to peer pressure from other candidates, who were proving their Christian witness to their own translators, nearly everyone declared for the Lord.

Now that the most ambitious young men had delivered their language and rejected tradition in exchange for bright prospects, they were expected to be Christian leaders, that is, carry out instructions to turn family and neighbours into Christian villagers. There was no room for free choice in the model bilingual school, because literacy and evangelical religion were part of the same package. 'I learned to read and write through Mr. [Will] Kindberg,' Wycliffe quoted Campa teacher Jose Flores in the presence of his translator in 1963. ' "If this had not happened, none of you would be learning. You would not be able to read the Bible and to be Christians." Then Will, adding his word of instruction, said: "Jesus is in heaven, and we accept Christ's resurrection as proof that there is resurrection and He will raise us up. . . . " After Will spoke, the students sang "Onward Christian Soldiers" in the Campa language.'[104]

Marching orders set the teacher on a collision course with traditional values. In Amazonian societies people generally share what they have, the power of a leader is generally limited to persuasion and the duty of a leader is to give, and give more generously than anyone else, so that he may end up the poorest man in the group.[105] In egalitarian societies where the leader was actually a servant, SIL was trying to set up an authoritarian leader who regarded his possessions as private property, and this in the name of humble Christian service! As the people tried to strip the teacher of his new possessions, his profession meant that he no longer had much time for hunting game and clearing a garden. The heavy demands not only shattered his dreams but threatened to make him destitute, putting him under pressure to break with patterns of sharing. Traditional exchange might claim even entrepreneurial profits. But SIL was trying to mould sturdy individualists, not mobs begging handouts, and tended to intervene accordingly. The result could be cultural misfits, men at odds with their own people and at the same time unable to approach the North American standard of living they had been taught to emulate.

The translators opened a Pandora's box when their teachers persuaded small, dispersed groups to come together to constitute 25 students necessary for an official salary. As newcomers who had to create their own foci of influence, the translators usually showed more enthusiasm for the practice than the Catholics, who could excuse themselves by appealing to experience. In the name of progressive education SIL was reproducing the notorious *reduccion,* a concentration of Indians whose instabilityiis typically blamed on native irrationality rather than ecology.

Since the branch was even more reluctant to explain its problems to Peruvians than to home supporters, eventually it fell to a Belgian anthropologist, Marcel D'Ans, to explain the consequences.[106] But in a 1970 Wycliffe publication we read how, in the consolidated Campa village of Quempiri, teacher Jose Flores 'became the arbiter of family squabbles, neighborhood disputes, garbage disposal problems and pet control — everything imaginable.' When an adult and a few children died of dysentery, 'a man became frightened and moved out, passing around the story that the white man's God was angry and was striking all the people dead.' Then a man saw a snake biting another snake and said that Quempiri was being overrun by serpents. 'Before the episode was over, a good share of Quempiri newcomers had pulled out, and Jose was left with a big public relations problem.'[107] A few of the 'public relations' problems noted by D'Ans — exhaustion of game and agricultural land, deteriorating hygiene, social tension and disorientation expressed by an increase in witchcraft fear, vendettas and sexual aggression — were mentioned by SIL's first anthropology co-ordinator, Dale Kietzman, several years later. The new settlement pattern around the bilingual schools in Peru, he explained, 'has created health problems they have never had before, placed strains on the food supply, and encouraged outside contacts which did expose the people to unfamiliar diseases.'[108]

Long before SIL acknowledged flaws in its Peruvian showcase, an outsider in 1961 grasped the trade politics at work. Matthew Huxley had been asked by Samuel Milbank, a New York businessman, philanthropist and friend of Cameron Townsend to write a book about Amazonian Indians. Huxley chose to study acculturation and gave considerable attention to his hosts, whom he hoped would help Indians avoid the seemingly inevitable progression from jungle to slum. The primitive Amahuaca had tasted of the white man's fruit — trade goods — and found them good, and their *Linguistico* was determined to teach them that they were basically bad: hence Huxley's title *Farewell to Eden*.

But in contrast to an isolationist Protestant mission and a Catholic 'factory for turning out Peruvians by destroying all things Indian', Huxley found SIL an encouraging middle ground. A number of its workers were trying to strike a balance between total assimilation and total protection. They were trying to prepare Indians for development as Indians. Huxley believed that the linguistic approach was responsible: since the *Linguisticos* were reluctant to destroy the languages for professional reasons, their method opened into a 'tribal denominator'. Where the culture was disintegrating, the *Linguistico* tried 'to encourage and reinforce what little tribal solidarity there exists, to knit the group together in a common psychological defense against the "outsiders" ' while helping them drive a more equitable bargain.

Huxley noticed that group solidarity could also be undermined, however. The gold-panning Amarakaeri were abandoning communal houses for individual huts so that they could lock up their new possessions. The manager of the Ticuna co-operative wanted a raise: if he did not get one, he would open his own store. To undercut a *patron*, a *Linguistico* spent years coaxing the people to switch to cash-and-carry. Finally he financed a headman's son to set up a store. The new businessman promptly extended credit and restored the old order. Now the *patron* was an Indian and even harder to deal with.

To prepare Indians for civilization the Bible translators were, after all, bringing it to them faster and sooner. To win Indian loyalty and keep the *patrones* at bay, SIL was accelerating the invasion of commodities into native groups. It was arranging for trade goods more cheaply and supplying more of them. It was encouraging Indians to transact in cash but, through a marriage of market forces and Protestant virtue, helping some become *patrones* themselves. Finally, as Huxley noticed, it was fuelling impossible expectations in Indians, dreams of wealth and grandeur which it would never be able to satisfy. Despite the revolutions they were setting in motion, most fieldworkers were still concentrating on their 'fundamental program' of Bible translation, literacy and church organizing. They were 'unwitting, frequently reluctant, and mostly unprepared revolutionaries'. Huxley told SIL that it should become an agency for 'both spiritual and technical development'. Hopefully, technical assistance would bring back to earth the visions of the Campa teacher Santos C., to Huxley the worry but to Wycliffe the promise, of the faith filling the void. A product of two or three Protestant missions, and the Army, before becoming a bilingual teacher, Santos saw in his boondock 'a jungle town like Atalaya, perhaps even like the bustling city of Pucallpa, with an airfield, a hospital, and coffee and cocoa plantations; with herds of cattle and lots of people in proper clothes and shoes, a city where every man, woman and child has found God.'[109]

The full measure of Santos' dream would not be disillusion, as Huxley foresaw, but the mounting *colono* invasions of his homeland. Under pressure from the demands it was generating, however, SIL-Peru did follow Huxley's advice more than any other branch: by the early 1970s it conducted more development programmes, centring on the government-supported occupational training system at Yarinacocha. The major lines of assistance have been new crops and domestic animals, to increase production for the market and improve the diet in ecologically threatened communities; small sawmills; stores; sewing machines and outboard motors. The community projects have been financed from a revolving loan fund provided by World Neighbors, an evangelical agency headquartered in Oklahoma, and the U.S. Agency for International Development. Having concluded that many jungle Indians possess a well-developed sense of private property, the branch has tended to give the low-interest loans to those individuals judged best suited to handle responsibility – they usually seem to be the more loyal evangelicals. They are supposed to use their new property – store, outboard motor, cattle – for the good of the community and inspire emulation, thereby promoting community development.

After SIL won its reprive from the government in 1977, branch director Lambert Anderson said that, together with the production of primers, community development was now its officially assigned priority.[110] Not long before, an anthropologist had surveyed the crop and livestock projects on which the branch has predicated the future of many bilingual school communities: his conclusion was that they had generally failed and would not provide a new economic base.[111] To the anthropologist's surprise, the translators were not upset with his findings. A few development specialists notwithstanding, they felt that they already had too little time for their most important task.[112] As underlined by the threat of expulsion, they preferred to concentrate on the same priority as in Huxley's time.

What remained most important to these translators was church organizing, as illustrated by their close co-operation with other evangelical missions. This is another aspect of the programme which has not been explained in Peru: since the 1950s the branch has recruited scholars for the Alliance Bible Institute at Huanuco in the highlands, as it also apparently did for the Indian Bible Institute at Tournavista and the South American Indian Mission at Contamana. But the most important of these liaisons is with the Swiss Indian Mission, whose Bible Institute Townsend helped establish near Yarinacocha in the late 1950s.[113] Reputedly more strict and dogmatic than its SIL partner, the Swiss Mission trains converts to be pastors. In return, the branch has helped the mission learn languages and set up stations, thereby relieving itself of the more sectarian tasks such as church discipline as well as providing an insurance against a premature departure.

Culture and Faith

Matthew Huxley believed that SIL-Peru showed promise because it was starting to ask questions. But, as he quickly added, only a few members shared his concern over the futile dreams of Santos C. One of the few branch members asking questions, a Ph.D candidate who wanted to do her dissertation on the bilingual schools and was forced to leave, summarizes the problems she sensed. These were a curriculum foreign to Indian needs; the effects of concentrating populations; the chasm between teacher-believers and their people, as if SIL was thrusting teachers into difficult situations and failing to support them; 'breaking up the power structure'; and 'breaking *mores* — supposedly we were replacing them with Christian love, but what about those who didn't accept it?

Most translators thought that Huxley had exaggerated the importance of trade goods in their mission. Since Satan was doing his utmost to undo their work, reverses were not likely to make much of an impression. Satan's attempt to rot the Lord's harvest was certainly confirmed by the first reported home, Esther Matteson's salvation of the Piro. Matteson found the Piro sunk in such an appalling moral condition that she could not include their folk tales in her primers for Piro children. Yet within a few years Piro headmen were asking her to reform their *patron*-dominated villages in a burst of enthusiasm for the Protestant Ethic. A government official was amazed by the sudden change. He needed food supplies for the penal colony at Sepa, but the Piro never had anything to sell because they were usually drunk. Soon he was shocked to see sobriety, new houses and gardens. The Piro had surplus food to sell and wanted to produce more. They were going to school and reading the Bible.

In only eight years Matteson finished the New Testament and 'witnessed the complete transformation' of the tribe.[114] After 15 years, in 1962, the *Peruvian Times* reported that 'the Linguists expect to be able to withdraw

125

soon, leaving observers to keep the tribe on the right lines for a few years.'[115] In the 20th year of the Piro work, Matteson reported that, despite many spiritual weaknesses which seemed overwhelming, the Piro church was prospering and God's Word prevailing against fear of evil spirits.[116] And as the Piro work approached its 30th year, Matteson's successors faced the same problem she had: except perhaps when a missionary was in the village congregations and Christian leaders carried on as they had prior to salvation.

Cameron Townsend had popularized the idea that language was the mao major obstacle to successful missionary work and that his translated Bible was responsible for the Cakchiquel church. Once translators 'broke' their languages and produced Scripture, they expected miracles. But even the Piro Christians were an unusual achievement and the branch was creating conflicts faster than it could manage them. The receding jungle around Yarinacocha provided several early warnings: here SIL had to reckon with the Pucallpa boom, an ideal Le Tourneau trinity of lumbering, settlement and cattle ranching. It had to deal with disintegrating native communities and others forewarned, the mistakes of previous Protestant missionaries as well as its own, and an increasing number of competitors.

At first the branch thought it had a fine pioneer of progress in the Cashibo strong man Bolivar Odicio. But the bilingual schools sowed conflict between young and old, frustrating evangelism and possibly hastening ethnic disintegration.[117] SIL decided that the origin of the problem was Bolivar's tyrannical campaign to civilize his people. By the 1960s, the branch shared Lake Yarina with the uncooperative Seventh Day Adventists and the Amazon Hospital of Dr. Theodore Binder who, unlike the translators, tried to work with folk healers rather than using Western medicine to discredit them. 'I listen to what the missionaries say,' he was fond of quoting a Shipibo medicine man. 'It goes in one ear. Some of it stays in my head. Much of it goes out the other ear.'[118] Villages were torn by three-way struggles between bilingual teachers, Seventh Day Adventists and traditionalists.

In 1976, a Shipibo explained that the principal problems facing Indians around Pucallpa were destruction of the forest and theft of their land. But the missionaries, particularly SIL and the Adventists,

> suppose that they must 'civilize the native with the Word of God'. Now religion is personal, free. . . . Directly or indirectly obliging someone to believe in certain gods appears counter-productive to me. . . . What they have done is to divide communities, turning brother against brother. Those who believe in the Bible are against those who do not believe. I suppose you know that we natives have believed not exactly in God, but in a superior being which means the same as God: the sun, the rain, the water, etc. But now there are people worried because they have been told that if they do not eat something they will not be saved and that they ought to pray because the end of the world is near. This is sowing division, confusion. Some say yes and others no. Some do not want to work on Saturdays [Adventists] and others do. I say that we

should believe in God, certainly, but at the hour of communal work everyone ought to work.[119]

The Summer Institute's theological forebears had rejected most intellectual developments since the 18th Century as unbiblical, particularly the divorce between reason and faith. Many members felt uneasy as their outstanding scholar and president, Kenneth Pike, demarcated faith and scholarship as separate spheres, and more liberal minds filtered into the organization. Asking tough questions was no more popular within SIL than it is today, but a few members began thinking about 'culture' as something more than a set of taboos. Their thoughts reflected a wider and evolving conception of what evangelical missionaries hoped to accomplish: from the 'authentic New Testament church' — which resembled the missionary's home church — to the 'indigenous church' — which was self-supporting, self-governing and self-propagating but still resembled the missionary's home church — to a truly 'cultural' indigenous church.[120] Gradually Eugene Nida's lectures on culture and a few members' doubts over the consequences of the programme produced a new framework for overcoming resistance to SIL's plans, managing the conflict they inspired and defending them against anthropologists, in something like the following stages:

1) In 1962 Kenneth Pike suggested that smashing moral systems was not in the divine plan and that Christianity should 'enter . . . a culture quietly, transforming its institutions, changing their forms to contribute more effectively to the culture.'[121] Many translators ignored the suggestion.

2) By the late 1960s a few members were acting as consultants in cultural sensitivity. Some of their colleagues paid attention, others did not. SIL no longer claimed to be undermining indigenous languages, but it still shared the widespread assumption that many were doomed to disappear (hence the claim to 'preserve' languages by recording them).[122]

3) By 1976, to refute accusations of ethnocide, spokespersons were making startling claims to cultural reinforcement which reflected neither their organization's record nor the practice of many members.

In keeping with his belief that the problem was one of sensitivity and communication, Kenneth Pike called the new approach 'building sympathy' or 'bridges' between cultures through 'shared components'. The translator had to work through the cultural system to stimulate desirable change or — reflecting the new concern for stability — resist undesirable change. Fieldworkers in Mexico pursued the same line of thought by trying to target God's Word against certain cultural components, stabilize others and, where necessary, encourage new functional equivalents.[123]

A few members never returned from their expeditions into anthropology, but others joined a new corps of evangelical ethnologists attempting to uplift fellow missionaries and ward off the missiles hurled by fellow scientists. Around 1971, the community development co-ordinator, Dale Kietzman, introduced the idea of the 'alternative' in societies with 'limited room for maneuver'. Now that teams were trying to extricate themselves from groups which had become dependent on them, Kietzman stressed the importance of native leadership.[124] Since strengthening leadership is easily translated as support for self-determination, it is now a frequently enunciated SIL aim. But was this to be a leadership representing both saved and unsaved, which was not likely to satisfy faith mission requirements, or was this to be merely a factional leadership representing the saved? The most important discovery of this period was perhaps the old distinction between culture and faith. SIL would merely have to avoid confusing the two, leaving North American 'cultural baggage' behind and advancing with 'Biblical' religion. Even more conveniently, the new distinction meant that indigenous religious beliefs and indigenous culture no longer had anything to do with each other. Now one could undermine the former and reinforce the latter all at once. So long as a group still spoke its old language, a translator could argue that its culture was being strengthened.

Cultural rationales did justify more flexibility, however, hinging upon what the translator considered pancultural Christianity. One issue in Peru by the late 1950s was whether Christians could drink *masato,* a fermented beverage which most jungle Indians drink in some quantity to get through the day and in even larger quantities at festivals, ritual occasions where friendships are reaffirmed and differences settled. Then too, as the branch's Dr. Ralph Eichenberger seems to have recognized, *masato* is also an important nutrient. Some translators tried to draw the line between nutrition and inebriation, hospitality and excess.

The destruction which the new rationales continue to excuse and disguise is suggested by the case of the Amuesha, a settler-besieged people who, a member reported in the 1950s, 'call the sun "our father", dance and sing to it, and deck themselves out because the sun is pleased when they look pretty.'[125] In 1961 two SIL women arranged an Amuesha-taught Bible school. The graduates attracted other Amuesha with Christian hymns and claimed that Jesus was the way to Our Father. The new religion seems to have been associated with the spread of coffee cultivation: Dr. Eichenberger discovered a community so preoccupied with producing coffee to buy clothes and transistor radios that it was neglecting its food crops.[126]

In the early 1970s, a North American anthropologist discovered that SIL was supplanting Amuesha sacred music with its own. Set to Amuesha words, all too familiar tunes like 'O My Darling Clementine' and 'The Battle Hymn of the Republic' were leaping out of cheap, playback-only cassette players which translators distribute from Peru to Guatemala. As for their own intricate ritual songs, most Amuesha now seemed too ashamed to sing them. From a dedicated convert, Richard Chase Smith learned how the bilingual school had arrived around 1957 with God's Word. As explained by the first teacher, the laws of the new order included a ban on holy *masato* beer, coca leaves and tobacco; an end to faith in the divining and curing powers of the holy men; and the replacement of traditional music and stories by evangelical hymns and the Word. The people made the exchange — the new rules in return for a school.

The bilingual teachers felt that the Amuesha were backward because they still believed in the old religion. Around a dozen schools the teachers drew a majority of their people. Smith heard one call his school congregation Jews because they did not have faith and were killing Jesus. A SIL-trained nurse called an elder a 'son of the devil' for not accepting the new order. The translators had appropriated the Amuesha term for the sun deity to label the Christian Trinity, sowing confusion among people trying to make sense of evangelical teachings in terms of their own categories. There was no choice in the schools, where reading and North American fundamentalism were taught together.[127]

To Smith, this was ethnocide disguised as a blessing, yet the SIL women believed that they had fortified Amuesha ethnic identity by putting the language into writing and translating the New Testament — now 'as much a part of the culture as the typical crown and necklace'. They believed that those Amuesha who had studied the Bible generally 'show greater discernment and stability' in the face of the pressures they meet. When the New Testament arrived in 1979, it was honoured as Wycliffe's 100th. Owing to the 'great change and confusion' coming to the Amuesha, the Book had arrived none too soon, the team's school supervisor observed. 'Improved roads are bringing floods of settlers and, with them, cultural changes, many far from encouraging.' But while Wycliffe proudly reported that one-fourth of the 4,500 Amuesha had learned to read in the bilingual schools and professed faith in Christ, the Amuesha team counted only 'several hundred believers'.[128] Despite their attempt to be evangelical Christians, the others apparently had failed to measure up to the new order. The consumer idols of the lower reaches of Western civilization were flooding into the 'faith void' SIL had done more than a little to create.

Spiritual Warfare

To undermine confidence in other religious traditions, the Summer Institute had to find common ground with them. Shared conceptions, such as the Creator God, life after death or the end of the world were only a start. As the contest grew bitter, the common ground became fear of malevolent spirits and belief in protective magic. Western rationalists hesitated to admit that they were operating on the same level as 'superstition', but by the early 1970s their generally disappointing spiritual results suggested that they were losing the war they had come to Peru to fight, a war with rival systems of spiritual power or magic. The branch turned therefore to Charismatic Renewal, as we shall see in Chapter 8, a Pentecostal movement associated with heightened consciousness of spiritual strife, faith healing and exorcism.

If the medicine man's bundle consisted of sacred feathers and stones, University of Oklahoma magic combined trade goods, Western medicine, air and radio services, prayer, the sacred written word and even the unfamiliar pale skin which set translators apart from Peruvians. Arriving in tow to the power and wealth of the colonizing society, presented or interpreted as the secret of the white man's supremacy, the Bible asserted its underlying property as a magical fetish. SIL members felt that prayers to alter events in their own favour were entirely different from 'magic spells', yet they encouraged Indians to substitute the one for the other to meet their spiritual requirements.[129] The sorry fate of Biblical witches and demons could be invoked to prove that the Christian deity was superior to any 20th Century spirits and sorcerers.

The shamans often welcomed the translators at first, and even provided sons to be trained as teachers, medical workers or pastors. But sooner or later their disillusion confirmed SIL's opinion that 'witchcraft' — divination, folk healing and lay magic, as well as sorcery — was the principal abode of Satan among Indians. As the clearest embodiment of Amazonian world views, shamanism was the cultural core which SIL hoped to destroy. It was the hollow sound, not just in the claim to respect culture, but the announcement of faith mission triumphs. The persistence of shamanistic beliefs became the most appalling discrepancy in the bilingual school congregations.

Among the Aguaruna, in the 1950s, the SIL team believed that Western medicine would undermine superstition. The Aguaruna were supposed to learn that germs rather than witchcraft were the source of their maladies, and that antibiotics rather than folk remedies provided the cure. But bacteria have not refuted evangelical belief in the potency of prayer: like all but the most agnostic Westerners, the Aguaruna interpret their well-being in spiritual terms. While they reclassified some maladies from folk healer to SIL nurse jurisdiction, the physical and psychological consequences of the new settlement pattern were beyond Western treatment. On the sly, even the more dedicated converts found the Aguaruna shamans essential to their security. By the 1970s, fear of witchcraft was so endemic in the churches that the ¬nguist's leading Bible translation assistant, a man planning to organize his own Bible institute, confessed to studying Western 'black magic', apparently for spiritual protection. The linguist suspected as much after watching him use 'a song for singing when we cast out demons' to help his sister, who had been possessed by the ghost of a dead person or *tunchi* and was singing 'the witchdoctor's song'. The ensuing exorcism was interpreted as a Christian victory, but the 'anger, lust and depression' of the assistant betrayed that he was now dabbling in the occult.[130] Such symptoms are not unusual in converts torn between SIL's demands and their own needs: after a 'witchdoctor cured the first Achual convert in 1974, the translator reported that his outstanding evangelist 'seems like a different man now — filled with hostility and bitterness.'[131]

Since fear of witchcraft expresses social conflict, the encroachment of the world market is likely to multiply it. Where shamans have earned a reputation as exploiters, such as in the Western Guatemalan highlands, a new religion may provide a spiritual haven for protest against them. By stabilizing the situation of a beleaguered group, missionaries may provide it with new defences against increasingly malevolent traditional spirits, as SIL-Peru claims to have accomplished.[132] But by destabilizing a group's situation, missionaries may dramatically increase fear of witchcraft. And while the Peruvian branch has never reported any such thing, there is good reason to believe that this has occurred. Since the life expectancy of known sorcerers is short, bans on homicide could lead to concentrations of witches in Christian communities.[133] Concentration of population, ecological breakdown, disruption of traditional sharing, and ideological disorder fuelled social tension, and, therefore the fears translators hoped to dispel. Finally, indiscriminate campaigns against 'witchcraft' undermined the magical safeguards of converts. Since sorcery itself is a secret affair while the remedial divining and curing ceremonies are public, it was far easier to disrupt protective magic than the harmful kind, which left converts defenceless.[134] Christian mission, in short, could easily breed its own diabolical enemy. [135] By reducing a religious system to their own principle of evil (Satan), translators could magnify the system's principle of evil (offended spirits) into a more oppressive presence for their converts.

The Summer Institute was becoming entangled in the same knot of beliefs which had stymied Catholic missionaries for centuries. Stefano Varese discerns a 'basically millenn[ial] ideological structure' in the Peruvian Amazon, particularly among those groups — Campa, Amuesha, Piro, Machiguenga, Shipibo— which united in the 18th Century to drive all Europeans from the central jungle. Rejecting subjection and dependency, they embarked on 'a search for a new identity and ethnic dignity' which continues to the present, guarded by the shamans and capable of re-emergence, as in the early 20th Century when the Campa managed to expel all outsiders from a zone south of Tournavista.[136] Even now, missionaries invoke the danger of a Campa 'holy war' against settlers.[137]

Intimations of communion and conflict between rival millennial systems are scattered across SIL's years in Peru. In 1958-59 terrible rumours swept along the rivers, particularly around Iquitos: *pishtacos,* always fair-complexioned foreigners and usually North Americans, were kidnapping Indians to obtain human fat for atomic weapons and interplanetary missiles. At Yarinacocha the *Linguisticos* melted them down. While the panic was variously blamed on communists, SIL's patronal and Catholic enemies, and Indian medicine men, the *pishtaco* dates to the Spanish Conquest.[138]

The harnessing of indigenous to evangelical millennialism is obvious in a Wycliffe account of the founding of Cushillococha. When Doris and Lambert Anderson arrived at the lake of this name in 1953, they found a dispersed, ritually intact Ticuna community drinking and brawling, in debt to the *patrones* of nearby Caballococha, a rubber boom town fallen far from glory. Just 12 years before, Curt Nimuendaju had recorded a Ticuna millennial movement some distance down the Amazon River. A white man had been identified as an immortal, who foretold an imminent cataclysm which would destroy all *civilizados.* Withdrawing from their mestizo *patrones,* the Ticuna managed to erect a large ceremonial structure before being suppressed.[139] As late as 1970, Ticuna closer to Cushillococha adhered to the Cult of the Cross, a millennial religion organized by a Catholic priest.

The Andersons scored their first success with the adolescents, the usual recipients of visions from the immortals, and in 1957 visited Ticuna attending Baptist services downstream in Brazil. Their assistant, Pachi, converted many Ticuna with his introduction of Christ 'as a personal friend'. On the trip home an old man asked the blond, Ticuna-speaking Anderson if he was God. That night Pachi persuaded a number of Ticuna 'to follow the God who could give them life after death'. Back in Cushillococha the Andersons asked Pachi to report the stirring events of the trip. 'Wouldn't it be a shame,' he told his people, 'if the Lord should come and we who have heard so much about Christ were left behind, while so many of our people in other places would go to be with him because they have truly received him into their hearts?' Most of the lake community converted en masse, gathering in family groups to weep, pray and confess. That same day they decided to build a church near the Anderson house. Soon they withdrew from the *patrones* by building a new, consolidated village around it.[140]

It is difficult to calculate the casualties of spiritual warfare, but Shapra (or Candoshi) Chief Tariri clearly was one. The case calls for a brief excursion into how Cameron Townsend promoted Wycliffe: to make his cause grow, as we know, the founder had to show results to the folks back home. The Amazon caught their imagination as Mexico did not, and since SIL's performance was ambiguous it had to be dramatized. Townsend had a gift for creating powerful, clear-cut images – his Good Neighbor smile, the University of Oklahoma linguist, the Bible in the brown hands of an Indian – to invest the most contradictory of situations with an appropriate significance. The Piro were the object of some moving testimony in the early 1950s – the slender female linguist standing on a river bank among a crowd of natives, as others embark in canoes to spread the Word – but they were mostly downtrodden, not savage, and posed little threat to the virtue of young North American women alone in the jungle.

Shapra Chief Tariri supposedly met these requirements. One puzzle is the Chief's record in severing, boiling and shrinking human heads before becoming a Christian. From modest estimates of Tariri's valour, his reputation as the terror of the Peruvian jungle grew through visits to Lima and Hollywood to reach gory heights at the 1965 New York World Fair.[141] A few years later, one of his translators cautioned that Tariri had never been a bloodthirsty killer.[142] A decade before the World Fair, SIL estimated that he was responsible for two deaths.[143] And except when encouraged to boast, Tariri denied that he had ever cut off a person's head, which could well be the case, as the very existence of Shapra headhunting is open to question.[144]

Then there are the rewards garnered by the Chief for serving as a Wycliffe promotion and upholding his testimony. By courtesy of the Ludens Company, in 1965 the Jungle Aviation and Radio Service delivered 500 pounds of candy to Shapra children.[145] There is also the Chief's otherwise glum luck as a Christian and finally the silence about him since the late 1960s, broken only by a trouble prayer notice in 1973 and a New Testament dedication seven years later.[146]

Fortunately, we have Tariri's own story, rendered plausibly by Ethel Wallis.

Until 1950 he seems to have been an ordinary headman with the possible exception of being in debt to a *patron,* whose kind the Shapra generally kept at some distance.[147] When two SIL women arrived in a plane, Tariri was afraid. His *patron* had to explain that they were merely white people, not goddesses. In exchange for trade goods and medicine, the Shapra were to work for the women and listen about God. As Tariri helped translate Scripture, he accepted Jesus, foreswore killing and witnessed constantly. In his prayers he asked God to provide game and protect his children from snakes.

But it was not just hard to be a Christian on Tariri's river: by SIL's standards it was downright impossible. A three-way collision between prayer, shamanism and Tariri's male progeny was the crux of one tragedy: Tariri thought he was cursed, the SIL women said that God was testing him. Since the translators had gone to some length to equate spiritual with antibiotic power, medical failure led to spiritual crisis and the discrediting of Tariri in the eyes of his people when they failed to save first one son and then another. He had tested the higher magic by killing a taboo animal; vitamin drops kept his son alive. He also consulted a shaman, staked down a boa-constrictor for conversation, was punished by God, and decided that talking with boas was not worth it. After the second son died, his faith was restored only after God killed the guilty sorcerer.

Another tragedy was political. Thanks to the many gifts he received for his Christian witness, Tariri became a wealthy man. But he was no longer supposed to participate in the inebriated festivals which maintained alliances and redistributed goods. In 1956, friends attacked Tariri as he tried to buy their animal skins with cloth: one of his men died and, if it had not been for an emergency flight to Yarinacocha, he would have too.[148] According to a Catholic missionary, SIL tried to obtain military protection for him. The Shapra team grew to five members and the more fundamentalist of the original women retired, a sign that something was amiss. But the founder was not to be deprived of his redeemed headhunter and, two years after Tariri was presented at the World Fair next to a bloodcurdling mural, Wycliffe requested prayer for him and other Shapra leaders under 'faith-testing pressures'.[149] Then we meet him on the Hefleys' 1969 tour, but only because they have the nearest aircraft in an emergency: a SIL man is adjudicating an armed confrontation between Tariri and heathen Shapra over the widow of a bilingual teacher.[150] Four years later the branch again requested prayer for Tariri: he 'needs much spiritual help'.[151]

Like its bitter convert, so did the Summer Institute. 'There has been opposition to the work from many sides,' the branch director had told the SIL/WBT biennial conference a decade before, 'but the Lord has proved sufficient to meet our every need. As we press on with greater prospect of completing the translation of the Word for all of the tribes of Peru, we should not expect the opposition to decrease. It will undoubtedly increase. Thus our prayer should be with Jehoshaphat in II Chron. 20:12, 15. . . . '[152]

References

1. *Pioneer News* July 1926 pp.2-3; (Camp) *Wycliffe Chronicle* August 1942 p.1; Hall 1959:151.
2. Robinson (1975) was among the first to outline SIL-Peru's patronage system and its implications. This overview is also indebted to a draft report by Stephen Corry.
3. Long 1970:32, 49-53.
4. Ibid. pp.31-5.
5. For the development of SIL's work among the Machiguenga, see Matthiessen 1961:259; Long 1970:37-53; Camino 1979.
6. Kensinger 1967:6.
7. Camino (1979) describes this process in a Machiguenga bilingual school community, Monte Carmelo.
8. *In Other Words* March 1977 p.3; Larson et al 1979:64.
9. 150,000: Ribeiro and Wise (1978:41), who present the translators' view of each group's situation including the number of bilingual teachers and schools.
10. Davis 1977:24-6.
11. *Peruvian Times* 5 April 1946 p.9 and May 1947 supplement 'A Report on Eastern Peru' p.viii.
12. Hefleys 1974:66, 72.
13. *Peruvian Times* 17 January 1964 p.3; the same newspaper's *Peruvian Year Book* June 1944 pp.9-10 and *Anglo-American Blue Book* December 1944 p.39. Mudd endowed Harvey Mudd College at Claremont University.
14. McCurry 1972:398.
15. Hefleys 1974:123-5, 129-33; Wallis and Bennett 1966:177-9.
16. SIL-Peru 1955.
17. Damboriena 1962:114. This Jesuit author (pp.118-9) describes SIL's misuse of the University of Oklahoma affiliation.
18. *Peruvian Times* 10 May 1946 p.9.
19. E.g. expositions by members Robert Schneider (27 April 1951 pp.9-10) and Rachel Saint (28 November 1952 pp.7-8), who does quote a Bible verse. The only reference to SIL's actual purpose is a list of primer contents which includes Bible selections (*Anglo-American Blue Book* February 1947 p.39).
20. *Peru Indigena* (Lima, Peruvian Indigenist Institute) and *Boletin Indigenista* (Mexico, Inter-American Indigenist Institute) published occasional branch reports.
21. *Peruvian Times* 2 August 1946 p.9.
22. Ibid. 7 March 1947 p.9.
23. Hefleys 1974:144-5 and *Anglo-American Blue Book* February 1947 p.39.
24. *Translation* July 1951 p.5.
25. *Peruvian Times* 28 November 1947.
26. Ibid., 23 July 1954 p.18.
27. Buckingham 1974:27, 47-9. For a ceremonial account, see SIL-Peru 1955:53-7.
28. Hefleys 1974: 160, 169; Buckingham 1974:25.
29. *Anglo-American Blue Book* February 1947 p.39.

30. *Peruvian Times* 14 November 1952 p.19; *Comercio* 19 September 1952 (reprinted SIL-Peru 1955:90).
31. Hefleys 1974:169.
32. *Peruvian Times* 10 April 1959.
33. Ibid., 28 August 1964 p.3; Hefleys 1972:107.
34. Bomb casings, Le Tourneau 1976:61-7.
35. *Peruvian Times* 22 May 1953 p.2.
36. *New York Times* 1 October 1953 p.11.
37. *Peruvian Times* 22 May 1953 p.2.
38. Le Tourneau 1967:246.
39. *Peruvian Times* 10 April 1953 p.1.
40. Ibid., 22 May 1953 pp.1-2, photo page.
41. Le Tourneau 1967:257-8; Townsend and Pittman 1975:27.
42. *Peruvian Times* 7 August 1953 p.3.
43. Ibid., 23 January 1953 p.16.
44. Hefleys 1974:175-7.
45. *El Comercio* 28 February 1953 pp.5, 18. Cuesta was responding to Martha Hildebrandt (Ibid., 15 February) and SIL's Robert Russell (Ibid)25 February pp.3, 4.)
46. Hefleys 1974:179-80.
47. *La Prensa* 8 August 1953 pp.1, 3.
48. Ibid., 10 August 1953 p.1.
49. Ibid., 12 August pp.1,2; *Comercio* 15 August 1953 pp.17-18.
50. *Prensa* 13 August 1953 p.2.
51. *Comercio* 19 August 1953 p.7.
52. *Prensa* 23 August 1953 p.1.
53. Hefleys 1974:180-81; Hall (1959:152-3) provides another Townsendian version.
54. (Camp) *Wycliffe Chronicle* September 1940 p.2.
55. McKinlay 1944:41.
56. Buckingham 1974:26-7; Townsend and Pittman 1975:52.
57. Hefleys 1974:177-8.
58. *Comercio* 19 August 1953 p.7; *Prensa* 7 August 1953 p.3.
59. *Translation* October 1953 and January 1954.
60. *New York Times* 30 August 1953 p.13.
61. *New York Herald Tribune* 26 February 1954 (in *Peruvian Times* 12 March 1954 p.4).
62. *National Geographic* March 1956 p.350.
63. Hefleys 1974:163, 188-9, 200-6.
64. *Translation* Spring/Summer 1958 p.3; Winter 1957-58 pp.3, 13.
65. Townsend and Pittman 1975:61-3.
66. Copied in the SIL library, Guatemala City, August 1978.
67. This quotation is a back translation of a Spanish translation of the original.
68. Translator cited in Hefleys 1972:152.
69. *Translation* Winter 1958-59 pp.14-15.
70. *Missions Annual* 1960 p.31; also ibid 1961 pp.22-3.
71. *Christianity Today* 27 October 1967 pp.41-2.
72. *Peruvian Times* 12 February 1954 p.22 for an English translation of the contract.

73. *Now* (Longview, Texas: Le Tourneau Technical Institute) 1 June 1957 and 1 January 1958. Airstrip: *Peruvian Times* 13 December 1968.
74. Nelson 1973:129-31.
75. *Peruvian Times* 22 December 1961 pp.3-4, 6, 8.
76. Ibid., 18 April 1958 p.26.
77. *El Expreso* 28 November 1964.
78. *Peruvian Times* 31 October 1969 p.8 and 9 October 1970 p.1.
79. *Anglo-American Blue Book* May 1950 pp.40-1; SIL-Peru 1955:10-12.
80. *Comercio* 25 February 1953 p.3.
81. Ibid., 15 August 1953 pp.17-18.
82. Ibid., 28 February 1953 pp.5, 18.
83. Morote Best 1961:305-7, 310-11.
84. Hefleys 1974:202-5.
85. Morote Best 1961:303-4, 308-9.
86. *Peruvian Times* 17 June 1955 p.2 and 15 July 1955 p.2.
87. Ibid., 1 July 1955 p.2 and 20 April 1956 cover.
88. Ibid., 29 July 1955 p.1.
89. Ibid., 2 December 1955 p.4 and 23 March 1956 p.1.
90. Vargas Llosa 1965 and 1971:24-45.
91. Najar 1976.
92. 'Amazonia: Extinction or Survival?', conference at the University of Wisconsin, Madison, 20 April 1978.
93. Author's interview, Ayacucho, 14 February 1977.
94. SIL/WBT 1964:117.
95. SIL-Peru 1969:31.
96. SIL-Peru 1955:67.
97. Paulston 1970:936.
98. James O. Wroughton, 'The SIL as a servant of Peru,' mimeo, 1975, p.6.
99. E.g. Wallis and Bennett 1966:198.
100. Morote Best 1957:9-11.
101. St. Clair 1958: 6 June p.10 and 13 June p.6.
102. Cowan 1979:252.
103. St. Clair 1958: 13 June p.8.
104. SIL/WBT 1963:55.
105. Clastres (1980) describes 'the leader as servant' among American Indians.
106. Cited by Solar (1972:39-42) for the First National Seminar on Bilingual Education.
107. Long 1970:35.
108. Pike and Brend 1977:78.
109. Huxley and Capa 1964:139-240. For a Wycliffe view of Santos C., see SIL/WBT 1963:92-101.
110. Authors' interview, Yarinacocha, 21 Febuary 1977.
111. Benson 1978.
112. Benson's comment to the author in this regard is corroborated by the branch's (*In Other Words* March 1977 p.3) presentation of its priorities to home supporters.
113. Hefleys 1972:137. For a fuller account of the relations between the missions, see Georg 1979.
114. Wallis and Bennett 1966:186-93; Hall 1959:143-6.
115. Bebbington 1962:13.

116. *Translation* Winter 1966 pp.10-11.
117. Gray 1953; Wistrand 1968.
118. Mendelsohn 1965:128.
119. 'Habla un Shipibo: Mateo Arevalo' *Marka* (Lima) 27 May 1976. In 1957-58 Hoffmann (1964) found that Shipibo relations with Protestant missionaries were limited to cash transactions. He ventured that Pucallpa area commercialization was increasing Shipibo independence and consolidating Shipibo culture. Georg (1979) paints a grimmer picture of evangelical influence.
120. Charles H. Kraft, in Stott and Coote 1980:212-3.
121. Pike 1962:43; Nida (1954:251-8) sounded a cautionary note earlier.
122. Wares 1974:vii.
123. Pike 1960 and 1961. Mexico, e.g. Beekman 1959. The same journal now called *Missiology*, has published much similar work.
124. SIL/WBT 1971:31-7.
125. Tanner 1957.
126. Eichenberger 1965:139-40.
127. Smith 1981.
128. Wycliffe views: *Translation* Summer 1969 pp.3-4, 14; *Wycliffe Associates Newsletter* March 1978 pp.2, 4; *In Other Words* September 1979 pp.1-3; *Beyond* (Waxhaw, North Carolina: JAARS) September/October 1979; Larson et al 1979:430.
129. E.g. Huxley and Capa 1964:144.
130. Larson 1974.
131. *Wycliffe Prayer Bulletin* August 1974.
132. Larson et al 1979:441-3.
133. E.g. Long 1970:35 on Quempiri.
134. Wilson (1975:78-82) describes such phenomena in Africa.
135. Lila Wistrand's (*Christianity Today* 24 February 1978 p.36) comment on a Mexican case is suggestive.
136. Varese 1975.
137. *Lima Times* 8 June 1979 p.1.
138. *Peruvian Times* 23 January 1959 p.2; Matthiessen 1961:53; Maxwell 1961:21-3; Hefleys 1974:203.
139. Nimuendaju 1952:137-40.
140. Rossi 1975:75-7, 147.
141. SIL-Peru 1955:19-22; flyleaf to Wallis 1965; *Christianity Today* 27 August 1965 pp.50-1; *Peruvian Times* 8 October 1965 pp.5, 6; Buckingham 1974:109.
142. Hefleys 1972:128.
143. *Peruvian Times* 19 August 1955 pp.6, 8.
144. Siverts 1979:218.
145. *Peruvian Times* 17 December 1965 p.21.
146. *In Other Words* September 1980 pp.1-3.
147. Ribeiro and Wise 1978:92.
148. Wallis 1965.
149. *Translation* November/December 1967 p.12.
150. Hefleys 1972:155-63.
151. *Translation* March/April 1973 p.11.
152. SIL/WBT 1961:62.

5. The Summer Institute in Peru: Part 2

Some of us don't understand that far from being away from the center of attention, it is the down-and-outer who is the focus of today's world. It is wrong to assume that these people are forgotten . . . . There are millions who care, and who put these down-and-outers *first* — to make them Communists. It is we in the Church who say that they don't matter. Neither God nor the devil says that.

The peasant is the focus of Communist attack in many areas. They want him and they get him.

Kenneth Pike, chapel talk at SIL-University of Oklahoma, June 1962.[1]

To SIL President Kenneth Pike in the 1960s it seemed that two trends — colonization and insurgency — were drawing new attention to pre-literate peoples. As the Summer Institute translated the Bible, it was riding with host governments 'on the forward wave of history'.[2] With Peru as a model of what it could do for a government, SIL had expanded rapidly in the previous decade. At meetings of the Inter-American Indigenist Institute, Cameron Townsend made new contacts, then dispatched linguist diplomats like Pike to negotiate agreements. Following advances into Guatemala and Ecuador, SIL moved into Bolivia, Brazil and, after much difficulty, Colombia in 1962.

The governments which welcomed SIL in the 1950s had come to power through some combination of popular unrest and the ballot box. Representing the national bourgeoisie, nationalist and reformist in rhetoric, they hoped to build on the measure of economic independence which some countries had achieved during the 1930s and early 1940s, when foreign investment declined. Sooner or later they succumbed to U.S.-trained colonels and generals. The subversion of reform in its name accelerated with the Cuban Revolution, moving the United States to organize the Alliance for Progress and brand any left-of-center movement as a likely pawn of Moscow.

As the United States battled insurgency and bank-rolled preventive colonization, SIL was already in place throughout much of the Latin American hinterlands. In Peru, General Mendoza, the Minister of Education who sponsored the first bilingual teacher course, alluded to SIL's prophylactic value in striking terms. While serving in the highlands, he learned that his officers

Map 5
Colombia

needed interpreters to communicate with their own Quechua troops. In Indian communities, we may infer, SIL was helping to bridge the gap between defenders of the public order and those to be kept in order. As Wycliffe explained in 1963, a Campa teacher was 'an effective direct link' between the tribe, national life and the government.[3] General Mendoza called Townsend a Godsend.[4]

It may seem even more miraculous that leftists took so long to form their own ideas about who had scattered North American evangelical linguists through their jungles and mountains. Townsendian friendship with men said to be Communists, the good name Protestantism still enjoyed in such circles, and SIL's value as a check on the Catholic clergy played their part. So did Marxist indifference to Indians and a belief shared with the rest of the political spectrum, that Indians would have to be integrated into the nation at the expense of their backward ways. Just as paper-shuffling revolutionary *doctores* who told Indians what to do were losing their credibility, guerrillas who could not even speak the language of the people they hoped to liberate would lose their lives.

Several changes in the intellectual climate for which Townsend had fashioned his presentations made SIL an anti-imperialist issue. One was dependency theory and the revolt against a leftist orthodoxy, which Townsend had found quite congenial. Until the 1960s, most Latin American Marxists assumed their main enemy to be 'feudal', the landed oligarchy and the Catholic clergy. Since only a national bourgeoisie could create the conditions for proletarian revolution, modernizing partnerships with North Americans were tolerated and even welcomed. Hence SIL's alliances with leftists in Mexico, Peru and Brazil. A few of these friends proved so loyal that they defended SIL through the controversies of the 1970s.

National front orthodoxy fell apart as the United States strengthened its hold on Latin America despite the professed aims of nationalist governments. Cuban guerrilla strategy and Maoist peasant revolution promised a faster route to socialism, which, in the opinion of many was the only one under Latin American conditions. According to the dependency theorists, far from creating the conditions for capitalist development, imperialism was maintaining Latin America in a permanent state of underdevelopment. The United States was therefore the principal enemy, encouraging the analysis of development programmes, the mass media and other seemingly neutral enterprises as instruments of control. It was indeed hard to find a Latin American boondock without its missionaries, Peace Corps volunteers and other North Americans of uncertain definition. Paths crossed. Did not SIL-Peru work in the same Campa territory where the young medical student Ernesto 'Che' Guevara helped the branch's sometime friend, the leprologist Dr Hugo Pesce, in the early 1950s? 15 years later, had not Guevara's men and then the Bolivian army occupied the village of Caraguatarenda, where SIL's Chiriguano translators worked at a station of the Evangelical Union of South America? (According to Wycliffe they were on furlough at the time).[5] With the failure of the guerrilla movements of the 1960s, sympathizers concluded that North Americans were strengthening state control over the countryside. If a government did not respect U.S.

wishes, on the other hand, North Americans might be in a position to destabilize it.

Another important change occurred in the Catholic and ecumenical Protestant churches. So long as the Catholic clergy maintained the demeanour of the Counter-Reformation, nearly any *evangelico* was bound to appear a model of progressive thinking and, along with other forces, erode its popular support. By the year 2000, evangelical missionaries were fond of declaring, Latin America could well be Protestant. Then the Cuban Revolution scared an influx of Catholic missionaries into slum and countryside, where they hoped to uplift the poor and save Latin America from Communism. As the Church built ecumenical alliances with Protestants against revolution, more priests and nuns were becoming acquainted with the conditions which gave rise to it. Country after country succumbed to dictatorship; the Church became a sanctuary for victims of official terror; and it began to suffer accordingly, turning middle-of-the-road clerics into rebels. Armed with the theology of liberation, they encouraged grass-roots lay leadership, supported peasant land claims and protested government violence.

A third intellectual change was led by anthropologists, chiefly Latin American and European. They were in revolt against the pillars of *indigenismo,* SIL's longstanding allies who had adapted anthropology to the task of Indian management as dictated by governments. By attributing the oppression of Indians to their cultures, indigenist policy was another expression of internal colonialism, which, in turn was the product of domination of Latin America by external powers in Europe and North America. Ethnocide, a play on the word genocide, came to refer to that vast swath of destruction short of physical extermination: the erosion of indigenous culture, identity and society which fed 'decultured' or 'marginalized' persons into the lowest class of the colonizing society. Support for indigenous self-determination, these anthropologists insisted, was the only legitimate end of their discipline.

Dissenting anthropology, dependency theory and liberation theology began to converge on SIL after 1971, when the World Council of Churches (WCC) brought a dozen anthropologists to Barbados to discuss the situation of lowland South American Indians. They noted the resurgence of indigenous ethnic consciousness, stood on the proposition that only Indians could liberate Indians, and presented a series of demands to governments, fellow anthropologists, and missionaries. The last were quick to note a professional bias: while the Barbados group had not demanded the abolition of the nation-state or its own occupation, it did call for the suspension of Christian mission to Indians. Until that could be effected, the missions were to end common practices such as concentrating dispersed populations, competing for converts, and using trade goods and schools to impose their religions.[6] Even though the Barbados Declaration condemned official policy as well, the implication was clear: government bureaucracies in which anthropologists could find employment would be more amenable to indigenous self-determination than religious agencies.

Missionaries proved more receptive than governments. The ecumenical

Protestants who had financed the Barbados meeting were leaving the mission field to their national churches anyway. Catholic missionaries were definitely offended by the Barbados demands, but many agreed that their work was badly in need of reform. As for most evangelical missionaries, they rejected the declaration entirely.[7] There had been abuses (chiefly by Catholics who were not really Christians in the first place), but the Barbados analysis did not apply to their own work. In fact, it was just one more proof that an apostate WCC had turned against the Great Commission and was openly pursuing political, suspiciously left-wing ends. While many evangelicals were still avidly apolitical supporters of the Vietnam War, the WCC opposed it, and was soon providing humanitarian aid to Southern African liberation movements. After the WCC discussed a moratorium on missions in 1973, evangelicals held their own congress, in which Wycliffe participated, and issued the Lausanne Statement. Quoted *Translation* in bold face: 'We believe that we are engaged in constant spiritual warfare with the principalities and powers of evil, who are seeking to overthrow the church and frustrate its task of world evangelization. . . . For we detect the activity of our enemy, not only in false ideologies outside the church, but also inside it in false gospels which twist Scripture. . .'[8]

Some of Wycliffe's animus for this statement came from a withering expose of its work, one soon to have a large impact. SIL had figured in the Barbados reports, but it was only one of many agencies to be questioned. The aura of scientific legitimacy evaporated after 1973, when a shoe-string anti-imperialist research body partially supported by WCC sources, the North American Congress on Latin America (NACLA), published Laurie Hart's 'The Wycliffe Translators: Pacifying the Last Frontiers'. Based on Barbados positions and Wycliffe's own literature, Hart demonstrated that SIL and WBT were one disturbing organization. Highlights included: 1) its enthusiasm for the Vietnam War; 2) its view of indigenous religion as 'Satan's stronghold'; 3) the Ecuadorian branch's use of airplanes, wing-mounted loudspeakers and converts to push hostile Auca Indians out of the way of U.S. oil companies and into a reserve; 4) the Colombian branch's alleged complicity in police and army repression of Guahibo Indians in 1970; and 5) its immunity from protest due to friends high in government.

The report found a nationalist audience in Latin America ranging from students to generals. With the important exception of the Guahibo charge, the factual basis was beyond dispute. But Hart moved directly from SIL's fundamentalist assumptions about Indians to their presumed effects on converts, submission to colonialism and revulsion against their own culture. It was as if missionaries imprinted alienation on putty-like Indians instead of being in constant conflict with them. And while Hart understood that internal colonialism led to conflict between Indian and 'national' interests, 'dependence' on missionaries ended up in a footnote. The implications — here termed alliances between Indians and missionaries, patronage battles over Indian followings and the expansion of state control — were not pursued.

Citing the Barbados declaration, a manifesto summarizing centuries of history, Hart identified SIL's function in the machinery of imperialism as:

1) contacting, concentrating and converting indigenous groups to facilitate their removal from areas desired by national and international corporations and lending technical assistance in the suppression of indigenous resistance; and
2) . . . imposing . . . 'criteria and patterns of thought and behavior . . . ' which fragment and therefore neutralize Indian communities and turn their members into 'marginal individuals, incapable of living either in the larger society or in their native communities.'

This permitted the emphatic statement that SIL 'serves the interests of U.S. imperialism and local exploiters, *not* of indigenous peoples.'[9] Its crisis in Latin America had begun to take shape several years before, in Colombia, to be taken up in the next chapter, and in Peru, to which we now return.

Spiritual Guides for the Settlers

By the late 1950s a few members of the Catholic hierarchy in Peru were throwing up their hands at the Summer Institute. If the futility of opposing its plans was plain, they also realized that they faced a more serious threat than Protestantism. In the course of President Odria's favourable investment climate, when most of the new foreign capital came from the United States, per capita income increased but was distributed more unequally than before, to such an extent that per capita consumption of calories and protein declined.[10] In 1958, the Papal Nuncio received Cameron Townsend, and the Peruvian bishops issued their first pastoral letter calling for redistributive social justice. The following year in Lima, Vice-President Richard Nixon set off the first of the riots which greeted him in each Latin American capital on his tour.

The Peruvian branch's mainstay continued to be military officers, who brought it through a third major crisis. After the armed forces voided the 1962 election, Washington slapped their wrists by curtailing loans. The branch found itself 'under terrific pressure' from a number of unnamed sources. The new minister of education 'planned to sink the whole program' by shutting down the bilingual schools and expelling SIL. The official subsidy had already been killed when General Salvador Garcia Zapatero drove onto the base. As chairman of the commission for jungle development, at a time when the Plan Peru-Via road-building programme was under way, the army officer was soon under Townsend's spell. 'I can see what is going to happen,' he exclaimed. '. . . these Indians, who are the guides in the jungle, humanly speaking, will become the spiritual guides for the settlers from the coast and from the highlands. I can see it because they have the Word of God. You are training them in the Scriptures, and they will be the guides of this area, to lead this whole great jungle region into a new way of life.' Garcia ordered the Minister of Education to reinstate SIL. Two air force generals, Vargas Prada and Granthom, renewed their service's contract with the branch. Again it

143

came out of crisis with more subsidy than before.*[11]

The year after General Garcia saved SIL-Peru for the decade's schedule of road-building and colonization, in 1963, Fernando Belaunde Terry captured the presidency with Alliance for Progress promises. In the highlands, where Quechua farmers were staging massive invasions of hacienda lands, Belaunde promised land reform and schools. To hungry men eyeing the huge coastal plantations and streaming into the cities, he offered the Amazon. A grandiose Marginal Jungle Highway would draw landless peasants from the highlands and strengthen government control along the eastern slope of the Andes, a forbidding terrain being forecast as a guerrilla sanctuary.

Townsend was still in step with the times: in March 1961 he had written to President Kennedy from Yarinacocha with 'suggestions to stimulate farming and trade in various areas of South America, by providing airlifts, building a transcontinental highway, etc; enclose[d] [is] a map of what would be the main highway.'[13] Penetration highways were indeed planned and financed from Washington as part of its Alliance for Progress counter-insurgency package.[14] Like other Christian missions, now SIL was not only to teach Indians their patriotic duties but serve as a warning system against subversion.

The mid-1960s under Belaunde were probably SIL's easiest years in Peru. Catholic opposition waned, thanks to ecumenism. Branch officials were welcome guests at the national palace.[15] In 1966 the Friends committee was replaced by the *Patronato,* which boasted a wider selection of distinguished Lima businessmen, claimed Belaunde as its honorary president and, according to *La Prensa,* enjoyed the financial backing of the National Society of Merchants (CONACO).[16]

The idyll ended in a turn of events which Fidel Castro compared to a fire breaking out at the fire station. Army officers seized power, not for the usual reason that an administration had displeased the United States, but because Belaunde had failed to stand up to it. Led by General Juan Velasco Alvarado (1968-75), they declared the Peruvian Revolution, which they said would be Christian, humanistic, non-Marxist and non-capitalist, and proved their anti-imperialist mettle by nationalizing (with compensation) certain unpopular U.S. investments.

In February 1970 President Velasco established a commission to study the now quarter century old SIL contract, and a year later the Ministry of Education imposed a more restrictive and demanding one. For the first time the branch's charter had an expiration date, just five years hence, in February 1976. If the government chose, it could even require SIL to train Peruvian linguists as counterparts and 'progressively substitute' them for members until the programme was in national hands.[17] Yet despite these unpleasant prospects and changes in bilingual school administration, the branch continued to operate as it always had. Soon after the junta seized power, according to SIL members,

---

* The 1963 government budget for the bilingual schools totalled approximately 2.45 million soles or ninety thousand dollars, including teacher salaries, new buildings at Yarinacocha and administrative expenses.[12]

it assured the branch that it was exempt from the new nationalism: whatever might be said about the United States in public, the junta knew what the linguists were doing and wanted them to continue. A North American noting the close ties between U.S. missionaries and their embassy considered SIL one religious mission which was not a symbol of cultural colonialism.[18] One reason was that it was so useful to the government's colonialist schemes for the jungle, plans now imbued with revolutionary significance. Hoping to surpass large oil deposits discovered to the north in Ecuador, the junta signed new contracts with North American firms for the latest stage in a decades-old offensive.

After decades of mutual celebration, however, an old partner in this noble cause was starting to defect. The Latin American professionals best equipped to criticize SIL's programme, the indigenists, had always supported it. The North American and European professionals in a similar position, the anthropologists, had kept their feelings to themselves. Now, in Lima in August 1970 at the International Congress of Americanists, Young Turk indigenists attacked SIL for the first time.

In the Manu National Park a patronage battle erupted over a bilingual school *reduccion,* pitting the branch against the park wardens and their anthropologist Marcel D'Ans. Whenever one of the institute's planes landed in the village for a few hours, the normally friendly Machiguenga would break off relations with the park post for at least a week. Without authorization from the Ministry of Education, JAARS helped the teacher and his faction move out of the park, leaving the others without facilities.[19] Linguist Alfredo Torero denounced a 25 year foreign intervention

> without any kind of supervision by Peruvian authorities. . . . The only connection of these tribes with the outside world is [SIL] . . . . [Its] purposes may be those declared or very different. In any case Peruvians do not have direct control over the jungle. We have to go to SIL to enter without problems. . . . [Indians consider] anyone, Peruvian or not, a foreigner if not from SIL. ... . subjects of a foreign nation dominate a large zone of our territory and have assumed the right to decide things within it.[20]

At the Barbados symposium Stefano Varese, an anthropologist comprising one of two persons in the Ministry of Agriculture's Division of Amazonian Populations, noted that the System of Bilingual Education (SEB) did not include a single Peruvian linguist or anthropologist. Since years of relying on foreigners had convinced Peruvians that they were helpless, they had allowed the system to remain under the control of SIL, which manipulated it for its own purposes. In particular, the North Americans had encouraged an 'isolationist and dependent feeling' in native groups, creating 'a series of water-tight compartments . . . which regard with extreme mistrust anything that does not directly or indirectly form part of the SEB.' Varese took comfort from the thought that, according to the new contract, SIL's personnel would gradually be replaced by Peruvians over the next five years.[21]

Cushillococha

The Ticuna of Cushillococha long served as a showcase of how SIL-Peru was integrating Indians into the nation. Freed from superstition, alcoholism and *patrones*, Cushillococha has also been said to represent a truly indigenous Christianity. Recently, Wycliffe author Sanna Barlow Rossi, called it 'God's City in the Jungle.' Since Cushillococha is reputedly the largest jungle Indian settlement in Peru, with 300 family heads, according to its President in 1976, no other branch accomplishment quite approaches the place. Yet as a showcase it illustrates trends reported elsewhere, providing a fitting site to inspect the Summer Institute's version of *Peruanidad*.

Soon after Doris and Lambert Anderson triggered Ticuna millennialism into a mass conversion in 1957, they arranged for JAARS to bring Efrain Morote Best, who offered a school and land title. Based upon the Andersons' plan, the Ticuna erected a model village around the couple's house and their new church.[22] The surprising result of their religious outburst, especially in light of traditional Ticuna aversion to living close together and putting walls on their dwellings, was a quadrangular, *criollo*-style town of houses with doors, including four two-story frame residences modelled after Yarinacocha.

The land title, school and evangelical discipline helped the Cushillocochans break out of dependence upon their mestizo *patrones*, making it easier to acquire the trade goods they desired. The Andersons drew upon the traditional Ticuna work party to initiate community labour days and a variety of group development projects, including a store and marketing cooperative.[23] As a reward for correct thinking, the Cushillocochans were showered with gifts and loans, a subsidy which was not repeated elsewhere and made their town an illusory model of development. Although the Andersons led the branch in promoting co-operatives, they apparently intended them to be a bridge to private accumulation. In this they were successful, borne along by wider tendencies in a colonized jungle producing an evangelical elite which sticks out like a sore thumb.

A coterie of younger men trained at Yarinacocha or the Swiss Bible Institute occupied all the new posts of authority inspired by the Andersons. They became the interpreters of the holy book, the teachers, elected village officials and entrepreneurs, as well as the community's most prosperous members. After 1964, the new system of authority came to revolve around one man, Leonardo Witanocort, whose ascendancy dates to a time when the Andersons were away on furlough and their Christian leadership faced a folk healing revival. Owing to his skill in reviving the moribund, a Cocama named Macawachi acquired a following. When the pastor/constable interfered with the man's drunken ways, his own son died. Macawachi's powers and threats threw Cuchillococha into turmoil; the district authorities ordered him to leave. After vowing to curse the village, he was murdered and the pastor forced to resign.

On the Andersons' return their third bilingual teacher Leonardo Witanocort was pastor. He went on to become their principal translation assistant, administrator of the community sawmill, municipal agent, village president and first supervisor of the Ticuna bilingual school system, which, by 1975, comprised 15 teachers.[24]

The rise of the elite and private enterprise was paralleled by a decline in the community work ethic for which Cushillococha had become famous. When I visited for two nights in April 1976, the men trained to run the store had long since gone private. There had been no electric light for six months because there was no money to buy gasoline for the generator. A storm had scattered 500 logs moored poorly in the Amazon, bankrupting the sawmill and associated community funds. The Ticuna lumberjacks wanted cash on delivery, not promises; when Witanocort returned, the sawmill would be reorganized and production resume.

Attendance at church — four or five services a week — was fairly good, perhaps half the visible population on Sunday morning. While the Andersons say that the Ticuna decided to build their church on simple New Testament principles, visitors have noticed that the result — prayer postures, hymns set to Ticuna words, the natty appearance of a small group who make most of the offerings, the message in the sermons — bears a strong resemblance to a North American fundamentalist congregation. Part of the Sunday morning sermon was in Spanish and this is what I heard:
1) Love becomes less and less, people more and more wicked in their ways.
2) Some people say there is no God, this is more testimony that rebellion is . increasing.
3) Science and knowledge grow more and more, but almost entirely in the service of evil.
4) Other dangers are the atomic bomb, cocaine and marijuana.
5) The Bible says that God will destroy the world because of men's wickedness.
6) Unless we think of God, Christians will be in danger as well.

I was surprised by this message of pre-millennial doom in a showcase of progress, but the Christian leadership had reason to be gloomy. Community spirit was not all that it might be, and thanks to inflation, Ticuna earnings purchased far less than before. The teachers and pastors knew that the Andersons and SIL were in trouble, and if that were not enough they themselves felt threatened by the government bureaucracy.

Besides problems with Ministry of Education officials, to whom they now reported instead of SIL, the Cushillococha leaders feared the National System for Social Mobilization (SINAMOS). The post-1968 dictatorship set up *sin amos* ('no bosses') to mobilize the masses for revolution from above. Several of the architects were survivors of the 1965 guerrilla forces: it was the government's help yourself and fight imperialism cheer-leader. In the jungle SINA-MOS was supposed to 'socialize' the same terrain which the junta was auctioning off to another cabal of foreign oil companies, by organizing Indians and non-Indian peasants into agrarian leagues, then setting up co-operatives with state loans to end exploitation and increase national production.

In the nearby patronal stronghold of Caballococha I found the local SINAMOS organizers in a state of frustration. The Cushillococha leadership wanted nothing to do with their plans. God's City in the Jungle was to become a 'social enterprise' with more cattle (the teachers already had herds), an expanded community sawmill and a community plantation in which the Ticuna would work three days a week. The profits would be distributed between the workers, community funds, and a national fund for further cooperative development.

The community plantation was not a popular idea, perhaps because the Ticuna work party has always been a labour exchange between family gardens (the group plantations promoted by Anderson and Morote had not been successful). Cushillococha was already burdened by its development projects: it would simply lose more autonomy and go further into debt. SINAMOS also had a reputation for promising but not delivering, taking control but not improving. Finally and most obviously, thanks to the many feuds between missionaries and SINAMOS organizers throughout the jungle, the proposed and faltering new order was highly suspect ideologically. Someone obviously had warned the Cushillococha leadership against Communists, but even without that kind of Christian service SINAMOS might have prompted a similar reaction.

Downstream, SINAMOS received a warmer welcome. Bellavista was one of two smaller, less developed villages pulled together by bilingual teachers from Cushillococha, their 'father' or 'leader' according to a town official. At Bufeococha the teacher carefully subverted the Cult of the Cross and replaced it with evangelical religion.[25] At the other 'little Cushillococha', an honour which the Bellavistans resented, I was told that they had come together to have a school and been provided with religious services as well. Bellavistans reckoned that festivities had continued until 1970, when *pastores* from Cushillococha said that dancing and drinking alcohol were contrary to God's Word, and replaced them with more religious services. Now everyone was an *evangelico* but, as a Bellavistan explained, 'the people follow the religion for a few years, then they leave it little by little.' There were fewer walls per house than in Cushillococha: some had only one for the view from the river. One of the two young pastors trained at the Swiss Bible Institute conducted evening hymn meetings in the school, which, after half an hour turned into SINAMOS meetings; the other, obviously a man with worries, said that he was no longer a pastor. The teachers from Cushillococha were said to be very, very disappointed with him.

In Cushillococha, where the evangelicals are supposed to be proud of their culture, the old religion has been proscribed so thoroughly that, according to a councilman, prior to the Andersons the Ticuna did not have one. Christian leaders call Ticuna outside their town and its satellites 'savage' or 'hardly civilized'.[26] But while they have rejected tradition as unmitigated darkness, they seem to be recuited in waves of millennial enthusiasm which envelop much of the community and then recede, leaving behind a comparatively few staunch young converts whom Witanocort and the Andersons select for higher education, positions of spiritual responsibility, and the material blessings these may entail.[27]

Remarkable stories emerged from a revival in the early 1970s, when the Andersons were away on furlough and the Ticuna church was in the doldrums. An old man whom no one knew walked out of the jungle, stopped a storm with a wave of his hand, brought down Pentecostal fire on the congregation and vanished without a trace. His name was Gabriel. A hundred people were baptized; young apostles spread the revival to Bellavista; and when the Andersons returned, they found a revitalized church.

The supernatural events seem to have been connected to the dependence of Cushillococha on the absent translators. Anderson himself minimizes his importance, but a councilman explained that, when in Lima, the founder of the town is obtaining necessary things for it and only returns when he can bring them. As visitors have noted for two decades, Cushillococha is waiting for his return. Gabriel's arrival is dated to the afternoon in 1971 when five SIL members died in an airliner catastrophe: there is much dispute over whether Gabriel is teaching the same message as Anderson. When he demonstrates his power, 'they knew it was God' and that 'God would really speak to them,' as if Anderson is the absent and offended culture hero of Ticuna tradition whom a group confession and rebirth will persuade to return.[28]

Young believers have tried to spread the revivals like earlier millennialists, but the widespread disaffection suggests that the break with tradition excludes more people than it incorporates. At Bellavista, the teachers, who still came from Cushillococha for the term, were not present and much of the population was in a mild state of sin. The regime would tighten when they returned, according to a Bellavistan, because otherwise the village would get in trouble with Cushillococha. According to a report corroborated by Wycliffe references to a sinful, backward element, even in Cushillococha the morals rebellion is unsuppressable. It would appear that, while evangelical religion has swept away traditional authority for many Ticuna, it has only provided a new spiritual foundation for a comparative few. The rest are unsaved or backsliders, which Cities of God have always produced in quantity.

The drastic changes required by the new order suggest that the new Ticuna identity is only Townsend's 'Indian costume', a shell for a new content. Ticuna millennial energy still pulses through the new order but SIL has channelled it in a particular way. One quickly notices the eagerness of young, monied evangelicals to acquire nylon stockings, high-heeled shoes, cosmetics, and other accoutrements of civilization. What Huxley called the Cushillocochans' 'urgent and expressed desire to become Peruvianized' suggests that the town is a model, not just of integration, but of assimilation with the sole distinctive of Ticuna language.[29]

Americanized may be closer to the mark than Peruvianized, however, for 15 years later the Christian leaders remained most distrustful of Peruvians and deeply attached to their North American founder, as if the old contrast between the mixed-race *patron* and the white immortal lives on. The traditional mythology made a radical distinction between the Ticuna and the 'rational' world which oppressed them. Periodic millennial upsurges brought Ticuna together with other Indian groups and, through such versions as the Cult of the Cross, incorporated detribalized people. But now young Cushillococha leaders disparage other Ticuna and explain that 'brothers' in the United States and Europe provided the sawmill and other improvements. The new social dualism is between believers and non-believers. In the opposed camp are not only Peruvians, as before, but most Ticuna and other Indians.

Who Preaches God's Word Down Here?

Much of the radio network in the Peruvian Amazon is licensed to foreigners, often missionaries, and well before the 1965 guerrilla campaigns the Summer Institute's radios, airplanes and schools made it a paramilitary resource at government disposal. After 1958 JAARS helped the Peruvian Army maintain its own short take-off and landing Helio-Couriers, a service it still performed 16 years later.[30] As the army prepared for guerrillas in 1964, pre-military instruction was introduced to the teacher training course at Yarinacocha.[31] The Minister of Education also approved SIL's first major project in the Sierra. The new Quechua bilingual schools would be proximate to the zone on the eastern slope of the Andes where, a year later, the Javier Heraud guerrilla unit went into action.

To the north in the jungle, SIL's Campa bilingual schools bordered the theatre of the Tupac Amaru guerrilla unit. Three years before *Life* magazine had included the Campa translators in its tribute to the young Americans of the New Frontier. In some of the most inaccessible terrain on earth, Will Kindberg had mastered the Campa language and could travel the jungle as skilfully as any Indian. Sometimes dressed like a Campa, he moved about the region like a circuit preacher on the old North American frontier. Impressed by his medical and radio powers, many Indians considered him to be super-human.[32]

Tens of thousands of Campa remained beyond SIL's reach, however, and at first they sided with the guerrillas. U.S. military advisers set up a camp in the region under USAID cover; government forces bombed Campa villages and killed hundreds of Indians.[33] SIL's place in the affair is unclear: according to local inhabitants, it was forced to close a post near Shaventini in the Gran Pajonal, then opened its present one near Shumahuani soon after the guerrillas were destroyed.[34] Then there was the government's aerial loudspeaker campaign 'in the native language'.[35] Although Campa have told visitors that it was carried out by SIL's small airplanes, how the branch's Helio-Couriers could be distinguished from the army's that were serviced at Yarinacocha is uncertain. When I asked James Wroughton whether his branch had played any role, he replied: 'We were asked to do a bit of transport. I couldn't say . . . . I was here in Lima. I should have known if one of our planes were involved. I think there were some flights for the Army or *Guardia Civil.*' But he did not know what the flights had involved since the army had its own transport. He did not believe that interpreters had been provided.[36] 'We know of no [SIL] flights made in that area at that time,' Eugene Loos wrote me several months later, 'and none of our linguistic personnel were working in the area at the time.'[37]

The new Highland Quechua programme was directed from Ayacucho, where educated native speakers had been recruited from the University of Huamanga. The U.S. embassy regarded Huamanga as a Communist machine: its rector was the branch's old friend Efrain Morote Best. Morote believes that SIL tried to avoid the CIA, but he recalls that the agency meddled in everything and infiltrated everywhere. As rector, for example, he encountered the strangest difficulties in licensing the university radio transmitter. Even a promise from President Belaunde was no help: in the judgement of the U.S. Embassy, the university would broadcast propaganda to Quechua peasants.[38]

The director of the Ayacucho project was Donald Burns, one of Townsend's young diplomats who had served as administrative secretary during the first years in Peru, then supervised early stages of the Guatemalan and Ecuadorian advances. In 1962 he occupied the first chair of linguistics at Huamanga and, like the Peace Corps, became an anti-imperialist issue – not for belonging to SIL, which was not understood, but simply for being a conservative North American with a two-way radio.

In 1964 the Minister of Education, Francisco Miro Quesada, was so impressed by the teacher graduation at Yarinacocha that he decided the Quechua needed a similar programme. Following a conference with the Minister, Burns designed a pilot project to open 'lines of communication . . . accommodating peasant cultural elements . . . to permit the peasant's voluntary and spontaneous adoption of models and norms considered in the national interests of the Republic.'[39] While he tried to uphold SIL's non-political principle, in 1966 the children at Palmapampa, who the year before had been 'terrified' simply to go to school, 'were out greeting and bringing food to soldiers, who came through to search out *"guerrilleros"*, even showing off their ability to read . . . the bilingual primers.'[40]

To home supporters Burns explained his ministry in the usual Wycliffe terms: 'We don't play a clerical role. But we can witness and study the Bible with individuals. . . . Uncle Cam convinced me that I could do much more for the Lord by keeping a low profile.' When the Hefleys visited in 1969, they asked: 'Are all the teachers believers – real Christians?' Replied Burns:

> Remember this is a government program and teachers cannot be judged on their religion. I can tell you this: all those who weren't believers when they entered have since accepted Christ. A few were evangelicals when they started. Fernando, the supervisor, was and still is a lay minister. We attend his church. Another lay preacher who came into the program had been stoned when he tried to preach in a certain village. He went back to this same place as a bilingual teacher and won thirty-five people to the Lord. The program is only three years

old and already we know of believers in over ten villages.[41]

Two of the teachers remember Burns as a good man, but they add that many colleagues surrendered to Christ in the heartfelt conviction that their careers depended on it. As a Huamanga professor, they say, Burns had invited students to his home for social occasions which turned into Bible and hymn sessions. Simultaneously he offered scholarships to Yarinacocha and Cornell University in the United States: three or four Quechua-speakers were saved in this manner and helped start the ministry project. In the villages, Burns and his assistants invited community leaders to the training centre near Ayacucho. This time the reward was a place in the teacher training course, eventually a ministry salary.

Since Burns could not refer to evangelism in his official reports, he omitted one of the reasons why the programme upset parents. The more strongly Catholic parents resented the fact that teachers were discouraging their children from making the sign of the cross and joining religious processions. If teachers respected parents' wishes in this regard, they risked the ire of Burns' wife Nadine, who did not have a ministry appointment but was referred to as the *subdirectora.* 'Her word was law,' her husband could not control her and she tyrannized each member of the teacher corps, according to our two sources. At her instigation, they say, 'several' teachers were discharged for 'not surrendering wholeheartedly to Christ' or failing to show her respect.

When the new military junta seized the International Petroleum Company in October 1968, jubilation swept the country. The project's general administrator, officially second in command, brought a patriotic poster from the Lima daily *Expreso* to class. The sight of it on the wall sent Nadine Burns into a rage. Demanding to know who was responsible, she humiliated the general administrator in front of everyone. Rebellion against the Burns gradually came into the open and, according to the two teachers, on 4 November 1970 the project's entire teaching staff sent a petition to Lima. They asked that the couple be dismissed for negative behaviour and using the Gospel against the national interest. A ministry commission arrived and the Burns were gone a week later. Most of the teachers abandoned their new faith.[42]

In 1973, the Peruvian branch dedicated its Ashaninca New Testament. Such ceremonies are important to Wycliffe: proceeding from homeland to SIL base to the recipients themselves, they ritualize the progress of God's Word from one centre to all the world. In 1931, Cameron Townsend and Trinidad Bac presented the first copy of the Cakchiquel New Testament to President Jorge Ubico. For the Ashaninca Campa 40 years later this exchange was reversed: Colonel Jose Guabloche, who had signed the 1971 contract for the government, presented the New Testament to Campa preacher Martin Cashantioite.

'I am a Campa, the Ashaninca Campa,' Martin told the assembled Campa, translators and government officials at Yarinacocha. He stammered about in Spanish and then switched to his own language:

Before the translator came, we didn't live well in our area. We had no identity with Peruvians; we knew nothing about planting crops. When someone in the family died, we burned the house and moved because we were afraid of the dead person's spirit. I knew nothing of the Lord because no one taught me. But thank God he sent linguists Will and Lee Kindberg to translate God's Word.

'Would he ever forget the official's words?' asked *Translation*. 'Although our geography and background are different,' Colonel Guabloche told the Campa, 'Christianity is the thing that unites us.' 'But what would the New Testament mean to [the] people? How would they respond. . . .?' wondered *Translation*. 'Who preaches God's Word down here?' Martin asked at the ceremony in Oviri. '. . . . I can't teach God's Word everywhere. You'll have to study it for yourselves. . . .' Martin had the same thought at the second ceremony, in Quempiri. After the Jungle Aviation and Radio Service landed with the cargo of New Testaments, the Campa and their guests sang the national anthem. 'God wants to speak to us in our own tongue,' the Peruvian Bible Society told the Campa. Teacher Jose Flores waved the red book above his head and shouted: 'Do you Campas see this? This is God's Word. It's good! Take care of it!'

And what was the popular response? For Oviri there is not a word, for Quempiri one line: 'After Jose's extemporaneous remarks some in the audience came up to purchase copies of the book.' Judging from the rousing reception at some New Testament presentations, this one was a real flop. The worry is plain. 'The last time I travelled downriver, there must have been 2,000 Campas in the churches,' Will Kindberg explained, 'but they need a lot of building up.'[43] These were bilingual school Christians, grouped around 34 sites lining the Tambo and Ene Rivers and their tributaries.

Like the rest of the Campa they face massive road-launched colonization projects, under way since the early 1960s when General Garcia told the founder that SIL's converts would be spiritual guides for the settlers. From west, north and south impoverished *colonos* backed by speculators are pushing along the rivers, displacing Campa as they go. Despite official surveys of Campa land, titles have not been forthcoming. Since 1979 Quempiri has been subject to repeated invasions. A wealthy architect laid claim to Oviri.[44] To the south in Otari, where there was no bilingual school, Campa had held an angry assembly two years before.

They treat us like savages but now, in this community of Otari, we are going to show them that we are not savages. They are the savages because since coming here they make us work without paying well and also deceive the women, leaving them abandoned with child. . . . I am not going to do like other Ashaninca chiefs who sell their brothers. . . . I am neither for nor against the Peruvian government. We only want justice. We want a high school and university just for the Ashaninca. . . . We are struggling to obtain schools, roads, machinery. . . . The

President of the colonists should come here personally to see all the problems we are having! We do not want the officials he sent because they are liars. . . . the officials help the hacienda owners. . . . knowing that they are swindling the government.

Long live [our Ashaninca] President!. . . .

We should support our brother peasants and make a true, authentic revolution. We should not ape the colonists who have a selfish revolution. . . . Here in time we shall have our own authority. A pure authority of the natives and we shall look on the colonists as foreigners. We shall import and export our products because the President will be Ashaninca. . . . This community will be a little nation governed by ourselves. Why are we waiting for the government to give us everything? It is never going to, simply because the President does not really know the problems we have. . . . No President has been concerned about us. For this reason, brothers, we must have an Ashaninca President who understands us well.

Long live our President!

We have to save our language, our ancestors and build our future. We cannot give in to the colonists, the evangelists and the other liars who try to destroy and enslave us. . . . those who claim to be the children of God are the real sinners. . . . they come here to fool us and make us fall into the trap that God exists [apparently the Christian God]. Do they practice what the Bible says? From what I can tell they do the opposite.

Yes! Yes! Yes! They are liars! . . . .

Right now the *Guardia Civil* is harrassing us. They are looking for our chief because they know he is concerned for the welfare of our community. . . .[45]

Within a few years the Campa settlements at this meeting had been destroyed. Their members were forced downriver into bilingual school territory, where the government stalled on long-promised land titles as lumber companies and settler associations established sweeping claims by force.[46] Thirteen years after North American counter-insurgency experts set up their camp near Satipo, in 1978, the Campa of this province held their fifth convention, the first free from SINAMOS. The delegates divided into six commissions: one ratified affiliation with the National Agrarian Confederation, which the government was now trying to dismantle. Another approved statutes emphasizing the rights of children, women and elders. Others discussed settler invasions, trade swindles, lack of medical assistance, the government's failure to grant land titles, and teachers who educate with contempt for tradition. The convention also decided to support a first national congress of native communities, not an idea in official favour.[47]

The Conscience of the Bureaucracy

By the time the Summer Institute seemed close to expulsion in 1976, Stefano Varese was having second thoughts. To illustrate his point he called attention to the Mayoruna or Matses, whose dependence on SIL he had once decried.[48] Since the rubber boom the Matses had killed any number of intruders. When a road-surveying party robbed their gardens in 1964, the Matses attacked and kept the well-armed group of men under siege for a week. The U.S. Panama Command sent rescue helicopters. The Peruvian Air Force bombed and machine-gunned Matses clearings on a daily basis.[49]

The year before the battle, a dead Matses had been laid out in the public square of Requena. The year after, the army took one alive and delivered him to Yarinacocha. In his year and a half at the base 'Joe' never gave his name, but he did come out of shock sufficiently to help SIL acquire his language. Between 1966 and 1969 two women spent a year camped by a river. Joe went home and did not come back; JAARS dropped gifts and concealed microphones to the Matses; and the breakthrough came when the linguist spotted pig skins on an overflight. 'Listen,' she loud-speakered down in Matses, 'if you want some help in trading those skins for valuable goods, meet us on the trail.'[50]

They did, and within a few years the Peruvian government was assigning tracts of jungle for a new round of oil exploration. Since labourers are reluctant to risk their lives for a few dollars a day, only SIL may have made the operation feasible. But according to Varese, Lima was not giving the least thought to the Matses. To the shame of the Peruvian Revolution, only SIL was. To prevent a mass encounter with outsiders, their weapons and germs, the branch negotiated a novel arrangement. Only technicians would be flown into its airstrip while the Matses did the manual labour.[51] The branch also served as intermediary, deposited Matses earnings in a bank for their use, and, along with Varese's Division of Native Communities and the Ministry of Agriculture, solicited a reserve covering most of Matses territory. Thanks to the possibility of further bloodshed, the army helped the Matses enforce the boundaries.

The branch was now stressing harmony in its presentations. It was the state's humanitarian arm and a valuable alternative to force, one part of the government which cared about Indians and had some idea of their needs. SIL said that it was giving Indians a chance to survive colonization: it addressed their resistance to expropriation with promises of brotherhood. SIL said that it was helping Indians adjust to colonization on their own terms, not those of someone else: faith mission required that it try to supplant a traditional system of meaning with its own. SIL was part of the juggernaut: its medicine was one of the reasons that the population of some groups had stabilized and begun to recover. The divergencies within a total pressure might determine whether Indians remained in a remote location or moved to a more accessible one; congregated or dispersed; had some animals to hunt or hardly any; worked mostly for *patrones* or mostly for themselves; sang old songs or new ones; continued to share their meat among themselves or did not; learned to

155

read; increased in number or declined.

Matthew Huxley had worried over the Amarakaeri, a people brought into contact by Catholic missionaries and being devastated by epidemics.[52] SIL worked with a single Amarakaeri group, about 100 persons, and not long before oil exploration arrived in 1974 a North American anthropologist came to live with them. Thomas Moore found the people at Puerto Alegre more isolated and under less pressure to conform to Peruvian ways than the larger number congregating around the Dominican stations. To pay for medicine, SIL had encouraged the Amarakaeri to pan for gold and instituted a money economy. But it also assuaged their appetite for trade goods with a relatively modest flow and kept them out of debt to *patrones*. The population was beginning to increase and Amarakaeri were still consulting shamans. Young men had rejected the traditional model of manhood in favour of trade goods prestige, yet the Amarakaeri still ate, distributed meat and co-operated like they had before.

When SIL's Robert Tripp was in Puerto Alegre, he conducted religious services every Sunday. To translate the concept of the Devil into Amarakaeri SIL had used the term *toto* or soul of the boa, occasionally linking *toto* with Communism, so that when Tripp asked the Amarakaeri to pray for the Millers captured in Vietnam they feared that the translators were being harmed by large snakes. While some Amarakaeri were now worried about the possibility of going to hell instead of their own, assuredly blissful afterlife, the only convert was the Swiss Mission-trained pastor. His attempt to be a Christian was bringing him into conflict with community life and he was losing the battle.

Moore says that the relative ethnic stability of the group was disrupted during two periods when SIL members were absent. In 1962-64 yellow fever took 20 lives and the Amarakaeri fled to the Catholics for medicine. Under pressure from more acculturated Indians at the Dominican mission, they abandoned their communal house and puberty rituals. But because the large concentration of people around the station proved stressful, they moved back to their old vicinity. During 1973-75, many translators, including Tripp, were busy at Yarinacocha, producing primers and linguistics to convince the government to renew the contract, and Scripture in case it did not. New state regulations on the gold and hide trade curtailed SIL's marketing and buyer service, so the Amarakaeri began trading with a government *Banco Minero* post. As the price of gold soared, the Amarakaeri acquired trade goods at a faster rate.

In 1974, an oil exploration contractor for Cities Service of New York turned SIL's airstrip at Puerto Alegre into a supply depot without consulting the branch or the Amarakaeri. As many as 19 flights a day disrupted the school. Despite many conflicts – sometimes there were 30 or 40 workers waiting for flights, running short of food, stealing chickens, getting drunk and harrassing native women – to the Amarakaeri the depot was their wildest dream come true. They begged, bought, thieved and started to quarrel over handouts, wealth differences and neglected group responsibilities. Some of the men learned to enjoy the prostitutes brought in to service company personnel.

Factionalized, the Amarakaeri curtailed sharing among themselves, abandoned their village to move closer to the *Banco Minero* and, because gardens had been neglected in the scramble for gold and trade goods, started buying food there. Some parents even took their children to the Dominican boarding school where they could learn Peruvian ways and Spanish more quickly. Moore concludes that SIL had retarded the ethnocide process but was being overwhelmed by it.

When the oil company tried to destroy fruit trees to lengthen the airstrip, again without consulting the owners, the Amarakaeri convinced the workers that it would be wiser not to proceed. Thomas Moore left for Lima to protest. Like Richard Smith, who in the 1960s, tried to get land titles for the Amuesha and found that SIL support never materialized, Moore was disappointed by SIL's failure to intervene with the authorities. It was not the translator's fault. Moore says that when Tripp was in the village he was often on the radio to Yarinacocha complaining about the company's latest misdeeds. 'Keep it cool, Bob,' branch administrators told him.[53]

After Morote Best's enforced departure in 1958, translators eager to battle for a reserve against a criminal *patron* or local official, had been restrained by branch administrators. Rocking the boat might endanger the more important, long-term goal of universal Bible translation. As a branch official put it in 1974, SIL had to maintain relationships with many people, including some whose interests were opposed to Indians, in order to continue helping Indians.[54] Since SIL was absolutely dependent on the state, far more so than Catholic missions, it could not afford to confront the government or its contractors. Against gross abuses it could not side with Indians, only try to minimize the abuses by mediating between aggressor and victim — sometimes — because branch administrators would not want to give higher powers the impression that SIL was a troublemaker. In profound political insecurity by the early 1970s, the Peruvian branch was stressing its 'service' ministry, ostensibly to everyone but with priority to the state.

In Search of a New Rationale

As was the case after 1953, crisis has forced the Summer Institute to legitimate itself in new terms. At the International Congress of Americanists in 1976, the branch's Eugene Loos, Patricia Davis and Mary Ruth Wise substituted an anthropological rationale for faith mission. The paper also illustrates their organization's capacity for selective amnesia: in what is apparently SIL-Peru's first published reference to the Wycliffe Bible Translators since the founder's confession 23 years before, the authors maintain that 'from the beginning, the public has been carefully informed of the functions of the two.'

It emerges that branch members analyse cultural traits in terms of their positive and negative values for the culture and its individual members. When confronted by a negative cultural trait, members present alternatives and permit the people to make their own decision. They 'try to maintain impartiality in regard to religious doctrines,' 'do not lend support to any political-economic system', 'fully respect . . . [indigenous] customs and their right to self-determination', and provide help only 'in response to needs felt and expressed by the group itself.' But since Amazonian Indians are already in contact with Western society, 'it is necessary to help them find alternatives so that they can retain their identity inside a viable, strong, united and just culture, whose values can survive cultural contact.' The alternative is, of course, Christianity. The authors are rather vague about what they mean by Christianity, however, to the point that their 'basic principles', which SIL members bring to the field, do not include the Wycliffe Statement of Doctrine. Were the authors to have included SIL's faith mission commitments in their presentation, it would emerge that Christianity 'as an option and not an imposition' entails 1) an *a priori* judgement that all non-evangelical belief systems are negative cultural traits; 2) a church to be established in each language SIL studies, and 3) the division of each 'united culture' into saved and unregenerate.[55]

The branch's most serious difficulties are not in the halls of indigenist congresses or even government ministries. Some of the contradictions threatening its position in native communities emerge from a 1979 summary of nearly three decades experience with bilingual education. Even though the volume reflects the usual political requirements, it suggests that SIL has much to teach its opponents. But the most notable feature is that, apparently for the first time, the branch has permitted a member to publish criticism of its performance, With assistance from Campa translator Will Kindberg, literacy specialist Patricia Davis circumspectly impeaches policies which helped turn the bilingual schools into an evangelical instrument. She recommends: 1) starting bilingual education with the adults (rather than the young who are more easily weaned from tradition); 2) avoiding the concentration of small, dispersed groups into large communities; 3) avoiding promotion of the teacher as leader of the community. Shared leadership will avoid any tendency for the teacher to turn into a *patron.*

The teachers are the object of special concern. Compared to other native people, they are more likely to suffer from tension — 'headaches, depression, psychosomatic disorders' — and 'at times' have killed themselves. After a decade of assurance that Christianity 'offers stability to face the problems and pressures of culture change', now we learn that the evangelists of the new order suffer more psychological distress than the unsaved [56] As the vanguard of change, the teacher must synthesize two cultures (three if one counts both Peruvian and North American) and is the locus of heavy, contradictory demands by outsiders and his own people. He himself may make heavy demands on his people, the 'more subtle' of which include becoming 'the involuntary initiator of materialism' and promoting 'differences in the world view.' Finally, he is confronted with a bewildering array of new and contradictory 'philosophical, ideological and religious tendencies.'[57]

These are cogent observations which probably displease the more fundamentalist members. But the Peruvian branch faces a knot of worsening dilemmas. The same government that rescued the branch in 1976 needs all the help it can get to keep Indians calm for its own, ever more unfortunate plans. Triumph in Lima has done nothing to remedy the deteriorating ecology of many bilingual school communities. But SIL's 'alternative' has paved the way for other religious and political groups, who are trying to make less demanding alliances with its clients.

One such contest is among the 20,000 Aguaruna, whose 120 bilingual teachers comprise more than one third of the entire bilingual system. In the 1950s, two sturdy SIL pioneers believed that thanks to modern medicine and the Gospel, the extirpation of superstition was imminent. In the late 1960s an anthropological consultant announced the achievement of profound cultural change, thanks to the bilingual schools and in stark contrast to previous mission efforts. Lately, the five member SIL team has been training the Aguaruna to handle their own problems, which they certainly have in abundance. In 1978 the translator reported that, three years after its dedication, the Aguaruna New Testament was in enthusiastic use.

> But we also talked to teachers frustrated by the pressures of civilization — pressures brought on by the coming of the road, the pipeline, and of many strangers. We talked to teachers struggling against discrimination, indifference, and injustice. We talked to pastors full of questions raised by the inroads of strange and new religions. These pastors carry a burden for believers preoccupied with the materialism of the new era.[58]

Like their well-organized Shuar cousins to the north in Ecuador, the Aguaruna are an Indian nation in the obvious sense of the word, By breaking off ceremonial warfare among themselves, local groups united to expel the invader from their rugged homeland as late as the 1920s. Even the Jesuits, whom the Aguaruna expelled in 1886, only re-established themselves several years after the arrival of the first SIL team. *Patrones* had made inroads among the more accessible Aguaruna, however, providing a constituency for the bitter contest between SIL and the Jesuits, which lasted into the early 1970s. Gerardo Wipio Deicat, a bilingual school supervisor, has recalled how the *patrones* mocked Aguaruna ways and took advantage of his people's illiteracy to exploit them. SIL recruited its first teachers from a small Nazarene Protestant mission and the Jesuit boarding school: since arithmetic, literacy and Spanish were a defense against the *patrones,* parents sent their children to school instead of bringing them up according to tradition.[59] Each year delegations arrived at the conference of teachers initiated by Efrain Morote Best to acquire one for themselves.

The higher objectives of the bilingual schools were to make the Aguaruna evangelical Christians and persuade them to accept colonization. As elsewhere, SIL eventually conceived of its religion as a new 'self-esteem' which it felt Indians needed to face the forces of which it was taking such advantage. Thus the individual Aguaruna 'no longer feels worthless and downtrodden. Christ died for *him*, and life takes on new meaning.'[60] Evangelical religion did become a protest against the old order, partly because the Jesuits had quickly rejoined it. Besides rejection of Catholic missionaries and initiation into economic individualism, the new identity required loyalty to the same government which was about to offer Aguaruna land to outsiders. In the words of Gerardo Wipio Deicat, the Aguaruna 'recognize the objective of our government to transform the jungle for the progress of the nation.'[61]

Bilingual education was so successful that it drew students away from the Jesuits, whose system eventually numbered more than 50 schools. The Catholic programme was taught by outsiders as well as Aguaruna, and had a significantly smaller enrolment, entailing less concentration of population. While the SIL team generally entrusted its concentration campaign to the teachers, a Jesuit reports hearing the leading fundamentalist using the language of millennial cataclysm to move a group to the main river around 1969. By this time, land shortage, hunger, illness, social tension and witchcraft fear were apparent around the bilingual schools.

When the Aguaruna learned about the new highway, SIL consultant Lila Wistrand reported in 1970, the elders proposed flight to the hills. Instead, SIL convinced teachers and elders to make their stand along the Maranon River, in the choice lands which they might otherwise lose forever. As the teachers' trading activities gave them 'greater insight' into the value of the approaching highway, the Aguaruna were acquiring 'a feeling for progress in the sense of accumulation of material goods.' Teacher salaries were 'the chief factor in economic change', according to Wistrand. Previously, family demands, jealousy and witchcraft had encouraged 'economic levelling', but the teachers 'experience conflict' because they do not want to give all their salary away.

The same year Peruvian anthropologists surveyed five bilingual school communities near the new road. They reported that often, only the teachers had money, which they used to buy prestige goods and hire labour. The *ipaamu* or communal work fiesta was starting to give way to wage labour in the production of cash crops. Since masato beer parties are part of the *ipaamu,* the custom was also threatened by the anti-masato campaign of certain SIL members. Teachers following their instructions 'find themselves in an ambiguous, distressing situation: caught between social sanction and the sanction of a new "ethic", they are forced to make a choice' between displeasing their people and displeasing the SIL missionary. But despite embryonic social stratification revolving around the teachers, the elders still commanded respect and played a leading role in community decisions. Although five years later reciprocity was said to have greatly declined, in 1970 new items, such as shotguns, were still being integrated into the system of sharing. Relatively little was being produced for market despite the arrival of the highway: the Aguaruna had little interest in cash crops, because they regarded profits and market fluctuations as incomprehensible and unjust.[62]

Lila Wistrand explained that the bilingual schools were supposed to enclose and preserve the core of Aguaruna culture' and relate it to the dominant one.

The schools were like buffers which regulated acculturation. But the balance was delicate and required state backing against the overwhelming power of colonization. Were the government to falter, 'anxiety drives and hostile actions might arise.'[63] While the Aguaruna were indeed refraining from violence, they were not doing as well as Wistrand hoped; and the government giving away their land was not among their allies. In the bilingual school community of Nazareth ten families lost their land to a government survey for settlers.[64] Soldiers had molested Urakusa, which was fighting official plans to set up a supply depot on its land: the land title obtained with the help of Morote Best and SIL had disappeared. As Aguaruna were forced from their homes, particularly around Nazareth, it was the Jesuits who entered the fray against the authorities.[65] If SIL came to the defense of its clients, it was behind the scenes and not reported.

By the early 1970s, the Aguaruna were the branch's most comprehensive operation, one conceptualized in terms of training the Aguaruna to take over the functions performed by SIL members. A dozen medical aides had been trained to deal with the hygienic consequences of the bilingual school concentrations. A community development programme was supposed to make the Aguaruna 'independent financially, able to buy and sell using money, and able to receive and give true value for goods and produce.' SIL helped the Swiss Mission establish itself in the language and encouraged an Aguaruna to start a Bible institute to assure 'church development.'[66] To bridge the divide between older traditionalists and young bilingual school converts, SIL initiated bilingual education for adults. The size of the educational system demanded that the SIL school supervisor begin relying on Aguaruna supervisors, an example followed by other teams managing extensive systems. By the late 1970s Aguaruna were studying linguistics, producing school texts, translating the Old Testament, running their own teacher training courses, and occupying higher posts in the educational bureaucracy.[67]

The Summer Institute has demonstrated that Amazonian Indians can run their own school system, which is no small achievement. No one else has provided the institutional room for them to prove this point on SIL's scale. The branch has gone further in its claims, however, by presenting the Aguaruna work as a model of support for self-determination. Some time ago, Lila Wistrand called the bilingual schools and teacher conferences 'a basis for tribal unity', which to some extent they perhaps have been. More recently, in the 1979 volume on the bilingual schools, Gerardo Wipio Deicat called the Bible 'the moral and spiritual base for our people.'[68] Yet a familiar discrepancy emerges: while the SIL translator claimed 'at least several thousand' believers in 1969, nine years later she noted 'hundreds and hundreds.'[69] The basis of Aguaruna unity undoubtedly remains, not SIL's dubious combination of the Bible, obedience to the government, and a few cultural forms like the language, but an identity opposed to the Peruvian, based upon distinct moral and religious values, and conscious of itself as an oppressed group.[70]

In 1977, a Jesuit thought that SIL was somewhat 'disoriented', having created situations which it could no longer manage. The 'materialism' which SIL laments is very much a product, not just of the new highway, but of its own policies. Unless its community development projects among the Aguaruna are an exception to the rule, they have not been very successful in maintaining the ecological balance of concentrated communities. When the branch realized that the government might be turning against it in the early 1970s, a change was noted, away from its old 'lord of the jungle' attitude. The truce between the two missions apparently helped to clear the way for the Aguaruna-Huambisa Council, which brought together local councils in 1977, and over which a variety of groups now maneouvre for influence. 'Political agitation has begun among the Aguarunas', a Jesuit reported. 'God willing that it be for their good and not so they can be used for the purposes of others, as always happens.'

References

1. *Translation* Summer 1962 pp.4-5.
2. K. Pike 1967:124-5.
3. SIL/WBT 1963:53.
4. Hefleys 1972:21.
5. Garrard 1970:44.
6. Dostal 1972:376-81.
7. For an evangelical analysis, see Tippett 1972. For a representative SIL response that the declaration is not applicable to its own work, see Kingsland 1980:140.
8. *Translation* September/October 1974 pp.2, 11.
9. Hart 1973:16, 26-9, 31.
10. F. Pike 1967:297.
11. SIL/WBT 1964:115-7; Townsend and Pittman 1975:5, 12-13.
12. SIL/WBT 1964:116-7.
13. 10 April 1961 White House route slip concerning 23 March 1961 letter from W. Cameron Townsend. John F. Kennedy Library, Boston.
14. Mangin 1972:206-7.
15. Hefleys 1974:229, 237, 241; Rossi 1975:115-16.
16. *La Prensa* 10 July 1966. For a membership list, see *El Comercio* 4 September 1966. Also these two papers and *El Expreso* 7 September 1966.
17. *El Peruano* (Lima) 8 February 1971 p.7.
18. McCurry 1972:405.
19. D'Ans 1981:148-62.
20. *El Expreso* 31 January and 1 February 1972.
21. Varese 1972a:128-9, 136-8.
22. Sullivan 1970:163, 173.
23. On the formation of Cushillococha, see SIL/WBT 1963:102-21; Huxley 1964:195-6, 213; Solnit 1964; *Peruvian Times* 17 December 1955 pp.4,6.
24. Rossi 1975:99-105, 117, 122, 124, 139.

25. Ibid. 103, 127-8, 147-8.
26. "Savage", Ticuna bilingual teacher cited in Cowan 1979:257. 'Hardly civilized', author's interview, Cushillococha, 11 April 1976.
27. See Rossi 1975:137-44.
28. Buckingham 1974:155-9.
29. Huxley and Capa 1964:195.
30. SIL-Peru 1975:84.
31. Larson et al 1979:136.
32. *Life* (New York) 14 September 1962 pp.76A-80.
33. Gall 1967:39
34. Soren Hvalkof, personal communication.
35. Ministry of War 1966:55, 60-4. Summarized in Gott 1973:423-31.
36. Author's interview, Lima, 23 February 1977.
37. Eugene Loos, personal communication.
38. Author's interview, Ayacucho, 14 February 1977.
39. Burns 1971:2.
40. *Peruvian Times* 30 September 1966 pp.12-13. For an analysis of one of the primers, see Escribens 1975.
41. Hefleys 1972:167, 170.
42. Author's interviews, Ayacucho, 14-15 February 1977.
43. *Translation* July/August 1973 p.10.
44. Chirif 1980:16-18.
45. Alencar and Yancan 1977:143-6.
46. Santos 1980:9-10.
47. *Marka* 28 December 1978 pp.24-5.
48. Varese 1972b:11.
49. A correspondent for *El Expreso* 19 March 1964 went along on one of the air raids. Peter Matthiessen drew upon the bombings as well as earlier contacts with SIL-Peru and other missions for his 1965 novel *At Play in the Fields of the Lord*.
50. Long 1970:16-19; Hefleys 1972:49-51, 77, 83, 115, 186.
51. Varese 1976a; 1976b.
52. Huxley and Capa 1964:177-8.
53. Moore 1981 and personal communication.
54. Latinamerica Press interview with James Wroughton, Lima, 30 January 1974.
55. Loos et al 1979:401, 406, 419, 426-7, 440, 444.
56. Ibid. 1979:441.
57. Davis 1979:232-7, 242, 248, 259.
58. *In Other Words* November 1978 p.3.
59. Deicat 1979:99-102.
60. *Translation* April/June 1972 pp.6-7.
61. Deicat 1979:104.
62. Varese et al 1970:18-20, 83.
63. Wistrand 1970:3, 8.
64. Varese et al 1970:69.
65. Siverts 1972:26, 30-72.
66. *Translation* April/June 1972 pp.6-7.
67. Larson et al 1979:381-99 summarize the transfer of functions.
68. Wistrand 1970:5; Deicat 1979:110-11.

69.   Hefleys 1972:151; *In Other Words* November 1978 p.3.
70.   Varese et al 1970:17.

6. The Summer Institute in Colombia

Colombia has come under a perpetual state of siege, the official declaration of national emergency. The crisis was said to be at an end in the late 1950s when, in the wake of civil war verging upon class war, the Liberal and Conservative oligarchies composed their differences in the National Front. This two-party system has ruled a nominal democracy to the present, but the *Violencia* in the countryside only abated and took on new forms. The most recent stage of Colombian democracy has been financed by the sale of cocaine and marijuana to the United States. With pressure from Washington to keep these principal exports illegal, the huge revenues have had a corrupting influence on officialdom and the armed forces, which use martial law to suppress political opposition. Under the 1978 Security Statute, for example, the government extended its vigilance to include 'unarmed subversion.' According to the Minister of Justice, that consisted of 'criticizing the authorities, censuring them, contributing to insecurity and stimulating subversive groups.'[1]

Like previous episodes of world market expansion, the marijuana and cocaine industries have had a violent impact on the internal frontiers populated by some 400,000 native people. Strife between landlords and small-holders has long sent refugees into these regions, where aspiring land monopolists commence the struggle anew. As marijuana cultivators invade the land of Indians, or they themselves take up the crop, suppression campaigns subsidized by the U.S. Drug Enforcement Agency target small farmers who cannot persuade the forces of law and order to go somewhere else. Among Indians traditionally attached to the coca leaf, entrepreneurs seize producing zones and deprive consumers of their supply.[2] Guerrillas, the armed forces and all-purpose gun thugs vie for control of regions disputed by landlords, homesteaders and native people.

When a Summer Institute recruit joined the weekly death toll in March 1981, it illustrated how many Colombians have come to understand the North American hunger for drugs and profits, national security and evangelism in terms of a vast, secret co-ordinating apparatus of empire, the CIA conspiracy. The execution followed more than a decade of controversy over SIL, which had been welcomed at the highest level in the early 1960s. Since the translators initially flourished as a check on the Catholic missions, the first to raise the anti-imperialist standard were renovated Catholic missionaries. Soon expanding linguistic and anthropological professions, capable of filling the technical vacuum SIL had occupied, learned that it was unmovable.

As the branch's CIA reputation flowered, Indian civil rights organizing was spreading throughout the country. In the eastern plains and forests, where the native population is more dispersed and linguistically diverse, the organizing was sometimes difficult to distinguish from patronage battle between rival brokers. But in the Andes, several Indian organizations directly challenged the local ruling class, which induced the army to militarize Indian homelands and had Indian leaders assassinated on the pretext that they were guerrillas and drug traffickers.

When Indian land was invaded, the government paid no attention. When Indians tried to recover their land, the police and army moved against them to maintain public order.[3] Many social scientists and a number of Catholic clergy found their own interests compatible with civil rights organizing: by reason of theology and state contract, SIL did not. That was why it continued to enjoy support at the highest level of government. Recently, the underlying conflict has emerged with greater clarity, in the government's attempt to use agitation against North American missionaries, quarrels among indigenists and the like to legislate dictatorial powers over Indians, legalizing repression of their civil rights movements.

Opening the Door

Only higher power, Cameron Townsend has reiterated, can explain his welcome in Colombia. As the home of a powerful Catholic clergy, it beckoned as that dearest of spiritual challenges, the closed field. For nearly a decade, from the height of the *Violencia* in the early 1950s, the founder's attempts to obtain a government agreement came to naught. Conservative priests were forcing Protestant missionaries to leave rural areas, sometimes inciting the slaughter of their converts as godless Communists. Then there was the Treaty on Missions, an official genuflection to the Vatican Concordat of 1887, which was strengthened during the same months in which Townsend broke a Catholic monopoly in Peru. Possibly with the University of Oklahoma linguists in mind, the January 1953 Treaty gave Catholic bishops total authority over education in the Indian territories.[4] Sooner or later, in any case, SIL's perform-ance in Peru had forewarned the defenders of the faith against a Protestant conspiracy. While Colombian Liberals regarded the Concordat as Roman imper-ialism, again and again linguist diplomats came to grief on St. Peter's rock. Then in 1961 their general director opened the door.

Townsend's explanation, that God had worked yet another miracle for the Wycliffe Bible Translators, begins in 1952. This was the year he met Alberto Lleras Camargo, the Liberal ex-president and head of the Organization of American States, in Chicago. Typically, even Lleras' return to the Colombian presidency six years later did not change Townsend's luck. His dilemma is illustrated by a 1959 encounter with another sympathetic Liberal, Gregorio

Hernandez de Alba. One of the fathers of Colombian anthropology, Hernandez de Alba had emerged from the Marxist *indigenismo* of the 1930s, a criole response to the Indian civil rights movements of that generation. Having witnessed many a setback to the indigenist cause, he made his life's work the establishment of a modern integration programme which would foster the cultural progress of Indians, protect them from abuses, and discreetly pry them loose from the Catholic clergy. Among the few allies he could count on were Protestant missionaries.[5] Now that Hernandez de Alba was persuading his friend President Lleras to sponsor a Division of Indian Affairs, he was eager for international assistance, which Townsend offered in his capacity as a Peruvian delegate to the Inter-American Indigenist Congress. If the founder wanted permission to evangelize Colombia's Indian population, Hernandez de Alba needed linguists to study their 50 or so languages. The Summer Institute could also provide flight service, create a public for government-controlled integration programmes and train Colombian linguists, all at little or no cost to tiny official budgets. It was a tantalizing offer: in return, SIL would enter Colombia's new indigenist bureaucracy on the ground floor. Two years later Hernandez de Alba drew up the contract, but in 1959 he said that the Vatican Concordat was insurmountable.

As North American alarm over the Cuban Revolution mounted, Townsend kept 'hoping and praying.' In September 1961, as the United States launched the Alliance for Progress, he turned down an invitation to visit England with the explanation that the Lord was keeping him on standby for Colombia. His prayers were answered in October when the Colombian ambassador to Washington, a Liberal named Carlos Sanz de Santa Maria, happened to visit the North Carolina businessman, Henderson Belk, who had just donated the land for the new JAARS centre near Charlotte. After conferring with the ambassador, Townsend winged southward to reintroduce himself to President Lleras, who promised the contract.[6]

Earlier the same October, through Colonel Kintner, Robert Schneider was offering SIL's help to the White House for the struggle against Communism. Two months later John Kennedy visited his anti-Castro ally, Lleras, in Bogota. And a few days before Townsend signed his contract in February 1962, a U.S. Special Forces team returned to Fort Bragg, North Carolina with a pessimistic report. 'In view of the propensity of most of the leaders in both political and economic fields to ignore their national responsibilities and to seek personal aggrandizement instead,' the team advised formation of a civil-military apparatus for 'clandestine execution of plans developed by the United States Government toward defined objectives in the political, economic and military fields. This would permit passing to the offensive in all fields of endeavour rather than depending on the Colombians to find their own solution. Although the latter would be preferable, there is no assurance that time exists to await developments.' The apparatus would be used 'to pressure toward reforms known to be needed, perform counter-agent and counter-propaganda functions and as necessary execute paramilitary, sabotage and/or terrorist activities against known communist proponents.'[7]

Since the Liberals were about to cede the presidency to the Conservatives as per the National Front agreement, a linguistic institute may well have figured in the horse-trading. According to the contract signed with the Minister of Interior, a Conservative named Fernando Londono y Londono, SIL would operate in co-ordination with the ministry's Division of Indian Affairs; attend to the 'social, economic, civic, moral and hygienic improvement' of Indians; and 'respect the prerogatives of the Catholic Church, according to the terms of the Concordat. . . .'[8]

Soon, the missionary bishops had their doubts about the last point. One of their secretaries, Manuel Lucena, had returned from the SIL session at the University of Oklahoma with an analysis of the dual identity. He suggested taking advantage of the contract by requiring SIL to train Catholic missionary linguists, who would then obviate the need for its services. At a meeting that Wycliffe describes in terms of Daniel meeting the lions, Townsend mollified the bishops with his language of love. The bishops were already under pressure from the Vatican to be ecumenical: they were supposed to marshall the faithful against a more serious threat than Protestantism. Townsend's director for the Colombian advance, Robert Schneider, asked him to help keep the truce, which he did by making Colombia his residence until 1965.[9]

The SIL base, Lomalinda, went up in the eastern plains or *llanos* on land donated by an air force general, Armando Urrego Bernal, near Puerto Lleras, Meta. Translators entered 20 languages by 1966 and 37 by 1974, with nine more in view. Each team was to produce a New Testament within ten years and all were to be finished by 1983 (the branch distributed its first in 1981), whereupon translators would devote more attention to community development programmes and conclude their work by 1985.[10]

The branch did not disclose its priorities to most Colombians: a Colombian supporter even argued that SIL's 'gigantic' effort in community development justified the delay in linguistic production.[11] As late as 1971, Victor Daniel Bonilla could only 'risk the statement' that SIL's fundamental purpose was 'spiritual'.[12] When film maker Brian Moser asked why the 'primary objective . . . to get the Word to the tribes' was not in the government contract, branch director Clarence Church replied that 'SIL is not a religious organization' — the official position.* He claimed that SIL's religious purpose 'has been perfectly known ever since the beginning' and that it put '90%' of its emphasis on linguistics.[13]

An official bilingual school system did not materialize, one reason being that the Ministry of Education was laced with loyal and wary Catholics. As

---

* Two years later, in 1972, the Colombian branch's Forrest Zander, and the Peruvian branch's James Wroughton, informed their official sponsors that 'our inspiration and motivation are invariably Christian. Nevertheless, we are not a religious mission, that is, we do not represent or propagate any particular Christian church or denomination' (like a number of other evangelical missions). Zander added: 'Therefore we are not a "catechizing" or "proselytizing" organization. In the 23 nations where SIL works not one baptism, one congregation, one pastor or priest exists by SIL's initiative.'[14] (God's Word and other missions were responsible).

for Colombian Protestants, the branch was content to ignore them, as Townsend had. SIL did not want Indian believers paternalized; it was hard to explain the 'other side' of the work without jeopardizing it; and Colombian brethren distrusted dual identity evasions, not least pledges to co-operate with their Catholic persecutors and a contract which acknowledged the Vatican Concordat. The Indian Affairs Division was so understaffed and powerless that both parties soon neglected each other: except for a brief official orientation in 1966, the branch apparently never was asked to train Colombian professionals. By way of compensation, it did cultivate the politicians passing through the top posts of the powerful Interior Ministry.

Circumspect and autonomous, preoccupied with taking the Word to the tribes and raising their children as North Americans, members isolated themselves from Colombian society. When the United States helped the National Front destroy peasant self-defense zones in 1964-65, transforming militias into guerrilla units and scattering them toward SIL fieldworkers, that was another example of how Communists frustrated the government's efforts to assure peace and progress. By spending their lives at Lomalinda, or flying in and out of native communities and concentrating on the vernacular, many members failed to learn passable Spanish.

Hopes pinned on the National Front slipped away, and so did the configuration of forces from which Townsend had extracted a contract. The government gradually shook loose from the Concordat; some members of the Catholic clergy began to oppose colonization; and the universities produced platoons of linguists and anthropologists, whose field ambitions were stimulated by SIL's. As the anti-Concordat rationale behind the contract unravelled, so did the need for foreign expertise. Indian civil rights organizing — 'unity, land and culture' — began to contradict evangelical plans. According to a New Tribes missionary, SIL members shrugged off an ever angrier horizon with comments like 'the [cabinet] ministers know what we're doing.'

Planas and CRIC

Two events in 1970-71, the Planas affair and the formation of the *Consejo Regional Indigena del Cauca* (CRIC), were something of a watershed in Indian politics. Planas is an oil-bearing region in the *llanos,* an hour's flight from Lomalinda, where cattle ranches have confined thousands of Guahibo Indians to patches of savannah. Stymied by a Guahibo co-operative, ranchers accused the white organizer of inciting a Communist guerrilla, which attracted the armed forces. After a number of sympathetic homesteaders and Indians were murdered, others tortured, the Guahibo fought back with the primitive weapons at their disposal. Priests and anthropologists brought the Guahibo side of the story to national attention. The official response confirmed that Indians could not expect justice from the authorities, some of whom claimed large tracts of the same area.[15]

As Indian policy was debated, the case against the Summer Institute began to emerge. It was only accused of helping to suppress the Guahibo resistance two years later, however, from New York. The North American Congress on Latin America quoted a February 1970 report in *El Espectador* of Bogota: SIL had 'entered into collaboration with the government's civic action program' to pacify presumed Guahibo guerrillas. Several 'professors' were working as liaison/interpreters and the Institute had 'provided the radio equipment to establish direct communications' between the police station at Planas and the department capital. NACLA added 'air support to these services, which have figured in polemics against SIL to the present.[16] But since the men who exposed the Planas atrocities did not mention such a role, nor does it seem to have emerged in Guahibo testimony, the only source is the newspaper report. According to SIL, whose team worked among Guahibo far to the east, its only service was a flight for Indian Affairs Co-ordinator, Alejandro Reyes Posada. According to one of the translators, her husband and Reyes found all but one of the Planas settlements abandoned: there they advised the people not to flee into the bush.[17] Following more inspections, Reyes helped to expose the origin of the conflict in rancher aggression, police brutality, and official indifference to Guahibo rights.[18]

Soon, evangelical missionaries in the Planas region were disturbed by the spectacle of priests less interested in saying mass than reviving pagan rituals. A few Catholic missionaries had defected from the common cause of destroying traditional religion: they were trying to decolonize their work by restoring Guahibo confidence in their culture. The most formidable adversary of this project was Sophie Muller, an elderly fundamentalist from New York City credited with her own empire: thousands of converts in eight languages scattered across the *llanos* and jungle of north-eastern Colombia, not to mention sweeping accomplishments in Brazil. When I met Muller in Bogota in 1975, she was no longer a member of the New Tribes Mission. Apparently the principal reason was that she kept getting it into trouble with the authorities. Like SIL she has been maligned but there is, as always, something to the legend. 'Destroying the culture?' she exclaimed that Sunday morning. 'I should hope so — drunkenness and wild dancing, you know dancing leads to immorality. The idiots had all this witchcraft, the men would drink and dance all night, then go off into the woods with girls and do their immorality.' She said that she was forever having to set Indians straight about who she was because they usually thought that she was from heaven.[19]

Muller came to Colombia in the early 1940s, as an independent missionary in search of the unreached tribe. She says that she was all by herself or 'beyond civilization' for the first 20 years, but she moved among groups mauled by colonial expansion and epidemic disease. Blaming their suffering on sorcery, native millennialists could be persuaded that deliverance lay in rejecting tradition for a white woman sent by God to warn them of the approaching end of the world.[20] Muller began work with the Curipaco, at Sejal on the Guainia River. Judging from her account of the first mass conversions, her pan-tribal messianic reputation grew out of an anti-witchcraft movement. Under Muller's direction, the first Curipaco converts threw their bundles of sacred objects into the river, axed the canoes where they made home brew and, because they feared the sorcery of their neighbours, took her to the next village to single out the guilty for a stern lecture. It went like this in village after village, Muller said: flotillas of canoes followed her from one to the next; and the Curipaco sorcerers became the elders of the new church.[21] They took the new religion to the Puinave, Cubeo and Guayabero. The Puinave evangelized the Piapoco, and both evangelized the Guahibo, Cuiva and Saliva. On the Isana River in Brazil, Maniba (or Baniwa) Indians constructed lodgings for their saviour in 18 settlements. They wanted her to bring trousers from heaven, make their crops grow well, protect them from illness, and chase away ants and evil spirits. Wherever her converts and reputation went, Muller followed, in the course of her journeys translating (after a fashion) the New Testament into three languages and portions into eight others.[22]

Muller reached the height of her influence during the *Violencia,* no doubt experienced personally by some of her followers. Frontier violence against Indians helps to explain the brain-washing and exploitation charges against her: other colonizers were disturbed by a policy of militant isolationism which suited Indians as well as their miracle worker. According to the Matallana Commission, which investigated SIL and the New Tribes Mission in 1974, 'the fundamental point of [Muller's] indoctrination is to convince Indians that any contact . . . with the "white" leads to the damnation of their souls. . . .[Arguing] that the highly communal Indian life is what God wants. . . . she always struggles to prevent the Indians from acquiring . . . the most common vices among the settlers.'[23] When Catholic missionaries forced her North American colleagues to leave during the *Violencia,* Muller hung on in areas which priest and policeman never reached. Unlike the Catholics, she recruited Indian pastors and did not erect mission stations which exploited Indian labour.

Yet by the 1970s, Muller's empire was crumbling, To younger, more cautious New Tribes and Summer Institute missionaries, it was a perplexing despair. They could not fulfil the supernatural expectations she had aroused. Nor could they ignore the traditional beliefs, such as fear of the Curipaco shamans, which she had consecrated into churches. Converts were in rebellion against her authoritarian ways. There was also more effective competition than before. 'Influence?' Muller responded. 'Not any more. That's a thing of the past when I could tell them what to do and they'd follow me. [Other outsiders] are coming in from all sides now, whole bands are going back to their old ways.' She was especially disgusted with the Guahibo and Cuiva, who she said destroyed their minds with a hallucinogen, just like her Guayabero converts do, as SIL has discovered. When Muller returned to a Guahibo village near Planas in 1974, only three families were still faithful. The others had painted themselves up and were dancing their dances. They would not allow her to stay in the village, and a spokesman told her that she had deceived them.[24]

Like the new wave in Catholic mission which she blames for such reverses, Muller was no friend of ambitious cattle ranchers. In 1967, a man claiming

8,000 hectares in Vichada Territory told a court that she had arrived on his property with 200 persons armed with bows and arrows and shotguns. Under her orders, the Indians worked day and night to erect a 500 metre fence, which deprived the rancher of most of his claim.[25] But Muller was no friend of the Guahibo co-operative destroyed in 1970 either. She considered its organizer a Communist, and her new Catholic rivals ('they're all for the Indians going back to their old way!') were clearly his successors. In the Book of Revelation there are two beasts, she explained, one red and the other white. One is to rule the world and the other is the false church. 'The first must be the Communists,' she said, 'they're the only ones who want to dominate the whole world, and the other must be ecumenism.'

> They want to get the *gringos* out first and then the [Colombian evange-licals] so that they can get control over everyone. A cooperative is just the thing for them to get started. They tell everyone to buy and sell there, they get all that under their control, and then they have it. That's what this Jaramillo did, he got the Indians into the cooperative and then told them to attack the white ranches. I told them not to join, I warned there would be trouble because the *junta* is directed by this non-believer who has other purposes. Join a cooperative with other believers, I told them. This is where the revolutions always start.[26]

In the wake of the Planas uprising all concerned, except perhaps Indians, anticipated another Indian uprising. Speculation centred on the Andes of south-western Colombia and, in particular, the Regional Indian Council of the Cauca (CRIC). Founded in 1971 by the Paez, a people famous for their military prowess, CRIC won the support of neighbouring Indian and non-Indian groups, became a model for organizers in other parts of the country, and has suffered accordingly. Its tactics date to early in the century, when the Paez faced the overwhelming firepower of a centralized government colonizing their homeland. Since *resguardo* (reserve) land was protected by law, the Paez turned to the courts and, like other small farmers, joined leagues to pressure officialdom. Following the *Violencia,* during which they fought and starved for the Liberal Party, they again faced a regime which supposedly was committed to land reform. Court and bureaucratic appeals having proved fruitless, CRIC encouraged the government to enforce the law by mounting unarmed invasions of stolen *resguardo* land and submitting to mass arrest. In a few years it recovered thousands of hectares. CRIC also joined the *Asociacion Nacional de Usuarios Campesinos* (ANUC, National Peasants Association), organized co-operative farms and stores, started to train its own bilingual teachers, and eroded the client vote with which the local landlord/politicians legitimized their rule.[27] Crying guerrillas, drug smugglers and subversion, the landlords unleashed gun thugs. The armed forces militarized the zone. By 1979 more than 45 CRIC leaders had been murdered without a single perpetrator brought to trial.[28] Members in official custody were tortured, a practice denounced by the local Catholic bishop.[29]

Evangelical missionaries have kept silence on the persecution: their churches are growing as a sanctuary from government violence, for which they, like the landlords who hire the assassins, blame subversives. Evangelicals with 'communist' political loyalties are to be found in the region; to the north, the army has even accused evangelical sects of sharing their tithe with the *Fuerzas Armadas Revolucionarias de Colombia*.[30] But among the Paez and neighbouring Guambiano, Protestantism has become identified with opposition to CRIC and collaboration with government schemes predicated on landlord interests. The Christian and Missionary Alliance is the principal evangelical mission: when I visited its compound near Silvia in 1975, Paez and Guambiano teachers said that they refused to support CRIC because it denied the (evangelical) God and did not respect the government. 'The government treats us badly but God has ordered that we obey,' one quoted Romans 13:1.[31] SIL's Guambiano translator felt that political militancy would destroy indigenous culture, a position I encountered elsewhere in the branch. He felt that Indians should continue to buy land outside their reserves rather than fight to restore them. In 1980 the translator was forced to leave when many Guambiano mounted a CRIC land invasion.

The Vaupes

Following the atrocities at Planas, translators and priests had some long talks. From the priests I gathered that their counterparts were unable to understand the implications of U.S. power in Colombia. the government they worked for and their own aspirations for Indians. From translators I gathered that their rivals were embarked on a dangerous course, stirring up Indians for political ends which would only rebound to their harm.

The new era in mission rivalry dawned earliest in Vaupes Territory among the Eastern Tucanoans, who have been disputed by Catholics and Protestants since the 1940s. The Colombian order entrusted with this corner of the Amazon jungle, the Javerianos de Yarumal, had been founded by the right-wing nationalist Msgr. Miguel Angel Builes. During the *Violencia* he called Protestantism 'an imperialist fifth column' to enslave Latin America to the United States.[32] Since a determined SIL distinguished 15 languages in the Vaupes, it assigned more teams than in any other Catholic jurisdiction. The Catholics responded with the theology of liberation. The power struggle stimulated the Tucanoans to move from shaman-led millennialism to evangelical religion and their first experiments with the council politics of tradition, unity and land. It also became a cradle of the national opposition to SIL.

The multilingualism and marriage exchanges of the 11,500 Tucanoans in the Colombian Vaupes justify considering them as a single people. When the National Front brought thousands of settlers into the western Vaupes (now Guaviare) in the late 1960s, the new road halted at that point. Except for a small number of rubber hunters and homesteaders, plus a missionary for perhaps every 150 Indians, the eastern Vaupes remained Tucanoan. They maintained a hunting and gardening economy, supplemented by labour for *patrones* and missionaries to obtain trade goods. Their relative isolation was subject to the usual pressures, however: if Brazil extends its highway to the border, Colombia may feel it has to build its own. The government has contracted for uranium exploration. And in the late 1970s, the cocaine mafias arrived with guns, massive quantities of trade goods and security forces in train. In some cases the mafias seemed to be using SIL's airstrips and, for their labour force, drafting some of the very Indians whose consumer appetites it had stimulated.

The first enduring Catholic mission was launched by Dutch Monfortians in the early 1900s. They destroyed *malocas* or communal houses, concentrated Tucanoans around stations and campaigned against their religious ceremonies. As the Javerianos undertook the expansion of this regime in 1949, Sophie Muller reached one of the most hard-hit Tucanoan groups, the Cubeo. A stiff Catholic blockade notwithstanding, the despair following a measles epidemic brought many Cubeo into the arms of the New Tribes Mission, whose many prohibitions — against tobacco, *chicha* beer, coca, hallucinogens, traditional dancing and singing — were part of a close, protective paternalism. The many Tucanoans to the south remained under Javeriano patronage; the Cubeo sorted themselves into evangelical and more traditionalist 'Catholic' villages; and a generation later the two remain peoples apart. [33] 'They stopped being Indians', a traditionalist mourned.*[34]

The Javerianos received the first SIL women cordially. But while both sides have claimed amicable relations during the 1960s, branch members relate how the more conservative priests tried to block new teams. The translators persisted, moving out from Catholic stations and switching villages when forced to leave. By 1970 ten teams were at work. The Javerianos found themselves at a disadvantage: dozens of religious infiltrators were mastering languages into which few of the Catholic staff had even ventured. Their so-called linguistics institute had a better logistics system and enough government backing to override Catholic protest. The Javeriano hold on Tucanoan loyalty was tenuous: movements like Sophie Muller's might emerge from SIL ouposts.

---

* They 'only want to become like white people' other Baniwa say of New Tribes crentes ('believers') across the border in Brazil. Baniwa millennial protest against white exploitation surfaced well into the 20th Century, Robin Wright reports, often led by shamans surnamed Christo, and disciples associated with Catholic saints. Although crentes remain uneasy about whites — in 1977 elders warned that a new military airstrip would take them from their homes — the young may go to some lengths to imitate merchants and missionaries. Literacy and Western medicine figure prominently in the new religion; villages bear names like America, Canada and Nazare. Crentes appear to maintain traditional exchange among themselves, particularly during the Muller-initiated conferencia (revival) circuits, but insist on cash sales to their kin in Catholic villages, who are still sometimes referred to as 'demons'. There is a 'half-crente' position, however: its adherents indulge in banned substances and some are known for their folk healing abilities.[35]

By fulfilling its unspoken task to the government, the branch was threatening the authority of a powerful Concordat mission.

Not coincidentally, after 1967 a new bishop and young priests began to reform their establishment in light of the theology of liberation. In Colombia this tendency's leading exponent was the soon suppressed Golconda Movement whose ranking member, Msgr. Gerardo Valencia Cano, had been the first Javeriano bishop in the Vaupes. Valencia's tenure as bishop of Buenaventura ended in 1972, when he and the other progressive in the Colombian hierachy died in plane crashes.[36] In the Vaupes, Msgr. Belarmino Correa carried on the new mission of *concientizacion* (community consciousness-raising). The Javerianos began to plead no contest to the defensive religious dualism of their charges, Catholic to outsiders and Tucanoan among Tucanoan. In 1969 and 1970 they organized 'Indian week' gatherings where, to the disgust of evangelical missionaries, Tucanoans danced their old dances and took *yaje*, the hallucinogen at the core of their traditions. To match the Protestants in cultivating Indian leadership, the Catholics hired their boarding school graduates to teach primary school in outlying communities. While not bilingual by SIL standards, the teachers used their own languages to make the Spanish curriculum more intelligible. Finally, the Javerianos organized the Tucanoans for political objectives. The first, more successful campaign was against the *patrones,* who were in straits due to declining rubber prices. In 1970 the Javerianos enlisted Tucanoans to suppress debt-peonage and set up co-operatives for those who wanted to extract and sell their own rubber.

The same year, the Javerianos turned their attention to SIL. After three new teams arrived along the Papuri River in the heart of Catholic domain, JAARS pilots found oil barrels and cattle on Catholic airstrips. One of the flights was carrying Brian Moser of Granada Television, who entitled his film on the two missions 'The War of the Gods'. In October 1970, as the campaign against the *patrones* led to the same kind of Red-baiting which had precipitated the Planas atrocities, Msgr. Correa lambasted the government's failure to protect Indians and their cultures. He also damned the contract with SIL, calling it a colonial force in the service of the United States.[37]

Escalation of mission-inspired conflict among the Tucanoans brought it to national attention. The non-religious SIL claimed to be innocent of any sectarianism. The Javeriano staff, their Tucanoan teachers and students pointed to religious strife among the Cubeo and tried to extract SIL teams from their villages. From 1969 to 1975 six teams — Guanano, Piratapuyo, Jupda-Macu, Tucano, Tuyuca and Desano — were dislocated. As best as I could determine, in three cases the villagers took the initiative; in others Catholic missionaries or their Tucanoan teachers were responsible, thus antagonizing SIL's following; and in only one was SIL's work ended.*

---

* In 1969- 70 the Guanano at the Catholic station of Via Fatima turned against a SIL team, which relocated. In 1971 the Piratapuyo at the Catholic station of Teresita

However successful the Javeriano reforms, their mission would remain the local seat of authority until such time as the government asserted itself. Were Tucanoan grievances, *concientizacion* and the example of CRIC to give rise to a political organization, it undoubtedly would come into conflict with the Javerianos. In 1973 the mission's Tucanoan teachers and boarding school students indeed organized the Regional Indian Council of the Vaupes (CRIVA), predicated not on Catholicism but tradition and cultural continuity. The following year CRIVA demanded that SIL withdraw from the territory, after a dispute in a Carapana village: an absent translator's supporters had ejected two of the Catholic mission's Carapana teachers for speaking against him.[40] CRIVA was also preoccupied by mysterious official survey teams and boarding school education, which led to confrontations with the mission. But the Javerianos supported CRIVA and, in the opinion of some, came to dominate it through teachers and students who did not necessarily get along with their elders.

'We know that if we are not united we cannot defend ourselves,' a Cubeo told *Alternativa* in 1975. 'But the pastors tell our evangelical brothers that we Catholics are demons because we smoke, chew coca, dance *carrizo* and wear feathers at our festivals.' The Catholic mission he accused of exploitation – with its purchase of handicrafts, hire of Indians to tend cattle, and stores. The Cubeo and his associates were about to make another attempt to organize a Union of Cubeo Indians (UDIC), at which the Catholics hoped to come to an agreement with the evangelicals. In the self-determination statement issued by that congress, UDIC condemned the missionary practice of Satanizing tradition and ended on the following note: 'In regard to the problem of the different religions . . . we are resolved to prevent it from blocking community programs. The religious question should be the private affair of each person.' At its second congress in 1976, UDIC decided that SIL ought to leave.[41]

For the time being, independent organizations seemed to have little chance of challenging the missions. Patronage was far more important to the Tucanoans

* (cont.) banished another team, owing to unfair business transactions which a colleague attributed to inexperience; the assignment was abandoned. In 1972 a junior member of the Javeriano staff burned the house of the Jupda-Macu team in its absence. According to investigators, the Jupda 'said that they had not had any part in the burning of the house and had even opposed those who did it. They petitioned the commission to ask the [SIL] women to return.'[38] Since the Jupda live astride the border, they were reassigned to the Brazilian branch. At the Catholic station of Acaricuara in June 1973, Tucanoan teachers, students and a priest turned back the Tucano team at the airstrip. According to SIL's Tuyuca translator, the priest went to the nearby village of Los Angeles and, in her presence, told the Tuyuca that they would have to expel her or break relations with the Catholic mission. The next year, Los Angeles and the Acari-cuara villagers welcomed back the SIL women. Soon two more teams moved into in the same area. When I visited Acaricuara in January 1976, the Tucano corregidor held a gathering for my questions. The sense of the meeting was that the 1973 blockade had been the affair of the Catholic boarding school, not the year-round residents of Acaricuara.[39]

than Christianity: when investigators for the National Council on Indian Policy visited SIL-occupied communities in 1972, they found leaders of seven — four in the Vaupes away from Catholic stations — very much in favour of the translators for reasons which read like a catalogue of their good works. The translators learned the languages; taught people how to read and write them; gave sick people medicine, sometimes flew them to the hospital, and taught how to extract teeth; provided new livestock and seeds; sold trade goods; and flew products to market in airplanes. In contrast, Tucanoans around the Catholic stations said that they opposed SIL for reasons like 'We're Catholics' or 'They come to impose dollar politics.'[42] Such arguments must have seemed rather abstract to the Tucanoans enjoying North American bounty. To attract the rewards of Bible translation, communities have even offered to clear airstrips.[43] But few of the SIL following had decided for Christ by 1974; except for the Cubeo, in each of the Vaupes languages the branch reported at best several believers.[44]

If opposition to the Catholic regime contributed to SIL's support, the agreement underpinning the CRIVA-Javeriano alliance was that Tucanoans would not face the disruption of more sectarian religion. This meeting of minds emerged in the Desano village which, in August 1975, asked its SIL couple to leave. According to the translator, a community leader explained that 'they' — the Catholic mission — had made it known that the village could not have a school unless he left. The Javerianos, the translator added, had frustrated his own attempts to set up a school. When I visited the village in December, the SIL airstrip seemed to dwarf the small collection of houses. The children were playing with home-made toy airplanes whose propellors spun in the wind. 'It's always a bother to have someone like this around,' a Catholic teacher home on furlough explained. 'The people always divide among themselves as the linguist does favours, brings gifts and pays wages, so that people on one side of the village are friends with the linguist, while on the other side they're friends with the teacher.' About 1971, the translator explained to a Lomalinda assembly, he was surprised when the village held a *yaje* dance, which he supposed they had given up. 'Even though the village is tranquil and they say they are Catholics,' continued the translator, 'this is what is deep in their souls, and we can see it in their reaction to medicine, to the primers, to any new thing that will better their lives.' The village leader who asked the translator to leave had a different perspective: 'The Catholics, the mission was here first and now we are with them, we do not want to change our religion again. . . . We do not want the Bible in Desano because it is the same as the Catholics have, we do not need it.'[45] This man understood the purpose of the Desano New Testament — to undermine his group's claim to be Catholic and the tradition this protected — and opposed it. While the SIL missionary was able to continue visiting and translating with his Lomalinda convert, the other Desano continued to reject evangelical religion.

The Appeal to the State

In December 1970 *El Tiempo* of Bogota reported the Javeriano case against their rivals. Noting that the priests were still lords of the manor, the correspondent treated their charges against SIL — hiding its evangelical aims, failing to train Colombian linguists, evading government controls on aircraft, Americanization of Indians, an 'independent republic' on national territory — with scepticism.[46] The branch brought a governor, generals, a congressional commission, high-level functionaries, social scientists and journalists out to Lomalinda for the base tour. They were impressed. In February 1971, *El Tiempo* championed SIL and the Vaupes rubber *patrones* against the Javerianos. The priests were accused of inciting poor rubber hunters and Indians against the government in order to capture the trade and make Indians their slaves. They were attacking SIL since its efforts to improve the lives of Indians were, without the slightest intent, threatening the Catholic empire.[47]

'Unfortunately', Clarence Church reported to the SIL/WBT biennial conference in May 1971, the Javeriano accusations had provoked a congressional counterattack on the Catholic Treaty on Missions. At the same time, an official commission of linguists and anthropologists studying SIL was being elevated to the status of National Council on Indian Policy. 'Interestingly enough,' Church reported, while there had been an attempt to make this body 'some sort of a permanent control over the work of SIL, our friends on the Commission, as well as the Minister of the Interior himself, made sure that this did not happen.' Church had reason to be pleased, but he sensed more trouble ahead. While there were 'no crowds in the streets yelling "Yankee go home!" ' nationalism 'with its several implications' was 'very much the mode' and 'the time is potentially short.'[48]

Planas campaigners had called attention to the fact that a Protestant mission was operating under a government contract parallelling the Treaty on Missions. They also took note of its potential for pursuing commercial aims or gathering intelligence.[49] In October 1971 there was a call for abolition of both mission agreements.[50] Politicians from frontier areas and the Ministry of Interior came to SIL's defense, proposing a new, reformed contract. 'More training for the country's professionals must be included,' branch director Forrest Zander explained. '. . . The new agreement must be more nationalist.'[51] The National Council on Indian Policy sent a team of anthropologists and linguists to inspect SIL in the field.

Their calm and measured report of March 1972 praised SIL's linguistic and humanitarian work, but it recommended more participation by Colombian professionals. That, rather than just linguistic training, was one warning flag. But for SIL, the most ominous recommendation was a ban on its unspoken evangelism. The commission's reasoning was simple: deducing that 'moral improvement' was the ultimate goal of the entity behind SIL, the Wycliffe Bible Translators it suggested that since the Constitution guarantees freedom of conscience, the state should not contract for 'moral improvement' with any entity.[52] It would have been a telling point in the United States.

Based on the commission's report, the Council on Indian Policy recommended that SIL be allowed a maximum of four more years; that its personnel be replaced by Colombians during this period; and that, if it continued to evangelize, its contract be revoked immediately. These suggestions were presented to the Minister of Interior, who ignored them.[53] The ministry also lost interest in the council and this was apparently its last accomplishment. On the branch's tenth anniversary, in October 1972, George Cowan was received by President Misael Pastrana.[54] While the Catholic Treaty on Missions was being replaced by more restrictive agreements, SIL had protected the autonomy it required for business as usual — at a certain cost. Opposition had widened from crusading Catholic clergy to middle-of-the-road academics. Now it was obvious that the government's review process was bankrupt and that there was no way to reform SIL. In the Ministry of Interior disguised North American missionaries counted more than Colombian indigenists.

They Divide Us Among Institutes

The sparring in Bogota caught the majority of translators at an early stage of their work, the cultivation of language informants as future church leaders. Hoping to anchor Indians around church sites, the branch proceeded to ingratiate itself with a far-flung multitude during the same years in which it became a national pariah. From the early 1970s to 1980 more than 1,000 native people were flown to Lomalinda, trained for six weeks in new agricultural methods, and returned with breeding stock under their arms. 'Here at this place thus he gave to me,' a Cuaiquer graduate stated, 'one pig, that is, one sow, one boar he gave to me. This is a good breed, they say. It's a pretty breed. This is not from here, they say. It is brought from afar. For breeding it was sent that we might have that they all among us might breed their own.'[55]

The more successful translators had been incorporated into the kinship system, would be defended by their followings, and had converted a few of their guests at Lomalinda, other missionaries usually having been responsible for the congregations in 11 languages.[56] The less successful were numerous even before the anti-imperialist wave: at the end of 1972, nine of the branch's 35 teams were at an impasse due to illness, lack of a field site or informants.[57] Along the western *cordillera* of the Andes the work nearly succumbed to physical adversity and Indian distrust: the Catio team, for example, required seven years to take up residence in a village.[58] Among the Tunebo, in the eastern *cordillera* of the Andes, the translators faced the conviction that paper and writing were related to disease. When informants returned from Lomalinda, they were divested of their religious baggage in a purification ritual.

The tension resulting from SIL's campaigns for information and neophytes provided ample material for national controversy. One mine of scandal was Putumayo Territory, where North Americans have performed a trail of good deeds along a militarized road leading to North American-operated oil fields. The Camsa, who lost most of their land to the Capuchin Mission

179

depicted in Victor Daniel Bonilla's *Servants of God or Masters of Men?*, showed little interest in the evangelical alternative; the SIL women therefore turned to children, one of whom was eventually imprisoned for burning down their house. Two of the Camsa visitors to Lomalinda, the convicted arsonist and Crispin Chicunque, are unusual in denouncing their treatment; more often informants say they enjoyed their stay. According to Crispin Chicunque, he was nearly 11 years old when, having been enticed by the superior technology of North American toys, his turn came for Lomalinda. He translated material into a tape recorder, spent most of his time in a room (until 1974 informants were not supposed to wander around the base or talk with informants from other languages), and emphasizes that for his trouble he received a pair of tennis shoes. At home, states Chicunque, the SIL women opposed *Carnaval* because of the drunkenness and fighting; urged the Camsa to bathe daily; told the parents they ought to give their children coffee (which must be purchased in a store) rather than *chicha* beer; campaigned against the distinctive Camsa haircut, by distributing pants and saying 'Now all you need is a haircut'; urged people to have only two or three children; and dispensed pills suspected of containing sterilizing agents.[59] (Following a sterilization scare several years before, the SIL nurse's practice seemed widely appreciated in 1975). Chicunque's successor liked Lomalinda so much that he went three times, for a total of one year, and wanted to go to the United States.[60] Three years after frustration led to the assault on his employers' premises, an elder recalled that he had returned from Lomalinda unwilling to live with his mother, work in the gardens and respect traditional ways.[61]

To the east, Siona elders told visiting students that Alvaro Wheeler had taken three of them to the United States, 'to display us like animals' at fund-raising events.[62] When the students publicized their findings and tried to raise the consciousness of the community, much of it seems to have rallied around the translator. Anxious to avoid further trouble, one of the travellers told me that he had enjoyed the United States and thought highly of its local representative. Another evidently felt exploited: Wheeler told them that they had raised enough money to purchase one and a half airplanes. Still another elder recalled various offenses — Wheeler had introduced and established himself as a linguist (standard SIL procedure), then pushed religion until the Siona (who claim to be good Catholics) asked a bishop to mend his ways, and been stingy in his accounts — but spoke warmly of him. Not long before the translator had saved the life of his son.[63] Two years later the Wheelers were soliciting prayer for their first converts 'because the pressures of the tribal customs make it extremely difficult for them to not participate in these as they always have.'[64]

Each group which benefited from SIL's good works could look forward to this rupture. 'They divide us among institutes such as the Summer Institute of Linguistics, among religions, among political parties,' Arhuaco stated. 'We do not have enough people to divide so many.'[65] In September 1974, the Indian commission of ANUC, including CRIC and members of a dozen other groups, came to the following conclusions:

We study the way in which the evangelical missions and the Summer Institute of Linguistics works. They claim to be interested only in the Bible and come to study our languages. In this way they can penetrate easier into communities which are already forewarned against the traditional methods of the Church.

But in many areas we have removed the Summer Institute of Linguistics from our lands because we have realized that it is they, also, who are destroying our culture, tradition and customs. As well as this, they exploit their knowledge of ourselves, of our lands and the riches of our earth in order to help the *gringos* who follow them to open oil wells, to extract timber and gold, etc.

The divisions which have been established within our communities, between Indians who adhere to the missions and to the evangelists, is used to keep us distracted, to keep our eyes covered so that we do not see how our real enemies are depriving us and destroying us.

In many areas we have observed that what we need is unity amongst the Indians whether they be Catholic or evangelists; and so we have begun to fight in unity to defend our land and our culture. In other communities, as we begin to organize ourselves, we must understand this issue clearly.

Our experience has shown that we should not attack one another because we profess one or another religion. On the contrary, we must reinforce our unity and strengthen our organization in order to win our struggles. And in the struggle we shall rediscover the roots of our own beliefs and traditions.[66]

While Wycliffe expects to confront Satan in every group it enters, he was getting rather well organized. Accustomed to isolated resistance by stubborn villagers, a shaman or an old-fashioned priest, the Summer Institute was in danger of being levered out of communities around the country. In each of the contests, translators detected outside agitators. As for Colombians, they had learned that SIL was unwilling to compromise its plans. When part of a community opposed the translators, another faction frequently defended it. Even when a group made clear that it wanted nothing to do with Bible translation, members persisted in defiance of evil powers which were not of this world. These conflicts fuelled the campaign to expel them from the country.

Occult Power

For its criminal reputation the Colombian branch may, in some measure, thank army generals. The branch had located its base in a region where insurgency is a folk tradition and contraband is a leading occupation, 60 kilometres from the fabled, reputedly mineral-rich Sierra Macarena. Mysterious or illicit activities, often by *gringos,* are constantly reported to the authorities. With the Summer Institute in the public eye, its base where several hundred North Americans administered their own affairs, its airplanes ferrying teams and their equipment throughout the hinterlands, rumour multiplied rumour.

General Abraham Varon Valencia had yet to be tainted by drug scandal when, in December 1973, as armed forces commander he sent a confidential memo to the Minister of Defense. Financed by an 'Instituto Wyckliff', SIL was suspected of clandestine activities, chiefly mineral exploration and extraction, throughout eastern Colombia.[67] Five months later, Inspector General Jose Joaquin Matallana, sworn enemy of guerrillas, corrupt officials and smugglers, landed troops on the Lomalinda airstrip. They sealed the base, and frogmen scoured an adjacent lake for evidence of uranium mining. Far and wide the commission helicoptered in search of the undercover SIL.

When the press obtained the Matallana report, in June 1975, it contained a number of surprises, First, the commission had found neither 'proof nor sufficient indications' that SIL engaged in covert activities. The commission even mentioned its 'excellent opinion' of members' integrity. Yet it had found suspicious excavations in the vicinity of a translator: since he seemed to be double-talking, it left this question dangling.

Second, the commission drew on NACLA anti-imperialism to make a nationalist case against the operation. It assailed the dual identity, contending that SIL had deceived the government in 1962 and failed to honour its contract. The programme created 'ideological confusion' among Indians, divided communities, and destroyed cultural values. There had been no national participation and, by its very nature, SIL was beyond government supervision. Not least because of the possible danger to national security, the commission recommended that SIL either be given a year to leave the country or be made a 'mixed institution', 50% of whose personnel would be Colombian, dedicated exclusively to science.[68]

Third, a year after a senior army general reached these conclusions, SIL was still in the Ministry of Interior, at its base in the *llanos* and in native communities, as if nothing had changed. Clearly there was more here than even the highest level military commission had been able to uncover.

Something had changed, however: the Interior Ministry was about to give SIL a new contract.[69] Not long before the new director of the Indian Affairs Division, Jose Gutierrez, had resigned in protest against his dependency: superiors had prevented him from exercising any authority over it, as they well might. From what Gutierrez could see, a foreign religious mission had no business in the Interior Ministry in the first place.[70] It was in the wake of these events, between mid-1975 and early 1976, that virtually all Colombian linguists and anthropologists, their departments and associations demanded SIL's expulsion. [71] At first some linguists suggested a transition, in the hope of learning from translators' experience, maintaining the channels of communication they had opened with native people, and avoiding disruption of necessary services.[72] As SIL again confirmed what Enrique Santos Calderon called its 'occult power' in government, they lost patience.[73]

The base labour pool, Puerto Lleras, produced another affliction. In November 1974 a young politician named Oscar Beltran prompted the town council to conduct its own investigation of Lomalinda. They found little or nothing amiss, declared their sleuth *persona non grata* and, during the congressional denunciations, proclaimed SIL's many services to the community. After the Matallana report appeared, Beltran claimed to have elicited dramatic revelations from the Lomalinda livestock expert: SIL had not only tracked down Che Guevara in Bolivia but supplied the aerial reconnaissance necessary to find the *llanos'* own Dumar Aljure, a Liberal ex-guerrilla who had controlled the Puerto Lleras region until his death in 1968.[74] It was an implausible story – the army had killed Aljure in or around his house, a known locale, after he had failed to deliver the vote in the last election – but it joined the press barrage.[75]

In November 1975, Agence France Presse reported that SIL was being expelled from Colombia, *El Tiempo* and United Press International that it was about to be given its (per the 1962 contract) one year dismissal notice.[76] These errors owed something to the hemming and hawing of SIL's friend in the Interior Ministry, Secretary General Hernan Villamarin, in reaction to two events. One was a vague 13 October pledge by President Alfonso Lopez Michelsen (1974-78) to nationalize linguistics.[77] The other was denunciation of SIL by a failing opposition party, the *Alianza Nacional Popular,* in congress. Marshalling copious documentation, Representative Napoleon Peralta accused the Bible translators of every offense known to imperialism, plus some which probably have yet to be invented.[78] Brandishing U.S. military maps with extraordinary security designations for the area, he went so far as to link Lomalinda to a secret North American rocket base in the Sierra Macarena.[79]

General Varon Valencia, now Defense Minister, and Interior Minister Cornelio Reyes came to SIL's defense, largely by denying the existence of the rocket base.[80] As a large landowner in Planas and champion of the Cauca landlords, assassinating CRIC leaders, Reyes believed that SIL's opponents were, in the main, subversives. 'The impresarios of the campaign,' he wrote as opposition swelled again three years later, 'are nearly always the same, headed by seditious anthropology professors at the National University, Marxists naturally. . . . The accusers are precisely those who identify themselves with the republic of Pato-Guayabero [a guerrilla stronghold], which wants to expand into the [Sierra] Macarena. . . .'[81]

Although the U.S. embassy minimized its interest in SIL, Ambassador Viron Vaky reportedly took up the matter with General Matallana. In July 1975, Vaky cabled Washington that, despite the lack of incriminating evidence, the general remained 'convinced that the SIL camp is involved in smuggling activities.' Following President Lopez' nationalization pledge in October, Vaky cabled that it 'may have taken the issue away' from the congressional opposition. 'The Lopez approach gives the appearance of a unilateral [government] decision, while in effect implementing the basic terms of the long-standing proposal for a new government agreement with SIL. The president's action will, we believe, eventually prove an effective way of removing the troublesome SIL question from the public eye.'

Nationalization, then, meant whatever one wanted to hear: it was a more mysterious way of going about business as usual. In September, the Interior Ministry mentioned that, under a more severe contract, the operation would become 50% Colombian.[82] As a national entity was organized, Villamarin explained two weeks later, SIL itself would be replaced in no more than four years.[83] And as Ambassador Vaky cabled on 20 November, the day after Villamarin confirmed that a Colombian Institute of Linguistics was under study and that SIL would be given a one year dismissal notice instead of a new contract: ' "Colombianization" .... is essentially what the SIL has proposed for its new contract. The Lopez move may, accordingly, provide an arrangement satisfactory to both parties while providing an appearance of [government] action that should placate most SIL critics here.'[84] Cameron Townsend visited Bogota twice, during the congressional tempest and then in February 1976, when he secured an endorsement from Minister of Education Hernando Duran Dussan, another large landowner in the *llanos*.[85] Despite setbacks — SIL's inability to rally Colombian brethren, visa problems with the Foreign Ministry, an official bilingual school subsidy which failed to materialize, a constitutional suit against the contract in the highest court of the land — by early 1978 the branch again hoped to sign a new agreement.[86]

Now, however, there was an impeccable competing project. SIL's official allies had argued that there was nothing to replace it, which would remain true so long as the government refused to finance such a programme. For some time, therefore, a caucus from the Ministries of Interior and Education, the Department of National Planning, and the Anthropology Institute had been discussing the proper administrative solution. Its argument against SIL was two-fold: 1) the government and universities were capable of meeting the needs of native communities, and 2) religious proselytism contradicted the official policy of respect for Indian tradition. Proposing to give the branch its contractual one year notice, the caucus stressed that its plan was within existing budgets.

President Lopez reportedly liked the scheme and, in July 1978, asked Interior Minister Alfredo Araujo to notify SIL of dismissal. But Araujo was displeased that the plan had gone to the President through Minister of Education Rafael Rivas rather than himself. That same month, in keeping with the ever-pending proposed contract stipulating gradual withdrawal, the Interior Ministry's Roberto Garcia ordered SIL to withdraw from the Sierra Nevada and noted that it could expect the same in the Vaupes and Amazonas. Araujo had the Garcia order revoked and deliberately delayed the Lopez directive until the newly elected president, Julio Turbay Ayala (1978-82), took office a few weeks later.

Unlike his predecessors, the new Interior Minister, German Zea, gave SIL's official opponents a hearing. On 7 November, 11 days before 900 North American sectarians killed each other and themselves at Jonestown, Guyana, Foreign Minister Diego Uribe said that a plan to 'finish with' SIL would be ready by the year's end.[87] On 13 November, Zea set up a commission: 15 days later its members, including Indian Affairs chief Julian Narvaez, reiterated that SIL ought to be given its one year notice.[88] Following Jonestown, the armed forces announced that Defense Minister Luis Camacho Leyva would join Zea in drafting a protocol of expulsion within two weeks.[89] Duran Dussan, now mayor of Bogota, reportedly took SIL's case to President Turbay who, like Zea, subsequently granted Cameron Townsend an audience. No more was heard from cabinet ministers about expelling SIL.

It was a crime, Townsend told *El Tiempo,* for the folkloric riches of native languages to die without anyone to study them. The Institute's linguists had discovered a relationship between languages in the Bolivian lowlands, Colombia and the southern United States! In view of the linguists' many accomplishments in preserving languages and elucidating grammatical marvels, he just did not understand how they had been misunderstood in Colombia. Still, against his own inclinations, he was going to clarify some aspects of the programme. There were, of course, the labours parallel to the strictly linguistic aspect. He was proud that witchcraft, alcohol, hatred, massacre, aggression, and the monstrous destruction of deformed infants had been replaced by the love, fraternity, understanding and spirituality which grow out of the translated divine Word. He recalled the case of the Cuibas of Casanare, whose artistic temperament the linguists had so encouraged that they now received tourists with paintings instead of arrows. Could all this be bad? If all that had been said were not so unjust, it would make him laugh. When the linguists finished their work within ten or fifteen years, everyone would realize how unjustly they had been treated.[90] The following year anthropologists, politicians, military officers and journalists again petitioned for SIL's expulsion, to no avail.[91]

Satan's Kingdom

> It is easier to find a Freemason than a defender of the Summer Institute of Linguistics.
>
> Daniel Samper, *El Tiempo,* September 14, 1978.

To Colombians following the case, a leading mystery was how, through crisis after crisis, the Summer Institute had managed to stay in the country. After the Jonestown massacre the press was shocked to report that SIL was just one of a hundred or more foreign, mostly North American sects operating within the national frontiers.[92] To hear Wycliffe tell the story, its Colombian branch was the victim of one of the most appalling sequences of treachery and betrayal in recorded history. The conviction grew: Wycliffe was the victim of Satan and his children. As Clarence Church reminded home supporters after the Cameron Townsend-Jim Jones charges,

the people who write . . . these things — the people who lend their names

> to advisory committees, and those who oppose the Gospel in such
> astute ways, are following the pattern of the one who was, according to
> the Lord Jesus Christ, a liar from the beginning. . . . This is Satan's world,
> and we who know the Lord have been snatched out of his kingdom. . . .
> those who have not yet been rescued can be devilishly clever in their
> attacks upon God's family. . . .[93]

I left Lomalinda with a vivid impression of sincerity and goodwill, and
naivete and intransigence. Members were bewildered and embittered by the
vendetta against their methods. 'They come out here, we show them around,
and they seem very impressed,' an administrator said, 'but by the time the
article comes out you wouldn't know they've been here. Someone's been
telling them what to do.' 'They have their own version of the truth,' a
JAARS technician added, 'and that's the one they print. Some people don't
understand that we're here to help. It's just not in their culture that people do
something only for good.'

'The organization is stupid politically,' a translator observed, 'in the sense
that it does things that make sense in terms of SIL's work but look very bad
to Colombians ' — like the DC-3 transport, when other North Americans used
cargo planes to ferry illegal substances.[94] Fundamentally, however, the branch
was trapped by the dual identity. While many members were eager to explain
their work, they were condemned to do so in the language of Cameron
Townsend. 'It is correct that we are connected with the Wycliffe Bible Translators because we are believers in the Lord,' government liaison William Nyman
Jr. told *El Tiempo* in June 1975. 'The Institute and the Wycliffe Bible Translators are the same people, but it is a question of two corporations dedicated
to different things. Ours is a scientific organization.'[95] Dual identity nonsense
concealed a cruel dilemma: were members to respond to the crisis as disinterested technicians, more than willing to leave when they were no longer welcome,
or as faith missionaries, fulfilling the prophecy of the Book of Revelation?
William Nyman stood on divine right. 'The powers of hell won't move us from
this country,' he laughed, 'not the powers of the left or the powers of the
right, until God tells us to and then we will. . . . We have friends! We're not
going to be leaving the country.'[96]

The branch politics pitted a 'conservative' majority against 'liberals,' plus a
few 'radicals' who wanted to abandon the base, move to a city, and send most
of the support workers packing. Since nearly everyone felt indispensable, it
was decided that the people at the base, not the base itself, were the source of
any failing on SIL's part; therefore Christian love, rededication and service
would eventually convince Colombians of the group's good intentions. At the
December 1975 branch conference two-thirds of the translators voted against
the re-election of branch director Forrest Zander, a former JAARS pilot; the
support personnel backed him in a two-thirds vote for the status quo. But there
would be an end to calling every criticism of SIL Communist-inspired, a
translator explained, because many were justified. Burglars began laying siege
to Lomalinda, and in August 1976 five members narrowly escaped a bomb

explosion outside the group house in Bogota.[97]

The most hard-fought issue was the integration of Colombians into the work, not just as menial labour and assistants but as linguists. The issue was also a farce, the result of years of mutually convenient misunderstanding between SIL officials and their politician friends. While even the Ministry of Interior was talking about 50% Colombian participation, adversaries pointed out that a religious sect could not be expected to welcome Colombian specialists. 'Every Colombian who joins the Institute,' Nyman told me in response to the government's 50% claim, 'is going to have to be a believer in Jesus Christ.' More to the point, at Lomalinda Colombian linguists learned that they could collaborate with SIL only if they agreed not to interefere with its evangelical goals. As Napoleon Peralta asked in congress, did SIL have the right to impose this condition when its contract did not authorize evangelism in the first place? [98]

Conservative members and their Colombian friends tried to dismiss indigenization on the grounds that, without an appropriately spiritual motivation, Colombians would not endure the discomfort of the field like SIL translators. Now that indigenization was supposedly a requirement, Colombian evangelicals were the obvious solution. But the branch would have to overcome long-standing distrust in these quarters, and many members felt that Colombian translators would be a financial burden. Since national churches would be reluctant to finance Bible translation as practiced by SIL, any deficit would have to be taken up by North American churches, who preferred to finance North Americans. Then too, Colombian translators might have to be remunerated at a level proximate to that of the North Americans, not of the 79 base employees whose monthly payroll and subsidy totalled about $3,190.* By 1976, nonetheless, some members were insisting that the branch had to offer Colombian evangelicals money. That brought them face to face with an even more fundamental difficulty: that many of their colleagues feared Colombians of any description and wanted as little to do with them as possible. At the close of a decade of controversy, after innumerable promises of national participation, the branch had introduced citizens into two or three languages.

* These figures (a 1975 monthly payroll of 80,300 pesos plus 25,000 pesos for transport subsidy, etc., where 33 pesos equal $1) were presented to President Lopez by the town council and citizenry of Puerto Lleras, an an index of SIL's importance to the community. Lomalinda is one of the town's principal industries and probably its single largest employer. The average monthly pay plus subsidy of $40 per worker was probably attractive for the area. The money apparently came from the faith support of 200 or so members, which in 1977 hopefully (but not necessarily) reached a monthly $240 for a single person and $680 for a couple with two children in grade school.[99] As a Colombian supporter explained, 'a foreign, non-profit, essentially philanthropic institute, with scarce economic resources from foreign donations. . . [cannot] expand the payroll of Colombian collaborators.'[100]

The Sierra Nevada

Another war of the gods is in the Sierra Nevada de Santa Marta, a mountain knot which drops to the Caribbean. Under siege for centuries, the 15,000 Cogui, Arhuaco and Malayo have retreated into remote valleys and higher, more inhospitable altitudes. They believe that, since the Sierra Nevada is the centre of the universe, the disruption of their ritual payments will cause ecological disaster everywhere. The violation of sacred sites by archaeological thieves, tourist promoters and mountaineers ('Do we climb onto the altars of your cathedrals?') is deeply felt.[101] In the 1940s, the Arhuaco organized an Indian league to defend their land through legal channels; in the 1970s they frustrated the local bosses with such skill that the army was necessary to 'maintain order.' Settlers push Indians off their land in order to grow the best marijuana in Colombia.

The Cogui were so reluctant to accept a SIL couple that they tried to poison the first informant, a man who broke the Cogui law of silence in exchange for flying in an airplane and seeing Bogota. Eventually, Western medicine earned the translator a Cogui cap and robe as a folk healer. But after the Stendals flew young informants to Lomalinda and took one to the United States, the refusal of the young men to chew the sacred coca leaf on their return upset their parents. 'We don't make any attempt to take coca away from them,' Patricia Stendal told me. 'Alfonso realizes that it is a drug and won't use it; this has been a big stigma for him. We believe that if the Lord speaks to them they will stop using it voluntarily. We tried to convince the Cogui that they shouldn't forcibly initiate young men into coca, and there was a big stir over this. It hangs over Valencia whenever he goes back because he's young.'

Since so much Indian tradition revolves around the consumption of coca, it has long been condemned by those who attribute indigenous misery to indigenous customs.[102] SIL has found ample grounds for disapproval: Stendal believed that it caused the men to neglect their gardens and made them irascible, damaging family life. Coca is also, as another member pointed out, associated with sexual symbolism. It is, in short, sinful.

> We respect their culture, [Stendal explained] we don't want to change it or their distinctiveness as a people. We would like to see them have a choice. Their present religion binds them to the coca, to being poor, sick, malnourished and underfed. The coca also makes them get married too early and to people they don't want. Girls get an especially raw deal. .. . . It's a real bondage, this culture and religion. Even from an anthropological point of view, we can't see how anybody would want them to continue in this misery. We would like to see them keep their culture, except replace their spirits with God, replace coca with the Holy Spirit, and the circles of men who do nothing but chew coca and be [ill-tempered] with the warmth of fellowship. . . . We've made great inroads at Mamarongo. Now they're planting enough food, they like

hearing Bible stories and listening to recordings. . . . We have fame throughout the whole tribe.[103]

In February 1975 leaders of the neighbouring Arhuaco accused SIL's three Sierra Nevada teams of using trade goods to impose their religion; stealing sacred objects from the lakes, and sterilizing women.[104] Several years before, according to Wycliffe, Arhuaco members had asked their team to leave, a request met by prayer but not compliance.[105] Then an Arhuaco congress had demanded withdrawal, denouncing the linguists as disguised Protestant missionaries sowing dissension and disintegrating the culture.[106] 'They make friends with gifts of radios and tape machines' Arhuaco told *Alternativa*

> Then they pay three or four pesos an hour for guides and information on our culture. They also preach their religion and we do not want it because it is a religion of domination and they want to destroy our learning which goes back many centuries. In their spare time they tour the Sierra and ask about everything. They have radios and telescopes and binoculars and make maps of everything. They ask what each Indian thinks.[107]

> A strange personage races through the *llanos* [an ANAPO scribe depicted one of the Stendal's informants at Lomalinda]. His robes billow out behind as he speeds along on his motorbike. From the sunglasses and chewing gum one would think that he is a *gringo* tourist, an eccentric. Except that his skin is copper, revealing his Indian ancestry. He is a laboratory rabbit which [SIL] uses for its penetration of Indian communities. He is an informant . . . and has returned from the United States. There he learned the new customs which he will try to implant in his community. . . .[108]

The Malayo translator, Robert Hoppe, blamed the accusations on the Union of Secular Missionaries (USEMI) organized by the late Msgn. Gerardo Valencia Cano. USEMI was trying to force the Indians to reject other outsiders, Hoppe said. One of his own informants had confessed to bearing false witness against him: e.g. that on the way to Lomalinda sacred objects in a box had cried out and tried to escape. But the man had been rewarded for his testimony and defended himself. 'The problem with you is that you are white,' he told Hoppe, 'that you will be an avenue for more whites, and that we do not want whites in our mountains.'

The previous year the Malayo had told Survival International's Stephen Corry that the couple were 'very good', apparently because they had learned the language and dispensed medicine cheaply. Incorporated into the group as a *mame* or folk healer, Hoppe said that his life had been threatened for trying to help the Malayo protect their land against colonists.

> I haven't done these things, [he told me with some anguish]. I wear

> Indian clothes, live in Indian houses, wear my hair long, work in the fields with them. They weave hats, I weave hats. . . . They are trying to say that cultural and religious are the same, and that's ridiculous. I have to start with my own personal belief, my conviction that I've found a faith which can help me overcome certain problems. . . . I feel I have a relationship with a person, Jesus Christ, a reason to live and a reason to die. . . . In the scriptures God is telling us that man is not a finite being, and that everyone has a right to know.[109]

The accusations against the three SIL teams came a few months after the formation of the Arhuaco Council. Pressure from a Capuchin Mission, land-lord/politicians and poor settlers have factionalized the group into what Corry terms 'puppets', who promote tourism and front for the bosses; 'hard-core traditionalists'; and 'progressionists', who accept Arhuaco values and lead the land struggle. The progressionists found an ally in the Indian Affairs Division, which checked the power of the Capuchin Mission and helped organize cooperatives. The cooperatives threatened the interests of the Castro family, the area's principal landowner and political power. After the Castros had several conscientious Indian Affairs officials purged on grounds that they were inciting the Arhuaco to guerrilla warfare, the Arhuaco progressionists and traditionalists organized their council. Subsequently USEMI Catholics and the Anthropology Institute helped the Arhuaco organize bilingual schools, complementing USEMI training of medical aides.

By 1976 the Summer Institute no longer functioned in the Sierra Nevada. The Stendals left to start an independent work in the *llanos*. By the time Robert Hoppe recovered from Chagas disease, the Malayo had turned against him. As for the Arhuaco translators, other members believed that they might never be able to return. The Tracys had faced steady problems from the beginning, not least the language itself. By late 1974, when the Arhuaco Council was organized, they felt that outsiders were responsible. Four years later, for *In Other Words,* Hugh Tracy told how he and his wife had returned to Sabanas del Jordan after a two year absence. It was hard to find language help. Everyone seemed to turn the cold shoulder.

> We were forced to conclude that we weren't really accepted by the religious leaders, the political leaders or the [Arhuaco] community. . . . We felt under heavy stress because there were no simple, easy answers. All we could do was ask the Lord to show us what practical steps needed to be taken: involvement of nationals? literacy work? language learning measures? or what?
>
> I'm certain the basic cause of all these problems was, and is, an intense spiritual conflict. The powers of darkness are determined not to let God and His work get a foothold in the hearts of the [Arhuaco] people.
>
> Under these stresses we've felt broken before the Lord and have made as deep a personal commitment to Him as we know how. . . .

190

He's led us to thank Him for our situation. . . .

We recognize that He's more powerful than our discouraging circumstances and that He can fill us with inner spiritual strength; give us cla clear direction; break down the enemy's stronghold; and receive praise, honor and glory from the [Arhuaco] people. 'Although we lead normal human lives, the battle we are fighting is on the spiritual level. The very weapons we use are not those of human warfare but powerful in God's warfare for the destruction of the enemy's stronghold' (II Cor. 10:3-4).[110]

Some translators were apparently starting to realize that 'outside agitators' were not even half the problem. While in 1974 Hugh Tracy blamed them, four years later he did not. Unencumbered by faith mission and state contracts, rivals were starting to offer Indians more attractive terms. But Wycliffe could conceive only of prayer on the one hand and better technique on the other, 'practical steps', the desperate 'involvement of nationals? literacy work? language learning measures? or what?' Respect for other religious traditions was out of the question.

The Summer Institute was not finished in the Sierra Nevada, however. In the midst of Arhuaco-colonist confrontations and threats to the lives of Anthropology Institute personnel, the department governor, Pepe Castro, accused the anthropologists and USEMI (which has received funds from the U.S. government's Inter-American Foundation) of being Communists.[111] As the armed forces militarized the zone, the Arhuaco decided to close the seven bilingual schools under their control. Soon the Tracys reported a new receptivity among the Arhuaco, one having to do with reading and writing their own language. Although the Hoppes now faced a serious penalty among the Malayo for giving out information — death — they were carefully reapproaching the group. A new Cogui team was so besieged by demands for medical help that there was no time for language study.

A Leftist Terrorist Bullet

The Summer Institute continued to hang on in Colombia, avoided by fellow Protestants, repudiated by indigenists and Indian organizations, harassed by the visa authorities, and protected from expulsion by a few powerful politicians. Even that bulwark swayed once more with the Interior Ministry's proposed Indian Statute, an attempt to criminalize the very existence of civil rights organizations like CRIC. Inspired partly by feuding anthropologists who lost control of their plans, a new Department of Indian Affairs would have the authority to deny outsiders permission to pursue Indian-related activities; cancel the legal status of native communities and associations; and appoint the lawyers defending native communities in court.[112] After the law stalled in congress, in 1980, its supporters tried to calm the opposition by adding a bill to expel SIL.[113] Since guerrillas were once again active in the *llanos* near Lomalinda, troops were assigned to protect it. Bible translators collided with the guardians of coca and marijuana plantations: if they called in the authorities, they might well call in the owners.

Into this magnificent picture stepped Chester Allen Bitterman III. 28 years old at the time of his death, he was the son of an independent mechanic in Lancaster, Pennsylvania and, like most other Wycliffe recruits, a product of the Christian home. It had led from Christian grade school to Columbia Bible College in South Carolina and back to Calvary Independent Church, whose 1,650 members give $400,000 a year to 100 missionaries around the world.[114] In these environs Bitterman met his wife — the daughter of Wycliffe's flight manager in Colombia — and decided to become a Bible translator. At the SIL sessions he was the sort of student whose determination was said to make up for his coursework. Despite their choice of Malaysia, the Wycliffe board asked the couple to go to Colombia, where they were led down such a rutted path that it was becoming impassable. During their year and a half in the country, Bitterman had been unable to start work in three different groups (in one case the Interior Ministry denied permission) before making exploratory visits to the world's last 120 Carijona Indians.[115] Once the pilot left, we'd be on our own, Bitterman wrote home.

> At least we have the radio, I thought . . . . The next morning we saw our
> first Carijona. His name was Luis. . . . One of the things we learned that
> day was that you always take an Indian's judgement of time or distance
> and double it. . . . And to say the trail was in bad shape was the best
> example of optimistic positive thinking I've ever experienced. The mud
> was over the tops of our boots. . . . We know God loves these people
> and wants them to come to enjoy a positive relationship with Him. . . .
> *Pray* with us that the Indians will begin to build us a tribal house... ;
> that God will continue to soften Carijona hearts, preparing them to
> receive His Word; that God will lead us to the two or three individuals
> in the tribe He has planned to be our language teachers.[116]

On 19 January 1981, seven kidnappers erupted in SIL's Bogota residence looking for branch director Alvaro Wheeler. Since he was not there, they took this novice translator instead. In a message to President Ronald Reagan, the kidnappers threatened to kill their captive unless his organization left the country in a month. As a matter of policy SIL, the U.S. and Colombian governments refused to consider terrorist demands. Not only did the branch plan to send translators into another 15 language areas without God's Word: it did not plan to leave the country until 1995.[117] After 47 days and much confusion over who the kidnappers were, Bitterman's body was found wrapped in a flag of the April 19 Movement.

The M-19 guerrillas take their name from the 1970 presidential election, which the National Front candidate is said to have won thanks only to official arithmetic. It was the congressional remnant of that disappointment, the National Popular Alliance, which five years later indicted SIL for complicity in nearly everything. As for the M-19, it caught the popular imagination like no other guerrilla group in recent years. Just before the Bitterman kidnapping, *Cromos* magazine released a poll purporting to show that two M-19 leaders were the most popular persons in the country. President Turbay was in tenth place, behind a beauty queen.[119] Prompted by the group's seizure of the Dominican embassy in 1980, a commission of the Organization of American States confirmed reports of widespread torture, sometimes murder, of helpless prisoners by police and military.[119] 16 days after Bitterman's execution, Turbay claimed that M-19 forces had been trained by Cuba and broke relations with that country, a move widely attributed to pressure from Washington.[120]

Before and after Bitterman's death, M-19 leaders denied responsibility and blamed a faction, which also disavowed any connection before and after the murder. At a meeting of the two M-19 groups on 14 February, they called the communiques in their name 'fake' and pointed the finger at military intelligence, perhaps even the CIA, which they said was trying to divide and discredit the movement.[121] The kidnappers continued to claim that they represented the M-19 faction, as did the government. Since the two sides undoubtedly have infiltrated each other, a third possibility was a consortium. To embarrass M-19 and perhaps remove moralistic, informing SIL teams from official cocaine and marijuana plantations, for example, a provocateur might have persuaded M-19 hardliners to carry conspiracy theory to its logical conclusion. Yet if a 100% M-19 faction did murder Bitterman, it would have found ample reason to claim that it had not.

The Summer Institute reaped a martyr's harvest. A previously sceptical press now sympathized with a young man who wanted to help the Indians and left behind a widow and two small children. Where was the secret rocket base? 'My eyes ran with tears', wrote a Siona elder.[122] President Turbay and his interior minister, who had once claimed to be expelling the branch, joined M-19 leaders in condemning the murder and extending their condolences. Among the 100 people arrested by the army was Alfredo Torres Pachon, an official of the WCC-affiliated Council of Latin American Churches, who had tried to mediate without SIL's consent and criticized its hard line. Other Protestant pastors received threats attributed to guerrillas, rallying them to SIL's cause. In the U.S., supporters accused opponents of intellectual responsibility for Bitterman's death.[123] Secretary of State Alexander Haig expressed his outrage at a terrorist act. Reagan administration spokesmen mentioned Bitterman in the same breath as the North American nuns murdered in El Salvador.

Every Wycliffe member now seemed publicly willing to die for Christ. All the confusion and hostility they had stirred up could be transformed into an age-old drama of sacrifice and redemption. Chet's death had been no accident: God did not make mistakes. Had not a gall bladder operation 'just happened' to bring him to Bogota when the kidnappers struck?[124] Back home in Pennsylvania, Mrs Mary Bitterman believed that her son had been born to minister to the M-19.[125] But while Chet's impact on his murderers remained a mystery, the results of his sacrifice for Wycliffe were clear enough: over the next year contributions jumped 22% and recruits 70%.[126] As the branch received further death threats and Colombian employees resigned, it asked home supporters to:

> PRAY for workers to enter the 15 remaining languages.
> PRAISE for God's protection at the centers as well as in isolated areas.
> PRAY that God will use attempts to hinder the work to advance the gospel.
> PRAISE for the support and interest shown by the Colombian Government.
> PRAY that Colombian leaders will have wisdom in their struggle against threats to peace in their land.[127]

'All men will hate you because of Me,' the DC-3 pilot quoted Jesus.[128]

References

1. *Uno Mas Uno* (Mexico, D.F.) 20 September 1979 p.10.
2. On the consequences of drug illegalization for Indians, see Antonil 1978.
3. Adolfo Triana, in Friede et al 1979:38.
4. Goff 1968:2/15-16.
5. Uribe 1980:284, 289.
6. Hefleys 1974:172, 209, 221, 224-5. Also SIL/WBT 1964:67-9, Townsend and Pittman 1975:15-17.
7. 'Colombia, South America, report of visit to, by a team from Special Warfare Center, Fort Bragg, N.C.,' NSF 319, John F. Kennedy Library, Boston.
8. University of Antioquia 1976:9-13.
9. Untitled memo, Bogota, September 1962, Manuel Lucena. Townsend and Pittman 1975:121-2, Hefleys 1974:225-9, and SIL/WBT 1964: 69-72.
10. 'WBT in Colombia and Panama,' WBT mimeo, 1970 and SIL/WBT 1971:73.
11. Morillo Cajiao 1978.
12. Bonilla 1972a:71.
13. Moser 1971.
14. Letter from James O. Wroughton to Jose Guabloche Rodriguez, Ministerio de Educacion 30 March 1972. Letter from Forrest Zander to Guillermo A. Gonzalez, DIGIDEC, Ministerio de Gobierno, 9 May 1972.
15. Perez Ramirez 1971 and Bonilla 1970.
16. Gossain 1970, cited in Hart 1973:25-8. NACLA had first raised the issue in February 1972, whereupon Colombians confronted SIL with it.

17. Author's interview, Lomalinda, 30 September 1975.
18. Bonilla 1970:17-18.
19. Author's interview, Bogota, 7 December 1975.
20. Goldman 1981 and Wright 1981b:4, 9.
21. Interview 7 December.
22. Muller 1952:52, 60, 67, 103, 107 and 1960:1, 3, 4.
23. Matallana Bermudez 1976:51-5, 73-4.
24. Interview 7 December.
25. Perez Ramirez 1971:79-80.
26. Interview 7 December.
27. Corry 1976:24-9 and Antonil 1978:229-69.
28. *NACLA Report on the Americas* (New York) July/August 1979:38-41.
29. *Alternativa* (Bogota) 14 August 1978:16-18.
30. *El Tiempo* (Bogota) 9 December 1978:9B.
31. Author's interviews, 3 November 1975.
32. Goff 1968:10/2.
33. Goldman 1981.
34. *Alternativa* September 22, 1975:16-17.
35. Wright 1981a.
36. Latorre Cabal 1978:54, 173.
37. University of Antioquia 1976:103-5.
38. Correal et al 1972:17.
39. For letters on the Piratapuyo and Tucano cases, see p.950
     Anales del Congreso (Bogota) October 15, 1975.
40. Ibid. p.951.
41. *Alternativa* 22 September 1975:16-17; *Unidad Indigena* (Bogota)
     October 1975:6-7 and September 1976:4.
42. Correal et al 1972:15-18.
43. Jackson (in press), who describes missionary-Tucanoan relations around
     1970.
44. *Communique* (Lomalinda) August 1974.
45. Lomalinda, 18 January 1967, and author's interview, Puerto Asis,
     22 December 1975.
46. German Castro Caycedo, *Tiempo* 27-29 December 1970.
47. Cesar Augusto Lopez Arias, *Tiempo* 2, 6, 18-23 February 1971.
48. SIL/WBT 1971:71-4.
49. Bonilla 1972a:70-1 and Perez Ramirez 1971:224-7.
50. *Tiempo* 18 October 1971:9A.
51. Ibid. 23 October 1971 and *El Espectador* (Bogota) 9 December 1971.
52. Correal et al 1972:12.
53. Friedemann 1975:28-9.
54. *Translation* January/February 1973:6.
55. Hefley 1978:71.
56. *Communique* August 1974.
57. Ibid. January 1973.
58. For an account of a SIL-associated prophetic movement among the
     Catio, see *In Other Words* November 1981:1-2.
59. *Anales del Congreso* 15 October 1975:956-7.
60. Author's interview, Mocoa jail, 16 November 1975.
61. Author's interview, Sibundoy, 14 November 1975.

62. *Anales del Congreso* 21 October 1975:991-2.
63. Author's interviews, Buenavista, 18-19 November 1975.
64. Wycliffe Associates prayer sheet, July 1977.
65. *Unidad Indigena* January 1975:8.
66. Corry 1976:41.
67. 'Un documento secreto', *El Estravagario* (*El Pueblo*, Cali) 26 October 1975. Varon Valencia scandal: Antonil 1978:116-18.
68. Matallana Bermudez 1976:48-50, 64-71, 88.
69. *Alternativa* 30 June 1975:30-1.
70. *Anales del Congreso* 15 October 1975:953, 957-8.
71. E.g., the National University declarations in University of Antioquia 1976:123-46; other statements *Anales del Congreso* 14 and 21 October 1975:940, 995; and director of Anthropology Institute, *Espectador* 28 March 1977.
72. *Anales del Congreso* 14 October 1975:940.
73. *Tiempo* 14 October 1975:5A.
74. *Anales del Congreso* 15 and 21 October 1975:952-3, 957, 995-6.
75. Maulin 1968:26-7.
76. AFP 18 November 1975; *Tiempo* (c. 17 November) cited *Anales del Congreso* 20 November 1975:1250; and UPI 19 November 1975.
77. *Tiempo* 14 October 1975.
78. For Peralta's case and many pertinent documents, see *Anales del Congreso* 1975, 9, 14, 15, 21 October and 14, 20 November: 927, 938-43, 950-8, 990-8, 1169-82, 1249-50.
79. Ibid. 14 November 1975:1180-1.
80. Ibid. 20 November 1975:1250 and *Tiempo* 17 October 1975:1-2A.
81. Morillo Cajiao 1978.
82. *Espectador* 10 September 1975:7A.
83. Author's interview, Bogota, 25 September 1975.
84. Cables, U.S. Embassy-Bogota to State Department, 2 July, 14 October and 20 November 1975, 'confidencial', signed Vaky. Released to author under FOIA.
85. *Espectador* 20 February 1976:5A.
86. Constitutional suit: see Fernando Umana Pavolini, *Dominical (Espectador)* 1977: 1, 3 and 24 April: 4, 10. Also *Espectador* 27 January 1981: 7A.
87. *Tiempo* 8 November 1978:6A.
88. 'Informe' mimeo, 28 November 1978, signed Julian Narvaez Hernandez et al.
89. *Foreign Broadcast Information Service* (Washington, D.C.) 1 December 1978:F1.
90. *Tiempo* 6 December 1978:3A.
91. *Uno Mas Uno* (Mexico, D.F.) 7 April 1979.
92. *Tiempo* 14 September (cited by Inter Press Service 15 September), 26 November 1978:9B and 10 December 1978:4A. Wilson (1980: 572-4) lists 72 North American Protestant Groups in Colombia fielding 1,043 missionaries.
93. *In Other Words* April 1979:4.
94. Author's interviews, Lomalinda, 29-30 September 1975.
95. *Tiempo* 27 or 28 June 1975, in University of Antioquia 1976:15-16.
96. Author's interview, Bogota, 16 September 1975.

97. Author's interviews, Lomalinda, 16-17 January 1976 and *Tiempo* 5 August 1976:1, 9A.
98. *Anales del Congreso* 14 October and 14 November 1975:939-40, 1171.
99. 'Colombia-Panama', WBT mimeo, April 1977:7. The Puerto Lleras petition was dated 4 December 1975.
100. Morillo Cajiao 1978.
101. This section is indebted to Stephen Corry (1976:29-35).
102. Antonil 1978:23-6.
103. Author's interview, San Martin, Meta, 3 October 1975.
104. *Unidad Indigena* April 1975:8.
105. *Translation* March/April 1973.
106. *Unidad Indigena* January 1975:2 and supplement.
107. *Alternativa* 14 July 1975:6.
108. *Anales del Congreso* 15 October 1975:954.
109. Author's interview, Lomalinda, 1 October 1975.
110. *In Other Words* February 1979:5.
11. Inter-American Foundation (Rosslyn, Virginia) *Annual Report* 1980:22.
112. *Survival International Review* Fall 1979:26-7.
113. *Latinamerica Press* (Lima) 13 March 1980:1,2.
114. *Christian Herald* June 1981:20-3.
115. *In Other Words* April:1-8 and Summer 1981:18-19.
116. Insert, *Wycliffe Associates Newsletter* March/April 1981.
117. *El Excelsior* (Mexico, D.F.) February 22, 1981:3, 6A.
118. *Uno Mas Uno* 10 January 1981:8.
119. *Washington Post* 31 July 1981:12A.
120. Penny Lernoux, *Nation* (New York) 27 June 1981:784-6.
121. *Foreign Broadcast Information Service* 17 February 1981:F1-3; *Excelsior* 16 February :3, 17A; and 13 March 3A, 1981.
122. 24 March 1981:7, 8A.
123. Richardson 1981.
124. Ibid.
125. *Chicago Tribune* 16 February 1982, section 3:1,6.
126. Blair 1982:31.
127. *Wycliffe Associates Newsletter* March/April 1981:1.
128. *Beyond* (Waxhaw, North Carolina: JAARS) September/October 1981.

7. Conspiracy Theory and State Expansion

God worked a mighty miracle in Peru! Now pray for another
miracle in four critical areas where Satan is stirring up concerted opposition to tribal work: in COLOMBIA, a meeting of
Indian leaders in Southeast Colombia has been called for the end
of November for the purpose of getting all foreigners out of that
area. This is an area of many Indian tribes and has long been an
agitation point for leftists. In BRAZIL our Director . . . was
advised by Indian Affairs that an order had come that our contract would not be renewed under any circumstances. . . .
MEXICO is feeling the same leftist agitation against our work
in Indian tribes, and . . . ECUADOR advises of a film put
together by the Central University in Quito in cooperation with
a group from Bolivia where evangelical foreign missionaries are
put in a very poor light as 'opening the way in the Andean areas
for foreign exploitation.'

Wycliffe prayer request, December 1977.[1]

The Summer Institute is not accustomed to leaving mission fields. It never did
until, after 40 years of expansion, the host regimes in Vietnam and Cambodia
collapsed. Despite the loss of six government contracts from 1976 to 1981 —
in Nigeria, Nepal, Brazil, Panama, Mexico and Ecuador — members only left
countries when forced to. In Latin America they stumbled from one crisis to
another but vowed to expand until every language had been given God's
Word. The language of Gospel advance was being translated into the language
of imperialist penetration: the police state paranoia of Latin American
intellectuals challenged the witchcraft fear of North American evangelicals.
Witch hunters chased each other in circles and confirmed each other's theories.
Whether a CIA conspiracy or Communist-inspired, the other side was part of
a grand design to conquer the world.

Anti-imperialist conspiracy theory united all feuding interests with a
grievance against SIL-entrepreneurs exploiting Indians, generals guarding frontiers, bishops, indigenists, disillusioned shamans, Indian political organizers —
into a nationalist cause. Had not SIL's advances into countries like Peru,
Ecuador, the Philippines and Vietnam coincided with North American oil or

counter-insurgency ventures? Why had some members of the Jungle Aviation and Radio Service found their way into the Lord's work from the armed forces of the United States? Did the distribution of all those teams reflect not a dozen dialects of some language, the evidence for which might be fabricated for all one knew, but mineral deposits and other geopolitical interests? Could all that high technology evangelism be subsidized by the U.S. espionage apparatus and transnational corporations? If SIL was too noble and selfless to run contraband, why had it used its duty-free import privileges to obtain, not just operational items like airplanes and typewriters, but the motor scooters, refrigerators and other paraphenalia which gave members such an enviable standard of living? If SIL was so concerned to build national unity, why did its converts identify so strongly with North Americans? Could its estimate of the number of languages in each country keep rising because it wanted to emphasize differences rather than overcome them? Why had two Latin American leaders opposed to Ronald Reagan's policy in El Salvador, President Jaime Roldos of Ecuador and General Omar Torrijos of Panama, died in plane crashes shortly after their governments had moved against SIL?

There was no end to questions like these, nor was there any way to answer many of them. It did not matter that only governments beholden to Washington would tolerate evangelical empire-builders; or that anyone who worked with Indians was proximate to something else; or that men engaged in nefarious activities would probably not settle at the scene of the crime with their wives, children and mothers; or that everything that SIL verifiably did could be explained in terms of a faith mission under contract to government and taking advantage of internal colonialism. None of that excluded more ominous possibilities. However coincidental the convergence of interests and interplay of functions, SIL was engaged in a good deal more than linguistics, literacy work and Bible translation. Its infrastructure — the knowledge, the logistics, the authority — could be put to a great many uses indeed. Although not much could be proven, it was certainly part of a much larger strategy. Each connection, suspicion and question led to the same conclusion: the Summer Institute was an agent of imperialist penetration.

Now who could conceive of such absurdities, members asked themselves, except communist agitators? For the translators conspiracy theory absolved Wycliffe of responsibility for its own global intrigue, projecting this onto ill-tempered coalitions which could agree on little, except that all would be better off without this particular group of North Americans. Why was the World Council of Churches trying to stop missionary work? Had not deceptive film-makers and anthropologists spread the climate of suspicion which killed Chester Bitterman? Why did the criticism of Christian missions go on and on when the worldwide expansion of Islam and Marxism aroused not the faintest objection? Wasn't so and so a known Communist? Were not the same accusations and lies heard first in one country, then all over Latin America and who knew where else? Who was coordinating all this? Why would left-wingers want to expel all Christian missionaries from remote areas ideal for guerrilla warfare? Some people did not realize that there were powerful forces at work in the world today to discredit all Christian missions, particularly those among tribal groups. There was too much of a pattern in the repetition of these vicious stories. Although nothing could be proven, the propaganda had all the earmarks of a disinformation campaign.

The Summer Institute's own system of misinformation had set off an avalanche. It was structurally incapable of acknowledging its central activity — the propagation of evangelical churches — for fear of endangering the government contracts and destroying the showcase value of its work for advances into other countries. Academic empire-builders often withhold or fudge data, but the dimensions of this empire guaranteed the most bitter controversy as critics challenged a sacred system of plausible denial. Soon rumours and speculation were being published, wire-serviced to other countries and turned into footnoted facts, burying the Summer Institute in further sediments of misinformation. Polemicists promoted one JAARS figure to captain and then general in five years.

Whether due to advice from allies or their own counsels, the branches were slow to reply in public. Instead, they went to the government with an 'objective' view of their work or the 'reality' of their programme. Objective reality revolved around the dual identity, the patriotic benefits of literacy and Bible translation, the alternative and so forth. Meanwhile anti-imperialism was being carried to extraordinary lengths, undermining the credibility of the opposition and vindicating SIL in the eyes of officialdom. By giving the other side all the rope it needed to hang itself, branches might even arrange a new contract or subsidy. Were a contract revoked, SIL called upon influential friends within and without the country — ambassadors, scientists, military officers, businessmen — to express their concern and hope that the government would reconsider its decision. Perhaps a representative of the ill-advised administration could be snared at a diplomatic event in Washington or Paris. But as branch officials used their whip hand on unruly indigenists, the establishment SIL had used to legitimate itself took notice. Club-footed university protest led to high level lobbying which finally outmatched SIL's in Mexico. Were a contract actually lost, the branches planned to carry on in the hope of once again demonstrating their value to the government.

As late as 1977 the Summer Institute still seemed lord of all that it surveyed. Everywhere in Latin America its adversaries had gone down to ignominious defeat. While the U.S. embassy was not to be discounted in Peru and possibly Colombia, the evident sense of loss felt by such entities as the *Guardia Civil* suggests that at most the embassy had played upon the implications of SIL's own alliances. As Townsend told the story, a military officer had greeted him with open arms and tearfully asked: 'Is there anything I can do for you? Two years ago I was dying at an inaccessible outpost and one of your airplanes brought me out to medical care and saved my life. Since then if there is anything I can do for Americans I certainly do it.'[2] To governments, SIL was not only useful but operationally and ideologically reliable, to say nothing of irreplaceable without unwanted expenditures. But to drive the point home, the Bible translators might have to appeal to military hardliners, politicians

representing landlords and other anti-Indian elements against 'Communists' —
former indigenist allies, Catholic clergy and Indian organizations. It was
as if the Apostle Paul had, instead of disappearing into a Roman prison, struck
a deal with the Praetorian Guard.

Then governments started to decide that SIL might be a useful sacrifice,
whether to give Washington a warning, expedite a new scheme to keep the
native population under control, or make a concession to Indian and indigenist oppositions. Already in Peru, the government had re-endorsed SIL only
after drawing back from SINAMOS, which might have socialized Indians as
production units for the state bureaucracy. In Brazil, the embargo against SIL
in late 1977 was probably a reprisal for the policies of President Jimmy Carter.
In Colombia, expulsion was offered to drum up support for anti-Indian civil
rights legislation. The Mexican contract was revoked in 1979: the indigenist
establishment had found the North Americans an embarrassment as it came
under attack from Indians and was entrusted with ambitious new projects
to respect their cultures and channel their protests. In 1981 SIL was expelled
from Panama and given a year to leave Ecuador.

Each government faced the same, disquieting phenomenon: increasingly
visible, militant Indian organizing. Indigenous nationalism was on the ascent,
a trend to which, like a number of other brokers, SIL had contributed in
largely unintended ways. Promotion of literacy, the trade language and inter-
group contacts helped members of scattered local communities identify
themselves as ethnic wholes. The attack on tradition in the name of Christianity and integration produced urban-oriented elites, which could no longer
rely on their old, localistic identities; faced discrimination due to their
origin; and formulated nationalist identities which bridged their increasing
class differences with the mass of native people.[3] A mission of political
socialization had created battlegrounds for other religious and political groups.
Unity organizing, nationalism and separatism were a response to increasing
factionalism in native communities along class and ideological lines.

The campaigns against SIL were part of this quest for unity, as well as of
another on the country level. The danger here was U.S. intervention, as
dramatized by threatening noises from Washington. Under pressure from
Indian organizing, governments could appeal to opposition forces by curtailing
a notorious North American organization. By sacrificing North Americans on
the altar of national unity and the defense of indigenous culture, governments
might also try to strengthen their control over native people. Or in Red-baiting
reaction to Indian militancy, they could restore SIL to favour.

God Intervenes in Peru

Since 1953 the Summer Institute had been referring to the day when it would
leave Peru, which at that time was said to arrive around 1970.[4] But in 1966
Cameron Townsend looked forward to another twenty years of service.[5] Four
years later a presidential commission established that SIL might be dispensed

with far sooner. By the time the new contract expired in 1976, it was assumed the government would have replaced the North Americans with Peruvians. As unease gripped the branch, a few anthropologists began submitting proposals for the transition. Somehow the small, powerless Division of Native Communities hoped to hand over base, school system and medical programme to Indians with a minimum of technical assistance. Its ideas were lost on the civil service and perished in bureaucracy. The Institute is civilizing the Indians, isn't it? Or be careful, colonel so-and-so is a good friend of the linguists. Or, do you expect Indians to run all that? Ironically, SIL itself was proving that Indians could run all that.

Another Native Division project, the Law of Native Communities and Agricultural Promotion, offered group land titles to all jungle Indian communities. But it saw the light of day only as amended by someone promoting private enterprise. To the added chagrin of the Native Division, the law would be implemented not by itself but the state machinery at large, and especially the National System for Social Mobilization (SINAMOS), under which it had been placed and with which it had disagreements.[6]

Organizing agrarian leagues and federations in the jungle for the official *Confederacion Nacional Agraria* (CNA) was the final assignment for 'No Bosses'. It planned to liberate the lower classes from patronal exploitation, then leave them to manage their own affairs with the help of a revolutionary state bureaucracy. But the Velasco government wanted to extract riches from the Amazon, not overturn the social order. SINAMOS grew into a huge establishment in Lima with little backing from the junta. By late 1975 its CNA clients on the coast and in the highlands were on the verge of revolt. Many observers suspected that turning jungle Indians into 'Peruvians totally integrated into the revolutionary process' meant making them work harder for an unreformed, unenlightened bureaucracy and bourgeoisie.

In early 1975, the Summer Institute still claimed a good working relationship with SINAMOS, which was supposed to supervise its activities. A Cushillococha evangelical was the first president of the agrarian league in that vicinity, and the local organizers seemed commendably cautious in their critique of Lambert Anderson's work. But the regional office in Iquitos was not so discriminating: the missionary profession was indicted for store-and-sawmill extraction of surplus value, ethnocide and political subversion. New to the Amazon or radicalized students from jungle towns, many organizers were blaming foreign missionaries for the activities of their own social class. Sweeping in and out of native communities, they learned of the conflicts which always exist between brokers and their followings; attacked the alliances between missionaries and Indians against more demanding colonizers; dismissed uncooperative Indians as 'alienated'; and ultimately reinforced their ties to missionaries.[7]

SINAMOS and the CNA would decide that SIL was standing in the way of their plans, but the campaign against it started elsewhere, at San Marcos University in Lima. In August 1975 the Minister of Education appointed the mandatory commission to study the contract which would expire the following

February.[8] The San Marcos linguists erupted when the ministry and the National Institute of Culture sponsored two SIL members to teach a course on a Quechua dialect. According to a restrictive clause added to the 1971 agreement, the branch was not authorized to operate in that language. Moreover, Wycliffe claimed Bible translators in as many as eleven other unauthorized languages.* Branch director Lambert Anderson stood on the clause for comparative studies ' of [authorized] languages. . . with the other languages of the world' .[10] This generous interpretation did not bother the education ministry: early in the contract review it legalized SIL in six of ten disputed cases.[11]

Until the year before, the branch could have counted upon sympathetic newspaper editors. But now the Lima daily press no longer belonged to oligarchic families such as the Miro Quesadas: it had been expropriated by the government and entrusted to left-wing intellectuals. Terse, spectacular wire service reports amplified the rumpus in Colombia; the Summer Insitute became a front page anti-imperialist scandal for week after week. Anthropologists explained how it had come to stand between the national and native socieites, blocking the path of the Peruvian Revolution.[12] CNA agrarian federations began to call for the immediate expulsion of SIL and other religious sects alienating and exploiting the natives.[13]

By early 1976, two official commissions had decided against SIL, the Prime Minister having appointed a second when the first failed to return a favourable judgement.[14] The second of the confidential reports cited the unauthorized languages, deficiencies in technical production, the failure to employ Peruvians in responsible positions and excessive radio communications capacity.[15] But as SIL's last days in Peru seemed at hand, another arithmetic asserted itself, the last days of the 1968 revolution. President Velasco had already been forced to retire due to various blunders, such as persevering with the expensive Maranon pipeline, even though the oil companies were finding little oil. The enormous foreign debt he had left behind demanded a policy shift to left or right. Conservatives in the armed forces purged their junior ranks of radicals and suppressed labour strikes; new foreign loans arrived and in March, all left-of-centre newspaper editors were fired.

Dismissing SIL would impress the CNA and the left, who were clamouring for a stand by the remaining army radicals. But the right-wing was not about to give more ground. After some vacillation the new President, General Francisco Morales Bermudez (1975-80) became the branch's saviour. Following SIL's rehabilitation, in February 1977, I asked its government liaison in Lima if the U.S. embassy had played any role. 'We don't know,' replied

---

* The 1971 contract permitted SIL to work only in those languages in which it already did, 32 to be exact. Two years later the branch was working in 38, At the May 1975 SIL/WBT biennial conference, the branch reported that 'translation goes ahead in 44 languages; nine groups still need linguists.' Luis Hernan Ramirez listed excursions into as many as 30 additional languages, but a number appear to have been within contractual terms.[9]

James Wroughton, noting that the 1971 contract barred diplomatic appeal. 'We maintain no contact with the U.S. embassy.'[16]

This was not true. Although Peruvian friends of SIL sometimes served as intermediaries, six embassy dispatches during the height of the controversey, from September 1975 to May 1976, cite direct contacts between a branch official, usually Lambert Anderson, and the embassy. When Ambassador Robert Dean left his post in mid-1977, Anderson sent a testimonial to President Carter: 'Ambassador Dean's professional correctness and precision, coupled with a warm personal interest and private words of support, without doubt contributed greatly to the happy outcome. . . . Being a private organization, we have never sought the official backing of the U.S. government, but we did appreciate the [ambassador's] judicious and thoughtful personal concern. . . .'[17]

Ambassador Dean had worked in State Department intelligence and been assigned to the Pentagon before serving as political counsellor in Brazil at the time of the U.S.-supported 1964 coup.[18] He visited Yarinacocha in mid-1975 and early the next year attended a reception for the founder. 'MinEd said further attacks from disgruntled academic and or leftist circles might be expected,' Dean cabled Washington on September 30, 1975. 'MinEd assured SIL its contract will be renewed.' This was during the exchange with San Marcos University over the unauthorized team, in which the ministry insisted that it was giving the contract a fair review. But by November 20 the ambassador was worried: 'The reported [expulsion from Colombia] will complicate the scheduled February renewal of SIL's contract. . . . The hostile leftist press, more than ever, is bent on treating the contract renewal as a political issue rather than technical decision.' A week later the embassy cabled that 'the SIL leaders seem sanguine. . . . that by February all will turn out satisfactorily.'

In late February or early March 1976 the branch was shocked to receive a letter of dismissal from its ally the Minister of Education, General Ramon Miranda Ampuero. On March 9 a 'Peruvian patron . . . and close collaborator' of SIL informed the ambassador that it had been a cabinet decision. A Velasco-era army radical, the new Prime Minister General Jorge Fernandez Maldonado, was 'considered to have played a key role.' Strangely, the government did not announce the decision. According to the ambassador's source, the Minister of Education had made it known that SIL was not to announce it either. While branch officials obligingly told persons like myself that they were receiving 'conflicting signals', at Yarinacocha, members began saying that they would have to leave the country by the end of the year.

'There was some feeling,' Dean cabled Washington on 19 April, 'that the recent . . . political shift [to the right] might aid the SIL in an effort to stretch out the transfer period. The fact that there had been no publicity of the decision not to renew SIL contract, was considered a hopeful sign which could lead to a postponement of SIL departure date.' But there was another line of thought in both the embassy and the branch leadership. As Dean had noted in his 10 March cable, the government might be trying 'to avoid another political controversy for the moment' — one which the left-wing in government could ill afford.

The branch official who disregarded the government's wishes and broke the news was base director Donald Lindholm. A graduate of Wheaton College, he had left his job as a USAID officier with the U.S. embassy in Lima to join the Summer Institute after the 1968 coup.[19] According to another member, he had caused problems on a number of occasions. This time he told *El Comercio* about the contract termination on April 12.[20] According to Ambassador Dean, a week later: 'Lambert Anderson told emb[assy] off[icer] that he was totally surprised, and somewhat dismayed to read the Lindholm interview.' Anderson's anger at his colleague was soon common knowledge, the only case I know where still-live differences between SIL administrators have been aired. The other possibility is that branch leaders were merely excusing themselves for disobeying the government.

Three days after Lindholm's disclosure, Prime Minister Maldonado announced the formation of a commission (the third) to transfer SIL's property and activities to the State by the end of the year.[21] At this point, *In Other Words* reported, 'God intervened' by purging the newspapers and marshalling an impressive display of support.[22] But as the founder always has maintained, God only helps those who help themselves. With the newspapers in friendlier hands, an ex-U.S. diplomat had provoked a public response from SIL's most powerful adversary, Prime Minister Maldonado, which his many enemies could use to embarrass him. By making SIL what Ambassador Dean would call 'part of the continuing broader argument over the future course of the revolution' (28 April), Lindholm was bringing the right-wing to the rescue.

Thirteen days after Lindholm's disclosure, a Peruvian-organized petition to reinstate SIL appeared in the press. It was signed by 65 persons of note and reinforced by another 66 names a month later.[23] Among the signers were five ex-ministers of education — Valcarcel, Mendoza, Basadre, Romero and Miro Quesada; old indigenist friends; academics isolated by the government's failure to suppress Marxism in the universities; businessmen; two Catholic priests; and the novelist Mario Vargas Llosa.

There were no linguists among the signers, but retired senior military officers made up for this and any other lack: they swelled to more than half the second list and comprised 40% of the total. While the branch had enjoyed its warmest relationships with the army and air force, the signing generals from these services (12 and 7 respectively, plus 6 from the *Guardia Civil*) were outnumbered by 19 navy admirals, a showing no doubt related to the navy's right-wing politics and leading role in attacks on labour and the left-wing press.*

---

* The most prestigious of the admiralty signers was Luis Vargas Caballero, the former navy minister whom President Velasco had sacked in 1974. The next minister investigated the navy's CIA liaisons, reportedly expelled a CIA officer named John Poulter, and was the target of terrorist attacks. When he accused the Naval Intelligence Service, a charge substantiated several years later, the college of admirals expelled him from their midst.[24]

According to SIL members (off the record) and the ultra-rightist Catholic priest Salomon Bolo, the campaign against the linguistic institute was the first step in an international Communist conspiracy to drive Christianity from Peru.[25] With only a few exceptions, however, the Catholic clergy stepped aside. While mission priests regarded many of the charges against SIL as scurrilous, they were not about to confuse one-time University of Oklahoma linguists with Christendom. But if religious freedom was not at issue, SIL's value as an agent of political control certainly was.

'A key SIL supporter has warned Morales Bermudez,' Ambassador Dean cabled on 28 April, 'of the political danger of terminating SIL activities only to allow leftist campesino organization to extend its operations among jungle Indians.' The supporter also reportedly had 'alluded to the possibility of the SIL center later becoming a focus for "guerrillas." ' (An aide to Prime Minister Maldonado had informed the embassy that the SIL base would be turned over to the CNA). President Morales appeared to be sympathetic. The name of SIL's intercessor with the president has been withheld, but on 2 June Ambassador Dean cabled Washington that 'former Min[ister of] Educ[ation] Miro Quesada has twice warned Morales Bermudez on erroneous Marxist allegations against SIL.' He added that Miro Quesada has 'lectured on [the] same theme to Peruvian war college,' the Center of Advanced Military Studies (CAEM).

On 26 May, Dean reported a week later, the president of the transfer commission told SIL that it would receive a five month extension from January to May 1977. The commission's Colonel Adrian Hueman had conducted his own investigation of the base and decided that most of the charges were false. A Peruvian friend of SIL told the ambassador that

> the extension was prompted by growing [government] awareness of the complexity and expense of takeover of SIL program. Director Anderson recently informed Mineduc that operational expenditures costing around 10 million soles per year are being curbed by the SIL as part of its phase out. This reduction has already affected services which SIL for years has rendered to military and civil officials. . . . We understand there have been many complaints by Guardia Civil and Guardia Republicana officials and by Army personnel, as well as civilians. Pay checks, mail and medical supplies are no longer arriving via SIL, and emergency transportation requests cannot always be met by SIL.

Noting the title of a Peruvian editorial which hailed its presumed departure, Ambassador Dean closed this final cable on the matter: 'ILV-Mission Accomplished.'[26]

Discreet, high level Red-baiting had turned the tide: the government was deciding that it could not forsake its North American blockade against leftist alliances with Indians. The dependence of the state bureaucracy on SIL also worked in its favour, a fact which branch leadership may have decided to dramatize by curtailing services before the transfer commission could arrange for their continuation. Thus, while SIL had been told only to turn over its facilities by the end of the year, not leave Peru; while it hoped to retain the private residences at Yarinacocha; while Anderson said that the branch hoped to continue its work even if the contract were lost; and while elsewhere, members have not left countries until obliged to, SIL made it known that some were leaving Peru eight months before the base transfer deadline.

At the end of June, the currency devaluation imposed by the international banks set off price increases and riots. When Prime Minister Maldonado suppressed a right-wing *coup d'etat* in July, the navy gave President Morales a 72 hour ultimatum to dismiss him. Morales complied and also dropped most of the remaining army radicals from the cabinet, bringing the 1968 revolution to a close. The government dismantled SINAMOS and the CNA swung into open opposition.

After a long official silence, in January 1977, the Prime Minister's office announced that the Summer Institute would be phased out over the next five years.[27] According to one report, the transfer commission had split: while the civilians continued to press for their stated objective, the military officers argued that the campaign against SIL was a Communist plot.[28] The official reason for the extension was maintaining the bilingual schools; Colonel Hueman's committee would report to the Prime Minister as it gradually transferred SIL's functions. The only press comment was favourable, because the armed forces had shut down the more offensive weeklies.

Some months after the five year reprieve, the branch received permission to operate in any language it pleased. Six Quechua teams planned to produce New Testaments in 18 dialects, while a nine person Campa team was to pursue its spiritual responsibilities in half a dozen dialects of that language.[29] With all the new opportunities, the branch doubted that it would meet its 1985 completion target.

SIL-Peru's Thirty-Fifth Anniversary

The contribution of Indians to the debate over the Peruvian branch was slight. With the major exception of the Amuesha Congress, which maintained silence, jungle Indian organizations had yet to come into being. The SINA-MOS-advised *Confederacion Nacional Agraria* represented some native Amazonians, but its mixture of cogency, equivocation and conspiracy theory made the Summer Institute a metaphor for capitalist expansion, without a word about the *patrones,* colonization and the state bureaucracy.[30]

One writer managed to publish statements by an Aguaruna and a Huitoto. While both found reason to denounce SIL, the Aguaruna made clear that missionaries were not the principal problem, and the Huitoto shortly allowed as much. According to the latter, Cecilio Jurafo, native communities were rebelling against SIL in growing number because they realized that it was trafficking in religion for political ends, specifically U.S. imperialism. But soon he added that the problems of native people would not be resolved by its departure. Perhaps there had been some demagoguery. While SIL had to be rejected, it was only a small part of a problem revolving around the *patrones* and internal colonialism. Native people needed a new structure controlled by themselves, official support but not more bureaucrats.[31]

In May 1976, bilingual teachers appeared in Lima with petitions to reinstate the Summer Institute. The Aguaruna school supervisor was received by President Morales, who offered the group all his support and stated that very possibly SIL would remain. 'We want the programs begun by the Institute to continue until we have been trained,' the supervisor told *La Prensa.* He also exhibited SIL's translation of the Universal Declaration of Human Rights, adding that it had been published in 23 other languages as well

The Machiguenga supervisor came to Lima to appeal an absurd bureaucratic decision; and ask for land titles. A Bible institute graduate, he had hoped to go to university, but decided to help his people instead. Thanking SIL members for their sacrifice, he told *La Prensa* that through them 'We have learned to love our fatherland, appreciate our heroes, work for our nation, beginning with our own community and brothers in language.' His people wanted technical assistance, the supervisor said. If SIL left, who would bring medicine and fly products to Pucallpa? [32]

During the few months in early 1976 when SIL's departure seemed assured, Stefano Varese composed his 'Open Letter to Triumphalism'. The Summer Institute had installed itself in an institutional vacuum and its expulsion would create a new one. Because the so-called revolution had failed to make any arrangements, such as he had proposed in vain from the Division of Native Communities, the vacuum would be filled by the local bourgeoisie in alliance with the local political authorities. 'The yankee agents of imperialism will go, to be replaced by the criole agents of imperialism: the first conscientious, refined . . . the second brutal, ignorant, physical aggressors.' To attribute all the problems of jungle Indians to SIL was irresponsible and chauvinistic, a trap which mystified dependency and would redound to the harm of native people. Far more was demanded than getting rid of the Summer Institute.[33]

In a fine series on jungle Indians and the Amazon, which ended when it was shut down again, the Lima weekly *Marka* celebrated Cameron Townsend's return to Peru in late 1978 with a reflection on his organization, the state, and what it called 'left McCarthyism', the rejoinder to which had been 'if it's gringo, it's good.' SIL 'was accused of being "the introducer of capitalism to the native communities"(?),' noted Pedro Amasifuen.

> We ask simply, where does this leave the state and the functionaries, the rubber-hunters and other extractors and 'conquistadores,' the traders and the Catholic missionaries, that is, the social and economic formation which has crystalized in Amazonia . . . and which evidently precedes the establishment of SIL? No analysis of SIL can ignore — as occurred during [1975-76] with a definite will to avoid the principal problem — the position and attitude of the state. . . . SIL is not the North American Marines who invaded Santo Domingo. . . . it is a

prolongation of the state.

Simply replacing North American missionaries with Peruvian bureaucrats was not a solution.[34]

The divine intervention which rescued Wycliffe guaranteed that workers, peasants, and especially Indians, would bear the brunt of austerity measures imposed by foreign banks and the International Monetary Fund. According to a Catholic missionary testifying to a U.S. Senate committee, the per capita caloric intake of Peruvians declined by one third from 1974 to 1979, to two-thirds of the FAO minimum standard, while per capita protein intake was halved to less than 50% of the FAO minimum standard. Much of the population had been reduced to eating chicken feed. Since the austerity measures, the missionary estimated, infant mortality had climbed to 80-100%. This would mean that 30,000 to 40,000 small children had died in 1979, who, four years before would not have.[35]

Jungle Indians had a special place in the economic recovery programme, a new support group observed. While the post-1968 Velasco reforms had acknowledged indigenous rights like never before, the structure of exploitation was left untouched. The contradiction became more acute after 1975: bowing to the demands of the international bankers, the bankrupt Morales government turned to the Amazon. It broke down legal barriers to the plunder of jungle resources and auctioned them off to the highest bidder.[36] In 1978 the land rights recognized by the Law of Native Communities were severely curtailed: only a few hundred of more than 1,000 jungle Indian communities had received the land titles promised five years before. Even where the titles had been granted, legal appeals were little defense against officially backed settler invasions.

The Summer Institute was performing humanitarian services for a regime which was, not just incapably, but hopelessly compromised by its ties to local exploiters. In exchange for propping up the government's credibility among Indians, a high-minded North American colony assured itself of generous opportunities for evangelism. The dilemmas which result are illustrated by recent conflicts over the bilingual schools.

In keeping with the national education reform, the System of Bilingual Education at Yarinacocha had been decentralized in 1972. Two-hundred-odd bilingual schools were distributed among 34 mestizo-administered nucleos responsible for all public education in their areas. Soon Indian teachers were complaining to their SIL translators about a range of problems, including blatant discrimination. Thanks to geography and the demise of a bilingual oriented central office, appeals were trying and futile. Unsympathetic administrators pressured many teachers into conforming to the standard programme. SIL's production of new bilingual texts declined, forcing many teachers to move their advancing students into a monolingual Spanish curriculum. For the Amuesha, bilingual education ended. Some teachers were purged to make their salaries available to mestizos; requirements for accreditation multiplied, forcing others to resign. By 1978, only one of seven

Candoshi teachers was left. Clearly the reform was a fine way to wreck SIL's patronage system, but in many cases probably at considerable cost to Indians for whom nothing better was on the horizon. In the branch's opinion the bilingual schools were being destroyed; a new central authority was needed; and it would have to resume the role of technical adviser.

By mid-1978 SIL had high-level ministry backing in Lima for an Office of Bilingual Education in the Jungle (OFEBISE), a central authority to be re-established at Yarinacocha and once again benefit from its expertise. But 'unforseen difficulties' arose: judging from an outline, OFEBISE was to be a purely SIL-Ministry of Education affair with no participation by the universities or Catholic missions.[37] Times had changed with the proliferation of rival, invading 'ideologies' which branch officials so lamented. Now there were other bilingual programmes for jungle Indians, proposed or in operation, which had been spurred by SIL's example but rejected the use to which it had put native languages.

Among the Napo River Quechua, French Canadian Franciscans boasted 21 teachers, 11 schools and nearly 500 students. In March 1977 three of their specialists visited the teacher training course at Yarinacocha. According to one report, they were received 'like you treat a dog when you're playing poker.' An observer for Survival International, which was funding Napo Quechua primers, believed that the Franciscan programme was compatible with the folk Catholic culture, in contrast to SIL's approach in many other languages.[38] When the Catholic bishops caught wind of OFEBISE a year later, they feared that SIL was restoring the old order and moved to 'balance' the scheme. The various parties failed to come to an agreement and, as of late 1979, Indians presumably continued to suffer for lack of a bilingual office. About the same time a number of bilingual teachers joined the national teacher's strike against the Ministry of Education. Non-Indian teachers replaced the Conibo and Shipibo strikers, who appealed for international support against the government and SIL.[39]

In July 1978, ex-Ambassador Robert Dean attended the first Townsend Institute of International Relations, a meeting of 26 Wycliffe government liaison men.[40] Half a year later, in Peru, the Prime Minister replaced the five year transfer committee with yet another commission, to draft a new contract.[41] Six months later, the branch's friend General Jose Guabloche, now Minister of Education, took time out from suppressing the national teacher's strike to attend its dedication of five New Testaments in Lima.[42] At last, in October 1979, the Ministry of Education and SIL signed their new contract.[43] The government had offered a 20-year term, according to Wycliffe, but it decided that ten would be enough.

When the branch's old backer, Fernando Belaunde Terry, was reelected to the presidency the following year, it was again on the premise that 'the conquest of the Amazon' would solve Peru's social problems. The new President even promised to build 50 new cities in the jungle and make lumber Peru's number one export.[44] A few months after Belaunde called ecological and human rights objections a global anti-development conspiracy, he awarded

Cameron Townsend a medal for SIL's contribution to his dream.[45] The Bible translators would continue to enjoy warm official support for their work of salvation.

Ecuador

After Ecuadorian and Peruvian troops disputed a jungle border in early 1981, the two Summer Institute branches fared rather differently. In Peru, the Belaunde administration announced that it was expanding the bilingual schools in coordination with SIL.[46] In Ecuador, the government gave the translators a year to leave the country. Under attack from university nationalists and Indian organizations, a branch modelled after its parent in enemy Peru was succumbing to unease over national security.

In Ecuador, the myth of the Amazon as national salvation is especially difficult to challenge. The country lost most of its eastern claim to Peru in a 1941 border war; U.S. diplomacy ratified the defeat. What remains has made Ecuador the largest oil producer in the basin, but only with the capital of U.S. corporations. Until recently the economy boomed and busted at the whim of foreign markets. Now oil money has freed the country from dependence on banana exports, turned it into a member of the Organization of Petroleum Exporting Countries, and opened up the Amazon to small farmers displaced from the Coast and Sierra. To North American-financed internal colonialism Ecuador owes what it is today: a middle and upper-class boom in consumer durables, urban real estate, military hardware and government bureaucracy, amidst a social order reminiscent of the Spanish hacienda.[47]

North American evangelicals have devoted considerable resources to the lowest, Indian strata of this social order, in the Sierra as well as the eastern jungle or Oriente. In the Sierra, the missionaries have set themselves against political protest, by counting upon Protestant virtue to help small farmers survive an expanding capitalist agriculture. In the Oriente, as Scott Robinson has reported, 'networks of trade-offs . . . assure the military's prestige and control, native defensive postures are repressed, evangelical missionaries work unmolested, and . . . tropical forest become[s] available for colonization and exploitation, thereby relieving agrarian tension in the Sierra.'[48]

SIL has concentrated on five language groups in the Oriente. Among the two which account for most jungle Indians, the Lowland Quichua with some 30,000 people and the Shuar with 15,000, fellow faith missionaries feel that the branch has failed to meet its evangelical responsibilities. When the government slashed bilingual teacher salaries, the Quichua school system disintegrated. Twenty bilingual schools survived among the Shuar, but the Shuar Federation operated an even larger system of bilingual radio schools with the assistance of the Salesian Mission.[49] In 1976 the federation's difficulties with evangelical religion centred on a more doctrinaire faith enterprise, the Gospel Missionary Union, with which SIL translated a New Testament and quarreled when the linguist refused to fire bilingual teachers for maintaining a traditional marriage pattern.

The branch's impact has been far more dramatic on three demographically precarious groups. When translators settled among some 700 Cofan and Siona-Secoya in the 1950s, fear of sorcery still maintained a dispersed, ecologically sound settlement pattern. Since then they have been hemmed in by oil roads, impoverished settlers and agribusiness. As a source of trade goods, wages and western medicine, the translators supplanted the authority of shaman/headmen, stimulated consumer appetites and encouraged production for market, conceivably on less exploitative terms than might have been the case without them. The demands of the new political economy (such as animal skins for trade goods) and an efficiently vaccinated, growing population exhausted natural resources around the Secoya translators. To make the best of the government's 50 hectare per family homestead policy, they encouraged Siona and Secoya groups to come together on good agricultural land much closer to colonization.

The translators introduced a 'new cleavage' in Siona-Secoya society, reports William Vickers. Shamanism, *yaje* ceremonies and *masato* parties were identified as sinful; the shaman/headman replaced by the bilingual teacher/ pastor; and converts discouraged from marrying the unsaved.[50] 'As the community development program grew,' notes a Wycliffe author, 'so did the number of believers' – to 90% of the village.[51] But as Wycliffe published its portrait of the Secoya church, the teacher/pastor lapsed spectacularly. Lured into *colono* civilization and stripped of old defenses, the Secoya were floundering in imported alcohol and debt.[52] As elsewhere, SIL's plans have paved the way for other ideologues. 'Politically the Secoyas are the target of ideological groups. . . ,' Wycliffe explained recently. 'Culturally their way of life is being challenged by those who think they should be westernized, and those who think they're in the way. Religiously they must contend with cults that are creeping in with doctrines it's hard for them to recognize as false.'[53]

Whether or not this can be called helping the Secoya adjust to change, SIL certainly was choosing their future. Since game reserves seemed likely to disappear, the branch was trying to prepare hunters to become stock raisers and more intensive farmers. This included efforts to devise an ecological agriculture for the government's 50 hectare plots. But SIL also tried to drum up Ecuadorian support for legal game reserves. To prevent its charges from abandoning their languages and translated New Testaments, the branch proposed what it called 'bilingual-bicultural' education in the face of the government's 'national culture'.

The adjustment policy came under attack from several quarters. The heavily North American and European preservationist camp included a tourist lobby, which was disappointed that Indians wore western clothes. A handful of anthropologists pointed out that even reserves undermined the ability of native people to adjust to change on their own terms. By indicting Ecuadorian racism and internal colonialism, they were liable to accusations of divide and rule imperialism. Leftists feared that reformist schemes created subservient local elites, consolidated state control and prolonged the agony of capitalism. To rally anti-imperialist sentiment they appealed to nationalism, ignoring the conflict between Indians and a colonizing society upon which evangelical missionaries have thrived.

SIL was roundly condemned for removing the Huaorani from the path of U.S. oil companies, for example, but only after they no longer endangered new oil fields, which the entire political spectrum considered sacrosanct. As the branch became an anti-imperialist issue in the mid-1970s, a government concession to a foreign company which threatened the Siona-Secoya game reserve did not. The only group which even raised the issue was SIL. Several years later *Nueva* magazine 1) applauded the opening of the Secoya oilfield and 2) criticized SIL for training Indian (including Secoya) mechanics, tailors, typists and authors, because such occupations were 'beyond their normal tasks and exceeding their necessities' — another example of how the North Americans turned Indians into exploited labour.[54] The translators persevered, by making obeisance to the government and doing something to satisfy immediate Indian demands — for schools, medicine, trade goods, land titles and other legal papers — which most of its adversaries did not recognize, were unwilling or unable to meet.

Much of the worry over SIL in the Oriente was inspired by the 'holy war' in the Sierra, where evangelical sects, leftist groups and renovated Catholic clergy competed for the loyalty of Quichua farmers. Despite identification of SIL as the mastermind of evangelism in the Sierra, it was actually the domain of three sister missions: the Gospel Missionary Union, World Radio Missionary Fellowship, and Christian and Missionary Alliance. Once territory had to be wrested from the Catholic Church, it had to be defended against Mormons, Jehovah's Witnesses and Pentecostals. The most spiritually fertile province was perhaps the most impoverished, Chimborazo: official abolition of feudalism, a truncated land reform and proliferation of the below-subsistence farm have produced the entrepreneurial opportunity and desperation in which evangelical religion flourishes. The Gospel Missionary Union counted 20,000 'Christians' or perhaps 10% of the Quichua population.

Chimborazo was also the diocese of Ecuador's leading progressive bishop, Leonidas Proano, whose support for peasant land claims offended the local ruling class. Claiming to be above politics, evangelical missionaries enjoyed the favour of the provincial authorities.[55] In a characteristic incident recounted by the bishop of Latacunga, Protestants drove their 'armored car' (loudspeaker van) through a folk Catholic community without permission; left three of their peasant partisans in the road, which started a riot; and then tried to obtain police protection for religious freedom.[56] Were North American neighbourhoods afflicted by Muslims preaching through loudspeakers, it would be outlawed as a public nuisance.

To many, the significance of such activities was plain: right-wing North Americans were fomenting religious turmoil to demobilize the peasantry.

> They are sent by the CIA, [a Quichua union leader said in 1976] . . . .
> They do not want us to reclaim our land. They do not want us to

struggle to change the society. We clearly see that they favor today's system. . . . But not all *campesinos* understand the political objectives of the Protestant missions. . . . The evangelical *campesino* does not drink. . . . Smoking is also a sin. By abandoning vice, he can administer his scarce income better. His house, his clothes and those of his family will be better than that of the 'pagans'. . . . Religious fanaticism replaces political militancy.

The battle extended to the airwaves: the World Radio Missionary Fellowship (Radio HCJB or 'The Voice of the Andes') broadcast in 17 dialects of Quichua to compete with Radios Havana and Moscow. The director of the Gospel Missionary Union 'complains about leftist influence in Ecuador,' *Christianity Today* reported in 1979, because 'it makes the Indians more concerned about their material rather than spiritual wellbeing.'[57]

In the GMU stronghold of Colta, Chimborazo, Blanca Muratorio suggests that evangelicals are forsaking folk Catholic burdens 'for a new identity to liberate them from a condition of humiliation.' Besides reviving pride in the Quichua language, reducing family violence and democratizing religious experience, the new religion is being used to strengthen the reciprocity networks necessary to survive growing land scarcity, competition and individualism.

By excluding non-Quichuas, *conferencias* (camp revivals) coinciding with folk Catholic fiestas reinforce ethnic solidarity. But

the conference only removes the peasants from social situations where they are exploited as peasants and as Indians, and by clouding class solidarity into a religious experience, it conceals the oppressive nature of the larger system of social relations. In this sense we can say that the function of the ideology is resolving the contradictions by excluding them.

Each year, the Association of Evangelical Indians of Chimborazo holds a mass meeting for government officials to affirm its dedication to citizenship and progress. While evangelical leaders ask for new services compatible with official priorities – roads, schools, water systems – they refrain from the basic issues – land rights and working conditions – which are not. Predictably, GMU-trained church leaders define most issues in individual moral terms. Should confrontation with the authorities loom, they offer the North American evangelical version of Romans 13:1. According to Muratorio, however, Protestant community leaders are conscious of the need to militate for peasant rights, to the point of subordinating religious to class issues.[58]

SIL only began working among the Highland Quechua after 1973, the year that a USAID official impressed by its literacy work in Vietnam, organized a national seminar on bilingual education. Until this point Ecuadorian universities had not been very interested in the subject: SIL led the way in the lowlands, followed by the Shuar Federation and the Salesians. In the highlands

Msgr. Proano's diocese had organized radio schools. An Inter-Andean Development Institute, staffed partly by the U.S. Peace Corps, was also at work. When the Ministry of Education established a special office in 1974, the mainstay was the Summer Institute, which prompted objections. Conceived as an integration and control device, bilingual education has come to figure in Indian demands and is always politically sensitive. Once introduced, often by North Americans against the wishes of Hispanicizing educational establishments, its growing number of partisans dispute who will control it.

In early 1975, anthropology students at the Catholic University in Quito accused SIL of robbing the Huaorani of their land. It had failed to live up to its contract and its studies were scientifically worthless. Finally, more capable and better trained Ecuadorians, 'more akin' to Indians 'owing to the very nature of our race', were being excluded from the bilingual scheme, which the North Americans would use to transmit values alien to the Latin American reality and reinforce the system of domination.[59] A reluctant Ministry of Education dispatched a commission to Lomoncocha, where it evidently concluded that SIL was a meritorious dependency. The Catholic University campaign fizzled out in vague charges that North American organizations were administering contaminated vaccines and castrating children. Regardless of political persuasion, all Ecuadorians would have to unite to save the fatherland from a terrible peril.[60]

The government's bilingual education office survived for a year, USAID having failed to produce a major subsidy. The Ministry of Education had never succeeded in fulfilling its budgetary commitments to the SIL system, which by 1977 consisted of 68 teachers, 51 schools and 1,200 pupils: each year the ministry provided an average of one-third the promised funds. The branch's occupational and medical training programmes had been underwritten by the Canadian International Development Agency.[61] The few Ecuadorian linguists felt excluded from ministry planning: they objected to the use of the schools as an evangelical instrument and suspected that they were not teaching Indians Spanish quickly enough. According to SIL, it wanted the schools in Ecuadorian hands because, once it left, the Bible translations would be 'nothing' without them; attempt after attempt to transfer the system to the education ministry had failed; and even the Catholic University did not want responsibility because it would have a still harder time squeezing money out of the government. Left to its own devices, the branch was trying to 'nationalize [indigenize] from below' by training Indians to produce their own texts.[62] It was also building a new teacher training centre at its Quito headquarters, for the Highland Quichua.

When Ecuador returned to civilian rule in 1979, the new Minister of Education launched an investigation.[63] Indian organizations proliferated and the government recognized Ecuador as a 'multi-cultural nation'. Early the next year it solicited Indian views on a proposed National Institute of Aboriginal Cultures and Community Action. Indian delegates from all over the country damned official policy. They called for a full land reform, indigenous control over the proposed institute and expulsion of foreign missionaries, particularly the Summer Institute.[64]

The government was not impressed. Over university opposition it entrusted SIL with bilingual-bicultural literacy in the Oriente, including a teacher training institute at its base.[65] But during the 1981 border clashes the Oriente was militarized. On 22 May, two days before President Jaime Roldos died in a plane crash, he and five cabinet ministers gave the branch its one year dismissal notice. According to the decree, SIL's activities were incompatible with national investigation and development priorities. It was the government's duty to take direct responsibility for SIL's contractual functions. These would be assumed by four cabinet ministries, two national councils, a secretariat, an institute, a service, and the universities.[66]

Most Indian organizations supported the government's decision, but the Ecuadorian Federation of Evangelical Indians took its case to congress. To Representative Alejandro Carrion it was clear that SIL was offering Indians Christianity, not imposing it; preserving their legends; and teaching them reading, hygiene and civilized forms of life. Religious unity did not have anything to do with the concept of culture, Carrion argued. Since proselytism is a liberty guaranteed by the Constitution, animist and evangelical Shuar were a direct product of democracy. In a world tending inexorably toward the most developed, complete and dominant culture, human beings could not be sacrificed to a monstrous state of cultural backwardness, isolated from other Ecuadorians, and condemned to remain a museum piece for the diversion of anthropologists. Behind all this raving regard for Shuar culture, Carrion detected Catholics indignant at ecumenism. (In December 1981 eight bishops called for SIL's removal and blessed a mass demonstration in Chimborazo to that end.)[67] Or the sinister hand of Moscow, whose minions had assassinated Chester Bitterman.[68] (Indian organizations affiliated with the Communist Party had joined with others in pressing for SIL's removal.) Welcoming a petition from the branch's Indian supporters for a new seven year contract, another congressman called ending the old one a violation of human rights.[69]

How, asked Daniela Guaman, did evangelizing Indians through a variety of pressures, encouraging them to wear western clothes and abandon folk healing 'recover' their cultural values as SIL's supporters claimed? How did ending a government contract endanger religious liberty? Enough of the castrating prejudice that Ecuadorians were incapable of forging their own nationality.[70] Alfredo Viteri of the Confederation of Indigenous Nationalities accused SIL of forging the signatures of entire communities to claim native support. By threatening to end its medical and logistical services, the Institute was spreading the fear that the government would not replace them. Instead of turning SIL's programmes over to independent Indian organizations, Viteri charged, the government was favouring university research centres. Why did the transfer commission include members of the army rather than the Indian organizations?[71] Amidst the confusion of the cabinet ministries, councils and universities there was talk of creating a single national institute.

Colonels for Christ in Bolivia

Now that many Roman Catholic clergy refuse to bless terrorist juntas, they must look elsewhere for sanctification. For some evangelicals the temptation has been too great to resist. When a SIL-Bolivia official arranged a presidential prayer breakfast for his old friend General Hugo Banzer in 1975, the President gave Argentinian evangelist Luis Palau five nights of prime time television to moralize the country. The New Testament became the official religious text in all Bolivian schools.[72] It was during these halcyon days, when illegal drug processing on the presidential estates could be ignored and official sadism had not reached recent levels, that SIL-Bolivia publicized its version of Paul to the Romans 13:1 in eight Indian languages: 'Obey your legal superiors, because God is the one who has put them in charge. There is no government on earth which God has not permitted to come to power.'[73]

Since then the branch has come under the charge of army officers who seized power to protect the cocaine trade with their Nazi-trained Special Security Service. Romans 13:1 was, after all, a favourite Scripture of the Fuhrer. Shortly after Colonel Ariel Coca awarded SIL a medal in his capacity as Minister of Education and Culture, the U.S. Drug Enforcement Agency confirmed his implication in the traffic.[74] Fortunately, his government too, wanted North American evangelicals to teach morality to the citizenry. 'In a mysterious way God is at work in the world,' Luis Palau explained to Wycliffe supporters before launching a mass media campaign in Guatemala. 'He is doing far more than we will ever grasp. Our duty is simply to be obedient soldiers and do what we're told. Too often we all try to be strategists. There is one commander-in-chief — the Lord Jesus. He's in charge. If we do just what we're told, He'll take care of moving the pieces on the chessboard and pulling the king and the queen around in His own way.'[75] *

This comforting confusion between Colonel and Christ was the logical outcome of Townsendian diplomacy in a country which is ruled from the barricades or the barracks, usually the latter. The founder had come to La Paz for the 1954 Inter-American Indigenist Congress. He presented Peru's new bilingual schools, which the congress commended to all member countries,

---

* It is hard to believe,' Wycliffe told home supporters in a confidential April 1982 prayer notice, 'that the vices and lawlessness of the American people could have an impact on the tribes in the jungles of Eastern Colombia and those in the highlands of Bolivia. However, the highly profitable and illicit trade in marijuana and cocaine is injecting unimaginable wealth right down to the village level among the Indians of these two countries. Although middlemen pay only a pittance to those who produce the raw materials for these two drugs, that pittance is immense wealth for many of these people who have only recently begun to understand a cash economy. The introduction of violence, alcohol, and even drug usage into the tribes unprepared for this onslaught of materialism is wrecking havoc. The only sure antidote is the Word of God in the languages of the people, but the lure of materialism is so great that it is difficult even to get language helpers at times.'[76] In 1981 the Bolivian cocaine mafias moved into the Beni jungle where SIL is headquartered.

and obtained an introduction to President Paz Estenssoro, whose *Movimiento Nacionalista Revolucionario* had come to power two years before when tin miners shattered the army. Weighing the odds in a bankrupted country, the United States launched a nation-building programme which included salvaging the armed forces. With Paz on the U.S. dole, not to mention high hopes for oil and cattle ranching in wide spaces occupied only by Indians, he approved Townsend's contract with few changes.[77] The first teams arrived the following year and carved out their Tumi Chucua base in the Beni jungle near Riberalta.

Lacking an indigenist establishment, the government came to rely on SIL so much that its La Paz representatives became officials of the education ministry. The branch learned to expect cabinet and presidential-level attention, which made the tenure of General Juan Jose Torres (1970-71) especially traumatic. Following expulsion of the Peace Corps, SIL was rescued by Colonel Hugo Banzer (1971-78), who made its base a vacation spot. After his government floated a plan to import large numbers of white supremacist refugees from southern Africa, SIL became involved in another, to resettle Hmong survivors of the CIA's Montagnard army in Laos.[78] Banzer's overthrow and revolving door government jeopardized the branch, particularly during the first weeks of President Lidia Gueiler, but the bloody 'cocaine coup' of July 1980 restored a note of stability.

The branch vows to finish its work by 1984, leaving behind Bible trans-lations and social services administered by the government, fellow evangelical missions and Indian church leaders. In the highlands, where religious and political groups compete for the Quechua and Aymara who make up the majority of the country's population, Indian nationalists not only spurn SIL's pioneering work in bilingual education: they want to expel all missionaries, rid themselves of anthropologists, and ban Spanish. The previously unreached Chipaya are the branch success story in the highlands: at the cost of much conflict, half this pocket of 800 people have joined five different churches which quarrel among themselves.[79]

In the lowlands, SIL and other evangelical missions stand accused of complicity in genocide, for their eagerness to lure free Indians into the perils of dependency, not least lethal epidemics and debt bondage. They are also accused of isolating Indians from Bolivian society.[80] SIL reports that the Chacobo, a group whom it brought into contact, increased from 135 to 250 persons in 25 years.[81] An official was so proud of their cultural Christianity and co-operative that he wanted to find an anthropologist to see for himself.[82] If native people are already trapped by colonization, Christian missions are probably their only source of educational and medical help. Many of the Siriono, who are ethnographically famous as the 'nomads of the long bow', the translators found on ranches in various stages of tuberculosis.[83]

As the branch prepared for withdrawal, the U.S. Agency for International Development stimulated official interest in bilingual schools with a $5 million loan to the Department of Rural Education. Members were hired to supervise the Quechua and Aymara projects, while SIL itself obtained $100,000 from USAID for its 1976-77 'leadership training course', a

combination of bilingual education, medical training and community development. Soon the branch's bilingual schools had more than doubled, and 60
teachers, 45 with government salaries, were operating in 12 languages. Three
SIL community development teams organized marketing projects: co-operatives, stores, bee-keeping, road and airstrip construction. The object was to
transfer instruction at the SIL base to Bolivians, increase equitable contacts
between Indians and Bolivian society, and construct a school system which
could be placed in the hands of a, hopefully bilingual-conscious Ministry of
Education.[84]

Brazil

The Summer Institute's crisis in Brazil broke the pattern established in the
Andean countries but obeyed a larger one. Until the branch was banned
from native communities at the end of 1977, governments could be counted
upon to rescue SIL from its enemies. In Brazil the enemy was the government, a right-wing dictatorship whose action underlined the group's expenda-
bility for reasons which had nothing to do with Indian rights. When SIL
showed signs of returning to official favour three years later, the government
was frightened by Indian militancy and fortifying itself against less
trustworthy missionaries.

Unlike other branches, the Brazilian has always been circumscribed by
national authorities. Universities tied it down with more academic requirements than elsewhere; the government only allowed SIL to enter Indian
groups on a selective basis, sometimes withdrawing permission, as in a mid-
1960s advance in the Xingu Park. Even when the branch negotiated a quasi-
standard contract with the Ministry of Interior's National Indian Foundation
(FUNAI) in 1969, it expired four years later and was renewed for only three.[85]
Like the Catholic missions, SIL's 44 language operation was overshadowed by
FUNAI, whose protectionist mission has been compromised by the Interior
Ministry's development plans.*

---

* When Cameron Townsend approached a Brazilian delegate at the 1954 Inter-American
Indeginist Congress. he fell foul of his institute's new reputation as an evangelical mission.
To establish SIL's scientific credentials he dispatched scholars such as Kenneth Pike,
who obtained the invitation from anthropologist Darcy Ribeiro. The authorities,
however, declined to incorporate SIL into their Indian policy. The first contract, signed
with the National Museum of the University of Brazil in 1959, was limited to investigation, required SIL to train national linguists and safeguard the museum's scientific
reputation.[86] For embarking on their true mission, therefore, some members were
ordered out of Indian areas. But gradually SIL prevailed upon the central authorities,
particularly after the United States encouraged the armed forces to overthrow an
elected government in 1964. With SIL's sponsoring universities under suspicion from the
military regime, it signed its first contract with FUNAI in 1969 as the Trans-Amazon highways were being announced. Reportedly for resisting the transfer of national educational
policy to a private foreign group, FUNAI's executive council was demoted to an advisory
body by Interior Minister Jose Costa Cavalcante.[87]

SIL's downfall followed several years of confrontation between the government and Catholic missionaries over the havoc wrought by the Trans-Amazon highways. Catholic activists of the Missionary Indigenist Council (CIMI) helped Indians hold national assemblies; in 1976 FUNAI tried to ban CIMI from Indian reserves and two priests were killed by police and colonists. The same year FUNAI disrupted three assistance projects, by invoking national security to force foreign anthropologists to leave border areas. But it encouraged SIL to enter one of the same regions, the Uaupes across the border from the Colombian Vaupes, where the Northern Peripheral Highway would soon reach a large Indian population.[88]

In November 1977, the year after SIL began raising money for its FUNAI-authorized advance into the Uaupes, the same agency informed the branch that it would have to leave all native communities by the end of the year. Nor would its contract be renewed. The president of FUNAI, General Ismarth de Araujo Oliveira, told branch director Steve Sheldon that he was personally unhappy with the decision but that it had 'come from above.'[89] According to a U.S. State Department source, 'above' was the President of Brazil, General Ernesto Geisel (1974-79), and his Interior Minister, Mauricio Rangel Reis.[90]

Of the available explanations, the official ones were least convincing. Influential speculators had already accused missionaries of political subversion and the plunder of Amazonian minerals. At first, therefore, the Interior Minister allowed that SIL had been doing secret geological surveys. When that drew mixed reviews, Rangel Reis denied having made any such statement, reiterated the same theme, and added that bilingual education was being placed in Brazilian hands. The year before, he had declared bilingual education a waste of time, declaring that Indians must be integrated into Brazilian society immediately. Ismarth volunteered that the National Museum had found SIL ineffective: after surveying branch linguistic production, the Museum sent him a generally favourable report. Alleged clandestine landing strips for cargo planes, as well as supposed gold and diamond smuggling, rounded out the indictment.[91]

At first SIL spokesmen professed to be dumbfounded by the ban, but as time went on they began to suggest that their defense of Indian rights was responsible. It is true that men like Rangel Reis instinctively distrust missionaries. Yet like other evangelical groups in the Brazilian Amazon, SIL is known for circumspection. 'They are more concerned with Bible translation . . . and spiritual conversion than with economic or political work,' a Survival International observer summarized the evangelical reputation. '[They] are usually far better prepared linguistically, which probably makes their religious work more effective than the Catholics. They have, however, been severely criticized for failing to take a stand on land rights and other indigenous political issues.'[92] While SIL would have been reluctant to report any act of defiance against the government, it may therefore have had none to withhold. The National Intelligence Service informed the branch director that 'SIL was not viewed as a security problem.'[93]

There is little doubt that the group had been chosen for reprisal against the policies of its born-again brother President Jimmy Carter. The same day that the U.S. Secretary of State arrived for 'frank, businesslike and friendly' talks the government announced that SIL's visas would not be renewed.[94] Before the branch could censor its reaction, translator Thomas Crowell called the ban 'vengeance' for Carter's nuclear non-proliferation policy, which disrupted the plans of Brazilian military officers for energy independence and the atom bomb.[95] Soon, other North American evangelical missions reported that no more residence visas were being issued, a misfortune attributed to Carter's human rights position.[96]

In another departure from Andean experience, indigenists either kept silent or came to SIL's defense. Not only was it still appreciated for having taught linguistics at the Universities of Brazil and Brasilia; national professionals had been largely excluded from FUNAI and had shown little interest in the Amazon. Then too, SIL could be considered important to the short-term welfare of some groups since its scruples and institutional connections might check certain kinds of exploitation. SIL's medical reputation was better than FUNAI's (although, reportedly, to avoid competition translators gave up their practice when FUNAI started a programme), and it had trained bilingual teachers in at least six Indian languages. Most importantly, even antagonists wanted no part in a campaign led by the Minister of Interior. Any ban on friends of the Indian could be a precedent for others.

When FUNAI officials, university linguists and anthropologists argued that SIL could not be replaced immediately, the government rejected a transition period. Universities were willing to contract members, but in February 1978 the government hardened: SIL would have to leave the country at an unspecified date. Following more indigenist protest, at the year's end Wycliffe reported that it would be allowed to stay in Brazil, but not on attractive terms. Fewer than 30 of 44 teams the branch had fielded were still occupied at the regional centres in Cuiaba, Porto Velho, Belem and Manaus; it was trying to recruit Brazilian evangelicals; and the authorities occasionally permitted a team to visit a group.

The embargo against SIL was followed by an official proposal to 'emancipate' Indians from protectionist legislation, for immediate integration. As native leaders organized the Union of Indian Nations in 1980, the government purged FUNAI of conscientious elements and replaced them with military intelligence officers. The state protectionist body seemed to be graduating from old-fashioned paternalism and neglect into an agency to watch and suppress civil rights movements. Now that Catholic missionaries had inspired a wider support movement, the government decreed new immigration laws which could force them out of the country.

After Indians in the Xingu Park killed intruders in August 1980, FUNAI head, Colonel Joao Nobre da Veiga, announced that his agency would return to its understanding with SIL. CIMI revived the 1977 accusations ('translators, geologists or spies?'). Linguists and anthropologists started to question SIL's trajectory: having used the universities to climb into official favour, it had made itself the transmitter of official policy in Indian languages. Were it to return to the Indian reserves now, some felt , it would be even more dependent on FUNAI than before.

'I like the Brazilians,' a Bororo elder had explained at the 1977 ban, 'but they do not understand the people and cannot help them. When something is needed here, Thomas [Crowell] tries to obtain it. Now the children of the people and the people themselves are going to die.' 'If there was a war with the United States and the Americans understood the Indians better than the Brazilians', Darcy Ribeiro maintained, 'there would be danger. But this is improbable.'[97] 'Many landlords . . . are trying to grab Indian land', a SIL linguist from Germany explained. . . .

> Various other groups try to incite the Indians to rebellion and violence. But such influence is slight where Indians have received, through the Gospel in their own language, an orientation which does not permit violence. [Instead], they tried to solve their problems with God's help. . . .This is why SIL . . . finds itself in a cross-fire of interest groups . . . which are each offended by the influence of the Gospel.[98]

Soon after Ronald Reagan was elected in November 1980, the government gave SIL a security clearance and it began negotiating to re-enter Indian areas. But while the authorities allowed more teams to visit the reserves, a year and a half later they still barred SIL's restoration.

Panama

The Summer Institute came to Panama in 1969 on a ten year contract with the Department of Education. It seems to have stepped into pre-existing enclaves of Protestant Indians. They preferred their North American mission-aries to Panamanians, whose efforts to free themselves from dependency on the United States include massive development projects on Indian land, to which opposition is frequently considered imperialist. During the wire service tempest of 1975, several patriotic fronts accused SIL of usurping functions which Panamanians could perform, committing espionage against the revolutionary process of General Omar Torrijos, and stirring up opposition to the government. In particular, SIL allegedly had incited Bayano Cuna Indians to resist expropriation for the Bayano hydroelectric project.[99]

At contract expiration in June 1979 the government gave the translators seven months to finish their work.[100] With the help of Indian lobbyists, they won an extension to teach Panamanians linguistics and even began to press for a new contract. Following several signs that they had exhausted official patience — loss of radio communication rights, then permission to live in Indian areas and operate an airplane — in July 1981 all 20 members were expelled on six days notice. The government was reportedly bowing to the wishes of Guaymi Indians, who had taken ten officials hostage over their many grievances.[101] While a new oil pipeline would be very difficult to sacrifice, a few Bible translators were not. Some months before a Guaymi representative had explained that SIL generated differences among Indians to impose systems of birth control.[102] Allegedly unauthorized radio transmitting equipment, which according to SIL had been placed in storage after the contract lapsed, was seized by police and presented as evidence of CIA involvement.[103]

Mexico

When we left the Summer Institute in Mexico, it was securely in the favour of senior indigenists and the government of the *Partido Revolucionario Institucional* (PRI). A secular constitution, official nationalism and respect for Indian culture notwithstanding, there seemed little reason to believe that this would change. Building on the friendships of the founder, SIL had maintained its lead as the principal linguistic agency in Mexico, indeed the only one working in more than a handful of languages. Since 1951 the branch had operated under contract to the Department of Education; it had authored as much as 85% of the department's indigenous primers, for a teacher corps numbering in the thousands; and it estimated that its Bible translations had brought three quarters of a million people to Christ.[104]

Under the mandate of official indispensability SIL-Mexico had entered 106 languages; officially completed its New Testament task in 39; and planned to enter 36 more. Only the Papua New Guinea branch surpassed it in size. A headquarters stood on government donated land in the Federal District; regional study centres had been built to the north and south at Ixmiquilpan, Hidalgo and Mitla, Oaxaca; and tucked away in the Lacandon Forest of Chiapas was Jungle Camp, established to teach survival skills for the Amazon and now the rite of passage for Wycliffe recuits. All 142 New Testaments were to be in the hands of the intended by the implausible date of 22 November, 1990, when the headquarters at Tlalpan was to revert to the government and SIL depart the land of its birth.[105]

To justify its position in national life SIL summoned the names of giants of Mexican indigenism who had blessed its work. The living embodiment of these figures was the *patronato,* a nominal supervisory body which typically included the President of the Republic, the Secretary of Education, members of the Saenz and Cardenas families, ex-cabinet ministers and eminent indigenists. The *patronato* dignified the convergence between the aims of SIL, the indigenist establishment and the institutional revolution. Since the time of Lazaro Cardenas, indigenists had been impressed by the group's success in mobilizing Indians against what they perceived, in the words of Rus and Wasserstrom, as 'the three pillars of Indian backwardness:' alcoholism, witchcraft and monolingualism.[106] Honouring, as always, official efforts, Wycliffe informed home supporters that a progressive government and the translated Word were bringing a new and better life to the Indians of Mexico.[107]

When SIL's future began to look uncertain in Peru, Colombia and Bolivia, the Mexican branch found old friends in high posts of the Luis Echeverria (1970-76) administration. 'Had [President Echeverria] asked us to name the arrangement [of government entities] and the people with whom we would most like to work,' the branch director reported, 'I do not believe we could have been more pleased with the results.' [108] Despite a flurry of anti-imperialist accusations following reports from New York and South America, Echeverria's successor Jose Lopez Portillo (1976-82) also accepted the honorary presidency of the *patronato*.

SIL's long tenure and its sudden fall in 1979 grew out of two contradictions in the institutional revolution. The first is the need to maintain control over a large peasantry being pauperized by capitalist development. To reconcile the demands of small farmers and their exploiters, the revolution gave rise to 'structures of mediation' which divert peasant aspirations into official channels.[109] The *cacique* (rural boss) is a central figure in the system: initially a popular leader, he was recruited into the PRI regime and joined the rural bourgeoisie. *Caciques* and their patronage networks are the basis of PRI control of the countryside: when the opposition gets out of hand, they hire gun thugs or use their political ties to call in the police or army. Opportunities for appeal in the huge state and federal bureaucracies are many and usually futile.

The second contradiction is the discrimination against seven million Indians, 15% of the population who, traditionally, have been blamed for the country's backwardness but provide much of its labour force.[110] The *Instituto Nacional Indigenista* (INI), organized by cultural anthropologists in 1948, became the nucleus of a large bureaucracy dedicated to forging national unity via 'acculturation' or 'Mexicanization'. In exchange for official backing, the indigenists agreed to accommodate Indians to ambitious development schemes which, despite all the talk of a new and better day, cost them dearly.

Together the *cacique* and the indigenist go far to explain the stability of the PRI regime in Indian regions, to say nothing of the contradictory accusations levelled against SIL in the late 1970s. When *cacique* oppression sparks popular revolt or hinders federal plans, indigenists have intervened with reform programmes, recruited popular leaders, and commenced the cycle of *cacique* formation anew. To older *caciques,* evangelical movements have posed a definite threat, protesting as they do against certain forms of religious and economic manipulation. Thus the Cultural Institute of the State of Oaxaca – a stronghold of *caciquismo,* the below-subsistence farm and repression where SIL fielded 52 teams – accused the North Americans of 'incit[ing] mountain settlements against the municipal authorities,' that is, the *caciques.* Since many translators had spent decades in the mountains, according to the Cultural Institute, 'their word is law and their wishes are carried out without the possibility of objection by official Mexican entities.'[111] But at the federal level, SIL was highly regarded for its ability to draw converts into reform programmes. In the words of *Punto Critico,* SIL and other missionaries in Chiapas 'attract the most restive *campesinos,* provide an ideology of accomodation and obedience, and channel them outside the zones of conflict.'[112]

As the Summer Institute secured its assurances from the Echeverria and Lopez Portillo administrations, four developments — agricultural crisis, Indian militancy, conflict within the indigenist establishment, and the switch to oil as Mexico's main development hope — combined to upset the equilibrium of forces in which it had thrived for so many years. In the early 1970s, open conflict over land erupted from the arid north to the jungles in the south. The agrarian explosion — land invasions, escalated repression and guerrilla movements — moved President Echeverria to accelerate land reform. The restoration of stability required federal confrontation with certain *caciques,* who entered left-wing PRI discourse as an obstacle to development.

In the course of these conflicts, thousands of young, literate Indian leaders ran foul of the *caciques,* allied themselves with disaffected traditionalists and raised the insignia of revolt, not only against local bosses but the paternalistic indigenists to whom they owed their education and anomalous position. As opposition political parties, religious missions and reformist PRI bureaucrats vied for protest followings, Indian leaders rejected the indigenist policy of acculturation. Ethnic conflict and the oppression of Indians, was due, not to the alleged cultural backwardness of Indians, but the unequal terms of trade in Mexican society. Denouncing manipulation by leftist sects, missionaries and indigenists as well as the government, Indians began to demand recognition as self-governing nationalities. Guillermo Bonfil Batalla has summarized Indian demands as: 1) 'recovery, expansion and control of productive resources' — land, water and subsoil rights — and the government assistance necessary to organize communities as modern units of production; 2) 'equitable relations with the national society,' first and foremost an end to *cacique* domination and state violence; and 3) 'legitimation of ethnic pluralism,' including an educational system controlled by Indians and appropriate to their cultures, not just the manipulation of their languages to undermine confidence in Indian ways of life.[113]

Indian protest discredited the indigenist establishment, which had been under attack from university Marxists since the 1960s. Senior officials acknowledged failure and promised reform; sceptics argued that the failure was in the very premises of *indigenismo* and the institutional revolution itself. Middle class radicals recruited into the National Indigenist Institute and other agencies faced an old dilemma, between their aspirations and the demands of career advancement. The INI expanded rapidly but remained a hamstrung bureaucracy, trapped between Indian demands, federal policy and local bosses.

To bring Indian militancy under control, in 1975 the Echeverria government created PRI- and INI-supervised advisory bodies, the National Council of Indian Peoples and its supreme councils in each ethnic group. The government also created a large development fund for small farmers, the INI-supervised National Plan for Deprived Zones and Marginal Groups (COPLAMAR). The exercise in PRI corporatism was only partially successful, however: some Indian political groups rejected it, some supreme councils became vehicles for protest organizing, and the national congresses could become unpleasant. As one critic put it, the new structure had not been 'able to function exclusively to present cultural and linguistic demands designed by anthropologists.'[114]

These developments set the stage for a house-cleaning in the indigenist establishment. In October 1975, a few dozen social scientists at the First National Indian Congress issued the Patzcuaro Denunciation. Several of the more prominent signers were INI officials, including adjunct director Salomon Nahmad, who two years before had addressed the SIL(WBT) biennial conference in Mexico City.[115] The manifesto accused SIL of being a pseudo-scientific agent of imperialist penetration fronting for the CIA. It had crippled Mexican linguistics, violated the Constitution and impeded the organization of Indians to defend their rights, by dividing communities and diverting attention from their fundamental problems.[116]

When Jose Lopez Portillo became President in 1976, he turned to oil as the solution to Mexico's economic crisis. The prospect of once again becoming a major supplier to the United States did not please the left: it would multiply Washington's 'national security' interest in their country's affairs. The announcement of vast reserves prompted a wave of protective nationalism. Journalists investigated North American religious groups with popular followings: there was some confusion between the Mormons (whom the CIA favours in recruiting case officers because they are so loyal); the Jehovah's Witnesses (who will not salute the flag or sing the national anthem because they reject national loyalties), the Seventh Day Adventists (who observe Old Testament dietary taboos and whose Saturday sabbath disrupts community work days); the Children of God (who were convicted of soliciting minors for promiscuous acts); World Vision (which was accused of using its child welfare activities to gather intelligence); the World Council of Churches (which was accused of distributing CIA and corporate money); and the Summer Institute, which was accused of nearly everything – from opposing school breakfast programmes to isolating Indians to preserve them as objects of study, thereby obstructing the necessary 'change in mental structure.'[117]

In 1978, some months before the Mexican Ambassador to Washington awarded Cameron Townsend the Decoration of the Aztec Eagle, directors of 12 INI regional centres in the south accused SIL and other foreigners of impeding their work. Many Indians refused medical assistance, for example, because foreign evangelists and anthropologists 'fostered distrust.'[118] The INI's Salomon Nahmad charged that U.S. intelligence agents were posing as scientists and missionaries, which of course they have done.[119] 'The risk of another Texas is being repeated in Tehuantepec,' an INI regional director warned the Mexico City daily *Uno Mas Uno* in early 1979: the functionary

> explains how in many places the INI's work is ignored and systematically belittled, while SIL's is eulogized and exaggerated. 'They are ahead of us because they have better resources. . . . It is hard for people to

226

recognize, but we try, sometimes heroically, to carry out our projects. . . . From us they demand, we are *government*. . . . While [the people] believe that INI workers are obliged to solve their problems, they welcome the linguists, listen to them, accept their advice. . . and help with the construction of buildings, schools, roads or landing strips' . . . . Without alarm, the anthropologist refers to this entire operation as 'a grand movement of separatism, like that brought to pass in Texas in the 19th Century.' [120]

Uno Mas Uno propounded conspiracy theory at some length in January 1979. It explained many ambiguities. While the branch had always presented itself as a scientific, humanitarian body, its work was associated with religious strife, even bloodshed, in a number of areas. One of the reasons — evangelical abstention from folk Catholic community activities — seemed to contradict its claim to respect indigenous culture. SIL said that it was teaching Indians to be good Mexicans: its converts were protesting exploitation by Mexicans and regarded North Americans as the bearers of true religion. SIL's information gathering network was ostensibly limited to language data: it could easily extend beyond this function, and members knew remote areas like few Mexicans. SIL claimed disinterest in politics: evangelical pastors often actively opposed political protest. Finally, was all this activity really financed by churches? Common traits in the SIL membership — dual identity reserve, distrust of Mexicans, right-wing political views — reinforced inferences based upon experience with the United States.

Dismissing SIL's explanations, conspiracy theorists interpreted its activities as a mode of North American infiltration designed to control strategic areas, facilitate internal repression, and establish a popular base for a repeat of history: eventual U.S. military intervention. The growing concentration of teams in southern Mexico was a pincer movement threatening the new oil fields, not a reflection of linguistic diversity as SIL claimed. Perhaps its computers evaluated natural resources instead of language data. Jungle Camp in the Lacandon Forest seemed to confirm that the organization was not telling the truth: as a carefully controlled rite of initiation into Wycliffe, the camp maintained tight security. While official visitors were received at Main Base, no outsiders were to trespass upon Advance Base or the survival trainees left alone in the jungle to subsist on roots and insects. The dispersal of Jungle Campers through 20 local Tzeltal villages — the Village Living section of the course — seemed to confirm that there were far more members in Mexico than admitted.

A few of SIL's old indigenist allies ridiculed conspiracy theory. It was idiotic to suppose that the tension the linguists caused in native communities was different than that produced by any outside element: were Indians to be put in a giant fishbowl? The North Americans were doing what Mexican linguists never had been willing to, work in the most remote parts of the country without conveniences of any kind and for little pay. But the onslaught threw SIL's position in Mexico into high relief, creating an audience for less speculative arguments. They revolved around the backwardness of a national language policy which relied upon missionaries from the United States; the unconstitutionality of the Department of Education contract; and SIL's retarding influence on Mexican linguistics. By making themselves so useful, the North Americans had minimized Mexican incentive to take the field and excused the government from spending money on linguistics. Thus the lack of Mexican expertise required SIL's services, and because they sufficed there was no need to finance training programmes, in an endless cycle of technological dependency. University linguists and anthropologists noted the group's long association with the INI and other agencies. Now that a secular state was acknowledging Indian demands to respect their traditions, why was it still mortgaging linguistics to evangelists who campaigned against those traditions? The very logic of indigenist reform since the early 1970s was turning against SIL.[121]

In February 1979 the Communist Party of Mexico called for expulsion and a professional body, the College of Ethnologists and Social Anthropologists, launched an investigation. With the INI in the van, senior officials of institutions long associated with the North Americans distanced themselves and called for an inquiry. The Departments of Education and Interior joined with the INI in investigating SIL's contractual compliance, finance, linguistic and literacy work. *Uno Mas Uno* obtained a memorandum to the Secretary of Education: four general directors recommended ending the contract because the *New York Times* was said to be preparing revelations which would cause an international scandal. If necessary, the directors advised, the department could contract SIL members on a personal basis.[122] The INI, the National Institute of Anthropology and History, and the Department of Education started a programme to train more Mexican linguists. In June 1979, the Mexican College of Anthropologists recognized SIL's linguistic services, questioned the espionage accusations and, for legal and constitutional reasons, recommended ending the contract. 'Pray the Lord will overrule all the powers of darkness,' Wycliffe had asked home supporters two months earlier, 'as they are making an organized, concerted effort to get the Summer Institute of Linguistics out of the country.'[123]

The turmoil in indigenist circles can be gathered from a single day's news items in the June 15, 1979 *Uno Mas Uno*. At a seminar, social scientists and students confront branch director John Alsop with the charge that SIL 'is the principal instrument of imperialist and ideological penetration which tries to divide native communities . . . to control the country politically.' The Archbishop of Oaxaca and nine bishops proclaim the 'good news of total liberation' to the poor. The 'frivolity' of the 'infinity of programs' in Indian education is condemned by one of the main contenders. Finally, an organization of teachers, called the National Alliance of Bilingual Indian Professionals, condemns the PRI, opposition political parties, the Church and the Department of Education for manipulating Indians. The bilingual teachers have closed their meeting to non-Indian intellectuals and especially linguists, whom they call 'dishonest' and accuse of intellectual exploitation.

The Alliance wanted SIL expelled as part of its campaign for a non-alienating, bicultural education. Several supreme councils — Otomi, Tlahuica, Matlatzinca, Mazahua — also demanded expulsion on the grounds that it was divisive and ethnocidal. But at the Third Congress of Indian Peoples, in July 1979, North Americans were not the principal issue. Delegates raised the familiar litany of demands: an end to official complicity in political assassinations, liberty for political prisoners, punishment of corrupt agrarian and indigenist officials, protection of land and water rights against large landowners. While the congress remained under official constraint, there were also demands for control of the INI by Indians rather than 'dishonest bureaucrats.'[124]

The Lopez Portillo government was accustomed to making symbolic gestures to the left. Although SIL had never offended the men who rule Mexico, it was becoming an attractive sacrifice on several scores. First, dismissing North Americans would demonstrate the administration's patriotism as it arranged for the sale of oil and natural gas to the United States. Second, it would send another signal to Washington that the oil belonged to Mexico, not the U.S., and that even vaguely suspicious activities in its vicinity would be discouraged. Finally, ending the contract would rid the government of an embarrassment and, as a news service headlined, 'herald a new deal for Indians.'[125] Hopefully it would encourage trouble-makers to rally to the new policy of indigenous participation and ethnic pluralism, demonstrating that the cause of the Indians was the cause of the government.

In August, a high official advised SIL to make an honourable exit by renouncing the contract. Townsend arrived in the belief that the Lord would throw back the tide. On 21 September 1979, two weeks after the College of Ethnologists released its findings and two days after the Lopez and Carter administrations closed an unpopular natural gas deal, the Department of Education announced that it had ended the contract. INI Director Ignacio Ovalle noted that, while anyone could do linguistics, a contract with a religious mission had been constitutionally anomalous. Salomon Nahmad hailed the decision because 'Mexican Indians will reconquer their identity and be able to seek their own cultural road.'[126]

'What have you done for the Indian people of our fatherland?' three Zapotecs asked SIL's indigenist foes. 'The only thing you do is insinuate that Indian people do not have . . . the ability to distinguish what is useful and useless. We ourselves would have thrown SIL's representatives . . . out of our towns if they had been harmful to our race.'[127] *Excelsior* columnists accused SIL's opponents of being jealous salon radicals and puppets of Soviet imperialism. Why would U.S. 'imperialism' do so many good things for Indians, one asked, when it would be easier to oppress them in their traditional backwardness and ignorance? Now indigenist bureaucrats could rest assured that they would be able to continue exploiting Indians.[128]

At year's end, the immigration office informed SIL that it would not receive more student visas, which would force half the branch to leave the country during 1980. Members began retiring across the border to the SIL centre in Dallas and to Tucson, Arizona, where Wycliffe supporters constructed new quarters. The exiled translators started to return on tourist visas and invite language informants to the U.S. Jungle Camp was renamed The Americas Field Training Course and retired to a ranch in the unjungled, Indianless plains of South Texas. Uncle Cam hoped to reopen the door.

Sundered Forever

The loss of the state contract in Mexico shattered the Summer Institute's indigenist image, but only as *indigenismo* itself had fallen on hard times. SIL's elevation to pariah was ratified in Merida, Mexico at the November 1980 congress of the Inter-American Indigenist Institute (III). A woefully financed, advisory body to members of the Organization of American States, the III had endorsed SIL as a legitimate international organization for more than 30 years. But now a forum called it 'an ideological and political institution' concealing its objectives under a scientific facade.[129] The delegation from Venezuela characterized the Bible translators as an 'incessant prospector of natural resources for the transnational enterprises' and 'an infiltrating agent for U.S. ideology.'[130] Despite opposition and abstention — from Chile, Bolivia (whose delegation was headed by SIL's government liaison) Brazil, Costa Rica and Paraguay — the congress voted to ask governments to investigate SIL's activities and, if appropriate, expel it.[131] A majority of delegations also voted to strip Cameron Townsend of an honour bestowed by the last III congress in 1972, as 'Benefactor of the linguistically isolated populations of America.' He was on hand for the motion and left the meeting after a seven minute ovation for it. The founder 'had believed himself a Bartolome de las Casas and used the name of Lazaro Cardenas . . . to neocolonize Latin America,' stated Felix Baez-Jorge of Mexico's National Indigenist Institute, 'but from now on the names of Townsend and Cardenas will be separated forever.'[132]

The credibility of the Inter-American Indigenist Institute was not much higher. Like Townsend, the indigenist politicians of the III had formulated plans for Indians, angled for official patronage and served as a doormat for state expansion. The founder's unequalled contributions notwithstanding, his final service to indigenism was expiating its sins. As delegates echoed the platitude that *indigenismo* had failed, an observer recalled the formulation made by Lazaro Cardenas at the first such congress 40 years before, when the future of the government-indigenist partnership seemed so bright: that the goal of *indigenismo* was to seek the 'effective emancipation of the Indian', a liberation tied to that of the proletariat and based on the right of native people to their own ethnic identity. Something of the III's success in emancipation could be gathered from the fact that the 1980 congress was the first to include Indian representatives.[133] Beforehand, some of the same Mexican supreme councils who had campaigned against SIL denounced the III as a 'farce' because it had failed to protest government atrocities against Indians.[134] Were the III to offend those dues-paying regimes which had systematically violated Indian rights, soon there might be no III left to hold the next congress.

230

Yet with the encouragement of the Mexican government, the organization was experimenting with new fundraising methods which might make it more independent.[135] Under attack from Indians, and conscious of its history as a pawn, even the III was trying to escape the indigenist reputation by redefining Latin American anthropology as an autonomous, critical discipline.

The Mexican 'new anthropology' seemed to offer the most reassuring vision of the future, in keeping with the leading intellectual role which Mexican *indigenismo* has always played. Felix Baez-Jorge could look forward to

> an anthropology which . . . performs support functions in two directions:
> on the one hand, orienting and critically questioning (for now to the
> extent which limitations permit) official actions; on the other, supporting
> those who constitute its object of study . . . in their struggles and
> demands, with the . . . knowledge they need to make them effective,
> in the context of the class struggle.[136]

There would even be some opportunity to combine the two, as in the Department of Education's pilot programme to train Indian ethnolinguists. Through *concientizacion* as advanced by the Catholic educator Paulo Freire, the programme would encourage 'consciousness of domination', which in turn would encourage Indians to revalue their languages and cultures and place the liberation struggle on an appropriate footing.[137] Since the government was conceding the right of Indians to ethnic pluralism and a greater role in programmes for their benefit, it could claim to support the struggle of Indians for their human and cultural rights. Those Indians who cared to ratify the exercise could pledge to struggle for, not just the liberation of their own peoples, but the revolutionary transformation of Latin American society.

Elsewhere it was harder for indigenists to arrange one big, anti-imperialist family. In Colombia, for example, there was far less room for manoeuvre between the state and native people. Carlos Uribe noted that criticism by his own, younger generation hastened the retirement of senior anthropologists, permitting it to take control of the profession.

> We still have not had enough time to mature as anthropologists and
> we lack clarity over the proper orientation for the science in a country
> like Colombia; we know that the academic option is not satisfactory,
> but we also distrust an irresponsible 'anthropological activism. And
> what is worse, we have neglected serious investigation in the fear of
> contaminating ourselves with academicism. . . . It is clear that it is
> ever more difficult to do anthropology in the country, especially in
> certain conflict-ridden regions. The missionaries distrust the young
> anthropologists, as do the security agencies and representatives of
> certain government sectors. Even many communities are sceptical of
> the benefits which anthropological investigation and action can bring
> them and resent the 'invasion' of anthropologists in their territory.

231

Gradually repression and political persecution fasten their grip on the country. To reflect on the human and the social in Colombia can be subversive now.[138]

A new ally had been gained, however, as becomes apparent in an Indian account of a 1980 anthropological congress. According to *Unidad Indigena,* the participants noted that the Summer Institute

does not simply try to study our languages . . . they are convinced that our customs such as drinking chicha or chewing coca are things of the devil. . . . . What they really want is for us to sing psalms and forget that we are people of flesh and bone, that we need our lands invaded by landlords, and that now we are not ashamed of our culture and customs. . . . They are fanatics who deprecate our beliefs. . . . [But] the Regional Indian Council of the Cauca approves of social investigators like the anthropologists who meet to . . . become acquainted with our situation and effectively support the struggles which Indians all over Colombia are waging.[139]

References

1. Prayer sheet, WBT-Huntington Beach, December 1977.
2. Dedication of 'Spirit of Kansas City,' 19 January 1958, Nixon, Vice-Presidential papers, Laguna Niguel Federal Archive, filed under SIL.
3. For an analysis of these trends among the Aymara of Bolivia, see Albo 1979.
4. Martha Hildebrandt, in *El Comercio* 15 February 1953 and SIL-Peru 1955:78.
5. SIL-Peru 1966:93.
6. Varese 1976a.
7. On SINAMOS, see Corry 1977b and Pierre Van Den Berghe, in Browman and Schwarz 1979:258-9.
8. *La Prensa* 30 September 1975.
9. Pike and Brend 1977:5 (1973); *In Other Words* November 1975 11; and Hernan Ramirez 1976.
10. Author's interview, Lima, 22 March 1976.
11. The two San Marcos denunciations were published in *El Correo* 28 September and 17 October 1975. The ministry responded in *Comercio* 30 September 1975.
12. Escribens 1975; Robinson 1975; D'Ans 1981:160-2 (*Comercio* 26 November 1975).
13. *Prensa* 22 November 1975; *La Cronica* 11 December 1975; *El Expreso* 15 December 1975; *Comercio* 29 February and 1 March 1976.
14. *Cronica* 24 December 1975.
15. *El Excelsior* (Mexico, D.F.) 22 April 1976:21A; Cano et al 1979:118-20.
16. Author's interview, Lima, 23 February 1977.

17. 7 June 1977, branch letterhead. Released to author under FOIA.
18. *Who's Who in Government* (Chicago: Marquis) 1977.
19. Hefleys 1972:22.
20. *Comercio* 13 April 1976:1.
21. *El Peruano* 17 April 1976.
22. *In Other Words* March 1977:2.
23. *Correo* 26 April 1976:3; *Prensa* 25 May 1976. There were also testimonials by Juan Mendoza (ibid. 2 February 1976), Luis Valcarcel (*Expreso* 15 May 1976), General Jorge Barbosa Falconi (*Prensa* 8 June 1976), Francisco Miro Quesada (*Oiga* (Lima) 21 January 1977:13-14.
24. *Latin America* (London) 26 March 1976:98; *Latin America Regional reports: Andean Group* (London) 12 December 1980:5.
25. Bolo, *ABC* (Lima) 16 January 1976:10-11; *Prensa* 10 June 1976. The branch arrayed its statistics in *Gente* 19 December 1975:39-421).
26. Cables, U.S. Embassy-Lima to State Department, 1975-6: 17 July, 'limited official use', signed Dean; 30 September 'limited official use', signed Dean; 20 November 'unclassified', signed Dean; 26 November 'limited official use', signed Barneby; 10 March 'confidential', signed Dean; 31 March 'unclassified', signed Dean; 19 April 'limited official use', signed Dean; 28 April 'limited official use', signed Dean, lines deleted; 20 May 'limited official use', signed Dean; 21 June 'limited official use', signed Dean. Released to author under FOIA.
27. *Gente* 12 January 1977:42.
28. *Documentos* (Mexico City: Centro Antropologico de Documentacion de America Latina) no. 2 May 1977: Per/46-7.
29. *In Other Words* October 1977:5; December 1977:6; April 1978:7.
30. E.g. *Comercio* 1 March 1976.
31. Najar 1976 and Cecilio Jurafo, in *Educacion en la Revolucion* (Lima: Ministry of Education) 10 June 1976; *Momento* (Lima) 26 March 1976:28-9.
32. *Prensa* 14 and 21 May 1976.
33. Varese 1976a.
34. Amasifuen 1978.
35. *Maryknoll* (Ossining, New York) October 1980:12-15.
36. *Centro de Investigacion y Promocion Amazonica:* cited in *Cultural Survival* (Cambridge, Massachusetts) Fall 1979.
37. Larson et al 1979:163-5; two mimeoed documents, 'Educacion bilingue de la Selva' (Yarinacocha, 27 April 1978) and 'Officina de educacion bilingue de la selva' (SIL-Peru, n.d.); *Cultural Survival* Spring 1980:3.
38. Corry 1977b.
39. *IWGIA Newsletter* (Copenhagen) April 1980:63-4.
40. *In Other Words* November 1978:6.
41. *Peruano* c. 27 January 1979.
42. *Wycliffe Associates Newsletter* October 1979:5.
43. *Marka* 7 February 1980:22-5.
44. *Guardian* (New York) 11 June 1980.
45. *Latin America Regional Reports: Andean Group* (London) 24 July 1981:6-7. *In Other Words* February-March 1982:7.
46. *El Comercio* (Quito) 8 June 1981,
47. For a more detailed picture of the pressures at work in the Ecuadorian

Amazon, see Whitten 1976 and 1981.
48. Robinson 1981:48.
49. For analyses of the Lowland Quichua, the Gospel Missionary Union among the Shuar, the Shuar Federation and the related Achuar (or Achual), see Whitten 1981.
50. Vickers 1981:59. For additional data, see the same author's article in Whitten 1981. On the Cofan, see Robinson 1979.
51. Steven 1980:139, 147.
52. Bloom 1981:260-8;
53. Circular, Wycliffe Associates, 20 June 1980.
54. *Nueva* (Quito) April 1980:21-9.
55. Ibid. May 1975:16-33.
56. Letter from Jose Mario Ruiz Navas, *Comercio* 2 August 1978:17, 20.
57. *Nueva* August 1976:44-7.
58. *Christianity Today* 5 October 1979:70-1 and 12 December 1980:72.
59. 'La educacion bilingue y la opresion a las masas campesinas', mimeo, Asociacion Escuela de Antropologia de la Universidad Catolica de Quito, and *Ultimas Noticias* (Quito) 7 February 1975.
60. *El Pionero* (Santo Domingo de los Colorados) April 12, 1975:1, 4.
61. SIL-Ecuador 1980:7-9, 16-17, 27-28.
62. Author's interviews, Quito, 1976-7.
63. *Comercio* 22 October 1979.
64. *Survival International Review* Spring 1980:23-5.
65. *Nueva* April 1980:24-9.
66. Decree 1159, *Registro Official* May 29, 1981:2-3.
67. *Punto de Vista* (Quito) 18 December 1981:5, 11.
68. Carrion, in *Comercio* 14 March and 27 June 1981.
69. *Comercio* 10 October 1981.
70. Guaman, in *Suplemento Cultural (Comercio)* 29 November 1981:4.
71. Viteri, in *Lucha Campesina* (Quito) November 1981:6-7. For other documents and national viewpoints, see Trujillo 1981 and Cano 1981:363-84.
72. Palau 1981:16.
73. SIL-Bolivia 1975.
74. *New York Times* 31 August 1981:1-7. *In Other Words* February 1981:6; *Uno Mas Uno* (Mexico, D.F.) 15 April 1981:8.
75. Palau 1981:15.
76. Prayer sheet, WBT-Huntington Beach, April 1982.
77. Hefleys 1974:187-8. The contract was published in *Boletin Indigenista* (Mexico, D.F.) December 1954:262-7.
78. Jeff Stein, Pacific News Service, *Latinamerica Press* (Lima) 21 December 1978:7-8.
79. *Translation* September/October 1974:7; *In Other Words* November 1976:1-2; Summer 1978:1-3; February 1980:1-2.
80. For criticism of the branch on these and other scores, see Riester 1975:49-55; Lewis 1978:11-16; Gesellschaft fur bedrohte Volker 1979:157-73; Pereira 1981.
81. *In Other Words* March 1980:1-2.
82. David Farah, author's interview, La Paz, 25 January 1977.
83. Garrard (1970:59-62), who sketches SIL's work in each group.

84. Grant no. 60074, documents from USAID-La Paz released to author.
85. The 1973 contract was published in SIL-Brazil 1974:6-11.
86. Hefleys 1974:188-90, Townsend and Pittman 1975:36 and 'WBT in Brazil', WBT mimeo c.1970. 1959 contract *Boletin Indigenista*, June 1961:112-17.
87. Leite et al 1981:61-2, 66.
88. *In Other Words* February 1977:5.
89. Cable, U.S. Embassy-Brasilia to State Department, 29 November 1977, 'confidential', signed Johnson. Released to author under FOIA.
90. Cable, State Department to Embassy-Brasilia, 23 November 1977, 'confidential', signed Habib, FOIA.
91. For press reports, see *Folha de Sao Paulo* 23 November 1977 (translated in *Survival International Review* Winter 1978:28); Associated Press 12 December 1977; *Christianity Today* 30 December 1977: 43-4; *Time* 9 January 1978:35.
92. Anna Presland, *Survival International Review* Spring 1979:16.
93. 29 November 1977 Embassy Cable.
94. *Washington Post* 23 November 1977:A15.
95. *Porantim* (Manaus:CIMI) September 1980:15.
96. *Christianity Today* 21 September 1979:57.
97. *Porantim* September 1980:1, 14-15; Leite et al 1981:59-67.
98. Ursula Wiesemann, quoted in Cano et al 1979:65. For another translator's response to the embargo, see *In Other Words* March 1979:1-3.
99. *Prensa Latina* 24 September 1975 and cable, U.S. Embassy-Panama City to State Department, 7 October 1975, 'limited official use', signed Gonzalez, FOIA. For an April 1976 position paper by the Cultural Workers Front of Panama, see *Documentos* (Mexico, D.F: Centro Antropologico de Documentacion de America Latina) May 1977:Pan /9-14.
100. *Christianity Today* 21 September 1979:54.
101. *Latin America Weekly Report* (London) 10 July 1981:12. Also *In Other Words* January 1982:5; Associated Press 7 July 1981; *Washington Post* 8 July 1981:A.20.
102. *Uno Mas Uno* (Mexico, D.F.) 20 March 1981:17.
103. *Christianity Today* 4 September 1981:59.
104. 1951 contract: *Boletin Indigenista* December 1951:332-9; 85% calculated from Bravo 1977:113.
105. SIL/WBT 1971:81, 83.
106. Rus and Wasserstrom 1981:165.
107. E.g., Beekman and Hefley 1974:22-3.
108. SIL/WBT 1971:80.
109. Bartra 1978.
110. Rus n.d.
111. *Uno Mas Uno* 10 January 1979.
112. *Punto Critico* (Mexico, D.F.) 5 October 1976:16.
113. Bonfil Batalla 1979:3.
114. Daniel Cazes, *Uno Mas Uno* 29 July 1979:7,
115. *Translation* July/August 1973:4.
116. Ochoa Zazueta 1975:78-81.
117. *Uno Mas Uno* 11 January 1979. Ibid. 15 January 1979 (Mormons);

uary 1978 (Children of God); 10-11 September 1979 (World Vision); *Proceso* 15 October 1979 (World Council):28.

118, *Uno Mas Uno* 15 February 1978:1, 4.
119. *Foreign Broadcast Information Service* 28 July 1978:M1; p.1A, 10A *El Excelsior* 7 May 1979:1A, 10A; *Revista de Revistas (Excelsior)* 16 May 1979:4-7.
120. *Uno Mas Uno* 25 January 1979.
121. For a chronology of the controversy and press references, particularly in *Uno Mas Uno* from January through August 1979, see College of Ethnologists and Social Anthropologists 1979:103-121. Also the weekly *Proceso* (Mexico D.F.) from 10 September through 15 October 1979, nos. 149-54.
122. Daniel Cazes, *Uno Mas Uno* 22 August and 24 September 1979:5.
123. Prayer Sheet, WBT-Huntington Beach, April 1979.
124. *Uno Mas Uno* 26 July 1979:1, 8.
125. *Latin America Regional Reports: Mexico and Central America* 16 November 1979:6-7.
126. *Uno Mas Uno* 22 September 1979:5.
127. *Excelsior* 2 October 1979:4A, 36A.
128. Ibid. 2, 4 and 5 October 1979:7-8A.
129. III 1980:219-20.
130. *Uno Mas Uno* 22 November 1980:1, 6.
131. III 1980:248; *Latinamerica Press* (Lima) 1 January 1981:4-6; *Excelsior* 25 November 1980:6A.
132. *Uno Mas Uno* 22 November 1980:1,6.
133. Jose Carreno Carlon, *Uno Mas Uno* 19 November 1980:3.
134. *Uno Mas Uno* 17 November 1980:4.
135. III 1980 explains these changes.
136. Baez-Jorge 1980:374-5.
137. Anguiano 1979:582. For Marxist critiques of the 'neoindigenist' or 'populist' positions exemplified by the refurbished III, see National Autonomous University of Mexico 1980.
138. Uribe 1980:305.
139. *Unidad Indigena* (Bogota) November 1980:13.

8. International Linguistic Center

Only the evangelicals are attempting to translate one text into every language in the world. No one else presumes to sow the dragon teeth of literacy in every extant pre-literate society, and recently Wycliffe was doing 80% of the pioneer work.[1] The task seems endless because Wycliffe is constantly distinguishing more dialects — in the Mixteco language alone the Mexican branch has identified 28 — which it feels require their own Bible translations. Far from 2,000 tongues to go, after 40 years Wycliffe counted 3,279 languages which definitely or possibly needed Bible translation.[2] The figure is likely to increase since much of the terrain has not been surveyed. In India, where Wycliffe's present definite/possible total is 216, it has informed other missions that 800 translations may be required.[3] At the present cost of translating a New Testament (perhaps five members per language x $6840 per member in 1980 x 20 years), India alone could require an investment of more than half a billion dollars.[4] Undaunted, Wycliffe maintained until recently that it would reach 'every tribe by '85' — 6,000 to 8,000 new members by that date to complete the Great Commission by the year 2000. As this dream faded, Wycliffe retreated to for 'each in his own tongue', declaring that it would persevere 'until the job is done or our Lord shall come.'[5]

The great obstacles to Wycliffe's plans are political: the Lord may not return until evangelical movements have swept every part of the globe including the Mongolian People's Republic. Since each language must have its saints to fulfil Revelation 7:9, a way must be found into the least hospitable polities on the face of the earth. Nor is Wycliffe very international: the 29% of the membership from outside the United States hails almost entirely from Europe and the white settlements of what was the British Empire.

At the 1975 biennial conference it fell to an Englishman, Africa Area Director John Bendor-Samuel, to present 'hard facts' to an organization which still flies the American flag.[6] To his observation that large numbers of North Americans can no longer be sent to the Third World, a member in Latin America asked, how can they stay where they already are? While faith in the homeland continued to thrive — Wycliffe's ranks doubled in the 1940s, quadrupled in the 1950s, doubled in the 1960s and doubled again by 1980 to more than 4,000 — Wycliffe may no longer make much sense in terms of what it hopes to accomplish. At the historical rate of multiplication and the recent rate of expulsion, how are 8,000 predominantly North American members going to occupy themselves by 1990? 16,000 by the year 2000?

Clearly a new strategy was needed to bring the millennial year back into range. It was to recruit citizens of host countries, people whose skin was not white, to produce many of those New Testaments. With that end in view, during the 1980s Wycliffe planned to finish 500 translations, including nearly every language in the Americas; devise strategies for China, Islamic areas and socialist countries; and recruit a relatively modest number of new translators and support workers — 3,000 — to undertake 800 more languages.[7] Were these plans to prosper, with the number of languages doubling again in the 1990s, by the end of the century Wycliffe would be approaching its goal of universal translation.

When Cameron Townsend retired from the general directorship in 1971, it was with some presentiment of the growing irrationality of the Wycliffe rationality he had set in motion. Judging from the Hefleys, precipitating factors included not just his age and liberties with his authority, but a series of unpopular proposals to broaden membership. Townsend had tried to bring fundamentalist stalwarts to heel ever since the backlash to his Mexican policies. At truce with wary Colombian bishops, he attempted to fulfil his non-sectarian pledge by shepherding a Roman Catholic into the membership. But even the argument that Paul Witte would impress the bishops failed to move the board of directors and the 1967 biennial conference. The main objection was the anticipated 'reaction of some members and supporters . . . a pragmatic concern: loss of support.' When Townsend sponsored a halfway arrangement for Witte, the Mexican branch protested and the board of directors ordered the Colombian branch to end it. By the late 1960s he was enjoining Wycliffe to recruit Latin Americans: in 1981 there were 15. He wanted to drop English as a requirement for membership — which the board rejected — and recruit North American blacks: none joined. He also tried to take SIL to the Soviet Union — which prompted an anti-Communist backlash — and criticized his organization's racism.[8]

At the 1969 biennial conference there were 'strong hints' that Townsend was too old to be general director. At the next he was elevated to founder. His parting salvo included 'incomplete adherence to our non-sectarian policy'; indulgence in 'missionary type activities' which could cause alarm in countries such as India and Nepal; discrimination against Pentecostals; intolerance toward the personal habits of some members (such as Lutherans who did not abstain from beer and wine); 'an almost unconscious going along with racist attitudes'; and 'over independence' on SIL's part in nationalist climates.[9]

At several biennial conferences Wycliffe discussed the obsolescence of the 'center pattern' — the base, two foreigners in each language, plus at least as many support personnel — and the need for making Bible translation more 'national', without much enthusiasm. There are technical arguments against entrusting Bible translation entirely to native speakers: should an indigenous translator have the background in trade language, Bible and linguistics which Wycliffe considers necessary, he may have been away from his people so long that he has lost touch with idiom and produces over-educated translations. Wycliffe philosophy presents another double-bind: since waiting for the indigenous church itself to translate the Bible 'condemn[s] the first generation . . . to living without the Scriptures' and is 'second-best', in George Cowan's words, Wycliffe wants to be present at the foundation wherever possible.[10] Last but not least, as Elaine Beekman notes, in the majority of languages there is 'no interest' in Bible translation.

Gradually, however, Wycliffe admitted the utter dependence of the foreign translator on his/her 'native helper', who is now being promoted to 'co-translator'. 'I couldn't get along without the . . . language helpers,' translators admitted by the early 1970s, 'but *they* couldn't do it on their own either.'[11] Yet none of the technical arguments explained why there were so very few Colombians, Filipinos and so forth in Wycliffe. In 1978 Third World membership totalled 14.[12] Several problems were at work. Since most national churches were free to perform any religious exercise they pleased, they preferred forceful evangelism to Wycliffe's subtle devices. Nor were they likely to finance two decades of desk work in each of countless languages when they felt that their own language, such as Spanish, sufficed to evangelize people whose languages were surely disappearing anyway. Nor had Wycliffe been especially interested in recruiting them.

Yet it was no longer such an asset to be a Summer Institute linguist. In many countries, the best to be hoped for was a relatively small team of highly skilled consultants, who each would enter a family of related languages to train native speakers or other citizens to do most of the work.[13] The national solution would be shaped by several constraints: since recruiting citizens of host countries into SIL/WBT could be self-defeating, parallel national agencies might be required. Since most of the faith in universal Bible translation resided in the United States, where churches preferred to finance their own people, translators with names like Juan Lopez might need dollars. And since Wycliffe considered Bible translation a profession which required supervision, it expected to play an advisory role in the new agencies.

The new Jerusalem of the Bible translation movement is rising out of trailers and dirt in a suburb of Dallas, Texas. To all intents and purposes the International Linguistic Center (ILC) is Wycliffe's own graduate school, accredited through the University of Texas branch in nearby Arlington. The ILC provides faculty to the university's Department of Foreign Languages and Linguistics, 22 of whose 43 professors and most of whose linguists were SIL members in 1980. In return, the university lists ILC courses in its curriculum. As the Summer Institute's world administrative-academic headquarters, the Center is to include departments of linguistics, translation, anthropology, literacy and bilingual education, as well as others for printing, academic publications and management training, not to mention a linguistics library, a museum, a medical facility and housing.[14]

Just as Wycliffe organized itself around the bases after the Second World War, a growing fraction of the membership seems to be congregating around the North American centres. The 500 staff and students at the ILC in 1978 were expected to double.[15] 150 members lived at JAARS headquarters in Waxhaw, North Carolina; perhaps another 100 at Wycliffe headquarters in Huntington Beach, California; and still others at the new Mexico Branch Center in Tucson, Arizona. This is an interesting trend in an organization which always has prided itself on a 'field first' policy. It includes a growing elderly membership for whom Wycliffe is building housing. But it also reflects a pressing need to professionalize the ranks: owing to rising disciplinary standards and faith mission limitations, SIL's competence has come into question in Latin America. The vanishing residence visa means that the work must be done more quickly — with more technology, especially computers — and much of it at a distance through brethren. As revolutions, ethnic conflicts and anti-imperialist campaigns drive Wycliffe from the field, more of its members' time is being spent in classes and cubicles in North American suburbs.

The International Linguistic Center is to be the training and consultation hub of an array of SIL branches and area offices, national translation agencies, and foreign missions inspired by Wycliffe's example, among them the Lutheran Bible Translators and Logos Translators, Pioneer Bible Translators, Evangel Bible Translators and Korean Translation Mission.* Were SIL to 'vanish' into a technical support role, so would much of the animus against it. No longer would members occupy the broker position or pioneer evangelism along the indigenous frontiers. But that is what Bible translation always has meant to Wycliffe and why it will only 'disappear' where forced to. Even at the ILC stage, many members remain in the position of the beleaguered colonial. Trapped in foreign enclaves which have become their homes, they believe they have a Biblical mandate, as much right to each Indian tribe as the sons of Abraham to the Promised Land.

Townsend seems to have recognized the besieged fortress into which he had led his followers and, to break out of it, encouraged a spiritual movement which he hoped would help them love their enemies and surmount a grave danger to the Great Commission. It took the form of Charismatic Renewal, a middle class version of the spirit-ridden Pentecostalism which has frightened and impressed missionaries when animists under their influence, such as the Montagnard churches in the last years of the American expedition, feel that they have been abandoned to evil. On Wycliffe's own darkening political horizon, a comforting fellowship of hugs and tears could become a springboard to millenarian thinking. As in Vietnam, apocalypse-smitten Christianity had the potential to justify any measure, however bloody, against those perceived as the Satanic enemy.

A question, then, runs through this survey of Wycliffe expansion around the world; its technical competence; the deeply embedded exchanges of commission and faith, dollars and youth upon which it draws in the United

---

* In 1979 the Lutheran body fielded 48 members in Liberia and Sierra Leone; 65 worked with Wycliffe in other countries. Evangel (Charismatic), Logos (Pentecostal) and Pioneer fielded 25 persons in all.[16]

States; the life at the bases; and the Peruvian branch's Charismatic Renewal in the early 1970s. The question is: does Wycliffe consider itself so close to the last days that it can only persist on its present course, or will it come to view the hammer blows of Satan as the Lord's perfect will? It is the divine hand, after all, which opens and shuts all doors.

To Every Nation

Wycliffe only began to move beyond the Christian pale in the 1960s. Having expended its youth against Roman Catholicism in Latin America, Wycliffe turned to Christian territory in the Pacific; South Vietnam, where Catholics ruled at the behest of the United States; and black Africa, which already reached out its hands to God. Even in Africa, however, Wycliffe found that its welcome could be short-lived; the same ethnic rivalries which called for linguistics, literacy work and nation-building invited distrust of its work. In Asia, where Wycliffe finally confronted other world religions, non-sectarianism was a flimsy pretext for university contracts and rapid expansion. Wycliffe also reckoned with bitter memories of colonialism: Christian missionaries who had sided with more receptive ethnic minorities against dominant groups, if they had not played the one against the other. As the Latin American strongholds came under siege and Wycliffe was driven from Vietnam, its initiatives in Africa and South Asia were either shut down or in clear trouble. Fearful that it was already too late, Wycliffe leap-frogged into African countries and petitioned at the gate of nearly every state along the south Asian rim, from Malaysia to Iran.

The founder took up the greatest challenge of all: 'deeply disturbed' by unnamed events in 1966-67, Townsend and his second wife Elaine Mielke (Elvira died in 1944) turned to the Soviet Union.[17] Whatever he was disturbed by, an advance into the citadel of world atheism would have restored the authority to deal with it. The association with Lazaro Cardenas provided an introduction to the Soviet embassy in Mexico City. Over the next decade the Townsends made 11 journeys, especially to the Caucasus, and produced an appreciative book about Soviet bilingualism. Their hopes were frequently invoked by SIL's Latin American friends to prove that it was above politics. But in the Academy of Science many a plan, including one involving the Colombian branch, came to naught. Finally the Townsends persuaded the Academy to translate an epistle into five of sixty Armenian dialects. That was where the Soviet advance stood when, in June 1981, *Pravda* denounced a 'nest of spies' for the CIA. 'Bible in hand and topographic map under cassock,' *Pravda* declared, 'the members of the Summer Institute of Linguistics do not hesitate to . . . traffic in drugs and precious stones as well.'[18]

India and Nepal

If several premature announcements of a breakthrough in the Soviet Union were not enough, experience elsewhere taught that the Summer Institute was not always the Lord's chosen vehicle. India was the first sign that Asia was rather different from Latin America: owing to diplomatic failure here, the 1976 expulsion from Nepal nearly cleared SIL off the map in this part of the world. When university contracts brought it into these countries in the mid-1960s, India was expected to become a major field. Under British rule, ethnic minorities – the 'tribes' – had shown some interest in Christianity. The missions had offended caste Hindus, however, and as SIL teams began work the diplomatic climate deteriorated. There was an upsurge of minority revolt against the New Delhi government; the Asia Foundation was barred from the country after its sometime role as a CIA conduit was publicized; and a scandal over Pentagon-financed university fieldwork led to a ban on any social science research funded by the U.S. government.[19] In 1969, New Delhi withdrew visas for members who did not hold Commonwealth passports, cutting the now-defunct branch from twenty-three persons to eight. Much diplomacy by Townsend, Kenneth Pike and others failed to reopen the way. By 1971 Wycliffe was discussing the possibility of an Indian translation agency, which might be independent of SIL but seek advice in training, candidate screening and linguistics. 'Such a program,' suggested a branch official, '. . . would not suffer as much, if at all from government opposition.'[20] Although even the national solution was slow to materialize, nine years later Indian translators were at work in perhaps four languages and a training course was under way.

When a country has been closed to Christian missionaries for two centuries finding citizens to translate the Bible is difficult. In Nepal, which happens to be the world's last Hindu monarchy, conversion to Christianity is unconstitutional. Yet recently the government has tolerated Christian social work and, except when compelled, averted its gaze from small but growing churches. For a decade, therefore, SIL enjoyed official and even royal favour. According to the 1966 agreement with Tribhuvan University, SIL is a 'private educational institution' associated with 11 public universities around the world and dedicated to linguistics and literacy work.[21] Five years later, the branch director warned that the laws 'demand our every caution.'[22] At the cancellation of the contract in June 1976, members were given until the end of August to leave the country: Nepali officials cited religious conversions.[23] The U.S. ambassador reported that SIL's religious programme had been an 'open secret' and long the subject of debate, having irritated conservatives in royal palace and government. Nationalists such as the Minister of Education, Harka Gurung, questioned the number of foreign scholars and their research priorities.[24] Since the government was promoting Nepali as the national language, Christian evangelism in vernacular languages was being taken as a divisive threat. The following year Wycliffe claimed believers in 15 languages and flourishing congregations in three.[25] Translators were also still at work in a dozen languages, by entering the country as tourists and inviting informants across the border. Even though converts were going to jail, Wycliffe reported new ones. And although a group of tourists was forced to leave Nepal in a hurry, that did not stop their work.

Africa

Recruiting indigenous translators and organizing national counterparts has gone further in Africa than anywhere else. Since Christianity continues to flourish in spite of decolonization, brethren eager to translate the Bible are to be found in many languages. Then too, in Africa, like several Pacific fields, the U.S. membership is matched by that from Europe and the British Commonwealth, some of whom will acknowledge that such a thing as Western imperialism exists.* The major competitors are Islam, whose rate of expansion Christianity may surpass, and the many animist traditions, which reassert themselves in the guise of world religion.

The Summer Institute started in West Africa in the early 1960s, at the request of missions and church leaders. Since then it has travelled in an arc across the Muslim frontier into East Africa, for a total of 13 countries by 1981. The second burst of expansion, in the late 1960s, was a diaspora from the Biafran civil war in Nigeria. The third, since the early 1970s, has brought SIL into eight more countries in as many years. The operations are small but efficient, involving few support workers: in 1981 SIL-Africa fielded 343 members in 93 languages. The style is changing: at first SIL took advantage of official interest in vernacular literacy to build 'center pattern' branches. Then it began to suffer from official anxiety over tribal separatism: one of the first four branches was shut down in 1976, and SIL is clearly preparing for the same in the other three. Now the plan is to build regional centres in the most hospitable countries, push a handful of linguists into as many others as possible, and train African translators from the start.

The architect of this policy is apparently the British linguist John Bendor-Samuel, who arranged SIL's first contracts in 1962 with state universities in Ghana and Nigeria. When the Biafran secession halted the Nigerian work five years later, several teams moved across the border to Cameroun, where Bendor-Samuel signed a state university contract in 1968. Seeking further diversification, he negotiated yet another in Ivory Coast.[27] By the early 1970s, SIL worked in 47 languages in this strip of countries, nearly half in Nigeria,

---

* Only 45% of the 266 SIL-Africa personnel in 1978 were from the United States. 58% of the 1,060 SIL-Pacific members were from the U.S: here the even split in Papua New Guinea was outweighed by the Philippines (75% U.S.), Indonesia (65% U.S.), and the ex-Vietnam branch (88% U.S.).[26]

where it was being overtaken by visa difficulties. Since Bendor-Samuel felt that 'only a thoroughly international and inter-racial' SIL would survive in Africa, the branch began to train Nigerian translators and set up a national counterpart.[28] In March 1976, after an unsuccessful putsch by military officers from an area where SIL operated, a government official informed the branch that Nigerians could do its work. It was to leave the country by the end of the month. According to a story circulating within Wycliffe, a Nigerian diplomat had been offended by a U.S. newspaper account of an airplane dedication and, on his return, disposed of the branch. While members were forced to leave at the end of June, the Nigerian Bible Translation Trust inherited the study centre at Jos and a visa quota for ten foreign consultants.[29] Two years later translators, many Nigerians trained and advised by SIL, were at work in 60 languages.

The Ghana branch has placed itself under the auspices of the Ghana Institute of Linguistics and Bible Translation which, hopefully, will take full charge of the work by 1990. SIL also plans to foster a national agency in Cameroun. Translators in Upper Volta and Mali have been administered from a regional study centre in Abidjan, Ivory Coast; others are at work in Togo and Benin. Another regional centre is being established in Kenya, for work in Ethopia, Sudan, Zaire and, in the future, Tanzania.

The Sudan is the largest of the new advances to date, with 11 translation teams, three literacy teams and, since 1979, $1.4 million from the U.S. Agency for International Development for literacy work.[30] Here SIL surveyed southern languages for the government in 1974-75, following a civil war between Arab Muslims, who control the state machinery in Khartoum, and blacks, many Christian, who were promised autonomy. Since then oil has been discovered in the south, hostilities with the north have escalated again, and the Reagan administration has tripled military aid. Based at Juba, where members have faced acute supply shortages, social disorder and epidemic disease, SIL is helping organize the Sudan Bible Translation and Literacy Association.

To the south, five teams have begun work in Zaire; to the west in Chad civil war forced several new teams to leave the country in 1979; and to the east in Ethiopia, which the first translator entered as a university researcher the year before the fall of Emperor Haile Selassie, several couples have stayed on under the Soviet-backed military dictatorship. Languages have been surveyed in Niger, Uganda and the Central African Republic, and SIL plans to do the same in Guinea-Bissau and Senegal.

Papua New Guinea

The Summer Institute's largest branch also promises to excel in promoting local Bible translation. It has concentrated on linguistic barriers because the political variety have scarcely existed. Since the Second World War most Papua New Guineans — according to a recent census 92% — have professed Christianity. In the early 1970s there was a foreign missionary — 3,400 in all

— for every 700 people in the territory.[31] Since the missions were indispensable to administration and schooling, perhaps even more so after Papua New Guinea became independent from Australia in 1975, SIL's official ties did not set it apart from other missions. The branch's most serious political problem may have been initial administrative distrust of vernacular education, for which it won a UNESCO award in 1979.[32]

Arithmetic, if nothing else, has prompted the training of Papua New Guinean Bible translators. The branch has entered 148 languages; six hundred others await their Scripture. According to a recent plan, new SIL teams will be assigned to families of three to six languages to train indigenous translators in each. For 1977-80 USAID followed $98,000 from the Canadian International Development Agency with $624,760 to train 380 teachers and community development promoters in 30 languages.[33] The branch has been a springboard to the Solomons and New Caledonia, Christianized islands where, like the scheduled advances into the New Hebrides and French Polynesia, the new style in Bible translation should thrive. Papua New Guinea may also prove to be the emergency evacuation site for a branch, working under a brutal dictatorship to the west.

Indonesia

The bench mark of recent Indonesian history is the 'abortive communist coup' of 1965, a military intrigue to which the CIA, a former officer has revealed, falsely linked the Communist Party in a propaganda campaign.[34] This provided an excuse for anti-Communist massacres and the present military dictatorship, hailed by Wycliffe and other evangelical missions for saving the country. A decade later the chief of state security said that perhaps half a million people had been killed; other estimates run to more than double that figure.[35] In the course of the slaughter, Pentecostal revivals provided a refuge for alleged Communists.[36] Since then, Christianity has found another boon in the government's promotion of religion as insurance against Marxism; since only Islam, Christianity, Hinduism and Buddhism are recognized as religions, animists have risked being classified as atheists, that is, Communists.[37]

Until its fall, the Soviet-allied Sukarno regime prevented the Summer Institute from entering the country. The University of Indonesia contract was only signed some years later, however, in February 1971. Eight months previously, President Suharto (in power 1966-) had visited Washington, an event which ended the low U.S. profile following the massacres, and opened the way for military advisers. Suharto's fellow triumvir, Foreign Minister Adam Malik, welcomed SIL after receiving a letter of introduction from his Filipino counterpart Carlos Romulo.[38] Of four possible areas — Sulawesi (Celebes), Kalimantan (Borneo), Halmahera and West Papua New Guinea (West Irian or Irian Jaya) — SIL chose to take the field across the border from its vigorous branch in (East) Papua New Guinea.

The work got off to a rather slow start. The authorities have insisted upon

245

university teaching and field training for Indonesians: the first contract included the extraordinary provision that SIL give a $25 a month subsidy to students at its field sites.[39] Other impediments may be Muslim officialdom and the government's outstanding corruption. Visas have been a headache from nearly the beginning: they always seem to depend upon the signing of some new contract. Starting fieldwork in West Papua New Guinea required long negotiations with the aviation authorities and the local Cenderawasih University at Jayapura (Hollandia). In 1980 visas had been complicated for more than two years pending signature of a new agreement with the central authorities in Jakarta.

West Papua New Guinea is, like the better known East Timor, recently conquered territory. Adam Malik has estimated that, in the former Portuguese colony of East Timor, 'fifty thousand or perhaps eighty thousand' of a 600,000 population were killed after Indonesia invaded the newly independent country in 1975.[40] West Papua New Guinea had been seized from the Dutch 13 years before, whereupon the Indonesians ruined the economy and suppressed Papuan uprisings. Large numbers of colonists have been introduced to the territory, with plans to bring more backed by a large occupation army. Mineral reserves worked by transnational corporations, chiefly North American provide one fifth of Indonesia's oil exports. The bloodshed has been on a lesser scale than in East Timor, however. In 1978 the Melanesian nationalists of the Free Papua Movement, which claims to control one fourth of the territory, estimated that 20,000 people had been killed in the bombings and paratrooper assaults.[41]

Christian missions are one of the few points of contact with the outside world, and they are in a most ambiguous position. Pledged to uphold the Indonesian occupation and indispensable to keeping the tribes-people under control, their sympathies undoubtedly lie with the Papuans, a probable majority of whom profess Christianity, rather than a basically Islamic regime which recently forced 200 Christian missionaries to leave Indonesia. When the Baliem Valley in the central highlands 'just blew up' in 1977, the Papuans reportedly attacked government posts but left the missions untouched.[42] The SIL base at Lake Holmes (Danau Bira) lies halfway between the Baliem Valley and the northern coast.[43] Labour is provided by converted Dani tribespeople, who have suffered heavily in the Baliem. SIL also has started to enter languages on the island of Sulawesi, under contract to Hasanuddin University in Ujung Pandang.

Post-Vietnam Asia

On the Asian mainland the Summer Institute's prospects might seem poor in view of social upheaval and rival world religion against which Christianity rarely has made much headway. Animistic ethnic minorities are another story, however: SIL plans to help thriving churches produce their own translations. The incentive for new advances has been reinforced by the ex-Vietnam translators, who regrouped in the Philippines as the Mainland South-east Asia Branch, produced Montagnard Scripture tapes for the Far Eastern Broadcasting

Company, and did their best to scatter to the winds.

Cambodia, where two teams followed the 1971 American invasion, and Laos, where cabinet ministers considered a SIL proposal in early 1975, were definitely closed. Burma had not been bombed by the Americans, however, and among the minorities there were strong Christian movements. Under British rule, unfortunately, missionaries had encouraged the arming of their tribal converts against the Burmese. The post-independence Buddhist dictatorship provoked minority revolts; the CIA subsidized a refugee Kuomintang Chinese army which proved less successful at fighting Communism than capturing the tribal opium trade. Then in 1966, after three American families went underground on the Chinese border, most Christian missionaries were expelled. Perhaps 40% of the countryside was beyond the control of the Rangoon government, tribal and Communist forces having made common cause against it. But as the government continued to lose ground, in the late 1970s it eased restrictions on contact with the outside world. Several SIL members started to help indigenous translators.

Thailand and Malaysia belong to the U.S.-sponsored Association of Southeast Asian Nations, but even here SIL's official welcome has been reluctant at best. In Thailand, where the military dictatorship is heavily involved in the opium trade, poppy-cultivating tribals have suffered at its hands and joined a thriving Communist movement. Post-China and Vietnam waves of Christian missionaries have antagonized Buddhists. Although a handful of SIL members found university posts or joined a literacy programme, the Thanin Kraivichien government rejected a 1977 proposal. Two years later Kenneth Pike and a Thai university signed an agreement which, hopefully, opened the way for half a dozen teams.

In the Malaysian state of Sabah, on the island of Borneo, tribal Christianity has flourished as it has in neighbouring Sarawak, another former British colony where SIL wants to work. But while the government appreciates literacy work, Malays plan to make Islam the state religion. Despite the same visa difficulties which have plagued older missions, a few dozen members started to enter languages in 1980 and local church leaders organized a support committee. Now that the ex-Vietnam translators had found new assignments, particularly in Sabah, the Mainland South-east Asia Branch was disbanded.

To the west, the reverses in India and Nepal apparently have made it harder to obtain contracts on the basis of linguistics and literacy work. In Pakistan, Townsend approached President Ali Bhutto (1971-77), an advocate of minority rights, with his book praising the Soviet bilingual system. Low-caste Hindu ethnic minorities have converted to Christianity in some number, but Muslim fundamentalists want their country to live up to its name as an Islamic republic, and the government apparently has rejected SIL proposals. Several couples have surveyed languages: an anticipated opening in 1979 for teams with British passports was closed. In Bangladesh, a 1976 proposal to the University of Dacca and the Minister of Education failed. A second, for a one year language survey, was accepted by the University of

Dacca but not the government. Here, too, what little success Christian missions have enjoyed is among the animist ethnic minorities, not the Muslim and Hindu Bengalis, and mission activities are being curtailed.

In Afghanistan SIL made a promising contact in 1971, but prior to the Soviet invasion nine years later it was still knocking at the door. Just before the fall of the Shah in neighbouring Iran, Kenneth Pike was scheduled to follow up a visit by Ethel Wallis. Several couples were already at work and apparently remained following the Islamic Revolution, requesting prayer for the wisdom to know when to leave.[44]

Latin America and the World

One might think the Summer Institute's only ambition in Latin America would be to conclude present business and extricate itself, but such is not the case. According to Wycliffe, another 142 translators are 'needed now' in this part of the world.[45] 200 more Latin American languages definitely or possibly require Bible translation, it feels. More than half are located in Mexico and Brazil, and a quarter in Colombia, Peru and Venezuela.[46] Despite talk of largely finishing Bible translation in the western hemisphere by 1990, there are enough languages to keep a new generation of members occupied into the 21st Century.

Venezuela has been a disappointment: SIL seems to have missed more than one opportunity here. Now that indigenists have discovered that the New Tribes Mission occupies an analogous position in their country, they vow that SIL will not get another.[47] Amidst the furor of the 1970s translators have moved into other countries, however. In Argentina a team has started in the Santiago del Estero dialect of Quechua; in Chile, where SIL has signed its third agreement with regional universities, two Peruvian branch teams have begun work on Easter island and among the Mapuche; and in Nicaragua a single team has been listed.

Of the nationalization pledges which most branches had adopted by the late 1970s, those in Latin America were least plausible. Here Cameron Townsend's methods may have destroyed the possibility of national Bible translation, because even for many brethren SIL's work has come to have the most unfortunate connotations. In Latin America there may be no turning back: the North Americans may have to finish the job by themselves, regardless of the opposition and at whatever cost.

Elsewhere SIL can derive some comfort from having won at least a foothold in seven countries — Indonesia, Papua New Guinea, Nigeria, India, Cameroun, Zaire and Sudan — which, in its present opinion, are the home of 57% of the 3,279 languages in definite or possible need of Bible translation. In each of these countries, and many others, national and indigenous translation holds some promise. Hope is also pinned upon Asian evangelicals, particularly Japanese, Koreans and overseas Chinese. Four Koreans have trained at the ILC and the Jungle Camp in Papua New Guinea; are being assigned to SIL-Pacific branches and it is hoped will train compatriots, all under the auspices of the Korean Translation Mission. Asian and Mideast students at Australian universities are to be recruited by a new centre near Melbourne.

In 1980 Kenneth Pike was teaching at a university in China. The Chinese, it is hoped, will take Bible translation to outer domains such as Tibet. A similar vision probably came to guide Townsend's seemingly Quixotic journeys to the Soviet Union: that linguists from non-Russian nationalities would join church leaders in an indigenous Bible translation movement. The ever lonelier expeditions of SIL members follow a long tradition in Christian mission to closed countries. By ones and twos and the half dozen, where necessary travelling as graduate students, businessmen or tourists, linguist-translators are introducing themselves to exiled native speakers or inviting language informants across borders, making church and academic contacts, encouraging local translators and carrying out surveys.

SIL Linguistics and Literacy Work

What lies behind the impressive Summer Institute bibliographies? Some list thousands of items and they have been termed 'perhaps our single most important publicity tool for academic and government purposes.'[48] The bibliographies now inspire disbelief in Latin America: fury over SIL's use of native languages and its influence on national linguistic policy has been accompanied by ridicule of its competence, not necessarily by those in a position to judge. Yet a faith mission whose priority is Bible translation has taken on heavy commitments in linguistics and literacy work, not to mention other responsibilities, at such a pace that admission standards and training have been kept to a minimum. University credentials have secured state contracts; linguistics has been used to disguise church-planting; and the need for linguistic expertise has been a faith mission's first line of defense. All combine to lend an air of fraud to its claims.

SIL's linguistic monopoly is a recent discovery, the product of an operation whose versatility, reliability and low cost benignly discouraged governments, and at one time universities, from bothering to break it. In country after country SIL was the first group of descriptive specialists in native languages. Through bilingual education it championed the legitimacy — although not full legal equality — of these languages when few others were. But much of SIL's academic work remained inaccessible in Latin America until its existence was publicly questioned. More often than not, promised training of national linguists never materialized. When national professions did start to emerge, it was generally without much help from SIL, and soon in express opposition to its plans. But such sentiments did not mean that national linguists had acquired much experience in native languages: when support for nationalizing SIL's functions finally appeared, a country might still lack the necessary expertise. The obvious solution, co-operation and the long-promised operational transfer, was not just difficult, as is usually the case with foreign projects: it was probably impossible, due to faith mission requirements and friends in high places. Whether or not attackers were ready to occupy those bastions which SIL deemed necessary to its work, it planned to defend them until it had completed that country's Great Commission.

The Summer Institute, then, leaves more than a little to be desired as a technical transfer organization. Nor is it the professional body depicted in public relations. But as a faith mission and arm of government, it has been a notable experimenter in the use of native languages for ulterior purposes, and it is doing so on a scale unmatched by any other agency in Latin America. The potential for manipuiating native language and consciousness has been the subject of much apprehension in academic circles. Now Indian organizations have begun to reject the very premise of a linguistic programme for every nation and people: that outsiders have the right to use languages to further an ideological programme of which, more often than not, the presumed bene-ficiaries feel no need. 'The use of language,' concluded Indian representatives at the 1977 Barbados meeting in repudiation of SIL, '. . . ought to be governed by the Indian people themselves within their own channels of creativity.'[49] As SIL spokesmen note with increasing regularity, the world has changed a great deal since their organization began.

For the first Camp Wycliffes in the 1930s, Cameron Townsend advertised his linguistic method like a magic weapon. After a summer or two at Camp Wycliffe, the average missionary supposedly could translate the entire New Testament and teach large groups to read it in ten years.[50] But by present Wycliffe standards the Cakchiquel New Testament was crude. No professional training went into the translation and Townsend may have taken credit for what was largely the work of his Mayan 'helpers'. One, Jose Chicol, claims to have rescued the founder from an impasse and be the true author.[51] Nor was the translation as intelligible to the Cakchiquel as Townsend thought it was. Following a revision by Chicol, eight SIL members are replacing it with dialect-specific versions.

Since the missionary was glorified at the cost of the local intellectuals who made his work possible, it became an article of faith that virtually anyone of the Lord's choosing could translate the Bible into any language on the face of the earth, regardless of its speakers' previous contact with Western civilization, their interest in evangelical religion, and penetration of the trade language. On each score the Cakchiquel had been an unusually favourable case. By recruiting for faith qualifications far more than academic ones, Wycliffe acquired some Bible translators who were led to believe that they had been brought into the world for a purpose which proved not to be the case. 'Not everyone makes a good linguist and some teams are just not doing good work,' a SIL professional told me. While academic admission standards have been raised again recently, SIL will be living with the previous results of rapid expansion for some time to come.

From the Peruvian branch's 1964 bibliography, Marcel D'Ans calculated that its investigators required an average of 14 years to publish a title in linguistics.[52] Nor was production impressive in Colombia: while the branch had published 25 phonologies by 1976, according to Jon Landabaru it had published only three grammars, which suggested that more than a few teams had spent much of their time in a mire.[53] According to a SIL member, 75-80% of the material produced in Mexico prior to the 1970s may be unusable because training, competence and technique were so inadequate.

Since linguistics is public relations to SIL – in the words of Kenneth Pike it 'has been our umbrella, our means of entrance and of staying in areas' – no hint of faith mission limitations appeared in its presentations.[54] For decades only a handful of translators were spared from the field to take graduate degrees: of these some were forced to leave owing to theological differences, divorces or other affronts to fundamentalist sensibilities. Yet under the guidance of Kenneth Pike, now SIL's president emeritus, the professionals who remained made the Summer Institute a respected name in North American and European linguistics. Among the testimonials Townsend presented to vindicate his August 1953 claims in Peru was one from the Linguistic Society of America.[55] Eight years later Pike served as president of this body.

The technique which met SIL's needs, Pike has explained, also served the linguistic profession in the metropolis. Early in his career Townsend had chanced upon the descriptive linguistics of Edward Sapir, a study of forms and how they function together as a behavioural system. Smitten by the same school of thought, linguists wanted data from as many exotic languages as possible. A vaguely religious linguistic institute became their single largest supplier. Then too, as the summer schools brought large numbers of missionaries into the discipline, SIL refined teaching methods which other linguists found useful for their own students. In the course of preparing field-worker data for publication, Pike worked out his tagmemic theory of descriptive linguistics. Since platoons of technicians were leaning upon a few professionals led by a famous system-builder, a tagmemic uniformity of method became the organization's hallmark.

But during the 1960s, when SIL's horizons seemed to stretch far indeed, it lost stature. With the transformational-generative grammar of Noam Chomsky, a more demanding approach, the study of cognition and meaning eclipsed the behavioural school. According to Pike, SIL found the new fashion unsuitable because it presupposed considerable knowledge about a language.[56] That is, many investigators could not be expected to move from descriptive preliminaries to more sophisticated work. Advances in the discipline left SIL vulnerable in terms of theoretical orientation and overall competence. While many linguists continued to respect the group as a data source, and its professionals were straying from Pike's system, rivals could use the gap between SIL's scientific mystique and actual accomplishments to question its alleged indispensability and use of native languages.

One such critic was Jon Landabaru, a French linguist working with the USEMI-Anthropology Institute Arhuaco bilingual schools in the Sierra Nevada of Colombia. SIL's 'view of language is now considered outdated by the majority of the world's linguists,' he told *Alternativa* after raising the training issue.

> It is outdated because it is too formal a view of language. It does not
> take into account the interpretation of grammatical categories; it does
> not take into account semantics in general (that is, the study of meanings);
> and it reduces the syntax of language to a purely formal machine, a
> system of rules of arrangement. Pike may have a more complex view
> but the publications do not show it.
>
> One aspect of the institution particularly disagreeable to a scientist is
> the way all its members follow the same theory, the same methodology,
> the same techniques. It appears that, in Oklahoma or elsewhere in the
> United States, Pike and his followers have arrived at a complete view of
> how languages function. . . . At least, nearly all SIL's publications around
> the world follow the same pattern. . . . Is it possible that this attitude
> has something to do with religious models? . . . Why don't they carry out
> research aimed at a deeper understanding of the indigenous mentality?
> Why is the underlying pattern always a formal view of language? Why
> don't they work on semantics? . . . Why do they see language as an
> arrangement of forms rather than a conceptualization of experience?
>
> In my opinion the answer is obvious. SIL theory is that which is best
> adapted to its missionary practice. The situation of the mission for SIL
> is as follows: the Indian has the form, the missionary has the content.
> The missionary has the truth, the Indian provides the form of express-
> ion. What the Indian is accustomed to express in this form, what the
> language reveals, what the Indian thinks is not important; it is ignorance
> and darkness. The missionary tells the Indian: 'Give us the form so that
> we can take care of the content.' Crudely stated, if you like, but this is
> at the bottom of it.[57]

SIL's professionals were painfully aware of its technical shortcomings well
before these were publicized. While some members have always taken themselves seriously as linguists, perhaps more so than as church founders, Pike's
charge to the 1971 biennial conference — 'our linguistic role is not just a
cover, or a subterfuge; it is not even just a tool' — indicates what they were up
against.[58] He and his associates did their best to make SIL professional, but
group priorities dictated journeyman standards. Townsend, for instance
maintained that quality was less important than getting the job done and
moving on to new languages.[59] Translators might reject theory on the grounds
that it was 'not practical' or refuse to deal with supposedly minor 'flaws'
which could ruin decades of work.[60] Members who already were having a
hard time translating the Bible and teaching people to read argued that they
were not supposed to be scholars; in their view, primers would meet government obligations. In a faith mission, those who appealed for more attention
to scholarship and contracts were a special interest lobby.

Unlike Townsend, the professionals appreciated the awesome dimensions of
producing an intelligible New Testament in an unknown language. And

unlike Townsend, they were responsible for seeing that SIL technicians fulfilled the staggering array of responsibilities into which their visionary founder
had led them. The professionals therefore campaigned to raise the training
standards which have contributed so much to theoretical regimentation. An
array of pressures forced the standards to be raised. One was frustration in
the branches, as translators realized that they were at an impasse or SIL professionals told them that their work was bad. The failure to produce New
Testaments became a major embarrassment in faith mission circles: by 1960
Wycliffe had published seven. Ten years later the figure was 20.[61] Long before
Marcel D'Ans posed the question, fellow evangelical missionaries were asking:
what does the Summer Institute really do? Finally, SIL professionals feared
that their charges would be ambushed by visiting scholars. In 1971, Pike
warned the biennial conference of a

> situation where other linguists come in, assert that our work is un-
> scientific and we would be without proof that our work is, in fact,
> based on an adequate linguistic foundation. Things of this sort have
> happened recently. . . . There may be — and has been — serious threat
> to our being able to stay in a country if they find (a) that we have not
> met our contracts in linguistic terms, or (b) if they see — even without
> specific contract — that we are not of service to them in the academic
> area (and if they consider that our translation efforts are at best
> worthless and at worst divisive) . . . [Were we to confine ourselves to
> literacy work,] a visiting Ph.D. would brush off such material as not
> being research at all, and the Institute as a fake, if it claims to be a
> research organization.[62]

In the late 1950s SIL formalized consultancy in its 'workshops': a more
competent member spends weeks or months with a circle of translators,
informants at their side, hashing out problems and working up publishable
material from linguistics to Scripture. During SIL's first 20 years the translator's task was best described as a lonely struggle; since then the translator
has spent more and more time at the base under the direction of specialists
and co-ordinators in linguistics, translation and, most recently, literacy. The
regulation this entails is suggested by a 1970 mimeo from SIL-Peru's Technical
Studies Department:

> The orthography for the language must be approved by the Technical
> Linguistics Section and the Executive Committee before anything
> beyond trial translations are duplicated. The *first* translator(s) from
> each team must have satisfied the basic grammar requirements of the
> Technical Linguistics Committee, and have begun work on level 5 of
> the production scale for evaluating language proficiency, i.e., he should
> have attained this level of fluency, before being recommended for
> official translation with a view to publication.
> Linguists are encouraged, however, to begin doing simple Bible stories

(not for publication) to help in their language learning and first attempts to communicate the Gospel when they are well into level 3 of the production scale.

A translation consultant should normally be assigned at this point to give orientation and help establish good techniques from the beginning. Tribe workers planning to translate any materials whatsoever should have orientation and techniques for translation.

Level 3 is also the point at which intensive study of cultural items and semantics should begin. Such study is, of course, necessary for the effective communication of the Gospel message. The translation consultant assigned to give orientation will expect the linguist to have gathered rather extensive data on tribal beliefs, especially with reference to the spirit world.[63]

Kenneth Pike describes several levels in the consultant structure: the member, not always equipped with a degree, who is familiar with problems in which colleagues need help; the 'frontiersman', often an itinerant trouble-shooter like Pike himself, who works out theory to solve new problems; and the 'engineer', who turns new material into pedagogical exercises for the summer schools.[64]

The feedback between the field, consultants and the summer schools kept alive not just SIL's academic reputation, but the hope that it could meet its commitments with a membership of technicians rather than professionals. There never were enough professionals, however: in 1961 1,100 members included only 16 Ph.Ds.[65] Members with doctoral or master degrees were forced to neglect their own assignments, perhaps hop from branch to branch; at times it was difficult to meet university requirements for Ph.D. staff in the summer schools. As SIL pressured the branches to release more of their members for graduate work, some argued that they already were too far behind to spare training furloughs, and that members sent to graduate school never came back. An increasing proportion of graduate students apparently have returned, however, perhaps because SIL now keeps most of them under its wing at the ILC and the bounds of the permissible have widened.

The continuing scarcity of professionals — in 1973 60-odd Ph.Ds. in a membership of some 2,800, and by 1980 perhaps 100 in a membership of 4,000 — fuelled the campaign to extend pre-field training from two to three summer school sessions.[66] SIL also became more selective in recruiting, recycled older members through the ILC for further training, and reportedly hoped to equip all new translators with a master degree early in their career. It will be difficult for a faith mission not to fall farther behind ever rising professional expectations, but SIL obviously is trying: the 1980 catalogue for the four sessions at the Universities of Oklahoma, North Dakota, Washington and Texas listed 43 courses beyond the first level.

Aside from protecting the Summer Institute's flanks, more training is supposed to improve its ability to introduce messages into indigenous societies and influence their behaviour. The content of the messages — in primers, intermediate reading material and translated Scripture — has caused much anxiety. Based upon extensive study of traditional beliefs, SIL (like some other agencies) reserves the right to appropriate terms for its own purposes and introduce new concepts into the language. Few if any outsiders can decipher even a single team's entire corpus of printed messages, and no other agency has the multilingual capacity to review all the messages produced by a branch in an array of languages. Bilingual publications, the social scientist who learns a language and finds something amiss, and comments by native speakers are the only windows on the subject.

It is no surprise, then, that SIL has been invested with near-magical powers of manipulation. In Colombia, an anonymous university scholar attacked SIL for allegedly adulterating Inga folk tales. Since an Inga story translated into Spanish included elements borrowed from Christianity and European folk tales such as 'Hansel and Gretel', it had to be fraudulent. Worse, when an Inga reads the foreign matter masquerading as his own, he 'falls into a state of confusion which permits him to be manipulated easily.'[67] Unfortunately, the Inga are so far from being a pristine society that, since their first contact with European folk tales in the 16th Century, some have served time in Venezuela for bank robbery. As highly commercial folk healers, they do cultivate a romantic image. Elaborating on the Hansel and Gretel conspiracy, *Uno Mas Uno* described how SIL's native writer workshops permit it 'to get inside the Indian subconscious, become acquainted with oral traditions and gradually change them to the point of devaluation.'[68]

Bernard Arcand illustrates the problem with more precision in another Colombian case. beyond the ken of anyone except a prying anthropologist, a SIL team has provided the Cuiva with mimeoed versions of their myths which incorporate Christian lessons. Thus the culture hero and creator Namoun (or Nacom) becomes God, and in the next story Satan is introduced as Namoun's antithesis. Although the official primers are more public and might seem very cultural, they too are loaded with remarkable messages, in the following case intended to influence the Cuiva to abandon their nomadic way of life for a sedentary one: 'A man cleans the land surrounding his house with a rake. He decides to leave and go plant corn in his field. Soon he returns home because he has forgotten his hat. That night, he hears a woolly opossum that has come to eat his chickens. He gets up from his hammock and throws a stick at the animal to chase it away. One chicken is dead and the man proposes to eat it in the morning ' Tidying up around a house, wearing a hat to protect oneself from the sun in an open field, protecting chickens from an opossum and eating a chicken (the Cuiva will only eat the eggs) all reflect the new way of life which the missionaries would like to inculcate.[69]

Some specialists and native speakers have roundly condemned SIL's primers and reading matter: they are said to be filled with errors, poorly structured and contain incomprehensible, dispiriting, culturally alienating or anti-national contents. As in the Inga case, some critics evidently have blamed SIL for Indian aspirations, stories or traits which contradict their own conceptions. Still, in a survey of Mexican branch production from the 1950s to the 1970s, Gloria

Bravo Ahuja corroborates some of the criticism. One problem, for example, is that some SIL authors apparently transferred their language-learning drills ad and linguistic analysis into primers for native speakers.* 'Many works have been published and to judge them all is a little presumpuous,' Jon Landabaur told *Alternativa.*

> I know of a few which, seen from here, appear interesting . . . there is a Guahibo publication on defending the land and others in Guambiano and Paez on caring for crops, using fertilizers, etc. . . . Nevertheless, a large majority of the texts are ridiculous, of extremely poor content. . . . I refer not to beginning primers but material for people who know how to read. What I have seen in various places is an attitude of ridicule by Indians towards texts which they consider unrepresentative of what they think and know. And really, if one compares the sophisticiation of indigenous intellectual systems with what is presented in these texts, one realizes that there is an abyss. An abyss of incomprehension and ignorance. . . . To do serious literary work the scientific, aesthetic and religious traditions have to be taken seriously. It is very difficult for someone who hopes to replace the majority of these values to be very sensitive to them.[71]

During the first decades, when SIL was alone in the field, Mexican and Peruvian educators hailed the psychophonemic method Townsend had devised to produce Cakchiquel readers. SIL viewed literacy work as one of the translator's simpler tasks: it was assumed that people could learn to read in a few weeks. But by the mid-1940s translators realized that psychophonemic method was not solving all their problems. A number of women, some ex-English reading teachers, were assigned to various languages to work out something better. Through trial-and-error experiments, then field training sessions and finally workshops, a corps of home-grown literacy specialists emerged. In 1965 Sarah Gudschinsky became the first literacy co-ordinator. She devised a curriculum for the summer schools and a literacy method 'heavily dependent' on Kenneth Pike's tagmemic linguistics.

The refinement of method made it obvious that many native people were not interested in reading SIL's offerings — generally a few primers and then Scripture. Translators therefore published 'a considerable body . . . of local stories, folk tales translated from other languages, health books, agricultural booklets, national hero stories and the like' according to Gudschinsky.

---

* As the founder of a scheme to teach Spanish through direct rather than bilingual method, Bravo assaults the premises of bilingual education as practiced by SIL and the Department of Education. Since the method moves from reading the native language to reading Spanish, she argues that it violates a basic rule in the teaching of second languages, that they first must be taught as spoken. She maintains that the means — literacy in the native language — has been elevated to an end in itself, to produce readers for Bible translations rather than speakers of Spanish.[70]

'Unfortunately, much of this translated material was of little interest to its intended audience, and some of it was very difficult reading indeed. It is difficult now to understand why the solution to this problem was so long in coming.' The solution was the native writer workshop. SIL discovered that people who had just learned to read, even illiterates, could produce their own literature on paper or through tape recordings. Gudschinsky dates the departure to 1970, in Mexico, and reports that more translators are relying on native authors to writer primer stories.[72]

Since SIL's professionals had anticipated much of the Latin American criticism, it vindicated their campaign for higher standards. Decades of data were hauled out of cupboards, workshop after workshop was held, academic publications poured forth and more were translated into Spanish (SIL's failure to publish much of its work in Spanish was one of two criticisms Efrain Morote Best allowed himself, the other being the failure to bring Peruvians into the operation).[73] Then there were all those primers, the only ones in many languages. Yet if SIL continued to have a good name in North American and European linguistics, to whose shelves it had long contributed generously, to many Latin American linguists it was now anathema regardless of what it accomplished.

As the nominal architects of state language policy, the Latin Americans were forced to deal with a range of problems posed or complicated by an ubiquitous institute. If language was a tool to break through political and cultural barriers to successful evangelism, as SIL had decided, sooner or later it was bound to cause endless offense. The potential field for linguistic research was unlimited, but the political opportunities for influence on government policy and native communities were not, and through decades of patronage battles SIL had done everything it could to build a commanding position. Not only was it using state-sponsored research and education to plant evangelical churches; possibly far-reaching linguistic decisions were being made by, not representative groups of native speakers or even citizens, but foreign sectarians and perhaps members of their religious followings.

Some disputes revolve around language definition and alphabet formation, the very skeleton of the growing literature in indigenous languages. Since SIL distinguishes mutually intelligible dialects for locally tailored Bible translation, it has been accused of, not just rationalizing personnel build-ups in certain areas, but encouraging the fragmentation of language groups.[74] Bible societies and SIL administrators also have tended to Hispanicize their alphabets, which facilitates the transition to literacy in Spanish and appeals to governments. In Guatemala, more indigenous systems have been circulated by the *Proyecto Francisco Marroquin,* started by North American linguists to revive Mayan literature and now in Mayan hands. Is the literature to be principally a tool for teaching Spanish or a cultural reservoir of Mayan nationalism? At last report SIL had the upper hand because its alphabets had been in production longer, it commanded superior resources and enjoyed better relations with the government.

Time being of the essence, computers may ease personnel shortages caused by visa losses and help translators meet the 15 year New Testament schedule which most have missed by five to fifteen. Since the 1960s SIL has computerized texts into concordances, a University of Oklahoma service made available to other linguists with funds from the U.S. government's National Science Foundation. Together with the University of Oklahoma and Cornell University, SIL also has computerized word lists, from 700 languages by 1974. Now the computers are moving out from a few centres to the bases, perhaps in the future to the villages, and performing wonders for overworked translators. In 1981 they were using nearly 100 machines at $5-8,000 each, the new JAARS computer division reported.[75] In experiments with grammar simulation the computer compares a proposed rule to previous rules and the material to be explained, identifying where the hypothesis breaks down.[76] At the Peruvian branch's new Quechua centre in Huanuco, the team in each dialect will translate a different part of the New Testament: a computer is then to draft each section in the other dialects.[77] Presently the most important function appears to be editorial, however: since publication of New Testaments in unusual alphabets can drag on for years, computerized copy-editing and typesetting have speeded up the recent flood of dedications. In 1981 Wycliffe completed its 150th New Testament, and during the next decade it hopes to finish one every week.

All that translation could conceivably affect the organization's view of the world. Owing to more graduate study, SIL is not the theoretical monolith it once was: in 1974 'most' of its grammars were reported to reflect Kenneth Pike's tagmemics.[78] By the end of the decade transformational-generative work was in evidence. Besides refurbishing its academic reputation, SIL hopes to deal with problems which have eluded its descriptive tradition. Through discourse analysis, for example, members are studying meaning in units larger than the sentence. Long ago the group rejected literal ('formal correspondence') translation in favour of idiomatic ('dynamic equivalence'). But translators still ran foul of indigenous narrative structure: that is, they unconsciously reproduced English or Indo-European forms of expression. With discourse analysis and other new work, the evangelical message will, hopefully, be cast in ever more relevant cultural form.

As SIL approaches the problem of meaning in indigenous languages, it may become harder to separate the form from content which Landabaru poses as the basic feature of group practice ('the missionary has the truth, the Indian provides the form of expression'). Centuries of experience teach that all to be hoped for is what Anthony F.C. Wallace called the 'partial equivalence structure', in which both sides bring their own understanding to a shared framework.[79] This is not satisfactory to fundamentalist Christians, however, motivating the campaign to replace indigenous beliefs with their own.

To SIL the Chomskyean transformational-generative approach may bridge the 'partial equivalence' dilemma because it posits universals in language. It offers an escape from the painful epistemological contrast between evangelical religion and Kenneth Pike's behavioural linguistics, whose implication is relativism. In *An Anatomy of Speech Notion* (1976) another SIL theorist,

Robert Longacre, uses the Chomskyean theory of universals to argue that language is a divine creation.[80] Should SIL demonstrate to its own satisfaction that God exists, allaying longstanding anxiety on this score, will this help it to accept the partial equivalence of belief systems, or will proof that God exists only harden its old resolve all the more?

Faith Finance

Money is a sensitive subject to the Summer Institute, one prone to paranoia and concealment. In the field, where most of the population has little, SIL obviously has much. At home, most of the money is raised according to the delicate euphemism of faith ritual — presenting the burden, asking for prayer, giving a blessing and so forth. In the belief that their money has been used for Godless ends, supporters have been known to interrupt its supply. 'Funding, funding, funding, that's all I hear!' declared an exasperated confidante. 'They're always telling me things and then saying I shouldn't tell anyone else.'

Sources in the United States apparently accounted for $22-23 million of Wycliffe's $26.5 million income in 1980.* Where it all comes from has been obfuscated ever since Cameron Townsend told Mexicans that individuals supported his work. Now the inquirer learns that the money comes from relatives, churches and friends who must remain anonymous. Much suspicion to the contrary, it is undoubtedly true that the middle class, mission-oriented congregation is the mainstay. The money is there for the asking and it does not take long to find a church which is giving it. In 1975 the 1,100 members of the Calvary Church of Santa Ana, California planned to give $230,000 to 65 missionaries, half Wycliffe members.[82] While Calvary obviously is a super-church, just 58 such mission budgets could have provided Wycliffe's $13.3 million U.S. income that year, as could 63,300 church members donating an average of $210.[83] The year before, Wycliffe claimed 66,000 donors, apparently just in the U.S., and several years later its monthly reported a 60,000 circulation.[84]

The Wycliffe support base is not to be confused with the statistical evangelical, who is slightly poorer than other North Americans, half again more likely to be a Democrat than Republican, and favours the small town and inner city over the suburb.[85]* Geographically, the support base does seem to be distributed like the Bible belt church, which is found all over the

---

* Members from outside the U.S. apparently have been subsidized by U.S. sources. In 1968, when 76% of the Wycliffe membership was from the U.S., 87% of its income was from there. Relative to the number of their Wycliffe missionaries, non-U.S. supporters were contributing only 54% as much as U.S. supporters.[81]

---

* Inner city evangelicals tend to be black, poor and show little interest in premillennial thinking or foreign missions.

country but is strongest in the South and weakest in the North-east. Yet Wycliffe is distinctively southern Californian in origin — three of four SIL/ WBT chartists were from here and a 1951 survey showed a heavily 'West Coast' membership — and southern California is a special place.[86]

The siting of the U.S. centres in Orange County and two other areas of strong support — Dallas and the environs of Charlotte, North Carolina where Billy Graham was born — skew Wycliffe's social terrain toward booming Sunbelt metropoli and parvenu Republicanism. People with small town values have moved into suburbs which threaten them. Financed by oil and Pentagon windfalls, right-wing jingoism flourishes. So does evangelical religion, transformed into salvation for a gilded age.[87]

In suburbs and the small town evangelical homeland, middle class orthodoxy and income provide a large public for mission appeals. The missions make alarming news from the around world understandable in the terms one hears in church every Sunday. They offer to make the world less threatening by making it more like the United States. And they appeal to the discrepancy between an ideology of sacrifice and lives dominated by consumerism. 'The American standard of living just doesn't fit in with so much of the world,' a Minnesota farm woman muses. 'We live sort of a pretend kind of life. Even spiritually, we've got it all. What about the rest of the world?' Following the 1976 earthquake in Guatemala, she and her husband go there for several months to help Wycliffe with reconstruction work. They discover that 'families are a lot closer than they are up here' and that 'life and death are real down there, not packed away in a sterilized room.'[88]

One of the reasons for Wycliffe's success is that it has promoted a clearly defined product, a fetish which is to be taken to exotic places, translated and work miracles. There is less sympathy for the missionary whom the Lord has called to minister to office machinery in a Los Angeles suburb, that is, for the administrative costs of the world's largest foreign faith mission bureaucracy. Since 'field first' has confined Wycliffe to a 10% administrative levy on donations to members, it must look elsewhere to meet the 17.9% management and publicity cost reflected in the 1979 financial statement.[89] Money for infrastructure is also difficult to raise: middle class congregations pledged to support the career and offspring of mission couples cannot be expected to finance yet another centre for the salvation of the world.

The Christian businessman can. Principal backers have always played a seminal role in Wycliffe, by financing the basis for recruiting members who, in turn, make a broader appeal to their own social networks. During the Depression the critical sum might be only a few hundred dollars, to finance the founder's next step; then in larger amounts after the Second World War, to purchase airplanes and erect bases; and now to finance Wycliffe's archipelago across the southern United States. Some of these funds come from Christian foundations such as the Billy Graham Evangelistic Association; the Fuller Evangelistic Association; and the Henry P. and Susan C. Crowell Trust, which in 1974 gave JAARS $42,500.[90]

The Wycliffe Associates (WA) was originally described as an organization of

Christian businessmen. But while it includes men like the one who provided the real estate for the Huntington Beach centre, the recent presentation as Wycliffe's lay support division is more descriptive. The business of most of the 12,000 associates is on the level of accountancy, construction sub-contracting, family farming and housework. The majority seem to be approaching retirement, free at last of child-rearing expenses but still near the peak of their income curve. They are willing to accept Wycliffe as a surrogate dependent, break with the etiquette of faith solicitation ('information concerning needs may be made known; funds will not be solicited'), and respond to appeals for Third World realities which a church mission committee would forego in favour of financing another North American soul winner, items such as the pickup truck demanded by the University of Ougadougou, houses for Dani base workers suffering from malaria, and travel expenses for Dr. Suharno to attend a conference in Montreal.[91] WA also has shouldered high publicity costs: during the first four years (1967-71) it spent $223,000 to transfer another $551,000 to Wycliffe (in 1981 WA transferred $1.7 million including services).[92] Translators may live in a house and work in an office built by WA tradesmen who spent their vacation for the Lord; entrust college-age children to WA 'aunts and uncles' in the United States; and on their own furlough in the U.S., drive about in a car loaned by a WA member and spend the night in WA homes.[93]

Wycliffe's largest undertaking to date, the International Linguistic Center, illustrates the fears that it could serve as a front for commercial interests or political extremists. More importantly, it suggests the boundaries of propriety which Wycliffe dare not trespass for fear of endangering support. In 1978, after more than a decade of witness in the banking and religious capital of Texas, the ILC board of trustees included five company presidents and five chairmen of the board of two Dallas banks, two Dallas manufacturing corporations, two Dallas insurance companies, five real estate and investment enterprises, and four oil and natural gas concerns. The trustees had donated half the $1.5 million invested in ILC construction, although one had pledged another $1.5 million in matching funds toward the $8 million plan.[94] Five sat on the boards of two of the largest bank holding companies in Texas, First International Bancshares and Republic of Texas, where they rubbed shoulders with directors of Texas Instruments and Halliburton, whose subsidiaries (Geophysical Service and Brown & Root, respecitvely) have explored for oil and built roads in the Ecuadorian and Peruvian Amazon.[95]

The most engaging ILC trustee is without doubt Nelson Bunker Hunt, son of the independent oilman and latecomer to the Lord, H.L. Hunt. Family generosity to Wycliffe may date to H.L.'s first wife Lyda, a Presbyterian churchwoman in Dallas from 1938 to 1955; or third wife Ruth, who in 1960 brought H.L. into the First Baptist Church of the Reverend W.A. Criswell, soon to be a Wycliffe supporter; or perhaps merely Bunker. In any case, Bunker is not the kind of person I would want on my board of trustees. He is not known for his scruples, and he owns oil and gas leases all over the world. In 1975, for example, Bunker and his wife Caroline were going to New Guinea where he would tend to oil business while she hoped to study a tribe of head-hunters.[96] Bunker also happens to be a board member and leading financier of the John Birch Society, the right-wing group named in honour of a funda-mentalist missionary turned intelligence officer who was killed by Chinese Communist troops in 1945.[97] Recently his money was thundering against the Red menace in Nicaragua, where evangelicals have found the Sandinistas understanding, and urging U.S. support for the same Guatemalan regime whose atrocities sometimes filter into Wycliffe prayer letters.

The ILC is modest, even humble compared to another of Bunker's charities, the Campus Crusade for Christ of Wycliffe supporter Bill Bright. By 1982, Hunt and Bright plan to raise $1 billion for world evangelism.[98] Colombians became acquainted with the scheme when an 'Alpha and Omega movement', led by a distant 'Guillermo Briceno' inundated the mass media with the same I FOUND IT! campaign which Campus Crusade has inflicted on other countries.[99] One of the three men in charge of planning Bright's Christian Graduate University in southern California, Charles LeMaistre is the University of Texas Chancellor who endorsed SIL's affiliation with that system.[100]

In such a small world, it is no surprise to find Cameron Townsend listed as one of several dozen Christian leaders in the Religious Roundtable, a New Right vehicle 'to fight in the political arena for pro-God, pro-family, pro-American causes.'[101] The Roundtable was organized in 1979 by a former Wycliffe Associates board member, E.E. McAteer, who had just introduced a flag and Bible entrepreneur named Jerry Falwell to his associates in Washington, thereby helping to launch the Moral Majority. The following year, both organizations helped elect Ronald Reagan and defeat six liberal senators opposed to military intervention in places like Central America.[102]

Wycliffe members have not been the last to recognize that they pay dearly for U.S. imperialism. 'What the United States does to Latin America,' Rachel Saint observed, 'Latin Americans do to us.'[103] If military force were used against Ecuador in a dispute over tuna fishing, as Ronald Reagan suggested in 1975, what would be the consequences for Bible translation? But if Wycliffe is being forced to leave the countries anyway and members blame Communists, they may feel they have little to lose. According to Christian extremists, America has done more to evangelize the world than any other nation; it must stay 'free' to finish the task; and to do that it must defend 'freedom' in places like El Salvador.

From small to large, Wycliffe supporters believe that their spiritual invest-ment ('the dividends are eternal' state the ILC trustees) will also make their world more stable.[104] Stability is in the eye of the beholder: were supporters to learn that McCarthyism has become a rationale for monopolizing the cocaine trade, to say nothing of an excuse for murdering the converts of their missionaries, they might be less susceptible to propaganda. But their own trusted missionaries never begin to tell them such things. Wycliffe is afraid of losing their support. For several decades now, that fear has been invoked to stave off changes. If supporters knew, they might stop sending us money; therefore we cannot tell them; and since supporters might not understand, we cannot do it. Wycliffe continues to censor information which could alarm supporters and marches into the arms of the New Right.

The Bases and the Members

The bases are Wycliffe's distinctive model of missionary work. It can function without them but prefers not to. Rationalized as a technological necessity, the bases reinforce institutional traits in the membership and set it apart from, not just the local population, but fellow missionaries. The gadgets and amenities, evangelical fame at home and elitism in the field, make Wycliffe a super-mission which is resented as well as admired. 'They're the most spiritual and materialistic of groups,' a colleague in Colombia said. 'I don't like to go to church as often as they do, but it seems they're in service, or prayer meetings, or a healing service so often that they don't have time to get out for a breath of fresh air and think critically about what's going on.' Actually there is a critical tradition within Wycliffe, even if some of its exponents have been forced to leave: in despair over the majority bloc in the Latin American branches, one characterized his associates as right-wing, middle class expatriates raised according to a closed circuit of evangelical doctrine, Bible training and little else. Despite Wycliffe's attempt to maintain that closed circuit, field-workers may be torn between, not just the expectations of home supporters and what has actually been accomplished, but faith mission objectives and their knowledge of the consequences.

Wycliffe's linguistic approach has appealed to students at evangelical liberal arts colleges and secular universities, diluting recruitment from the more fundamentalist Bible institutes and colleges which produce so many faith missionaries.* But it appears that more than a few aspirants attracted by the intellectual, seemingly non-sectarian approach are discouraged by the Statement of Doctrine — especially eternal punishment of the lost and Scriptural inerrancy — or turned down because they are too liberal. According to a 1961 survey, two thirds of the recruits were Baptist (40) and independent fundamentalist (29), with Presbyterians (9) a distant third and a few Congregationalists, Lutherans, Dutch Reformers and so forth (23 in all) bringing up the rear.[106]

With its ups and downs, recruitment has increasingly failed to measure up to Wycliffe's sense of urgency and crisis, hence the high hopes placed on Chester Bitterman's martyrdom. There were 180 new members from all countries in 1970, an average of 130 a year in 1975-77, and about 200 in 1979, with approximately two-thirds from the United States. There was a drop to 169 in 1980 and a recovery toward the 200 level in 1981, with a martyr's

* In 1961 recruits who had attended secular universities and colleges (46), evangelical arts colleges (36) and technical or nursing schools (39) outnumbered those with experience at Bible institutes and colleges (53) and theological seminaries (14).[105]

crop entering the training pipeline.[107] Whether the prospect of being kidnapped and accused of working for the CIA will appeal to young evangelicals is uncertain. 'Questions such as "will I like it?," "will I be happy?" or "will I be successful?" crowd into the mind,' Wycliffe's candidate secretary reports of the self-fulfillment generation.[108] Like other of the more image-conscious missions, Wycliffe has offered fulfillment for some time. In their 'calling' young members tend to describe, not a striking religious experience, but a middle class career decision sanctified by a Christian upbringing. 'What the Bible did in my own life' is a common theme.

Preparing for the field usually takes several years. Most non-Bible majors require a year of formal training to pass Wycliffe's examination in this subject.[109] In the late 1970s, aspiring field-workers were attending three semesters of Summer Institute, studying a trade language, attending an ILC orientation and, after the first Summer Institute, spending four months at Jungle Camp — one of the Field Training Courses for the Americas, the Pacific and Africa. Throughout this process, and for two years probationary membership on the field, recruits are indoctrinated in Wycliffe policies, evaluated and culled. Jungle Camp is particularly rugged for North American suburbanites: that contrast, not any similarity to the field conditions a majority will enjoy, is the main point of the exercise. It is Wycliffe's version of army boot camp. Physical and spiritual pressure — the group regime, Bible study, staff command and evaluation — encourage doing things Wycliffe's way.[110] 'Most things inside come out,' an administrator observed. Each candidate gives his/her testimony — how the Lord led one to become a Christian and then to Wycliffe — at group assemblies. Those whose overall testimony fails to impress the staff, reportedly less than 10%, are rejected.[111]

Except for 500-odd short-term assistants, who are not considered members and do support work, Wycliffe is supposed to be an exclusive life commitment. During the first decades the attrition rate seems to have been far higher: of the 19 young pioneers in Peru, only three remained active members 25 years later.[112] One of the more obvious costs of the commitment is Wycliffe endogamy, to guard against unchristian influences and divided allegiance. Were 660 single women in 1978 so inclined, they could be selected as a spouse by 88 single men. To guarantee their independence, women must apparently remain single: the groom is supposed to come to the fore even when he marries into a previous field assignment, and nearly all directors and officers in a 57% female organization are male.[113] Another cost is often early separation from children advancing through school: 'missionary kids' are the subject of much reassurance in the Wycliffe monthly. But there are powerful emotional rewards for staying: one has found something to do which seems far more significant than most occupations at home and, by the very fact of being a North American in the Third World, climbed upward in the social scale.

The organization prides itself upon egalitarianism — 'it seemed like the closest thing to a classless society I'd ever seen' — and conceptualizes itself as a democracy. Although the branches are subject to the board of directors, they are supposed to be autonomous. Each year their members elect branch administrators. Every two years, members choose delegates to the SIL/WBT biennial conference, which elects the board of directors. The board appoints most administrators above the branch level, where a circle of Townsend's proteges, survivors of pioneer days in Mexico, are leaving the top posts to a more diverse second generation.[114] In view of the delicate balance between home, state and field requirements to which administrators must subordinate members, bureaucratic stability is the dominant note.

The rationale for all the support services, that they make for greater efficiency, is ridiculed by some members and brethren. They argue that the bases distract attention from the task at hand, arouse suspicion, disorient informants, make local people jealous and isolate members from the country in which they are living. It is hard to criticize the technological geniuses who have provided one's electricity, telephone and plumbing, not to mention flight and radio service, but there is some feeling among the field-workers that JAARS complicates their lives. These members recognize that the base is a cultural affair from its all-important efficiency to the deepest attachments of its residents. In the words of an evangelical writer, Yaninacocha is 'a little bit of America transported into the heart of the jungle.'[115] The children — Wycliffe had 2,800 in 1976 — are paramount.[116] Most parents want to raise them as North Americans. And while some members find the bases suffocating, many more want to live in an evangelical North American community even if there is nothing quite like it in the United States, a community of the saved who not only pray but live and work together, a community of saints without sinners. Life is regulated by production quotas, progress reports, committee meetings and lunch hours. Even women with small children have a part-time job, and everyone reports to someone else. All are subject to the group will as expressed in its spiritual life, the intensity of which varies from base to base and over time as a branch responds to crisis in the capital or trouble in the tribes.

The most serious threat to little America is the Bible translator. While base personnel tend to feel marginal and JAARS is a group apart with its own defensive *elan,* the Bible translators are regarded with some awe. Many spend more time at the base than in the field, and their attempt to live like the people may convince only the visitor expecting a mission hacienda. But unlike support personnel, who acculturate chiefly to the base, translators and other field-workers must also adjust to native communities and then, periodically, the homeland. It is easy to infect one milieu with behaviour appropriate to another. Except perhaps for administrators, who are usually inactive field-workers, the translators see more of the programme from what is said at home to what happens in native communities than anyone else. For base and homeland they must translate their experience in native communities into faith mission terms, usually not an easy task. They must live with the consequences for the people they want to help.

Most importantly, translators must contain the influence of native people on their faith, a danger dramatized as their children — more open to cultural influence than adults — turn into 'little Indians.' The great peril is that the translator will be converted by the people s/he hopes to convert. Instead of injecting a missionary content into indigenous forms, the fallen translator accepts an indigenous content and, if indiscreet, parades as a pagan in missionary form. Although relatively few translators have ended their careers in this way, a far larger number apparently have had to struggle against it. Prophylaxis against the danger, perhaps more sever than in other faith missions owing to the emphasis on language and culture, is the central reinforcement function of the base. Despite increasing talk of cultural exchange, to change other cultures to satisfaction Wycliffe must protect its own against their influence.

In the eyes of a rebel, a City of God becomes a system for social control. As one such translator recalls the Peruvian branch when the founder himself walked the base, Townsend frequently reminded members of Wycliffe principles, why they were adopted and how they were Scriptural. His wife Elaine took notes of members' sermons. Attendance at church was important: if one's absence was noted, the administration delegated someone to pay a call out of personal concern. For spiritual renewal ministers from the homeland were introduced for a week or two of meetings and house to house pastoral care. They reminded members of their duty to God, their brethren and the lost, in that order. There was also a pat on the back, but the message of this naive visitor representing the expectations of home supporters was duty. It was frowned upon to be out in the tribe for more than six months at a time: even those who would have preferred otherwise needed a break for spiritual refreshment.

However carefully the faith is guarded, the collision between faith mission objective and experience gives rise to dilemmas. One is the discrepancy between home fantasies and field reality, a gap which Cameron Townsend's flair for promotion widened. Guilt that one has failed the high Wycliffe calling is common as members prepare for furlough, one year in the homeland after four or five in the field, which is required to keep members in touch with their prayer and financial constituencies. According to an undated manual, members are 'increasingly dreading furlough ministry.'[117] Their anxieties have come to be treated as the 'pre-furlough syndrome', an indication that, like much else in Wycliffe, the affair has become steadily more managed.[118] Having been dispatched to the field with high expectations, members return to find themselves near the U.S. poverty level and endowed with more sanctity than most ministers enjoy. As missionaries they are presumed to have forsaken the comforts of home for hardship, if not danger, and achieved substantial victories for the Lord. 'Such ideas!' a field-worker exclaimed. Even more disturbing, perhaps, members return to the society which sent them abroad in the first place. 'You feel the world has gone on and passed you by', a translator explains:

> You see kids you knew now grown up and married and you feel a lot older. The affluence and the inflation almost knock you over. You don't

know how you'll cope and how your kids will do. . . . We were going
through a residential neighbourhood with beautifully manicured
lawns, when I suddenly said to Madeline, 'Where are all the people?'
Compared to crowded Asia . . . this was like a graveyard.

Members are now prepared for such feelings as 'reverse culture shock.'[119]
   The path to safety usually leads back to the mission field which has
become one's home. It is a lesson which does not make another any easier,
the conflict between Wycliffe demands and those of the local situation. Field-
workers may come to regret the cost of the programme to native people, or
its irrelevance to their felt needs, or its failure to help them defend themselves
against other forces, producing one or another degree of disillusion with
Wycliffe.[120] This leads directly to a third dilemma, one faced by the entire
membership: the constraints imposed upon a range of emotions — defiance,
satire, despair — with which human beings protect themselves against the
institutions which control their lives.

   The Wycliffe family makes very high demands on its members' loyalty.
Bound to carry out group decisions, members also apparently are to refrain
from public criticism. All publications from prayer letters to scholarship
must be approved by higher authority.[121] Dissent which goes beyond certain
rather narrow limits is likely to be interpreted as a spiritual crisis, whereupon
appropriate supportive measures are applied. If one does not find balm in
more religion, it is time to leave Wycliffe. As the founder himself stated at
his 1971 farewell: 'God has been good to us. He led us into our unusual
policies. Let's be true to them. Folks who do not accept them should not
join us. Folks who want to depart from them should resign and thus avoid
jeopardizing our situation especially as regards "closed" countries. God will
raise up substitutes for them.'[122]

   If Wycliffe is so very close to God, members have little choice but to blame
their institution's contradictions on themselves. In the 1970s a troubled
Wycliffe became more introspective: while supporters used to read mainly
about external obstacles to Bible translation, now they also learn about
members' personal problems: family difficulties, pride, jealousy, frustration.
Until recently psychological disorder was usually interpreted as a sign that
the victim was out of touch with God and living in sin. To put the afflicted
under professional care would have been to admit that the answer was
beyond the fundamentalist system. Now, thanks to the construction of evangelical psychology, Wycliffe relies upon conformist therapies of adjustment
whose vocabulary — coping, everyone has their hangups, like yourself and so
forth — finds its way into the group vocabulary. Pop psychology does not
explain the mounting opposition to the divine plan, however, the bewildering
rage which threatens to destroy members' life work and turn them into men
and women without a country they can really call their own. To deal with
that the Summer Institute still relies on demonology.

Charismatic Renewal

Evangelical missionaries choose their response to adversity by interpreting it
as Satanic opposition or the Lord's will. If affliction is the Lord's will, then
Satan is at work only in the sense of tempting one to reject it. The Christian
prays for the long suffering patience of Job, a trait much in evidence in the
Wycliffe membership. But if Satan has orchestrated the assault, the Christian
prays against an Enemy who may well wear a human face. Once prayer fails
to stave off defeat at the hands of the forces of evil, it turns into prayer to
seek the Lord's perfect will, the divine plan which encompasses all setbacks
and will ultimately lead to victory. Since Satan never admits defeat, the
contest begins anew.

In North America, Christian belief in diabolical conspiracy and protective
magic is as old as the Puritans. The devils lurking in the forest were Indians,
from whom prayer and firearms delivered God's people. Now that the Summer
Institute is invading Satan's last indigenous strongholds, prayer is just as
crucial. And as befits a modern age, it is radio co-ordinated. Kept in touch by
mail and shortwave radio, homeland networks of prayer partners and prayer
warriors direct their petitions to spiritual needs on the field. At the bases,
which function as relay and booster stations for the prayer power Wycliffe
casts into the battle against indigenous magic, members may be organized into
prayer partnerships and circles. When the radio dispatcher at Yarinacocha
learns of an emergency, she activates a telephone network which unites the
base in petition to the Lord.[123]

Whether chanted by a witch doctor or printed in a newspaper, Satanic
opposition demands a corresponding response. Since the Summer Institute
considers itself dedicated to everyone's highest good, its prayers are entirely
good. Yet it wants divine intervention in its favour. When the Guatemalan
branch reported that the *Proyecto Francisco Marroquin* (not identified with
Satan) had proposed alphabets which 'may be linguistically sound in themselves' but would not benefit Indians, it asked for 'prayers that the proposal
either be dropped or turned down.'[124] When an offending sorcerer is killed,
that may be an answer to prayer; when the Peruvian government purged the
press, that was an answer to prayer; and when all those North Vietnamese
attacking the bunker were killed, that too was an answer to prayer. However
good it may be, prayer may therefore entail not only frustrating but harming
the adversary. By Satanizing human opposition, SIL makes the functional
equivalent of a witchcraft accusation. By praying for the overcoming of
adversaries, the linguists cast the curse of the godly.

As spiritual warfare intensified during the 1970s, it gave rise to a remarkable departure within the Summer Institute. Until recently, middle class
evangelicals have considered baptism in the Holy Spirit dangerous. Pentecostals
have frequent encounters with the Devil, are eager to discern the miraculous,
and often have been accused of confusing the two. When C.I. Scofield
confronted ecstatic religion among poor Blacks and Whites, he relegated New
Testament references to the Pentecostal gifts (or charismata) to a past

dispensation: they were no longer available to the Christian. The most common charismata are faith healing and speaking in tongues, but some Pentecostal sects have become known for their visions and prophecy, extra-Biblical revelation which supersedes that which orthodox evangelicals hold most dear.

For several decades Wycliffe discriminated against Pentecostal applicants and rid itself of the newly Spirit-baptized in its ranks. Since Pentecostals claim special spiritual gifts, other members resented them, perhaps responding with the kind of personal concern which becomes unbearable. But Cameron Townsend prevailed upon the 1949 biennial conference to accept 'compatible' Pentecostals and protected them when he could.[125] Gradually, baptism in the Holy Spirit proved irresistible: in the mid-1960s speaking in tongues is said to have broken out in the Colombian branch, with the result that U.S. headquarters dispatched someone to restore order. But soon Pentecostalism was achieving middle class respectability in the United States. The Neo-Pentecostals or Charismatics were careful to curb excess and demonstrate the legitimacy of their faith: while maintaining denominational ties, they felt closer to other Charismatics. Under the new dispensation Roman Catholics and evangelical Protestants came together in good faith.

Wycliffe has been cautious about sharing its Charismatic movements with home supporters, but they seem to owe something to the Townsends. If the founder always opposed discrimination against Pentecostals, his wife Elaine is said to have brought back the Holy Spirit from the oppressed congregations of the Soviet Union. They proceeded to settle into their retirement home at the first Wycliffe centre to publicize its Charismatic Renewal, JAARS headquarters in North Carolina. Hoping to make some headway against this bastion of Wycliffe ethnocentrism, the Townsends furthered their campaign against racial discrimination by joining a black Presbyterian church. It could not have been easy for the Jungle Aviation and Radio Service to break race taboos in rural North Carolina, as the founder prodded them, nor were many likely to have applauded his expeditions to the Soviet Union. In the struggle to rise to Townsend's challenges, the Holy Spirit made sufficient inroads for a Charismatic, Jamie Buckingham, to be asked to write the JAARS story.

Buckingham and Wycliffe writer Hugh Steven describe Charismatic phenomena in Papua New Guinea, the Philippines, Brazil and Peru.[126] There is also reason to believe that, after some resistance, by 1977 a movement was under way again in Colombia. The Peruvian renewal is attributed to branch administrator Jerry Elder, who is said to have returned from furlough in the U.S. 'a new man' dissatisfied with the Yarinacocha machine he had done much to engineer. 'For years the Wycliffe Bible Translators in Peru — and I in particular — had been self-reliant people,' he told Buckingham. 'We were highly trained, skilled technicians, We knew our jobs and prided ourselves that we were the best in the world.'

After Elder's first attempts to renew the branch are said to have failed, on Christmas Eve 1971, a Pucallpa-bound airliner disappeared in a storm with five branch members and 90 other people. During the search a certain hysteria gripped Pucallpa and Yarinacocha, where shortwave radio operators activated a worldwide prayer chain. All over the jungle it was reported that an airliner had been heard, or seen, flying low over the jungle, hours after it proved to have disintegrated at 10,000 feet. One passenger actually survived the fall — along with perhaps a dozen others who died from insects and hunger — and walked out to help.[127] This was the making of a ghost airliner.

> During those days of uncertainty, [Elder continued], when our men were combing the jungles hoping against hope our friends were still alive, something happened in the hearts of the people on base. Love, more love than we'd ever dare express, was poured out toward the families of those lost in the jungle. And when the bodies were finally returned to the base, that love increased. It spread to others on the base and flowed out into the jungle toward our Indian friends. It leaped the boundaries of doctrinal differences, as we began to love and respect our Roman Catholic friends who were part of the same crisis.

The base held a communion service — Charismatic fare — and, according to Buckingham,

> didn't get around to serving the bread and wine until after midnight. It seemed that everybody on base — more than four hundred — had something to confess, and wanted to do it publicly. Men, women and children rose to their feet, tearfully confessing such things as pride, selfishness, haughtiness, intolerance, envy and resentment.

At the Yarinacocha Bible Conference 'there was more confession. People admitted their hypocrisy, they confessed their fears and failures, they publicly cried out to God for help.' The base divided into small groups for weekly body ministry. Every month a day was set aside to pray for one another. The base doctors began laying hands on their patients.[128]

Carried from the United States, Charismatic Renewal met the Peruvian branch's needs on several levels. One was the 'jungle', which had swallowed the bodies of five comrades and threatened to devour an entire faith mission, in the sense that North American evangelicals felt themselves in danger of being overcome in their contest with heathen powers. 'I had thought of demons as figments of the imaginations of primitive peoples,' wrote the Aguaruna translator who discovered her Bible translation assistant dabbling in the occult. . .

> My relation to God didn't involve power over evil in such an alive form . . . . Two weeks later we learned that [a demon possessed woman] had died. Doomed to eternity in hell with real demons! The torment I had seen in her eyes haunted me. Where was the power to save others like her? With all my heart I longed for such power.[129]

270

Charismatic Renewal offered that power, or so it was hoped. A majority of Latin American *evangelicos* are Pentecostals: beyond the control of North American missionaries, they steal into flocks which the North Americans have wooed away from Catholicism, preach the necessity of yet another baptism, divide congregations and perhaps snatch them away entirely. The reason for these triumphs over North Americans with far more patronage power is apparently that Pentecostalism permits traditional spirits to be acknowledged by, admitted to, and brought under control within the Christian scheme. Thus, in Ecuador, SIL's Secoya translators were dismayed by Pentecostal services which reminded them of the hallucinogenic trances they thought they had banished.[130] Pentecostalism is likely to flourish in the wreckage of legalistic church-building triumphs which suppressed protective magic, increased social conflict and heightened fear of witchcraft.

Such a ruin is perhaps Cushillococha where, on the very afternoon of the lost airliner, the Archangel Gabriel is said to have appeared and prophesied that a mighty revival would sweep the jungle. The Ticuna who received him were in radio contact with the SIL base, and sooner or later Gabriel's deeds made a large impression on Yarinacocha.

> From the day I arrived [reported Buckingham] . . . I began hearing rumours about miracles among [the Ticuna] . I heard . . . almost unbelievable stories about meetings where the Indians were anointed with tongues of fire, where they spontaneously spoke in unknown tongues, stories of large water baptismal services, and even resurrections from the dead.[131]

By sanctifying native eruptions, Charismatic Renewal provided a bridge to wavering followings.

The movement also led to love and respect for Catholic clergy whom the branch had officially been loving and respecting since 1953. Conveniently, while Charismatic movements in Latin America have been heavily Catholic, many have been shepherded by North American evangelicals. In 1979, Cardinal Anibal Munoz Duque of Colombia warned that 'Alpha and Omega' — again, Bill Bright's Campus Crusade for Christ — was infiltrating the Church for uncatholic ends.[132] Even more conveniently, Charismatics generally frown upon the theology of liberation: their renewals are acclaimed for uniting people of all classes from matrons to their maids rather than dividing rich from poor.

In Peru, where most Catholic missionaries had reconciled themselves to SIL but scarcely numbered it among their blessings, a newly Charismatic branch made unprecedented overtures in the Holy Spirit, notably to the Jesuit Mission in the Maranon. During the late 1970s contract negotiations, one of the branch's leading Charismatics, its public relations director, was holding a weekly Bible class for 600 Catholics. According to *Christianity Today*, he argued that evangelical Protestants could relate to Catholic Charismatics more easily than to ecumenical Protestants because (like the evangelicals) Catholic Charismatics oppose the theology of liberation.[133] In other words, Charismatic religion could produce an alliance between right-wing Catholics and Protestants against left-wing Catholics and Protestants. The Jesuits and Dominicans of the Amazon missions did not seem impressed. They welcomed the chance to improve relations, but this particular flood of Holy Spirit looked like another political manoeuvre.

The Yarinacocha movement was more than a hunt for allies, however, or even a deeply felt response to the 'jungle' which might restore the confidence of Indian followings. At bottom, it was a reaction to disillusion with one's associates and Wycliffe. The Peruvian branch owes more to Cameron Townsend than any other except the Mexican. It put the total programme together like no other in Latin America. But the methods employed created undying enmities and exacted a high moral cost. The branch never learned to feel secure and came to regard itself as the pinnacle of creation. A man who knew the base in the 1960s recalls that he never knew a community where 'witchcraft' tension – petty jealousy and suspicion – was so obvious. Each Christian seemed to feel the others a little less so. Worse, it seemed that all had been for naught: out in the tribes many believers were in open disobedience as they are today. Then, during the 1970 contract negotiations, government officials took pains to emphasize that Peru was in charge, not SIL, and that within a few short years it might be dispensed with. No wonder that members felt insecure and spiritually filthy. Clearly they needed a new kind of help.

As everyone confessed their sins, the only performance which escaped scrutiny was that of the branch, the institution which had fostered so many sins. Divinely ordained Wycliffe, which some might hold responsible for the sorry condition of the membership, was definitely not the object. The guilt in the heart of each member was. Charismatic Renewal remystified the Lord's work and its leadership. According to the JAARS-Peru Director, 'it was the difference between giving God directions and learning to take orders from Him.'[134]

The Pentecostal movement at Yarinacocha was a faith mission's cry for survival on the, now junk-strewn Amazonian frontier it did so much to pioneer. By restoring the aura of sanctity about the institution, Charismatic Renewal united a membership divided by petty bigotries against external danger. From formal contacts to casual encounters, God's people were drawing their wagons into circle to fight off the hostiles. When Buckingham visited Yarinacocha around 1973, he sensed 'a real depth of spirituality'.[135] Yet judging from my own experience and that of others, Charismatic Yarinacocha displayed a hostility and bitterness toward potential adversaries which neighbouring, non-charismatic branches did not. The enemy was 'Communism and the Devil', members informed confidantes. During my brief visits it seemed that cult discourse – 'the Lord' this and 'the Lord' that – was more common than in other branches. Looking into the faces of several members, it was as if I were the Devil in human form.

For Latin Americans who no longer gave SIL any credence, for home supporters to whom it could not explain its desperate position, for members themselves, something more was needed, to transform a demoralizing morass into another evangelical drama and aggressors into victims. With threats to the lives of members on the upswing, well before the Bogota kidnapping Wycliffe was preparing to redeem itself with missionary blood. 'To serve Him is costly as the Bittermans have found out and as those five brave young men killed by the Aucas [in 1956] found out,' Billy Graham told Wycliffe's Golden Jubilee rally two months later:

> But the rewards are overwhelming in this life and the life to come. It's already been demonstrated time and time again that the death of those brave young men in Ecuador led to a whole new dimension of missions in this century. And Chet Bitterman's going home to glory I believe was planned in the providence of God to open up a new chapter in missions. To call up the young men and young women to say, 'I'll go and take his place so that Chet Bitterman will be multiplied hundreds and thousands of times over until this job is finished. . . .'
>
> There can be no argument or even discussion about this when we face the command of Christ. It's only about the where, the how and the when. There are three thousand languages yet to go. Wycliffe can now absorb about five hundred new translators and backup personnel a year. This means that every one of these language groups can be touched and occupied within this decade of the eighties. . . . You know what the primary problem is? It's the volunteers who are willing to go and put all on the altar as Chet Bitterman did. . . . I believe that God is calling hundreds of young people here tonight to say 'yes, I'm willing to do that. . . .'
>
> I'm convinced that we're approaching the last days. We must work before the night comes and we come back to our text. . . 'the Good News about the Kingdom will be preached throughout the whole world so that all the nations will hear it, and *then,* and *then,* and *then,* the end will come!' I don't see but one thing standing in the way of the coming of the Lord. Now I believe He could come tonight. But there's one thing . . . that puzzles me in the signs. All nations must hear. And this is what Cameron Townsend has always believed. . . .
>
> When Cortez landed in Mexico with that handful of men, he ordered them to burn the ships, so they couldn't go back to Spain. He was determined to stay until he conquered. I'm asking you to burn your bridges and burn the ships and say 'Lord here I am, I'm yours.'[136]

References

1. *In Other Words* March 1976:2. On the implications for pre-literate societies, see Goody and Watt 1963.
2. Grimes 1978:vii, x, 13-14.

3. Hoke 1975:223.
4. $6840: *In Other Words* Summer 1981:32.
5. *Translation* January/February 1975:15.
6. *In Other Words* August 1975:4.
7. *Wycliffe Associates Newsletter* May 1981:4.
8. Hefleys 1974:243-71; Buckingham 1974:87-9.
9. SIL/WBT 1971:1-3.
10. Cowan 1979:189.
11. Elaine Beekman, *Translation* January/March 1972:2-3.
12. Calculated from WBT 1978.
13. Pike and Brend 1977:185-8.
14. ILC 1977.
25. Haas 1978.
16. Cowan 1979:224; Wilson 1980:264, 354-7, 426.
17. Townsend and Pittman 1975:102.
18. The journeys: *Translation* July/September 1969:13; *Christianity Today* 9 May 1969:41, 13 October 1972:57, and 11 January 1980:46, 48; *Wycliffe Associates Newsletter* March 1979:2; Hefleys 1974:251-62. Townsend 1972. *Pravda,* cited *El Dia* (Mexico, D.F.) 7 June 1981:19.
19. *Nation* (New York) 10 November 1969:505-8.
20. SIL/WBT 1971:77-9.
21. Included in 11 page airgram, U.S. Embassy-Kathmandu to State Department, 'limited official use', 14 May 1969.
22. SIL/WBT 1971:80.
23. United Press International 14 August 1976 and *In Other Words* August 1976:6.
24. Cable, U.S. Embassy-Kathmandu to State Department, 8 June 1976, 'limited official use', signed Maytag.
25. *In Other Words* March 1977:2.
26. Calculated from WBT 1978.
27. For an account of Bendor-Samuel's work and WBT-Britain, see Thompson 1974.
28. SIL/WBT 1971:54.
29. *Nigeria Times* (Lagos) 6 May 1976:1, 4 and 12 May 1976:13; *In Other Words* August 1976:6 and March 1977:2; *Christianity Today* 10 September 1976:71-2.
30. *Washington Star* 28 February 1981.
31. Hoke 1975:518-19.
32. *In Other Words* December 1979:6. For an account of a branch showcase, the Sepik Iwam at Hauna, see Hall 1980.
33. AID/Asia-G-1250: *Current Technical Service Contracts and Grants* (AID) October 1978/September 1979:53.
34. Ralph McGehee, in *Nation* 11 April 1981:423-5.
35. Chomsky and Herman 1979:208.
36. Peters 1975:102-3.
37. Hoke 1975:280, 283.
38. SIL/WBT 1972:48.
39. SIL/WBT 1971:58 and 'Indonesia Profile', WBT pamphlet, 1975.
40. Chomsky and Herman 1979:175-6.
41. *Guardian* (New York) 20 September 1978:18.

42. Sharp 1977:6.
43. *In Other Words* April 1975:5. *From Baudi to Indonesian* (Suharno and Pike 1976), a publication financed by the Asia Foundation, illustrates the branch's attempt to identify with Indonesian nationalism, particularly propagation of 'the national language'. It also suggests the social chasm into which SIL has stepped, as if its role in Latin America were being caricatured.
44. Compiled from WBT notices and Hoke 1975.
45. '401 Translators Needed Now', WBT flier, 1980.
46. Grimes 1978:vii, x.
47. For an account of the Venezuelan controversy over New Tribes, see Marquina 1981.
48. SIL/WBT 1971:11. For the most recent, see Wares 1979.
49. 'La Politica Colonialista del ILV', in Bonfil Batalla 1979:397-400.
50. *Camp Wycliffe Chronicle* August 1936:2.
51. Author's interview, Patzun, 22 August 1978.
52. D'Ans 1981:146-8.
53. Landabaru 1979:6.
54. SIL/WBT 1971:5.
55. *El Comercio* 19 August 1953:7. Townsend cited *Bulletin* July/September 1948:4.
56. SIL/WBT 1972:18-28.
57. Landabaru 1979:6-7.
58. SIL/WBT 1971:5.
59. Ibid p.1.
60. Pike and Brend 1977:8.
61. Calculated from *In Other Words* September 1979:8.
62. SIL/WBT 1971:5, 14.
63. 'Minimum language proficiency goals', TSD Adv. Com., 29 October 1970, mimeo.
64. SIL/WBT 1972:26.
65. SIL/WBT 1961:74.
66. Sixty: Pike and Brend 1977:60. One hundred: tallied from WBT 1979.
67. Anon. 1976:111-21.
68. *Uno Mas Uno* 8 and 10 January 1979.
69. Arcand 1981:79-80.
70. Bravo Ahuja 1977:100, 118, 141, 251.
71. Landabaru 1979:7.
72. Sarah Gudschinsky, in Pike and Brend 1977:39-56.
73. Author's interview, Ayacucho, 14 February 1977.
74. Bonfil Batalla 1979:399.
75. *Beyond* (Waxhaw, North Carolina: JAARS) November/December 1980 and July/August 1981.
76. Joseph Grimes reviews SIL's computer work in Pike and Brend 1977:129-46.
77. *Annual Report* 1981:6 Wycliffe Associates (Orange, California).
78. Calvin Rensch (in Pike and Brend 1977:92), who (pp.85-128) reviews SIL's contributions to linguistics.
79. Cited by Daniel Hughes in Boutilier et al 1979:204.
80. Reviewed *Christianity Today* 6 May 1977:40, 42.

81. Calculated from SIL/WBT 1971:19; *Translation* September/October 1967:20 and Summer 1969:15.
82. *In Other Words* September 1975:1-3.
83. Ibid. September 1976:6.
84. *Translation* May/June 1974:9; *In Other Words* March 1979:5.
85. Results of Gallup Poll reported *Christianity Today* 21 December 1979:17-19.
86. *Translation* March 1951:6.
87. Miles 1980:261-66, 280.
88. *Wycliffe Associates Newsletter* May 1978:5.
89. *In Other Words* October 1980:6.
90. BGEA: *Sojourners* September 1977:8. FEA: Huntington and Kaplan 1981:11. Crowell: Foundation Center 1976:145.
91. SIL/WBT 1963:11.
92. SIL/WBT 1971:101 and *Annual Report* 1981:2 Wycliffe Associates (Orange, California).
93. For a description of WA, see Hefley 1978.
94. ILC 1977.
95. 'The ties that bind', in Oppenheimer and Porterfield 1976. *Texas Monthly* (Austin) April 1976:77.
96. *New York Times* 29 February 1976:48.
97. *Texas Monthly* April 1978:185; *Newsweek* (New York) 7 April 1980:57.
98. *Texas Observer* (Austin) 20 June 1980:2.
99. *Alternativa* (Bogota) 29 January 1979:12-13.
100. Quebedeaux 1979:174-5 and ILC 1977.
101. *Conservative Digest* (Falls Church, Virginia) 12 November 1979:12-13.
102. For an analysis of the Religious Roundtable, see Huntington and Kaplan 1981. On the Moral Majority, see Fitzgerald 1981 and *Christianity Today* 4 September 1981:22-31.
103. Author's interview, Dallas, 20 March 1980.
104. ILC 1977.
105. SIL/WBT 1961:87.
106. Ibid.
107. SIL/WBT 1971:17; *Wycliffe Associates Newsletter* January 1980:1; *In Other Words* December 1981:4.
108. *In Other Words* December 1981:4.
109. 'Training for translation with Wycliffe', sheet distributed May 1981.
110. For a description of Jungle Camp, see *In Other Words* April 1976:1-6.
111. Buckingham 1974:22.
112. *Translation* April/June 1972:2.
113. 660/88: *In Other Words* October 1978:4. 57% calculated from ibid. and Haas 1978.
114. Cowan 1979:227, 235-42.
115. Buckingham 1974:139.
116. *In Other Words* February 1976:6.
117. 'Furlough planning', SIL-Guatemala library.
118. *In Other Words* March 1980:3.
119. Hefley 1978:119-20.
120. E.g., Turner 1972:89-93.

121. Cowan 1979:235, 240.
122. SIL/WBT 1971:2-3.
123. Hefleys 1972:117,
124. SIL/WBT 1971:70.
125. Hefleys 1974:163-4.
126. Buckingham 1974:214-15 (Papua New Guinea); Steven 1974 (Philippines) and 1978 (Brazil).
127. *Reader's Digest* February 1973:100-4.
128. Buckingham 1974:138-55.
129. Larson 1974.
130. Bloom 1981:262.
131. Buckingham 1974:155.
132. *El Tiempo* (Bogota) 3 December 1978.
133. *Christianity Today* 1 December 1978:52 and 7 December 1979:46.
134. Buckingham 1974:154.
135. Buckingham 1974:138.
136. Golden Jubilee Rally, Anaheim Convention Center, Anaheim, California, 9 May 1981.

9. The Huaorani Go To Market

In 1956 five North Americans lost their lives trying to bring the Gospel to an unreached tribe. The Aucas or Huaorani defied the world market like few others at mid-20th Century, by controlling valuable jungle 150 kilometers from the capital of Ecuador. A 100 or so Huao spearmen, divided into four bands at war with each other, defended 7% of a republic against anyone.

The missionaries had landed an airplane in Huao domain after passing up an opportunity to learn the language. They acted in secrecy and haste, calling their plan Operation Auca and code-naming the landing site Palm Beach. Their speared remains were recovered by colleagues, the Army of Ecuador and the U.S. Air Force Rescue Service, Panama Command. Although the five men had fired their guns and the consequences for the Huaorani were unknown, a martyrdom was broadcast around the world.

Evangelical missions felt their lifeblood quicken with a thousand volunteers in a few weeks.

> Those five brave men . . . have paved the way for advance, not just in Amazonia but along all pioneer fronts, [a visionary proclaimed]. . . . In out-of-the-way corners of the earth there are some 2,000 tribes speaking 2,000 Bibleless languages. A tidal wave of missionary advance must engulf them all for Christ. From the tiny blood-stained strip of sand along the Curaray River in Ecuador to two thousand Bibleless groups. . . . A mighty crusade can now be brought to pass that will reach every tribe for the Lord Jesus Christ in this generation.[1]

The Huaorani (their own word for 'people') make their first unmistakable appearance in battles with rubber hunters around the turn of the century. Their adversaries were usually other jungle Indians, especially Lowland Quichua who, as the indispensable guide and labour of patronal expeditions, suffered most of the casualties and undertook most of the reprisals. The Huaorani decided that all outsiders were cannibals, owing possibly to an experience in the flesh. Their own ferocity made them known as *aucas,* the Quichua word for savages. They committed their most serious offense in the 1940s, however, by harassing the oil exploration teams of Royal Dutch Shell.[2]

278

Less than three years after Palm Beach, in 1958, a widow and a sister went to live with the band which had speared their men. One was the Plymouth Brethren's Elisabeth Elliot, whose books about Operation Auca and her husband were making her a best-selling author. The other was Wycliffe's Rachel Saint, whose brother had piloted the missionary plane into Auca land. They joined the band with the help of three Huao women including Dayuma, whom Saint had found on a hacienda. Sure enough, the men who had killed the missionaries turned into the elders of the Auca church. The drama of the five Auca martyrs, the five Auca killers, Elliot, Saint and Dayuma became an unsurpassed evangelical legend, probably the best known evangelical mission in the world, and did much to make the Wycliffe Bible Translators what it is today.

Years later, flying out of Wycliffe's tranquil Limoncocha base, pillars of smoke come into view as the airplane lifts above the jungle. The smoke proves to be rising from certain clearings, each at the end of a long dirt road. As the plane passes between the pillars of smoke, it comes in view of the tongues of fire which lick from the top of steel towers. The jungle here is one edge of the Lago Agrio oil field, which has made Ecuador a member of the Organization of Petroleum Exporting Countries. Lining the roads leading up to the wells are hundreds of tiny habitations, strips of tumbled-down jungle and corn plantings. These are the homes of peasants who have followed the oil companies into the jungle.

South-east of Lago Agrio, in what is now the Auca oil field, the Summer Institute removed most of the people of this name from land which the government had leased to North American oil companies. Airplanes flew Huao converts over their people, showering presents, loudspeaking messages and dropping concealed microphones from the sky. The converts brought their kin and enemies into the mission outpost; the Summer Institute obtained a reservation of sorts. Here it tried to protect the Huaorani from competitors and was invaded by the oil companies.

At their height, the removals met with no challenge because the plans of everyone from the Gulf and Texaco corporations to the Lowland Quichua depended on subduing or exterminating the Huaorani. SIL performed well in comparison with many pacifications, for the simple reason that most Huaorani survived it. In the mid-1970s 600 were increasing at a rate of more than 2% a year.[3] By clearing the way for the corporations and ending a vexation to the government, the missionaries also ended spear raids on Quichua settlements and most of the fighting between Huao bands.

The Huaorani only found their champions after they were available for other projects. The Summer Institute had performed an important function, but its plans were soon shattered as a mission-arranged armistice led to the next step in the transformation of aboriginal jungle into private property. Recent events suggest four stages in the conversion of the Huaorani into commodities: 1) war; 2) divine mission, in which the Huao struggle for survival is turned into a symbol of savagery and redemption for consumption in the United States. While a few Huaorani are plucked from the jungle for

Map 6
Huaorani Territory in Eastern Ecuador

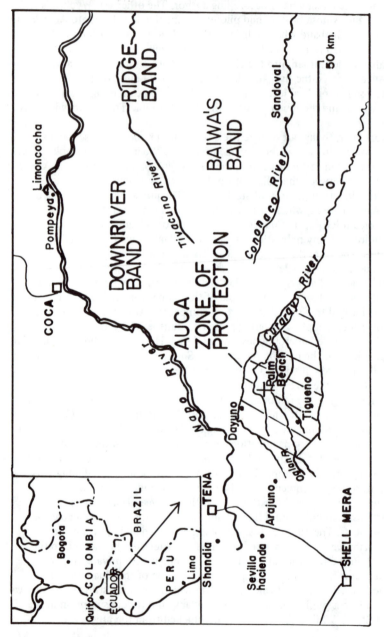

temporary display, most are exploited symbolically, to raise funds and recruits for Gospel advance on other frontiers; 3) tourism, in which missionary images of the Huaorani are appropriated to exploit them directly as ethnic curiosities; 4) the conventional labour commodity, as Huaorani hire themselves to oil companies.

The rupture of Rachel Saint's patronage system can be traced to the removals, which produced a disoriented, highly dependent population. SIL tried to restrain the hunger for trade goods it had done so much to stimulate. But as a member observed, most Huaorani seemed less interested in Christianity than in acquiring possessions and becoming as much like their Quichua enemies-turned-trading partners as possible. A protectionist policy was failing to meet the demands of the new Huao bondage and the larger system. A North American bailiwick dedicated to the glory of God was being nationalized by Ecuadorian entrepreneurs.

Wycliffe's nemesis proved to be its most famous convert, the first Auca Christian, Dayuma, and her son Sam Padilla. By 1976, the two were planning to turn the Huaorani, the Palm Beach martyr ground and even Rachel Saint into a see 'em, photograph 'em tourist attraction. In desperation the Ecuadorian branch was trying to fortify the people it had uprooted and disarmed. It also was trying to retire Wycliffe's most famous missionary against her will. Rachel Saint hoped that, if the tourism became too destructive, the Huaorani would become angry and put a stop to it themselves.

The Palm Beach Martyrs

In 1923 the Pioneer Mission's Howard Dinwiddie toured the Oriente and photographed a spindly, malnourished 'Auka' captive, one of two boys captured by a hunting party.

> Owing to the robbery, stealing of their children and carrying off of their maidens by the lawless rubber hunters, and the burning of their homes, the friendly 'Aukas' have become hostile, [Pioneer reported]. [The captive's] place on the plantation seemed to be that of a new animal. He was fed, watched, discussed and exhibited to visitors. . . . He represents hundreds of those taken yearly to become the slaves of the whites. How long, Lord, how long shall these captives of the Amazon watershed wait for the messengers of Liberty and of Life?[4]

The first of such messengers arrived in an Oriente which North American and British-Dutch oil companies were scheming and bribing to snatch away from each other. The settling of scores is said to have included an imperial bush war: Ecuador (seconded by Royal Dutch Shell) disputed territory with Peru (backed by Standard of New Jersey, now Exxon). In the 1941 war Ecuador lost most of its Amazon claim. The new, U.S.-imposed border respected Shell's concession, and Ecuador remained with what it had leased.[5]

Three years before, Shell had started to blast the first motor road from the highlands into the jungle. From the staging area at Shell Mera crews advanced into the forest to clear airstrips. Provoked by the incursions, a handful of Huao raiders speared Ecuadorian workers, panicked entire base camps, and forced settlers to abandon the eastern bank of the Napo River. Thanks to the Shell motor road, the population west of the Napo grew rapidly. In 1949, Shell and its new partner Standard of New Jersey suddenly and mysteriously withdrew, leaving the Huoarani to the Lowland Quichua, their *patrones* and Christian missionaries.

To the missions, reaching the Aucas with Cross or Bible was now the supreme and generally avoided challenge. As Italian and Spanish priests extended their stations along the Napo frontier, North American military veterans swelled the smaller evangelical missions. The post-war technological breakthrough arrived with the Missionary Aviation Fellowship, a flight and radio service organized by two ex-U.S. Navy officers. Its first pilot in the Oriente was Nate Saint, an ex-Army Air Corps mechanic whose plane knit together a few dozen Protestant missionaries at nine stations, some in abandoned oil camps. The Shell Mera airfield began to turn into an evangelical centre. Despite the alleged collapse of their oil prospects, Shell executives occasionally passed through. Once they brought along their vice-president General Jimmy Doolittle, a U.S. war hero who inquired after the health of Saint's one man air force. A few years later so did General William Harrison Jr., chief of the U.S. Panama Command.[6] Situated in a strategic mineral reserve, the missionaries were junior members in a vast partnership dedicated to freedom and the like, pioneers for Christ who would become spiritual giants to thousands of other missionaries and millions at home.

At 32 years of age, Nate Saint was the oldest and most experienced member of Operation Auca, with seven years in the Oriente. Three others were Plymouth Brethren missionaries to the Lowland Quichua, college men with new wives and about three years in the region. The fifth, an ex-paratrooper named Roger Youderian, worked with his wife and the Gospel Missionary Union among the Shuar and Atshuar to the south. Owing to raids and contact epidemics, it had been a tough two and a half years. At the time Youderian joined the others, he was in crisis over his work and preparing to quit.[7]

Two of the Brethren men were graduates of Wheaton College, a recruiting ground for the evangelical missions near Chicago. Before carrying the Gospel to a foreign land, Jim Elliot and Ed McCully had tried to bring it to sinners on their own. 'I do not understand,' Elliot wrote, 'why I have never seen in America what missionaries write of — that sense of swords being drawn, the smell of war with demon powers.' But by persisting he felt that they were 'delivering our souls of the blood of the community. They know we are here, and that we are having meetings regarding the reality of the Lord Jesus. If they do not want to hear, then their blood is on their own heads. Elliot prayed that he could be like a fork in the road, 'that men must turn one way or another on facing Christ in me.' Although North American Christians had 'sold their lives to the service of Mammon,' he and a few confederates would spark the evangelization of most of the Andes.[8]

In Ecuador, the three Brethren boys joined Dr Wilfred Tidmarsh, an Englishman dating to the time of the first Shell crews. His confrontations with the Italian priests of the Josephine Mission had led Ecuadorians to wonder whether the Second World War was still being waged in their vicinity.[9] On contested turf at Shandia, the Lowland Quichua disappointed the new Brethren. To Elliot they seemed like children: cheating on wages and trade, begging, and playing Catholic and Protestant missionaries against each other for maximum advantage. The Quichua did not seem concerned about their souls, which Elliot attributed to lack of concerned prayer on his own part. The new Brethren learned Quichua, however, and near the end of their lives were reporting dozens of decisions for Christ.

Operation Auca materialized suddenly in September 1955. While the evangelical accounts excuse the secrecy and haste as a measure against godless adventurers, this does not explain why the Brethren failed to inform their senior partner Tidmarsh, who was visiting England and probably would have advised against their plan. Nor does it explain why Nate Saint failed to inform his older sister Rachel, whose ruling ambition was to reach the same people. Stranger still, from a hacienda labourer Rachel had learned more about the Auca language than anyone else. Nate's sister, it now seems obvious, was the heart of the matter. The reason for the secrecy, the haste, the martyrdom and glory of Operation Auca was probably evangelical competition for the prize of the unreached tribe.

The Summer Institute had come to Ecuador in 1952 as Jose Velasco Ibarra succeeded Galo Plaza as President.[10] The evangelical missions welcomed Robert Schneider, but they were taken aback by his disclaimers of SIL's religious mission. Despite the rupture of confidence, or perhaps to keep an eye on Wycliffe, they urged a base site near Shell Mera. Cameron Townsend did not want to associate the new branch too closely with other evangelicals.[11] By early 1955 SIL no longer relied on MAF flight service, because of its refusal to transport Catholic clergy, and soon the branch moved to its present location at Limoncocha.

Now that SIL was assigning a non-competitive translation team to each language, the stage was set for a collision of the headstrong: between the divine will as revealed to Rachel Saint, and that same divine will as revealed to brother Nate, Ed McCully and Jim Elliot. Fellow missionaries blame sibling rivalry: each Saint had an unshakable faith in personal destiny and neither was to be crossed. Their mother had found the Lord and married an artist below her station in Philadelphia society. In adolescence, Rachel is supposed to have turned down a chance to rejoin the gentry, an heirship from one of her father's patrons. To this occasion, in 1932, she dates a vision of a brown tribe in a green jungle, her first sign from the Lord. It must have felt like she had missed the next one: rejected as a missionary to China, Rachel spent 12 years drying out alcoholics in New Jersey, at the Keswick Colony of Mercy where Charles Gallaudet Trumbull had intoned the Victorious Life.[12] In hindsight, the Lord's hand is evident: taking bottles away from drunks was superb training for laying down the law to Auca killers. She learned to be the equal of any occasion, acquiring a sense of humour appropriate to picking men out of gutters. Finally, in 1949, at 35 years old Rachel joined Wycliffe. In Peru she was apprenticed to women who had already reached their Bibleless tribes, the soon famous Piro and Shapra. On visits with brother Nate she noticed that the Aucas were a household word in Ecuador. By 1953 several signs from the Lord had established that the Huaorani were 'my tribe'.[13]

Brother Nate and his friends did not share this conviction. In 1954 the McCullys moved out to an abandoned oil camp on the Arajuno River. Here, they were so certain to meet Huaorani that the local Quichua pioneers always retired to the far bank before dark. Then in September 1955, following Rachel's first language-learning term with the hacienda peon Dayuma, her brother and Ed McCully searched for Huao clearings from the air. They found several near Arajuno and code-named them Terminal City. Nate's biography includes a 'Dear Sis' letter to be held until further notice: Ed McCully has been chosen for the vanguard role. Rachel has been kept in the dark because she 'might feel obligated to divulge this information to save me the risks involved.'[14] Rachel 'was very possessive over the Aucas,' Elisabeth Elliot explained recently, 'and was convinced that God had intended her to be the *only* one to work with the Aucas. . . . If Jim and the others had asked for her help, she would have put in so many obstacles that it would have been impossible.'[15]

The Brethren understood the importance of language: several had taken the SIL course. But if Nate's sister was not to know of the plan, they could not ask for data or even spend much time with her informant, whom they did visit a few times to extract word lists. Nate's technological vision led to another blunder: although local men would play an important role in the 1958 contact, he and the Brethren blamed 'skittish' Quichua for the failure of previous overtures. They replaced native wisdom, upon which outsiders depend for their lives under the most ordinary circumstances, with an airplane. Still another mistake was wishful thinking about self-defense. In the mission accounts the martyrs do not plan to sacrifice themselves to avoid injuring Huaorani. Instead, they hope that firearms, apparently revolvers and .22 carbines, will 'discourage an attack that could result in fatalities.' Somehow they felt that shooting to scare, shooting not-to-kill, digging foxholes or piling into a small airplane would be a non-lethal defense against Huao spearsmen, whom they knew always ambushed and were very quick.[16]

To make friends before hitting the ground, the men dropped presents into the Terminal City clearings. This was an old Shell tactic which Saint improved with his 'spiralling line', a method for lowering and retrieving objects, which mission pilots no longer use because it is so difficult. Between October and December 1955 the team made fourteen drops — of pots, clothes, candy, salt, cutting tools — which the Huaorani soon reciprocated, by sending something up — a feather headband, parrots, cooked fish — for every present spiralled down.

The importance of secrecy pushed the men into an early landing. As the

Huaorani did their own reconnoitering around Arajuno, the missionaries staked out gifts which made the Quichua jealous. Gossip might reach the wrong ears. A few miles from Terminal City, Saint found a sandbar where he could land his plane by dipping the wing around a tree. On Friday 6 January 1956, three Huaorani arrived at Palm Beach. The missionaries showered them with gifts and despite the word lists, could not understand a word they said. The Huaorani did not return on Saturday. Saint worried about the mistakes he and his friends might have committed. On Sunday the five wives lost radio contact with their men, the next day called for help. SIL's Larry Montgomery contacted General Harrison at the Panama Command.[17] While the first mission account said the burial party had found no evidence of struggle, Elisabeth Elliot reported the bullet hole through the airplane windshield.[18]

The Conversion of Dayuma

In the field remained the MAF and Plymouth Brethren remnants on the one hand, SIL's Rachel Saint on the other. Saint would have been in an uncomfortable position whatever the outcome of Operation Auca: her own brother and friends had tried to steal her tribe. Anger at her brother and the widows vied with the respect due martyrs. The sacrifice became part of the Lord's plan for her own eventual vindication.

Once it was apparent that Terminal City was delighted by MAF's renewed gift drops, Wilfred Tidmarsh chose a slower approach, which would bring Huaorani out rather than push missionaries in. South-east of Arajuno in a border zone, where the Oglan River joins the Curaray, Tidmarsh built a hut, left presents and visited on week-ends. Huaorani came by in his absence, then plundered the axe and machete stock. A month later, in November 1957, three Huao women walked out of the forest at a nearby Quichua village. One ran away, and Elisabeth Elliot introduced herself to the other two, Mintaka and Maengamo. Huao raiders killed a Quichua man, whereupon Elliot retired with her charges to the safety of Shandia. Here the Huao women made themselves at home in a Quichua household. With the help of data sent by Rachel Saint, Elliot quickly caught up in the language. Maengamo, she discovered, wanted to take her back to the Terminal City band. The MAF-Tidmarsh-Elliot team had obtained an invitation, which it now extended to the Summer Institute.[19]

Saint's contribution was Dayuma. Probably never have the transactions between a missionary and a key first convert been paid more attention than in Ethel Wallis' *The Dayuma Story,* whose raw material is a rebellious language informant. It becomes clear that, following Palm Beach, Saint rigorously conditioned Dayuma to undertake a programme she feared. When SIL faced competition for Dayuma's time and loyalty, it skilfully removed her to the United States and kept her there for nearly a year until she seemed ready to do the job.

Unlike her Aunts Maengamo and Mintaka, Dayuma did not want to return to her people. Having fled from the Terminal City band in fear for her life, she had adjusted to life on the hacienda as a Lowland Quichua. They had taught her to despise her kin as savages and she would have remained a Quichua for the rest of her life. Since SIL's plans hung entirely on Dayuma, she could destroy them and certainly tried, time and again revolting against Saint's slow, calculated unfolding of the Lord's plan. When she did return, it was on Quichua and, to some extent, Saint's terms, least of all on Huao terms. Owing to Dayuma's hacienda expereince, the bridge between Christian mission and the Huaorani in the forest was peonage.

The *patron* in question, Carlos Sevilla, had come into the possession of seven Huao women in the course of his rubber gathering career. But when Saint and her SIL partner Catherine Peeke visited Sevilla's hacienda for the first time in February 1955, only Dayuma could recall fragments of the Huao language. Her arrival dated to the Shell era, eight years before, when fratricidal spearing had decimated her band. After three attempts to escape the hacienda she learned that her Huao enemies were still at large, embraced Quichua ways, and was baptized by one of Tidmarsh's Italian foes, Padre Cesar Ricci. [20] She had a son, who has attributed his paternity to a son of Carlos Sevilla, then lost a Quichua spouse surnamed Padilla in a measles epidemic and tried to kill herself.[21] Saint's probes for language summoned up the past, throwing Dayuma into tantrums in which she cursed a man named Moipa who had speared her father and kin. Intra-tribal murder was a refrain in her recitals: the Aucas appeared to kill each other more often than they did outsiders. To Saint's horror, Dayuma also recalled infanticides and the customary live burials of the dying, sometimes with their small children.

Missionaries sometimes purchased peons to set them free, but when Saint returned to the Sevilla hacienda in March 1956, three months after the Palm Beach killings, she found that the value of the only available Huao speaker had multiplied many times. Sevilla promoted Dayuma to house servant, which in Saint's opinion should have opened up new vistas in her work. Yet even after JAARS inaugurated service to Sevilla's new airstrip, Dayuma's manual labour obligations were so important that Saint did not have enough time for language study and Bible stories. Worse, Dayuma was being courted by a series of competitors whom the *patron* welcomed as he had SIL. Only Dayuma's reluctance frustrated Sevilla's plan to use her as a guide for a new expedition.[22]

In the United States, aroused men of God were urging the Ecuadorian branch to make another contact. Saint scotched their schemes: she still did not command the language and Dayuma had yet to be saved.[23] Cameron Townsend was 'anxious that the challenge of the tribes be continued while [Palm Beach] was still fresh on the minds of most Americans.' But Saint declined to lend herself to Wycliffe rallies because 'we might be intruding on something that doesn't belong to us.'[24] Less than a year and a half after Palm Beach, Townsend came up with a better plan, whose outline I shall venture as the following: 1) promise Sevilla fame (fortune); 2) with Sevilla on his side, trick Saint into bringing Dayuma to the United States; 3) exploit Saint and Dayuma for publicity; 4) keep Dayuma in the U.S. long enough to get her out of Sevilla's clutches for good.

After the founder had channelled an initial ruse through Dayuma's *patron,* Saint drew the line at taking Dayuma to Hollywood to appear opposite Sevilla on a television show about an 18th Century North American Indian fighter. She was 'aghast', 'reluctant' and refused, until the Lord assured her that she could share her burden for the Bibleless tribes and Dayuma would not die of some germ.[25] So it was that on 5 June 1957, Saint, Dayuma, Palm Beach and, most importantly, Wycliffe were trotted before 30 million television viewers on Ralph Edward's *This Is Your Life!* Despite similar objections from his translators, Chief Tariri was also imported for the occasion.

With this unforgettable night, Wycliffe began to appropriate the fruits of Huao resistance. Townsend had no good answer to missionaries who accused him of abusing Indians for publicity and glory-snatching, but that hardly mattered. The spoils were in future, rather than immediate income, from the incalculable fame accruing to Wycliffe among a growing public. Henceforth Wycliffe would be known as the mission bringing Christ to the Aucas, an equation which has passed through the minds of most recruits and supporters and been a comfort to many a hard-pressed translator. But there was no substance to the triumph Townsend had promised the world: Dayuma had not even agreed to return to her people. Vindication was in the Lord's hands; everything hung on Saint's success with Dayuma.

The evening after Dayuma's television appearance she was in bed with a burning fever. When the attending doctor delivered his testimony and asked if she knew the Lord, 'Yes!' was the answer. 'I think of Him day and night!'[26] That was Dayuma's first declaration of faith. The faith of the *patron* Sevilla seems to have been sorely tested. He had only loaned his servant for a month and, to ensure that she was returned, kept her son behind in Ecuador. Eventually Larry Montgomery delivered the child, after ferrying the 'Spirit of Kansas City' Helio-Courier to Quito for ceremonies with the Minister of Education.[27]

Despite homesickness, Dayuma learned to like living and travelling around the United States. In early 1958, the Ecuadorian branch reported that she and Saint were raising funds to buy a Helio-Courier.[28] The previous summer Kenneth Pike had conducted a grammar workshop around her at the University of Oklahoma, and at summer's end, the first Auca Christian gave her testimony at the Billy Graham crusade in New York City. Soon after, she began talking about the jaguars living inside her grandfather. To deal with Dayuma's lapses Saint prayed for wisdom and guidance, searched Scripture for appropriate truths and applied them to promote spiritual progress, specifically 'to plant the seed of desire for returning to her own home in Dayuma's mind. Perhaps Jesus might some day ask *her* to go home to [her] family and friends and tell them of His power. Rachel said she would willingly go to the Aucas — would Dayuma go, too?'

After Dayuma nearly died of Asian flu, the Word 'began to penetrate her thinking deeply.' But when her Aunts Maengamo and Mintaka came out of the forest in November 1957, Dayuma did not share Saint's enthusiasm for

287

returning to Ecuador. Realizing that 'the girl was not ready to go,' Saint launched a series of tape-recording exchanges which became so traumatic that Dayuma seems to have had a nervous breakdown. From her aunts she learned who had been speared during the last decade. Upon hearing that her number one enemy Moipa had been killed, she shouted for joy. Learning that a brother had been killed, reportedly her older brother Wawae, she wailed ' "I will never go back!" ' . . . In a firm voice Rachel began to check the rising anger which threatened to undo the spiritual progress of recent weeks. . . . "You are the *only* one of your people who knows God," [Saint told her]. ' ". . . . You may be the *only* one who can tell them of Jesus." '

Since Saint could not understand the tapes without Dayuma's help and could not control her until she knew what was on the tapes, the only solution was to replay the messages day after day to make Dayuma translate, which kept her in a state of nervous disorder. But through the storm and fury there was a gleam of light: in Saint's words, 'the girl is nearly crazy waiting to know if her mother still lives.'[29]

The Foundation of Tigueno

Missionary women made the contact on the assumption that they would be less threatening than men. They were shielded by the three Huao emigres, who decided to test the mood of their male kin before bringing in the outsiders. Following another of Dayuma's revolts against the divine plan, this time at SIL's Limoncocha base, Maengamo and Mintaka reintroduced her to her people, in September 1958. Dayuma halted at the Tigueno River, only about half the distance from the Quichua settlement near Oglan to the band's clearings. The morning after her first kin came to see her, she was making them fell trees 'so the plane can come low.'[30] This was the origin of mission headquarters, the new centre for the Terminal City band.

After more than a decade Dayuma was an alien. Contrary to the 'searching for Dayuma' theme in the Wallis account — her kin claimed never to have stopped looking for her — they probably had long since given her up for dead. The reborn Dayuma dressed like an outsider.and was a doctrinarian. When she reappeared in Arajuno a month later with a gang of Huao women and children, Elisabeth Elliot taped her report: 'I began to teach them right away. I said, "Why do you kill? Why do you live like dogs? Don't you know we are all of the same family?" When I spoke thus, two of them cried.' While Dayuma said that she was willing to resume living with her people, she 'would run back to the foreigners' if they threatened her. After taking her son to meet her mother, she planned to put him in school somewhere else.[31]

Rachel Saint wanted to meet her brother's killers alone; SIL came to Elliot's rescue.[32] In October they walked into Tigueno with Elliot's three year old daughter Valerie, their Huao entourage and six armed Quichua men. Only one Huao man, Kimo, was there to receive them; the Quichua tarried and soon were trading with their enemies. Two people died in a contact epidemic;

Nimonga threatened to spear the missionaries and their collaborators but it blew over.[33]

The Dayuma-missionary ascendancy at Tigueno was based upon trade goods, the standard lure in any pacification. The Huaorani had long appreciated steel cutting tools, for which they sometimes raided. Now, after several years of gift drops, which paved the way for peaceful Huao-Quichua encounters and Dayuma's reunion with her kin, trade goods drew the band over to Tigueno and gradually resettled them there. With every excursion to the outside there returned pots, machetes, trinkets to be coveted and exchanged for something, which Saint interpreted as interest in Christianity.

Dayuma was a pivotal figure in the new order, as a channel for Saint's plans and a power in her own right. Having decreed the seven day week, she would call everyone together for a lesson each Sunday, coached beforehand by Saint. But Dayuma also had her own distinctly Quichua ideas, a product of discrimination against her on the hacienda. On arrival, Elliot was surprised to find that she had given every male within reach a crewcut. With Saint's support, Dayuma also did her best to stuff the group into clothes. From the beginning she campaigned against aspects of Huao culture which the missionaries considered innocuous, telling her people that not only their nakedness but their wooden earplugs, hair style and eating habits branded them as savages. Empty, dangling earlobes became the sign to Quichua that a Huao was civilized, therefore not to be shot on sight.[34]

Saint claimed a number of converts by 1960, but a year later Elliott referred only to one. Dayuma. Saint's once and future SIL partner, Catherine Peeke, explained why Bible translation was so difficult:

> There are deficiencies in vocabulary because the Aucas have apparently lived without any cognizance of what the civilized world about them is doing. In this category lie the concepts of buying and selling, or even of trading; any form of specialized labor . . . any religious or governmental organization, any concept of village or city; any idea of law, trial or authority . . . . Market places and political boundaries are unknown to them. They know no master-servant relationship, no rich, no poor. Teaching-learning situations are not recognized.[35]

Elliot noticed that the language seemed to have no basis for the idea of petition and prayer. God's son translated as the offspring of a certain species of fish.[36] But Saint was not one to worry overmuch about cross-cultural communication. The message she wanted to impress on the Huaorani sprang directly from her understanding of the divine mission, was drummed into Dayuma and spoke to the Huaorani in terms they understood: vengeance.

> For us to be willing to live with them cut straight across the pattern for revenge, [she explained two decades later]. They killed our men. Dayuma's brother had killed my brother. Yet we were asking to live with them instead of taking our revenge. Then one day they found

that our men had had guns with them when they were attacked and . . . chose to die rather than shoot the Indians. Nothing less than this kind of commitment would have broken the Aucas' cultural mindset.[37]

Saint had forsaken revenge in favour of a more sublime chastisement, salvation. Dayuma and her people were beholden to Saint because they had killed her brother; Christ had died for their sins; and the various sacrifices were presented to the Huaorani as something to be reciprocated by obeying new rules. Even if the Huaorani were poorly equipped to understand sin and salvation, they knew a truce when they saw one since Huao enemies occasionally patched up their differences. But while Saint's jungle theology produced quick results, there was a flaw: her perception of Palm Beach (no injuries inflicted on the Huaorani, therefore martyrdom) was not shared by the people who had been there. Saint kept her distance from the subject, uncertain of the Huao point of view: judging from the mission accounts, Dayuma sometimes said that her people were sorry about Palm Beach, other times that they ridiculed the idea that the five men had been their friends.[38]

Cameron Townsend knew that it was time for another round of publicity. Not only had his own, Elliot's and other efforts fuelled a mass appetite for redemption; except for a November 1958 story in *Life* magazine (the third) starring little Valerie Elliot, the books and articles did not have much to say about Rachel Saint and Wycliffe.[39] Hollywood needed a follow-up. As Saint and Elliot survived their sixth month in Tigueno, Townsend therefore dispatched the Mexican branch's Ethel Wallis to write what became Wycliffe's all-time bestseller. Perhaps due to pressure of time, Wallis worked almost entirely with Saint and through her Dayuma, so that the Huao contact became *The Dayuma Story*. During the six weeks between Saint's session with Wallis and Saint's reading of the proofs, she obtained the first conversions as recorded in her triumphant epilogue.[40]

The central tenet of the new order was 'thou shalt not kill.' But if the missionaries were insurance against other outsiders, they were none against Huao enemies. Fortunately, the downriver enemy never flashed into Tigueno, and Christianity became part of the band's ritual discourse. 'Believing in God, we pray only to Him — and take the medicine that [Rachel] gives us,' former war leader Gikita lectured a newcomer refusing a pill.[41] When missionaries ask converts to testify, a standard response seems to be: 'Not knowing/ understanding, we killed your men, but now we have a new life. There are others still living badly and we must try to reach them.'[42] The 'not knowing we killed' is a ritual apology to a missionary corps who, for some Huaorani, have been steadfast patrons. The 'new life' refers to the ban against killing people and is a claim to be accepted as peaceful.

If Saint has always been very sure of her convictions, Elisabeth Elliot wrote books about her doubts. She was from the same genteel class of Philadelphia which Saint and her mother had forsaken; Elliot's father was a member of the Pioneer Mission board of directors in the mid-1930s. She had been induced to launch her writing career with two best-sellers about the martyrs —

Through Gates of Splendor (1956) and *Shadow of the Almighty* (1958) before it could be confirmed that they were martyrs: we might expect some complications. In *The Savage My Kinsman* (1961) Elliot avoids indicting the Huaorani and evidently makes her rejoinder to Saint's interpretations in *Dayuma Story* (1960). Following a protracted struggle over such questions as the Biblical status of polygamy and the priority to be placed upon checking Huao sexual license, Elliot left the work in the early 1960s and was replaced by SIL's Catherine Peeke.[43] Now that Townsend had appropriated Huao savagery to enhance Wycliffe's evangelical reputation, and Elliot had been pressured into leaving the field, the Aucas belonged to Wycliffe.

The Savage My Kinsman was poorly received in some quarters; instead of castigating darkness, Elliot seemed to be celebrating it. 'Because their forms of cruelty were different from ours were they therefore worse than ours?' Suggesting that she and her audience had confused 'inhibition with virtue, refinement with righteousness, propriety with purity,' Elliot complimented the Huaorani for their freedom from various sins of civilization, said that she had never seen any sign of friction between spouses, and ventured that a polygamous family got along beautifully.[44] In a novel published five years later, seemingly autobiographical in feeling, Elliot hit bottom with many readers. She raised the problem of evil — God is all powerful, God is all good, and God not only permits evil but condemns human beings to eternal punishment — in a very particular form: the potential convert killed by missionary error before he can be shown the way to salvation.[45]

The Removal

> Lord, you give us our land,
>   and here happily serving you
> we will live.
> > Dyuwi's first hymn[46]

The missionaries pacified the first of four bands in its own territory. The Auca Christians maintained a hunting and gardening economy, protected by their reputation as much as the missionaries. To pacify the next two groups the missionaries uprooted them from their land and turned Tigueno into a refugee camp, destroying a brief experiment in primitive Christianity.

The removal took shape in the converging plans of corporations, governments and a service-oriented linguistic institute. Since Ecuador lacked the capital to consolidate its eastern frontier, well before the Huaorani learned to pray their reward was mortgaged to the world market for oil and the reserve lists of transnational corporations. The corporations, whose annual sales each dwarfed the country's gross national product by a factor of five or more, would decide when Ecuador secured its Oriente in the name of national security and development.

Around Tigueno, the Protestant missions had ended warfare, but to the north and east colonists were probing Huao territory. Spear reprisals were on the increase and Tigueno taking the blame. To the east, on the Cononaco River, the army decided to plant the flag; Rachel Saint says that she warned the army commander.[47] In August 1962 a new garrison at Sandoval killed a Huao man, one of two reportedly besieging and attacking the post. In November the Huaorani killed three soldiers and escaped with their own casualties; the garrison evacuated in a helicopter.[48]

Ever since the Shell-Standard withdrawal in 1949, oil giants had occasionally leased large tracts of the Oriente only to allow their rights to lapse. When a Texaco-Gulf consortium arrived to negotiate in June 1963, the government was in the hands of Carlos Julio Arosemena, a nationalist reformer displeasing the United States on several scores. His policies were rectified a month later when the U.S. embassy arranged for him to be ousted.[49] The new military junta organized the Institute for Agrarian Reform and Colonization (IERAC); it also gave SIL-Ecuador its first bilingual education subsidy.

When the junta toured the frontier on 12 February 1964, the Day of the Oriente honouring colonization, citizens and priests in the Napo River settlement of Coca asked the generals for protection from Huao raids. 40 kilometres downstream at SIL's Limoncocha base, Huaorani from Tigueno sang and blow-gunned for the generals. The performers also asked for a reservation. In exchange, Dayuma had offered to help bring the whole tribe into the Tigueno area, 'thus opening the remainder of the jungle for commerce.'[50] Three weeks after the Huaorani sang for the junta, it leased Texaco-Gulf 1.43 million hectares, and oil exploration resumed in earnest.

Texaco started work from the Limoncocha airstrip, which belongs to the government. But the branch says that it made only one flight for the consortium, to a Helio-Courier airstrip at a Quichua bilingual school.[51] Helicopters brought in bulldozers, and Santa Cecilia became the first big oil base. Within a few years the jungle north of Huao territory was swarming with aircraft. The first well came in at Lago Agrio in 1967: Texaco-Gulf built a pipeline and road across the Andes. Thousands of settlers crowded boom towns and tried to scratch out a living next to oil company roads, encircling small pockets of Cofan, Siona and Secoya Indians. Consortiums representing dozens of companies snapped up leases for the entire Oriente.

The companies, the government and the Summer Institute found each other the solution to a shared problem. As contacts with the Huaorani multiplied, their rejoinder would increase the pressure for a military solution. But while exterminating the Huaorani was a popular idea among their neighbours, even bombs and bacteria might only have guaranteed that numerous survivors would fight to the last man. Besides, with its band of Auca Christians SIL was more than willing to provide a humane alternative. The companies would provide free helicopter time and spare the expense of terrorized workers. The government, which could see the wisdom of collecting the Huaorani in one place, would give SIL exclusive rights to the group, maybe even a reservation.

Now that the evangelical lustre has vanished, the decision whether or not to intervene in the latest crisis is a torment for those few SIL members on the scene. But as Dayuma's son Sam Padilla recalled in 1976, at first the branch was full of enthusiasm for removal. Prospecting schedules were the way to bring the rest of the Aucas to the Lord, not least because the Auca Christians whom experience taught would have to make the ground contacts, were not exactly burning evangelists. In the early 1960s they told Saint that, if God sent them, they would go, and it seemed like the Lord's marching orders never came through.[52] Oil exploration became an excuse to goad reluctant Tigueno Christians into fulfilling their duty to the Great Commission.

'Not in so many words but in hidden ways, or through others [Dayuma],' Sam Padilla explained, 'Rachel would say, "My brother died for you, and I have sacrificed my life for you because of the love of God. It would be so good if you could go to the others, to save them as well" '. While Tigueno saw the advantage of extending the spearing ban to its Huao enemies, the few to be stirred would soon be overtaken by second thoughts: they might not live to enjoy the new era.

> And here, [continued Sam], the linguists would step in. 'No, don't worry, that's not a problem, we can give you a radio, we can drop you food and medicine, we can drop this machine into their village and record their names, you can talk to them from the air.' The Aucas didn't understand radios or how all this worked, but it didn't matter, the linguists did all that part for them. . . . The oil company said, 'We're coming in three months,' and this was just their chance.[53]

Trade goods, kin ties and romance — bands seeking spouses from other bands — were the bait which drew the rest of the Huaorani into dependence. Manipulated by the missionaries, these attractions and bonds eventually gave the removals their own Huao momentum as the people learned to value patronage and peace. But to start the campaign Saint decided that she needed another Dayuma, or rather a better Dayuma who not only was separated from her kin but eager to see them again. Already she had dozens of refugees from the down-river band at Tigueno, but none were interested.

As Saint formulated her prayers in early 1964, Quichua homesteaders and Huaorani were ambushing each other along the Napo River near Coca. The Capuchin Mission still believes that Tigueno rebels were responsible for several assaults: raiders reportedly sported bathing trunks, leading to rumours that Dayuma had vowed to destroy the Catholic settlement.[54] SIL assigns all guilt to the down-river band, which several years later would be the first in the way of the oil companies. A month before the military junta visited Coca in February 1964, Huao raiders killed three people and kidnapped another. Two weeks after the junta departed, Huao raiders skewered a woman in her house. 'AUCAS CONTINUE ADVANCING IN COCA REGION,' *El Comercio* screamed in August. 'SETTLERS ABANDON THEIR PROPERTIES.'[55]

When an army-settler posse shot and captured a Huao woman on 19 May 1964, she was placed in the care of the Sisters of Mother Laura at Coca. After putting up some resistance, the mother superior reported, the patient took to playing with children from her bed. A Capuchin nurse attended her thigh wound, administered antibiotics and vitamins; she ate and slept well.

As soon as Saint heard about the captive, probably over the military radio, she claimed her. 'From the first I knew [the girl] could be the key to a successful contact,' she wrote. Unfortunately, the Catholic mission had the same idea. On the evening of 21 May the Jungle Aviation and Radio Service flew Saint into Coca with an army doctor. She says that she found Oncaye in terrible shape: in fever, pain and full of hate, the girl had not eaten any food in days. On arrival, according to the mother superior's report, Saint announced that she wanted to take the patient to the military hospital at Shell Mera. The nuns protested, the army doctor deferred to his formidable companion, and the arguments made it impossible to leave that night.

Proceeding with the Catholic version, inter-faith relations got off to a poor start the next morning when Saint declared that, in her and Oncaye's opinion, another raid was imminent. A sister suggested that perhaps Saint was orchestrating the attacks. It nevertheless was agreed that doctor, Oncaye and a nun would take the first flight to Shell Mera, while Saint would wait for a second. But Oncaye put up a fight during the move to the airplane and Saint entered after her. According to the rector of the Coca high school, Mr. Flores, the citizenry of Coca poured onto the airstrip to block the take-off. The army doctor ordered Saint to leave the plane.

At the military hospital in Shell Mera the tide turned against the Catholics, according to mother superior thanks to Saint's friendship with the commander, Colonel Jaime Paz y Mino Salas. Around midnight the contenders surprised each other in Oncaye's room, Saint reinforced by two of Oncaye's kinswomen from Tigueno, the sisters by two Capuchin priests who hoped to settle the matter in 'the rational and European way.' Each side accused the other of trying to steal Oncaye. To mother superior, the arrival of Oncaye's kin confirmed that Saint was responsible for the attacks on Coca. When Colonel Paz y Mino arrived the next morning, Saint accused her adversaries of trying to purloin the patient, whereupon the colonel banished the sisters from the hospital forever.

This was the 'kidnapping' of Oncaye, a familiar story in Ecuador, but not to Wycliffe readers since the manner of her arrival is sanitized. After the Capuchin bishop appealed to the colonel twice, the mission solicited generals, the Minister of Defense, the papal nuncio and foreign ambassadors, all in vain. On 20-21 June 1964 Saint took Oncaye to Tigueno. The military junta rejected an appeal.[56] While the army had reason to prefer SIL, it was no light matter to cross the Catholic Church so rudely. The composition of the ruling junta did not hurt SIL's chances; Philip Agee names two of the figures who gave the Capuchins the runaround, Generals Aurelio Naranjo and Gandara Enriquez, as CIA liaison contacts the year before.[57]

In Tigueno, Oncaye joined the others memorizing Bible verses. She learned to pray and lived with Saint, who 'won her complete loyalty' and prayed that the Lord would work it out for her as he had for Dayuma, We are told of long hours of planning for the expedition to bring Oncaye's mother to Tigueno. Yet by February 1965, when it seemed to Saint and Catherine Peeke high time to begin, a banana harvest was seducing the Christians into a delightful round of song and dance parties.

'All thought of the savage groups was lost in the pleasures of the moment,' Saint wrote. 'When any mention was made of the matter, it was evident that the people were beginning to count the cost.' For one, as she noticed, they were afraid that the down-river crowd would steal their (trade) possessions. For another, even the loyalists were afraid that they might get killed. No one knew the trail and Dayuma was saying: 'when you get ready you send Oncaye.' A prayer meeting changed everyone's attitude and a ground party set out. A few days later they straggled back saying that Oncaye's wound hurt too much, a tree had fallen on them and they had lost their way.[58]

One reason for the haste of February 1965 was probably Catholic, chiefly Capuchin activity with the same objective. Saint says that she was 'cognizant' of these ventures.[59] It would have been hard not to as many were out of Pompeya Mission an hour's walk from Limoncocha. Capuchin records date first stirrings to 1957, after Dayuma went to Hollywood. On the Cononaco River, far to the southeast opposite another Huao band, the Josephine Mission blamed the army's bloodletting for its failure. Smarting over the loss of Oncaye, in September 1964 the Capuchin bishop led his mission's first expedition into the downriver territory. While SIL's first ground expeditions were ending just as quickly, the Capuchins prepared for another round: three expeditions in June, July and August 1965 out of Pompeya. In January 1966, just before SIL burst into action again, the Capuchins made another. And as the Protestants turned to airborne technology, the Capuchins took to the skies themselves. From March 1966 to April 1967 the mission logged 30 flight hours, dropping clothes, seeds, birds and other things into Huao clearings. The Capuchins felt that all they needed now was a helicopter, which the government and the oil companies never provided.[60] More to the point, the Catholics did not have any Huaorani to shield them.

The Summer Institute faced two problems, reluctant Christians and down-river dislike of aerial surveillance. More technology, exhortation and Oncaye's family ties were the solution. When JAARS discovered Oncaye's family fled to a new clearing in February 1966, the angry ground reaction reinforced the doubts in Saint's believing family. Despite technological improvements — ground party radio, wing-mounted loudspeakers, radio-coordinated food drops — the next sallies came to naught. Even though the voices from the sky spoke Huao, the down-river band continued to burn its houses and flee. The ground parties kept running back to Tigueno with real or imagined enemies at their heels. By now oil exploration was imminent and the Quichua on the Napo River were losing patience. To justify SIL in the Oncaye affair there had been talk of speedy relief.

So that Oncaye could pinpoint her aerial invitations to Tigueno, JAARS began dropping radio transmitters for air-ground conversation. Since the recipients smashed the first transmitters, JAARS wove the next ones into false-bottom baskets loaded with gifts. In February 1968 Oncaye's brother demanded an axe; when it dropped at his feet, he agreed to start up-river the next day. As the sixth, radio and medicine-equipped ground party made its way out of Tigueno, Oncaye's family tricked the rest of the band and fled. From the air JAARS brought the two parties together. When the dozen down-river runaways arrived in Tigueno, they were dismayed to find an outsider there. 'In the excitement,' explains Wallis, 'Oncaye had neglected to inform her family of the foreigner living right in their midst.' Most of the rest of the down-river band – 92 people – struggled into Tigueno in July 1968, sick and malnourished. In the interval, spearings had splintered the group, quite possibly – like the hunger and sickness – a consequence of the SIL campaign. Ten people fled in another direction: by 1980 they were the last Huaorani rejecting all contact with outsiders.

The Summer Institute had harassed, bribed and tricked the terror of Coca out of the way of the oil companies and into Tigueno, doubling the population to more than 200. Saint 'had never dreamed that so many down-river people would all come at once.' The epidemic lasted six weeks, food ran short, and down-river men wanted to spear Quichua and up-river men. Saint banned JAARS landings, food supplies were dropped and loyalists forced down-river people leaving for home to return to Tigueno.[61] The marriage fever sweeping the two bands meant that polygamy had to be discouraged. Christian girls tried to drown their 'illegitmate' babies and one pregnant Christian killed herself.[62]

The casualties and strife began to worry the branch. 'I suppose we are all very much aware,' Catherine Peeke wrote in her journal in October 1968:

> that we are not offering the people any better way of life from the material standpoint. For what are a few machetes and kettles compared to the unrestricted game reserve they have always enjoyed? And we are offering them unknown territory for known, a foreign land instead of home, dependency for self-sufficiency, subjection to outside powers instead of resistance, and hunger where there has been plenty. It is a miracle that Oncaye's group ever agreed to this, even with her here.

> There is something pathetic, [Peeke added five months later] in the plight of those who, having failed to find isolation through remoteness, are driven to hide their thatch huts under the trees, thus exposing themselves to natural dangers (snakes and falling branches in a windstorm) which they would normally avoid. How can they assume good will when we ferret them out so relentlessly, approaching from the very sky, the sphere which they do not control? They are desperate to hide from forces which they do not understand – but how much more desperate they would be if they really did understand! The swallowing up of

their resources, their liberty, even their identity is inevitable. And they will meet the even greater frustrations of modern man.

Two bands remained to the east and in the path of the oil companies. Despite disillusion with oil company terms and what Peeke called 'the resistance of almost the entire Christian community to further advance', fear of spearings and a military solution kept the operation rolling.[63] The admonitions booming out of aircraft angered the Huaorani on the ground, but through the concealed transmitters they learned to demand 'throw me down an *axe* . . . a *machete* . . . some *beads*.' Oil company helicopters quickened the pace. When approaching crews delivered an ultimatum in mid-1969, relatives dropped by helicopter persuaded Baiwa's group to come see their relatives.[64] But before SIL could turn full attention to the fourth and last Huao group, it lost control of the three it already had.

Two weeks after the arrival of Baiwa's band, in August 1969, the first person fell sick with polio. Two people died and dozens were struck before it was diagnosed. Against the advice of missionary doctors, Saint had decided that immediate vaccination and its side-effects would disturb the new people too much.[65] Now she decided that a (male) doctor could not be introduced until potential killers were too paralyzed to spear. Virtually all the Huao refugees contracted polio and Saint came down with it herself.

By October, 16 Huaorani were dead, another 16 crippled for life. Witchcraft was blamed: two long-time Tigueno 'rebels', at least one a baptized Christian, were responsible for the two revenge spearings. Hungry and leaving behind three dead, Baiwa and half his band escaped for home. According to Saint, she would have left them alone if the army had not called her in a year later. They are said to have killed six people before being corralled.

Prospecting schedules demanded speedy pacification of the eastern-most band, the Ridge Huaorani. Here, SIL lost its first Huao martyr, the Tigueno schoolteacher Tona. His family had been reluctant to receive him and, in June 1970, chopped him in the back with a gift axe. Later they explained that they had been 'misled into believing he was an outsider.' The next year Tona's people carved out a helipad and then an airstrip, permitting the introduction of Tigueno women. Since there were far too many people on the Ridge – nearly 300 or about half the language group – to bring to Tigueno at once, marriages were contracted, medical flights made and instructions provided in proper behaviour toward oil crews. Company helicopters offered so many presents that the Ridge people made up magical songs to attract more of them. The oil trails were also appreciated: they made hunting easier. The branch began flying the Ridge people to Tigueno, a dozen or so every few months.[66]

Several years later, in 1975, the evacuation was nearly complete when a SIL anthropologist persuaded the branch to halt it. By this time SIL counted only about 75 Ridge Huaorani left in the east, with 525 Huaorani in the Tigueno area. Two years later, Dayuma's son Sam Padilla prevented the branch from completing the removal, to the displeasure of his mother and Rachel

Saint. Instead, Sam relocated one of the two groups of Ridge remnants for his own purposes. The only other Huaorani known to exist were the ten to twelve fugitives from the 1968 down-river removal. In their old territory north of Tigueno, now abandoned by the Huaorani except for hunting forays, access roads were being built to service the new Auca petroleum field. Lumbering operations were underway and settlers homesteading along rivers.

Protectorate and Pursuit of Liberty

In 1975, the Catholic University of Quito devoted a conference to U.S. philanthropy, particularly the Summer Institute and its Auca work. Calling SIL a function of penetration by foreign capital, economist Fernando Velasco attributed its advent to the need to control future petroleum fields. Masquerading as the Voice of God, the airborne linguists had employed diverse methods of cultural aggression against Indians, such as putting them into reservations. According to the Shuar Federation, the Aucas addressed Rachel Saint as ' "Star" and "Queen" . . . a mystical image which produces complete submission.'* SIL had closed important zones of the Oriente to scientific investigation, the German naturalist Erwin Patzelt declared. From the Aucas he had learned that the five SIL missionaries killed in 1956 had shot one Auca in the forehead. Although most of the tribe was now under missionary control, 60 persons had escaped from Tigueno in search of liberty.[67]

More or less pacified Huaorani were indeed in revolt against their benefactors. According to Rachel Saint, she had not had enough time to teach Christianity to the objects of the removal operation. The branch's new anthropologist thought that a politics of trade goods was replacing a politics of war.

After the 1968 removal, SIL finally had persuaded the government to cede the Huaorani a reservation, or rather, the closest thing to a reservation that they were likely to get. The government had never been willing to title Indians to the land needed for a traditional hunting economy: 50 hectares (120 acres) per family was the rule. But because the Huaorani were a special case, in April 1969 the colonization agency IERAC granted them 'reasonable time' to incorporate into the national culture. The reward for the removal was a 1,600 square kilometre 'zone of protection.' This was one thirteenth of the 21,000 square kilometres which the Huaorani had controlled, but for 600 people it was still about 270 hectares (one square mile) per person.

The Protectorate had no bearing on oil exploration or royalties, because the Ecuadorian state retains mineral rights. It did mean that IERAC would temporarily refrain from titling other parties to the same land. In return, SIL was supposed to 'accelerate its beneficial concentration of Auca families in certain areas of the zone.' IERAC would then title the Huaorani according to the number of families in each nucleus, throwing open the rest to colonization.[68]

---

* In the 1950s Dayuma named Saint Nimu (Star) in memory of a sister.

At its most generous, IERAC would cede 50 hectares per family, for a total of perhaps 6,000 hectares, or 1/27th of the Protectorate and 1/350th of the pre-pacification territory. SIL was not happy with the arrangement but accepted what it could get. Perhaps a future government would be more generous. In the interval, the Huaorani regarded the Protectorate as their land; SIL encouraged them to defend it; and, as of 1979, IERAC was not proceeding to the final stage.

By complying with ultimatums SIL had earned official backing to concentrate the Huaorani free of competitors. A writer says that Anglo-Ecuadorian Oilfields offered to fly him anywhere in the Oriente except the Huao zones: the companies had an understanding with SIL. So did the army. When the conference at the Catholic University accused SIL of barring Ecuadorians from their own national territory, a government spokesman called the charge absurd: it might be a question of national security.[69]

Saint's exclusive claim to the Huaorani had an invincible rationale, a long string of murders. Since the missionary example inspired Huao confidence in the possibility of peaceful contact, she stressed the danger to discourage voyages into the unknown. A missionary's possessive instincts were almost impossible to distinguish from cautionary measures, isolationism from protectionism. What Saint called 'Auca patterns' kept resurfacing, even in Dayuma, and the only solution was a Huao adaption of Christianity. It turned out that God wanted the Huaorani to stay Huaorani. While they would dress decently and go to church, stop killing, sleeping around and fooling with witchcraft, they would continue to chant Huao chants, dance Huao dances, spear pigs and blow-gun monkeys in the forest, now with God's blessing. Saint did not want Huao men to work for the oil companies, Carlos Sevilla's son Vicente explained, for fear that it would 'throw them into civilization' — alcohol, firearms and prostitution.[70]

The branch sometimes allowed visitors to confirm that everything was above-board in Tigueno, but most emphatically it discouraged forays among its new and uncertain clients on the Ridge. Here the schoolteacher Tona had been killed in June 1970. The down-river splinter twice attacked oil workers. A North American anthropologist is said to have dropped a dozen rifles into a Huao clearing before going home in a hurry.[71] But since the Ridge people were beyond effective missionary control, within easy reach of oil camps and receptive to barter, they exercised a powerful appeal as 'the last of the Aucas.'

SIL's defenses here were breached by Erwin Patzelt, a man determined to photograph and film visibly savage, naked Huaorani. Since his expeditions were expensive, he eventually produced documentaries and a photograph collection. He also split the cost with two other Germans who published on the last of the Aucas, Peter Baumann and Karl Dieter Gartelmann. Patzelt's other major accomplishments were to expose a flaw in the Palm Beach legend and, together with Wycliffe, introduce Dayuma's son Sam Padilla to the exploitation of the Huaorani for personal profit.

In July 1971, Patzelt flew out to the oil base at Tivacuno. A few months before, SIL had made its first non-lethal contact with the eastern band; and the down-river fugitives had put 26 spears into an oil crew cook. With the help of Western Geophysical Service and Howard Stephen Strouth, a U.S. geologist credited with the discovery of profitable oil in the Oriente, Patzelt hired helicopters for forays into the eastern bands. His interpreter was Sam Padilla, whom SIL had sent to the Tivacuno camp to prevent further killings.[72] On Patzelt's third sally in September 1971, he and Catherine Peeke each touched down at the same place in their own whirlybird. 'Don't worry about my life, ma'am,' he says he told her, 'I'm doing just fine handing out presents.' When he tried to hire a helicopter for a fourth expedition, the company refused.

Patzelt had not yet begun to fight. Accompanied by a man in civilian dress, in early 1972 he once again tried and failed to charter an oil company heli-copter. Rachel Saint refused permission. Unbeknownst to SIL, Patzelt's companion was Colonel Carlos Espinoza, sub-director of the Military Geo-graphic Institute. A few days later, during one of his lectures at the military academy in Quito, Patzelt mentioned that even military officers were unable to inspect certain parts of their fatherland. This brought the secret police into the case: SIL capitulated with a chaperoned tour.[73] Henceforth Patzelt visited the Ridge in military as well as oil company helicopters, taking along officer friends, authors and even the German consul to the last Aucas unspoilt by civilization.

Around Tigueno, SIL's protectionist policy was also falling apart, not least because the Huaorani shared their leasehold with an oil consortium. While the well drilled three kilometres from Tigueno in 1971 proved 'uneconomical', the state oil firm CEPE came through again four years later and will probably be back. The Huao reward was oil company booty, the like of which Tigueno had never seen: soon every house had a corrugated roof except for Rachel Saint's.

Many of the oil workers were Lowland Quichua, the largest Indian language group in the Oriente. Displaced by colonization, they are a growing, land-hungry people who have reason to resent the Protectorate. The Upper Curaray always had been a trade route, into which their mortal enemies had moved within living memory. Now the government was giving the Aucas exclusive rights on a scale which the Quichua were denied. Working for the oil companies was an opportunity to explore in safety and become acquainted with the new, hopefully temporary, proprietors.

Neither of these pressures was the most serious threat to SIL's protectionist policy, however. That came from the Huaorani themselves, in the form of demands which SIL did not want to meet and power plays within Rachel Saint's patronage system. The clearest sign that something was very wrong were the defections from Tigueno, the so-called escape to liberty.

By 1971 a band of 'rebels' was moving, not east like the spearing Baiwa the year before, but west toward the Napo River, as if they were looking for better trading partners. They included one of Saint's five redeemed Palm Beach killers, Nimonga, and they were led by one of the former Sevilla peons, Zoila Winaemi. Like Sevilla's other Huao women, Zoila spoke Quichua and a bit of Spanish, which made her one of the few Huaroani capable of functioning

as an intermediary with outsiders. Since Dayuma's special relationship with
Saint gave her a near monopoly in mediation and its rewards, she and
Zoila quarrelled bitterly.

The branch dates the final rupture to a 1971 confrontation between
Zoila and Dawa, Saint's number two woman. When a helicopter dropped an
oil crew into Zoila's vicinity between the Protectorate and the Napo River,
the crew panicked on contact. According to the crew boss and contractor,
Captain Nelson Villalba, he mastered the situation by inviting Zoila's band
into camp. Another version includes a timely shower of gifts from a Texaco
helicopter.

Perhaps a week after the friendly contact, according to Villalba, Dawa
arrived in an ugly mood with 14 other men and women. Dawa shoved the
captain, telling him to get out because his men were going to rob Huao game.
Zoila intervened on Villalba's side and the two women fell to a screaming
match, in the midst of the two armed Huao parties and the labourers.
Believing that the women were exchanging spear threats, Villalba radioed
Texaco which radioed SIL. A helicopter arrived bearing Catherine Peeke, who
persuaded Dawa and her people to leave.[74]

An accommodating man like Villalba was just what Zoila and her people
were looking for. He took four of the men to meet President Rodriguez
Lara; they refused to leave the palace until given armloads of antique shotguns
and .22 rifles. Villalba passed the band on to David Miller of the Christian
and Missionary Alliance (C&MA), who helped it settle a day's walk away
from the Napo River, at Dayuno on the northern boundary of the Protectorate. A Quichua pastor, the C&MA's Pedro Chimbo, began teaching school
at Dayuno in December 1973.

Among the first outsiders to visit this Quichua-Huaorani trading scene were
Erwin Patzelt, Peter Baumann and the army's Major Tito Parreno. Through
Pedro Chimbo and Zoila as interpreters, they heard disturbing stories about
Rachel Saint's regime in Tigueno. Chimbo called it a 'mission prison' where
SIL prevented the Huaorani from learning anything about the outside world
and recalcitrants were bound hand and foot.[75]

Dayuno was also the first settlement to attract large numbers of tourists,
weekly groups of young, mostly North American and European back-packers
escorted from the Napo River by a guide. When my group of seven spent a
night in Dayuno in October 1976, the atmosphere of many-cornered distrust
and opportunism was palpable. The Huao children were lively and receptive,
the young men alternately sullen and sarcastic, the older people mostly glum.
Half a dozen Quichua men were passing through on a hunting excursion. The
Huaorani tried to sell the tourists toy blow-guns, necklaces and the like;
some begged for ladies' underwear and aspirin.

A journalist was so impressed by Zoila's authority that he classified Huao
society as a traditional matriarchy straight from Lewis Morgan's Middle Stage
of Savagery.[76] My impression of Dayuno was a middle stage of disintegration.
Pedro Chimbo proved more accessible than Zoila; he was considered a brave
man because Dayuno included men upon whom the Gospel had made little

impression. They still had scores to settle from the last battles in the 1960s; in a rage, any outsider would do.

Chimbo was thinking of leaving because the group gave him a hard time; he doubted that the education ministry would find a replacement. He thought that the Huaorani begged too much and received too many presents for their own good, but the worst was that our tour guide gave most of his bounty to Zoila, who did not distribute it to the others, who became angry and sometimes muttered about spearing the tourists. During dinner a young man arrived in anger and was quickly hired to paddle us upstream the next day.

When I belaboured the tourism issue, Chimbo added that it was unfortunately in the hands of men like our tour guide (from the coast) rather than the Quichua. The two accused each other of cheating the Huaorani on their handicrafts. A month after our visit, a spearing scare ran up and down the Napo River: Pedro Chimbo was in danger, maybe dead. Early the next year he tried to ban tourism, which made Zoila and her people angry.

SIL Sends an Anthropologist

In January 1976 the Wycliffe monthly printed Ethel Wallis' update on the Huaorani. They had new goals: trade routes, visiting Quito, building airstrips, buying sewing machines and cattle. Four young believers were preparing to be the first Huao schoolteachers since Tona. The Huaorani had a better idea of fair price for their labour and purchases; they were struggling to learn Spanish and wanted to be registered as citizens. The Sunday after a Huao-organized Bible conference 50 were baptized; backsliders and the unsaved interrupted the Quichua preacher to confess their sins.[77]

The Summer Institute had arranged an armistice among hostile Huao bands, ended their raids on Quichua settlements, and helped Ecuador take possession of its oil lands. The credit belonged to the Lord, of course, and the branch's greatest pride were those men who had clearly found a new life free from killing. By the time Wallis' bright picture reached Wycliffe supporters, the branch executive committee had decided that SIL's influence on the Huaorani was 'negative'.

Since the removals had come home to roost at Tigueno, it had grown harder and harder to take Rachel Saint's faith on faith. The judgements of Catherine Peeke and two other women brought in to prop up the work – a North American schoolteacher and a nurse from Germany – began to contradict their senior partner's. After 1968 Saint had forbidden SIL men from spending the night in Tigueno on grounds they might be speared. When branch leadership began suggesting an evaluation around 1972, Tigueno was still such a dangerous place that she could not guarantee a man's safety. No one was accustomed to giving her orders: at Limoncocha visitors noticed the air of authority trailing her about. Patience at branch headquarters snapped after the publication of Ethel Wallis' *Aucas Downriver: Dayuma's Story Today* (1973), whose text Catherine Peeke had refused to approve. Wallis' fairy tale optimism conflicted strangely with Saint's claim that not a single male colleague could live in Tigueno without risking his life.

The branch director assumed responsibility for the safety of a new arrival from the United States, an anthropologist. SIL has only a few: they have been expected to tour branches, hold seminars and do short studies, not intervene in field disasters and antagonize translators. James Yost had left the University of Colorado to join SIL: his official mission was a study of pre-contact Huao culture. But he was also to evaluate the branch's performance and became deeply involved in what was supposed to have been a temporary assignment. Saint smelled a rat and he soon ran foul of her.

On arrival Yost was so protectionist that he opposed Huao acquisition of Quichua and Spanish for fear that it would threaten their cultural identity (unlike most SIL literacy work in Latin America, its programme for the Huaorani was still monolingual). He shared a conviction with Rachel Saint, the German adventurers, myself and many others: that a recently contacted people facing the worst yet to come should somehow remain like they were and apart from the world, with the sole exception of one's own programme.

Yost soon learned that Huao anxiety over outsiders vied with a consuming passion for trade goods. Until the rise of Dayuno, the leading port of entry had been the airstrip at Tigueno. Around it remained many of the Huaorani from the removals, not just for booty but because missionaries and converts wanted to make sure that they did not kill anyone. Controlling the distribution of patronage were 'cultural brokers', a few Huaorani whose language skills made them mediators of contacts with outsiders. At the core of this group were the former Sevilla peons, and especially Dayuma, upon whom Saint had always leaned heavily. They proceeded to introduce hacienda methods of exploitation into SIL's patronage system, by using their power over Huao clients to extract protracted labour obligations from them. Although Tigueno always had been Dayuma's turf, a wide open field in new fiefdoms led to serious competition from her hacienda peers. Huao refugees found their own reasons for leaving Tigueno and, under the leadership of former Sevilla peons, moved out to the edge of the Protectorate.

Compared to the missionary-regulated Tigueno, the new centres were free ports where Dayuma figures exchanged Protectorate game for trade goods. The most treasured item was the shotgun, which Rachel Saint had tried to ban on grounds that many men were still not stable enough to be trusted with them. The firearm ban was also ecological, but it gave oil crews and Quichua hunting parties an edge in the competition for animals. By 1976 Yost counted 40 or so shotguns in Huao hands — most through Dayuno — which had obtained another consignment, along with registration as citizens in a second audience with President Rodriguez Lara. Other improvements gaining ground in the Protectorate included dynamite (obtained from oil crews) and DDT (from malaria spray teams) for fishing. The new methods were depleting game so rapidly that longer and longer journeys were required for meagre returns. Circulation into other parts of the Protectorate would help, but modern technology would wipe out game wherever it was used.

If that were not enough, SIL was still moving the last of the Ridge Huaorani into the Protectorate. Saint wanted them all under her wing and so did Dayuma; her people were badgering her for spouses and this was where she could get them. Gardens were supposed to be planted in the Protectorate for new arrivals, but after 30 people were flown to Tigueno Yost noticed that they were getting thinner. In early 1975 he persuaded the branch to postpone the next flight, then postpone it again.

Now that people transferred from the Ridge had their spouses, the anthropologist tried to persuade some of them to go home. There were no takers. 'Trade goods are at the bottom of it,' he told me. Another idea was to make the Protectorate larger. Technicians from the United Nations Food and Agricultural Organization (FAO) were surveying for national parks throughout the country. Soon FAO was proposing one to the south-east of the Protectorate: perhaps there could be a land bridge and Huaorani serve as wardens.

A much larger jungle Indian population might want the same land to satisfy its own needs, however. And at the current rate, soon there might be no Huaorani left to protect. Many of them resented Quichua intrusions, but they were becoming dependent on the same men for rubber boots, flashlights and the like, which made them afraid to anger their new trading partners. Forced to prove that they had not reverted to savagery, first the Dayuma figures and now other Huaorani were doing their painful best to identify with the Quichua. Stripped of their duty to defend the group, the young men spent far too much time looking in pocket mirrors and combing their hair. Rachel Saint harangued them for singing Quichua songs instead of their own. They were not impressed by the argument that the only answer to discrimination was pride in being Huaorani.

Six SIL members were now alternating between Tigueno and Limoncocha, certainly enough to do whatever could be done. They decided that the best thing that they could do was to leave, for a while. All but one felt that the Huaorani around Tigueno were too dependent on SIL, and all but one did not like the way Dayuma manipulated her following. The Huaorani would have to be left alone to figure out their problems by themselves. The risk was that they would all decide to join the wild crowd in Dayuno. But Dayuno was the child of Christian Tigueno and, unless something changed, the pattern of the future for other Huaorani.

In 1975, members began to urge dispersal, underlining the point by curtailing the flow of trade goods into the Tigueno airstrip. The next year, with some difficulty, all members were pulled out. Dayuma and her confederates were incensed that Saint had been taken away and their main trade goods channel cut off. Huao medical trainees found that they were more capable than they had thought. There was also an increase in witch and spear anxiety, Yost believes because missionaries were not around as a guarantee against mayhem, and dispersal took families away from church service, whose primary function he calls reinforcement of the spearing ban. On return, SIL members reduced their consumption of outside goods, stopped acting as trade agents and bypassed Dayuma in executing their plans. They stepped up the training of Huaorani to handle their own school programme and continued to reduce their time in the Protectorate.[78]

The weaning programme indeed accelerated dispersal from Tigueno. But contrary to the anthropologist's hopes, the Huaorani continued to relocate to maximize their contacts with the outside world. Like the Dayuno band had been doing for several years with tragicomic results, more Huaorani went out for the grand tour of Quichua villages and settler towns. More Quichua became *compadres* (godparents— to Huao children to gain access to the Protectorate. The Huaorani quarrelled over their demands, but *compadrazgo* provided a trading partner and intermediary in other transactions, a place to stay and a niche from which to observe outsiders beyond old boundaries. To earn money for trade goods, by 1976 a few Huao men from Dayuna and Tigueno were working in the east for an oil company — which hoped that they would prevent trouble with the last of the group still at large. Obviously the Huaorani would have to learn Quichua and Spanish to defend themselves.[79]

Nampa

The rupture of SIL's patronage system brought to light a conflict between sanctity and honesty. Accounts of the Palm Beach martyrdom had changed over the years in undeclared homage to Dayuma's younger brother Nampa, who died some weeks or months after the missionaries. According to Ethel Wallis, word that Nampa was no longer alive led to Dayuma's last rebellion before rejoining her people in 1958. Strangely, this important news took 'a few days' to emerge in non-stop conversation with Aunts Maengamo and Mintaka. It came up as Dayuma pondered the death of Nate Saint. And Dayuma turned on Rachel Saint as if she were to blame: 'I am never going back. . . . I won't teach you any more of my language—'[80] Even more strangely, according to Elisabeth Elliot she had already learned of Nampa's death in the tape exchanges.[81]

The likely cause of Dayuma's revolt was not the fact of Nampa's death but how he had died, in the words of the 1980 Kingsland account: 'The aunts described with great relish the wound in his head from one of the missionaries' rifles. . . .'[82] Yet the aunts blamed Nampa's death on witchcraft and a boa constrictor, leading Wallis to conclude that Nampa 'had been cruelly crushed by a boa while hunting in the forest. Black and blue and very ill, he lingered for a month. He had been cursed by the down-river Indians, Maengamo said, and finally died a horrible death.'[83]

Saint was aware of the bullet no later than her 1960 epilogue to *The Dayuma Story*. Here, reportedly as she learned from Gikita in his hour of confession and faith, we read that 'one bullet grazed the head of young Nampa,' who was 'hiding behind the plane' as the missionaries shot 'into the air.'[84] The trajectory of the magic bullet is corrected in Saint's 1965 epilogue to *The Dayuma Story*, as reported by her second convert Dawa. Now the accident occurs when Dayuma's own mother Akawo grabbed for a missionary gun and a shot went off, grazing her own son who was hiding in the forest on the other side of the plane.[85]

The enduring result of the Saint-Huao exchanges on Palm Beach was the most noble, graceful death to which Huao enemies have ever been privileged: 'One by one the foreigners had fallen. Although they fired shots into the air, warning the Aucas that they had means of defense, they chose to be killed by Auca spears.'[86] In 1959, Huao informants told Saint that one of the missionaries had climbed into the plane, looked back and rejoined his comrades (implication brother Nate).[87] A few years later Minkayi told her that the action had been much too fast for such heroism: 'before [her previous informants] were afraid' and this was 'talking wild' — Huao for nonsense.[88]

In early 1974 Erwin Patzelt interviewed one of Saint's legendary 'five killers' at Dayuno. From Nimonga, through Zoila and Pedro Chimbo as interpreters, he heard about the sixth casualty of Palm Beach. On Patzelt's tape, with Nimonga in the background, Chimbo explains that the last missionary to die shot Nampa as if he were trying to save himself. Later Patzelt asked Dayuma's son Sam Padilla what had happened to his uncle Nampa. 'He died after the massacre of the five missionaries,' Sam replies on Patzelt's tape. 'Why?' presses Patzelt. 'With sickness, I believe,' answers Sam. In June, Patzelt presented his evidence to Sam, eliciting the taped statement that 'one of the bullets came out and hit [Nampa] in the head, but it was not deliberate, it was an accident which happened. After the five were killed, Nampa was a little bad, he went home, felt bad and nearly died. The bullet was still in his head. . . . After some months he died from the effect of the bullet.'

When *El Comercio* mentioned Patzelt's version of Palm Beach in April 1974, SIL protested but also asked its new anthropologist to investigate. James Yost discovered that 'he met a boa and he died' was the first Tigueno response to inquiries. Perhaps a month after Palm Beach, the story went, Dayuma's brother had gone hunting by himself. On his way home he encountered a boa coming out of a hole. The boa talked to him. Nampa tried to run away but the boa talked to him again. 'Now I know I'm going to die because the boa has spoken to me,' Nampa said.

Obviously this was a spirit boa, one associated with sorcery, which animists may regard as the cause of death even when they know that something else was the immediate agency. Whether the bullet lodged in Nampa's head or left a furrow which became infected, Yost's Tigueno interviews led him to believe that Nampa had not died from a boa attack but probably because of the bullet wound. When he asked Nimonga how the missionaries had shot Nampa accidentally if he was in hiding, Nimonga laughed and said that Nampa had come armed with a spear to kill. Contrary to her early 'five killers' motif, even Saint now has three of four women in the party participating in the assault and only Nampa, old enough to go hunting by himself, aloof. According to Sam Padilla, everyone helped.

For various reasons — the lapse of time and the Huao definition of time, the problematical Huao photo identification of whom they killed in what order, special interest lobbies among the Huaorani – it is probably impossible to determine precisely who shot Nampa, how he was shot and how soon he died. Among Saint's loyalists, Yost reports, the 1965 accidental version that Nampa's own mother was responsible seems firmly established. When he suggested that the bullet killed Nampa, Dayuma flew into one of her tantrums and insisted that it was the boa. Since then her son Sam has used a two week bullet death to bludgeon SIL.[89]

In 1976, Rachel Saint was standing her ground: 1) if the five men had tried to shoot attackers, they would have been more successful; 2) Nampa was off the beach and in hiding, therefore the shooting was accidental; and 3) he died six months after Palm Beach, therefore the relation to the shooting is dubious.[90] But since learning the seven day week, the Huaorani have scrambled their old term for the lunar cycle into it: six months could be six weeks. Saint also evidently influenced her converts to tell her what she wanted to hear. The martyrdom is basic to her understanding of Huao Christianity because, without it, the blood debt between herself and the Huaorani becomes mutual: while Dayuma's people killed her brother Nate, Nate and his associates killed Dayuma's brother.

With the imposition of Saint's views in *Aucas Downriver: Dayuma's Story Today* a fresh memory, and now Nampa, several branch members asked SIL President Kenneth Pike to put a stop to misleading publicity. They were told that new publicity would reflect the situation more accurately, but not dwell on past errors, and that inquiries would be answered accurately. In a rejoinder Saint sent her notices to the United States without branch review, an infraction which led to a third round of protest from her co-workers.

Rachel Saint Removed

To some SIL-Ecuador members, particularly the Huao team minus Rachel Saint, the burden of maintaining the Auca legend had become too heavy. Wycliffe supporters and members expected to hear that the Lord was still doing mighty works. Less respectful bystanders accused them of genocide. But this was the least of their problems with a famous missionary accustomed to steam-rolling her opposition.

Saint found it impossible to accept the anti-dependency campaign of 1975-76, undermining as it did her regime of 15 years standing. No one knew the Aucas like she did. Hadn't she saved the tribe from spearing itself to extinction? The next item on the agenda might be to ease her out of the work, the last farewell to people who had become her family and home. She tried to keep on as if nothing had changed, digging in her heels and refusing to leave Tigueno along with the others.

At first, in early 1976, I heard that Saint was about to retire for reasons of health. But in July she was still holed up in the tribe and showing no sign of leaving. In August visitors saw a subdued Saint deplaning at Limoncocha. She had made some 'serious mistakes', a member said in October: the branch executive committee would take them up at its next meeting.

If the most pressing issue was Saint's refusal to bow to the will of her colleagues, another was surely the offense she had given a series of military officers, whom branch officials would then have to placate. In 1970 a journalist had recorded one such figure's discontent with the 'halo of mystery' which prevented anyone from visiting Tigueno without Saint's approval. 'She gives the impression that the Aucas are her personal property' was a common complaint.[91] In 1974, Major Tito Parreno, one of Erwin Patzelt's partners on Ridge expeditions, helicoptered into Limoncocha to ask for help in counting the Huaorani for the national census. According to a member of his party, over lunch Saint 'became angry'. She did not want the national census to visit the Ridge because something bad might happen; therefore, she would have no part in it. Major Parreno did the census with the help of Zoila Winaemi. In his report he mentioned that many Huaorani had asked to visit Quito, especially Dayuma, who also asked for a shotgun for her husband Komi, to whom it would be a great help in stocking the family larder. Major Parreno concluded that depopulating a zone on the Peruvian frontier was not in the national interest.[92]

Then there was the danger lurking behind Huao dependence on SIL: Saint's dependence on Dayuma. Although Dayuma never really had reconciled herself to the divine plan, Saint seems never to have faced the possibility that her protege was not its proper instrument. Dayuma needed her missionary even more thanks to what Saint understood as a battle between the material and spiritual, the attraction of 'possessions' and a life more comfortable than the Huao forest, from which Dayuma still longed to escape.* Yet in 1975-76 Dayuma won the upper hand, when SIL put them both in a difficult position and an emerging power broker promised to surpass her old mentor.

In November 1976 the branch executive committee heard Rachel Saint's appeal, apparently of a retirement order which had pulled her out of the tribe in August. As I learned later, her trump was the fame bestowed by the Wycliffe publicity machine: she was threatening to start a scandal in the United States. The outcome was that Saint could not return to the Huaorani without leaving Wycliffe, although she might be reinstated at a later date. In March 1977 she was in Tigueno briefly to say goodbye and then out again to Quito,

---

* After Dayuma testified at a 1961 Billy Graham crusade in Philadelphia, she refused to return to Ecuador in what Saint called a 'conflict of material and spiritual values. The thought of leaving this land of plenty, where everyone had been so kind to her, to go back to primitive tribe who completely lacked possessions seemed too great to ask. Dayuma did not want to leave the States, and she began to react.'

'As far as I was concerned it was primarily a spiritual battle. We were planning to go right ahead with the translation of God's carving as soon as we got back. Here was the first hindrance. My informant did not want to return and was unhappy with me for expecting her to. We were to leave on the plane early the next morning. The conflict became so strong and dark. . . .'[93] For her 1966 and 1971 tours to Europe and the United States Saint chose other converts.

preparing to go home on furlough to think things over. One subject to ponder were the plans of her virtual foster son Sam Padilla.

The Palm Beach Shrine

Since SIL's plans required that Dayuma return to the Huaorani, her son had to go along with her. In mid-1959 around the age of seven to nine, following transfer from the Sevilla hacienda to the U.S. to school in Limoncocha and/or Quito, Sam Padilla was introduced to Huao life. While Ethel Wallis describes a happy adjustment, he apparently did not learn the language.[94] Rachel Saint wanted him to stay in Tigueno with his mother, but Dayuma refused to have her son grow up to be an 'Auca' (savage) and demanded a school education. From approximately 1961 to 1968 Saint arranged for Sam to attend school in Quito and return to Tigueno for vacations. After 1968 he learned the language yet continued to live and dress like the outsider he was, refusing to sing Huao songs or dance Huao dances.

In 1971 a journalist asked Sam whether he felt like an Auca.

> Half and half, [Sam replied]. Because my father was from the outside. So I'm in-between, you know? My life's been almost everything. I've been more to the outside world. . . . I don't mind [the Auca life], it's just the same for me, but I'd rather be outside, because there's more things to do and see, you know. I have to work for my living. I'll have to stay around the cities. I go [back to Tigueno] now for one week, two weeks, something like that when I have time.

He thought Rachel Saint was doing a great job. She had been like a mother to him since he was little. The missionaries were trying to help the Aucas so they wouldn't be like they used to be.[95]

Earlier that year, as advance man for rallies featuring Saint, Gikita, Kimo and Dawa in 27 North American cities, Sam learned at first hand how Wycliffe exploited the Aucas and their image. Back home he fell in with what SIL regarded as bad company, Erwin Patzelt. Sam was such a valuable associate on Patzelt's expeditions that Saint sent him to the United States again, this time to Bible school. But before Sam left, he was peddling Patzelt's photographs of naked Huaorani as his own. In the U.S. he managed to escape from a grim fundamentalist institution to the Florida Bible College, installed in a former resort hotel near Miami.[96]

After several years of training in American girls, stereos and boutiques, Sam went to work for Metropolitan Tours of Quito on its 'Flotel' — an improbable 180 ton, floating, semi-navigable property which promised the wealthier class of tourist the 'untouched, unexplored, undiscovered' Amazon. Its home port was the oil dock at Coca. As tour guide through Quichua villages and Limoncocha, Sam was perhaps the Flotel's only success. He was billed as the man who had made the transition from the Stone Age to the Space Age.

He made contacts with wealthy North Americans and Ecuadorians, occasionally taking off in the middle of the tour with a few select, bored customers for a charter flight to the Ridge Huaorani.

As a presumed member of a famously savage tribe, Sam now realized that he had quite a future in the Oriente. But this was not, as he would later style himself, as the tribune of his people. True, he had good rapport with some Huaorani and was a capable intermediary for oil companies. He had leverage against the missionaries; access to government, the press and universities if he cared; and was well situated to deal with Huao-Quichua conflicts. Yet when I met Sam in 1976 during his Flotel days, the theme of Huao welfare was absent. He appeared to be motivated by 1) his personal grievances against Rachel Saint and SIL, and 2) his pursuit of an affluent lifestyle in Quito at Huao expense, by commercializing them and spending money entrusted to him for their benefit on personal needs such as a large collection of toiletries. In Tigueno he was his own glory, to the confused young men looking in mirrors the watch-and-sunglasses epitome of sophistication, which they tried to emulate in the middle of the jungle. According to the missionaries, he even brought in dynamite to blast the fish out of the water.

By early 1976 Sam and Dayuma had a plan, according to Sam his mother's and according to SIL Sam's: move Tigueno to Palm Beach, clear an airstrip and build a shrine where the martyrs are buried so that visitors could pay their respects. Owing to the SIL reforms, Dayuma was falling far behind her rivals Zoila and Olga in the competition for trade goods. With her son as an unbeatable promoter, tourism would redress this injustice. Conveniently enough, Tigueno had been planning to move toward the Curaray River for fresh land and better game.

In November 1976 Sam outlined his plans and demonstrated their superiority to the Flotel, which he described as expensive and dull. The superior feature of Sam's tour would be Aucas. 'Small groups' — 15 to 20 tourists — would be flown from Quito to Pastaza to Primavera, a Napo River hacienda where the Flotel tied up after a short drift downstream. Here, the owner was building half a dozen tourist cabins. Customers would tour the nearby SIL base and, after four or five days, be flown to the 'Palm Beach Village'.

Sam emphasized that, while Flotel made everyone go around in a group, he would offer his customers alternatives:

> If you're a botanist, I know where you can find the most fantastic flowers and plants you've ever seen. If your thing is insects — you wouldn't believe what some these people are into — I'll show you that. If your interest is anthropology, then I'll take you where you can watch the native people and see how they live.

Whatever their interests at Palm Beach village, Sam explained, his customers would be free to pursue them: hunting, chasing butterflies, or just hanging around the village 'looking at the natives and how they go about their daily lives.' To each tourist Sam would assign a Huao: 'If a gentleman wants to fish, fine. I know a great place for you to fish, here's a native person who'll take you with him and, man, that tourist is excited, he gets what he wants. He comes back, tells the others all about it. He's had the time of his life.' Sam would also take his customers by boat to the massacre site, where the incident would be retold with 'some of those who participated' on hand to explain their part.

The next day Sam would fly his amateur anthropologists, etc. to an abandoned oil company airstrip in the Cononaco region. Here, at last, they would be able to photograph and chat with genuine, naked Aucas, one of the two small Ridge groups still in the east, aside from the down-river fugitives. As Sam explained with some firmness, his customers would be allowed to stay only three hours, no more, to avoid spoiling the natives. But if a few wanted to return, he would be happy to arrange a special charter.[97]

Rachel Saint is supposed to have had a fit when Dayuma broke the news about the Palm Beach shrine. But as was increasingly the case, she had to come around to doing things Dayuma's way or not do them at all. While Saint did not want to talk about it, she was plainly troubled: if the move to the Curaray was motivated by financial greed, it was not Huao greed but that of outsiders, people who had lived on the outside. Sam had not been the same since he went to work for Flotel. It was not really him but his backers. Dayuma always had a special place in her heart for Palm Beach. As Saint prepared for exile in early 1977, Dayuma and son were urging her to leave SIL and come to live at Palm Beach village. If you want to see the most famous missionary in the world, Sam could tell his customers, I know where you can find her.

In the east, the last two groups of Ridge Huaorani were heating up. The one to the north was harassing oil crews, which prompted the Capuchin Mission to interpose itself with SIL's blessing.[98] The group to the south was at war with the down-river fugitives, who killed three oil workers in 1977. Erwin Patzelt and Karl Dieter Gartelmann found a helipad planted with stakes: from the air they watched previously friendly men scramble for their spears as women and children rushed into the jungle.[99]

When James Yost visited the southern Ridge group in mid-1976, they said they were going to the Cononaco airstrip at Sam's request. In August Yost found them at the airstrip. They said they had arrived when they were supposed to, but some time had passed and no Sam. Since they had no gardens in the area and no one else was around, it had been a tough period. When I asked Sam why the Huaorani had gone to the Cononaco airstrip, he answered 'they have a better deal going.'

Even if Sam could persuade the Huaorani to take off their T-shirts and helicopter seat belts for his customers, he had a more serious problem. SIL was about to bow to the demands of his own mother and Saint by bringing the same people to the Protectorate. Each time Yost visited the Ridge, young men begged to come to Tigueno because there were no more spouses in their reduced groups. Fortunately for Sam, the colonels and generals he was now lobbying could see the wisdom of keeping the Ridge remnants in the east. They were impressed by a young Auca who had become the epitome of civilization. His message was that the eastern Huaorani were a national patrimony, who had to be preserved and could help guard the frontier.

If SIL members opposed his plans, Sam threatened, he would have them kicked out of the country. For Rachel Saint, who was still predicting a scandal in the U.S. over the branch's betrayal of her mission, Sam had an offer. If she returned to Ecuador as an independent missionary, he and his mother would tell the government to expel SIL because it was not doing anything for the Huaorani anyway. According to Saint, her foster son was 'two bits': the branch was simply using him as an excuse not to bring in the Ridge. But Sam was tying the branch into knots. Not long before, his boss and probable backer at Metropolitana Tours, Eduardo Proana, had overcome SIL's aversion to the weekly Flotel tours through Limoncocha. He simply pointed out that he was introducing influential Ecuadorians to the Oriente. They might be perplexed, unhappy, even angry to learn that mysterious North Americans had declined to let them visit their facilities. JAARS made its stand by telling Sam that, if he was going to fly any more 'friends' into the Huaorani, he was not going to do it in JAARS. Sam went to the Minister of Defense and offered to fly officials to the east on Oriente Day 1977 in his accustomed airline. Reluctantly JAARS reserved a plane: Sam took his military party out from Coca in a helicopter.

Authentic and Ruined Aucas

When I left Ecuador in early 1977, Sam Padilla, Dayuma and Rachel Saint were squaring off against the Ecuadorian branch and the rest of its Huao team over what remained of Wycliffe's most famous mission. By halting the removal in 1975 and curtailing its patronage, the Summer Institute created a wider opening for Sam and Dayuma's tourism plans. But the triple alliance was shot through with contradictions: Saint wanted nothing to do with tourism. While Sam was promoting heathenism, his mother and Saint wanted to bring the eastern Huaorani into the Protectorate and stitch them into clothes. Sam fell out with both of them, and the eastern Huaorani stayed where they were. In early 1980, Saint was still with the Summer Institute and still hoped to retire among the Huaorani; SIL seemed determined that she should retire somewhere else.

'The worst enemies we have are the missionaries,' Sam ('Ceantu' or 'Caento') told *El Comercio* in February 1978. He intended 'we' to refer to the Huaorani rather than his business partners. According to Sam's new biography, during his first stay with the Huaorani 'I learned the Auca language, their customs and rituals.' After a year in Quito, he returned to his tribe and stayed with them for four years, then, at the age of fourteen went to the United States for several years of study. Here, explained *Comercio*, he 'assimilate[d] some of the essential cultural values of the most advanced nation in the world.' Yet once again he returned to the jungle, 'that free world without time and without fear,' to 'help his people face civilization . . . so they will not be abused.'

Missionaries were the only affliction Sam mentioned. They had forced the
Aucas to wear clothes, told them not to do this and not to do that, read
them the Bible and sown confusion in their simple, pure minds. They had
introduced his people to a series of necessities and now they were in the
settlements, practically begging because the money they could scrape together
did not meet their needs. The missionaries had taken away their blow-guns,
given them shotguns and exploited them with the handicraft trade so
cruelly that, 'according to . . . this representative of the Auca tribe, at least
five hundred are presently ruined by [mission] work.' Stressing his faith in the
Huao witches, Sam called upon the national authorities to protect his tribe
from foreign interference. He had already presented the Auca case, to a concerned General Cabrera Sevilla, for the defense of that part of the tribe still
uncontaminated by civilization.[100]

To free themselves from dependence upon SIL and the Dayuma figures,
western Huaorani continued to multiply their contacts with outsiders. By
late 1979 James Yost counted more than 70 Protectorate men (60% of the
total) who had worked for oil companies at least once, compared to 33 a year
earlier and less than ten before 1977. 13 single women were working as
servants in towns. 80% of the married couples in the Protectorate now had
Quichua *compadres,* compared to only 14% two years before. Each week,
Huaorani carried out large quantities of smoked meat to their trading partners
some of whom were pressuring their Huao *compadres* for Protectorate land.
The popularity of *compadrazgo* spelled disaster for the Dayuma followers:
while they had thrived upon Quichua contacts, as more Huaorani established
their own ties the broker position was withering away. To stay at the head
of the pack these women stepped up their Huao-Quichua matchmaking –
which increased pressure on Protectorate land from growing numbers of
Quichua in-laws – and tried to attract more tourists.[101]

Dayuma's move to Palm Beach was not without its difficulties. Her son's
airstrip 1) had to be much longer than the one at Tigueno to bring down a
15 to 20 seat aircraft, requiring that much more work, and 2) was so poorly
planned that a second had to be cleared. Because Sam now considered his
mother and her people 'ruined', she found herself neglected in favour of the
more lucrative Huaorani at the Cononaco airstrip. To prevent more of her
shrinking following defecting to Dayuno, she had a trail cut to the Napo River
to bring in back-packers. By 1979, next to the thicket which has swallowed
the missionary graves, Dayuma was therefore firmly established as an 'Auca
queen' – the sales pitch of the small-time tour guides. Since the guides paid
only the 'queens' for the lodging of their several expeditions per week,
Dayuma was still on top. Two other groups of Huaorani, including those
remaining around the missionaries in Tigueno, were cool toward tourists
but getting them anyway as guides sought out more 'savage' Indians to keep
up their trade.

Now that Sam had become a champion of his people, he acquired an author
in Rosemary Kingsland. From her *A Saint Among Savages* (1980) emerges
an enchanting trio in the person of Sam ('a classic example of a universal

young man'); his mother Dayuma ('a very special person . . . radiates humility, grace and humour); and of course Rachel Saint, who comes in for some hard knocks but, like the others, is ultimately the victim of the Summer Institute. Both Saint and branch officials blame their troubles on their critics, particularly anthropologists who want to turn Indians into zoo specimens.

Persecuted by the Summer Institute, *out of his own pocket* the philanthropic Sam supports an entire group of Huaorani on the Cononaco River. In contrast, SIL has virtually abandoned poor Dayuma, who pines for the banished Saint and politely indicates that she has no further use for her friend's cruel brethren. Sam and his mother have differences to patch up, but this too is the fault of SIL, which is preventing Saint's return on grounds that she is too emotionally involved with the Huaorani.

Unlike the blood and guts German authors, whose readers learn that an Auca contact is not to be undertaken without putting one's affairs in order, Kingsland paints 'Sam's Rio Cononaco Wagrani group' as a highly accessible, harmless bunch, so long as one has Sam along. Naked, touching, laughing, warm and friendly, these are just the sort of unspoiled natives which thousands of liberated consumers would like to visit themselves. A fifth author in search of the last free Auca, introduced to the same people by Sam, suggests that they be protected from tourists and SIL missionaries by a small group of guardians, including his guide.[102]

In the United States, yet another of Sam's partners was advertising tours for the 'anthropologically curious' to a 'once-forbidden Auca village'. It sounds wonderful:

> The Aucas live in rain forests where rushing rivers and high mountains form a natural barrier, isolating them from the outside world. The Indians literally live off the bountiful land . . . .
>
> The tribesmen wear little more than G-strings.
>
> They have no monetary system. All food and materials are shared equally by all inhabitants.
>
> The Aucas are unconcerned about the use of cameras, so there are no obstacles for visitors wanting to take photographs.
>
> Trips are led by a young Auca man who speaks fluent English, Spanish and his native tongue. He's called Sam.
>
> Sam was brought out of the jungle by missionaries and educated in the United States. According to ['Adventures in Ethnocide'], he is interested in enlightening the world about his Auca kinsmen while trying to preserve the society of the jungle people whose culture has remained unchanged for so long. . . . Tour groups flown in by ['Adventures in Ethnocide'] offer sacks of corn and rice as good-will gifts on arrival.[103]

Ethnic tourism can sometimes bring benefits to all concerned. But in this case recently contacted, immunologically defenseless people are being treated to a constant flow of germs from several continents, for which addiction to

Western medicine is no remedy. Tourism to the Huaorani is also a breeder of ultra-dependency and a total invasion of privacy. Rather than inspecting some handicraft, skill or model village behind which the people can screen themselves, a stream of clumsy, gawking strangers is, in Sam's words, just 'looking at the natives and how they go about their daily lives.'

With the Quichua, the Huaorani share much common ground as jungle Indians. The two are ending a history of bloodshed by establishing ties of some advantage to each. Indeed, the Quichua seem to be a super-ethnicity composed partly of merging Jivaroan and the near-extinct Zaparoan peoples, whose road many Huaorani seem anxious to follow by becoming as Quichua as possible. But they are also absorbing new experience at a dizzy rate, which may force them in another direction. Perhaps Quichua discrimination and Huao resentment of their inroads will lead to a new Huao orientation, one capable of peaceful relations with outsiders on more equal terms. In either case, whether the Quichua prove to be the model of acculturation or the foil which saves Huao identity, the Huaorani are not 'ruined' except for exploitation as human curiosities.

In 1979, the year after Kingsland toured, James Yost summarized the impact of tourism as 'hard to see as good in any way. Much illness, dissension, transformed personality of the people from the previously free, uninhibited warm people [Elisabeth] Elliot [1961] describes and I know. Those most out of reach of tourists remain refreshingly kind. The others seem jaded by the visits.' He attributed two deaths within four months to tourism and soon counted two more.

> In Tzapino a Quichua guide brought in a few tourists, one of whom coughed all night according to the Huaorani. They objected to the guide and told him not to bring sick people in there. He, of course, did not understand Huao and never got the point. A few days later the entire village had colds, and a week later one man was dead and several others came very close to it.
>
> The other death was at Cononaco a few weeks after Sam took a load of tourists in there. Again, the Huaorani told me that one of the tourists had a cough and sniffles. They were only there a few hours, but the entire community ended up with colds and an infant died. They claim they asked Sam for medicines on a return visit but he refused to give them. That may mean nothing more than the fact that he just didn't have them along. At any rate, following that second visit a child got worse than when he was there and died.
>
> The Huaorani of course have no say on who comes or goes into the territory. Stripped of the right to kill, they have no mechanism for defending themselves against entrepreneurial guides and insistent tourists, who will not be denied their right to make money and watch savages. . . . The folks at Cononaco tell me they lived there almost two years before planting, always expecting Sam to fly food in to them. Rice and canned tuna were the big carrots.[104]

By early 1980, Zoila's band at Dayuno, the earliest to be inundated by tourists, had moved to the provincial capital at Tena. There they hoped to 'live forever as outsiders'.[105] Now Huaorani could be seen stumbling glassy-eyed through the settler towns. For the time being they could still return to a Protectorate secured by the Summer Institute of Linguistics and their fighting reputation.

References

1. *Translation* Spring 1956:19.
2. For a summary of pre-SIL knowledge about the Huaorani, see Blomberg 1956.
3. Yost 1981:687.
4. *Pioneer News* July 1926:1-2.
5. Galarza 1974:107-36.
6. Hitt 1973:152, 230.
7. Elliot 1974:135-9.
8. Elliot 1970:59, 119, 132-3, 146, 189.
9. For a Josephine account, see Spiller 1974:107-10, 203-13, 151-2.
10. First contract: *El Comercio* (Quito) 28 June 1952:7.
11. Hefleys 1974:173-4.
12. Bledsoe 1972:130; Kingsland 1980:19-40.
13. Wallis 1971:23-7.
14. Hitt 1973:240.
15. Kingsland 1980:97.
16. Elliot 1974:144; Hall 1959:249; Hitt 1973:243-4.
17. Elliot 1974:184.
18. Savage and Andrade Crespo 1956:35; Elliot 1974:199.
19. World Radio Missionary Fellowship 1976; Elliot 1961:18-63.
20. Patzelt 1976:1.
21. Kingsland 1980:67-8.
22. Wallis 1971:74-80.
23. Ibid. p.75-6.
24. Hefleys 1974:193.
25. Wallis 1971:80-1.
26. Ibid. 1971:84.
27. Ibid. 1971:117-18, 120.
28. *Boletin Indigenista* (Mexico, D.F.) March 1958:41.
29. Wallis 1971:91, 95, 97, 106-7, 113.
30. Elliot 1961:74.
31. Ibid.
32. Kingsland 1980:107.
33. Wallis 1971:193, 197.
34. Wallis 1971:182-4; Elliot 1961:82, 94, 156; Yost 1981:689-90.
35. Cited in Wallis 1973:38-9.
36. Elliot 1961:156-7.

37. *Christianity Today* 2 January 1976:14-16.
38. Wallis 1971:151-2, 183 and 1973:13.
39. *Life* 30 January 1956, 20 May 1957, and 24 November 1958.
40. Wallis 1971:10-11, 214, 217-23.
41. Wallis 1973:32.
42. Rachel Saint, author's interview, Quito, 10 November 1976.
43. Kingsland 1980:117-19.
44. Elliot 1961:129, 144-5, 151,
45. Elliot 1966.
46. Wallis 1973:25.
47. Author's interview, Quito, 9 December 1976.
48. Parreno Ruiz 1975:39-40.
49. Galarza 1974:158-66.
50. Wallis 1973:25.
51. John Linkdskoog, author's interview, Quito, 12 November 1976.
52. *Translation* Winter 1961/62:7; Saint 1965:288.
53. Author's interview, Quito, 9 June 1976.
54. Santos Ortiz 1980:29-30, 41-45.
55. *Comercio* 16, 17 and 20 August 1964:1.
56. Saint's version in Saint 1965:293-4 and Wallis 1973:26-8. Catholic version: from documents of the Aguarico Prefecture (Coca) including 'Informe de la madre superiora, Madre Cesarina. . . .', 24 May 1964; Feliciano de Ansoain, 'Que hay de la entrega de la auca "Onkay" a la Mision Capuchina', 11 July 1964 and 'Por la reduccion y evangelizacion de las tribus aucas del Napo', 6 July 1965.
57. Agee 1975:609, 615.
58. Saint 1965:294-302 and Wallis 1973:30-7.
59. Author's interview, Quito 9 December 1976.
60. Spiller 1974:261-2; Santos Ortiz (1980:59-78), who also describes the attacks on Coca and the Oncaye affair; and document of the Aguarico Prefecture, 'Operacion aucas para la reduccion y evangelizacion de estas tribus salvajes', 8 September 1967.
61. Wallis 1973:36-7, 47-71 and SIL-Ecuador 1969.
62. Kingsland 1980:127.
63. James Yost, personal communication.
64. Wallis 1973:73-9, 85-93.
65. Author's interviews.
66. Bledsoe 1972:151-2; Wallis 1973:80-84, 94-121; Yost 1981:688.
67. *El Mercurio* (Cuenca) 18 January 1975.
68. Resolution, Comite Ejecutivo, Instituto Ecuatoriano de Reforma Agraria y Colonizacion, 14 April 1969.
69. *El Tiempo* (Quito) 18 January 1975.
70. Author's interview, Puerto Misahualli, 19 October 1976.
71. Baumann 1975:89; Kingsland 1980:155.
72. Baumann 1975:13-14, 216-17.
73. Erwin Patzelt, author's interviews, Quito, 24 February and 9 June 1976.
74. Nelson Villalba, author's interviews, Quito, 29 October and 17 November 1976.
75. Baumann 1975:93-114.

76. *Comercio* April 29, 1974:1, 15.
77. *In Other Words* January 1976:4-5.
78. Yost 1979:16-20.
79. Yost 1981, and author's interviews.
80. Wallis 1971:141.
81. Elliot 1961:63.
82. Kingsland 1980:107.
83. Wallis 1971:141, 199, 212.
84. Saint 1971:221.
85. Saint 1965:290.
86. Wallis 1973:44.
87. Saint 1971:221.
88. Saint 1965:290.
89. Kingsland 1980:130.
90. Author's interview, Quito, 10 November 1976.
91. Cisneros 1970:100.
92. Parreno Ruiz 1975:41-2.
93. Saint 1965:279.
94. Bledsoe 1972:152.
95. Ibid. 1972:154.
96. Kingsland 1980:132-6.
97. Author's interview, Quito, 5 November 1976.
98. Santos Ortiz 1980:79-159.
99. Gartelmann 1977:189-90.
100. Aillon 1978.
101. Yost 1981:699-701.
102. Broennimann 1981:179-80.
103. Swem 1979.
104. Yost, personal communication.
105. Yost 1981:702.

Table 1
Summer Institute Branches, Field Areas and Advances, 1981*

Branch	Work Begun	Languages Undertaken	Personnel	Contracts/Remarks
Australian Aborigines	1961	22	101	Ministry of Education and Culture
Bolivia	1955	17	87	National Indian Foundation, Ministry of Interior (1969-76).
Brazil	1956	44	241	
Cameroun/Chad	1968	21	81	University of the Cameroun and Research Institute. Chad entered 1978, evacuated 1979. Operates as Societe Internationale de Linguistique.
Central America	1952	34	112	Ministry of Education (Guatemala) and Institute of Anthropology and History (Honduras, three languages since 1960). Nicaragua, one language.
Colombia	1962	36	250	Ministry of Interior.
Ecuador	1953	12	108	Ministry of Education (1953-81).
Ghana	1962	18	49	University of Ghana. Operates as Ghana Institute of Linguistics.
(India)	1966	9 (1970)	20	Deccan College. Work continues under Asia Area Office.
Indonesia	1971	19	109	University of Indonesia, Cenderawasih and Hasanuddin Universities.
Ivory Coast/Upper Volta/Mali	1970	25	73	Universities of Abidjan (Ivory Coast) and Ougadougou (Upper Volta, six languages since 1975). Ministry of Education (Mali, three languages since 1979).
Malaysia	1978	3	34	Sabah State.
Mexico	1936	114	328	Department of Public Education (1951-79).

Table 1 continued

Branch	*Work Begun*	*Languages Undertaken*	*Personnel*	*Contracts/Remarks*
(Nepal)	1966	18 (1976)	83	Tribhuvan University (1966-76). Work continues under Asia Area Office.
(Nigeria)	1962	22 (1976)	71	Universities of Nigeria and Nsukka, Ahmadu Bello University (1962-76). Work continues under Nigerian Bible Translation Trust and Africa Area Office.
North America	1944	41	108	Includes United States and Canada (12 languages since 1955).
Panama	1970	5	22	Department of Education (1969-79).
Papua New Guinea	1956	148	656	National government.
Peru	1946	45	262	Ministry of Education.
Philippines	1953	64	287	Departments of Education and National Defense.
Solomon Islands	1977	14	12	Technical assistance group working with local translators.
(South Vietnam/ Cambodia)	1957	21 (1975)	66	Department of Education. Work discontinued. Cambodia, two languages 1971-75.
Sudan	1977	11	52	Ministry of Education, Southern Regional Government.
Suriname	1967	7	25	Ministry of Education.
Togo/Benin	1967	6	25	National Scientific Research Institute. Benin, one language since 1981.
Displaced Languages Project		6		Works with expatriates in Europe and North America.
Field Area Offices Africa				
Ethiopia	1973	6	60	Administers work in Nigeria.

Table 1 continued

Branch	Work Begun	Languages Undertaken	Personnel	Contracts/Remarks
Kenya	1978	1		University of Nairobi.
Zaire	1978	5		
Asia			64	Administers work in India and Nepal.
Advances: Bangladesh, Burma, Pakistan, Thailand.				
Europe			11	Works with expatriates.
			7	
Latin America				
Chile	1976	2	4	Regional universities.
Argentina		1		
Pacific			24	
Advances: New Caledonia, New Hebrides and French Polynesia.				
Total		*797***	*3,192****	

* Most personnel and language totals are from WBT 1981. Parentheses indicate a defunct branch.
** While Wycliffe has undertaken the study of 902 languages according to *In Other Words* (Summer 1981), work has been completed in 39, abandoned short of New Testaments in 55, and halted in 83 (e.g., Vietnam), leaving 725 languages in which members are active.
*** This total does not include defunct branches, whose personnel have been assigned elsewhere.

Table 2
Wycliffe Home Divisions and Other Sending Countries, 1981*

	Members	*Short-Term Assistants*	*Total Personnel*	*Percent of Total*
Australia	285	17	302	7.2
Austria	2		2	
Belgium	1		1	
Brazil	4		4	
British Isles	211	7	218	5.2
Canada	266	65	331	7.9
Colombia	1		1	
Denmark	2		2	
Finland	25	3	28	.7
France	4		4	
Germany	66		66	1.6
Indonesia	1		1	
Japan	17		17	.4
Mexico	3		3	
Netherlands	48	5	53	1.3
New Zealand	48		48	1.2
Norway	6		6	
Panama	1		1	
Peru	6		6	
Republic of South Africa	14	1	15	.4
Sweden	15	5	20	.5
Switzerland	77	7	84	2
USA	2,525	431	2,956	70.9
Total	*3,628*	*541*	*4,169*	

*Personnel figures are from WBT 1981.

Bibliography

Aaby, Peter and Hvalkof, Soren (eds.) (1981) *Is God an American? An anthropological perspective on the missionary work of the Summer Institute of Linguistics*, Copenhagen: International Work Group for Indigenous Affairs and London: Survival International.

Academy for Educational Development (1978) *Guatemala Education Sector Assessment*, for Agency for International Development, in American Statistics Index 79:7208-18.

Agee, Philip (1975) *Inside the Company: CIA Diary*, New York, Stonehill.

Agence Latino-Americaine d'Information (1978) 'El ILV, Instrumento del Imperialismo', *Nueva Antropologia* (Mexico, D.F.), October, 3(9):117-42.

Aguilar, Alonso (1968) *Pan-Americanism*, New York: Monthly Review.

Aillon, Eliodoro (1978) 'Ceantu: El retorno a la vida y a la libertad de la selva,' *El Comercio* (Quito), 5 February

Albo, Javier (1979) 'Khitipxtansa? Quienes somos? Identidad localista, etnica y clasista en los Aymaras de hoy', *America Indigena* (Mexico, D.F.), July/ September, 39(3):477-528.

Alencar, Jane de and Yancan, Walter (1977) 'Nos dicen que somos ociosos, salvajes. . .', *Amazonia Peruana* (Lima), July, 1(2):143-8.

Alsop, John R. (1979) 'No despreciamos al indigena', *Proceso* (Mexico, D.F.), 1 October (152):6-12.

Amasifuen, Pedro (1978) 'Reflexiones sobre el ILV', *Marka* (Lima), 7 December (100):24-5.

American Foreign Service Journal (Washington, D.C.) (1939) 'Education among Mexican Indians', April:200-1215.

Anderson, Robert Mapes (1979) *Vision of the Disinherited: The making of modern Pentecostalism*, New York: Oxford University Press.

Anderson, Thomas P. (1971) *Matanza*, Lincoln; University of Nebraska.

Anguiano, Marina (1979) 'La etnologia como factor de reforzamiento de la identidad etnica', *America Indigena*, July/September, 39(3):573-86.

Anonymous (1976) 'Hansel y Gretel del Instituto Linguistico', in University of Antioquia 1976:111-21.

————— (1978) *Otro Zarpazo: Cia. Linguistica de Verano USA*, Editores Audio Visuales.

Antonil (1978) *Mama Coca*, London: Hassle Free Press.

Arcand, Bernard (1981) 'God is an American', in Aaby and Hvalkof:77-84.

Baez-Jorge, Felix (1980) 'Reflexiones sobre el quehacer de antropologia en Mexico', *America Indigena*, April/June, 40(2):367-80.

Fishers of Men or Founders of Empire?

Barr, James (1978) *Fundamentalism*, Philadelphia: Westminster Press.
Bartra, Roger et al (1978) *Caciquismo y Poder Politico en el Mexico Rural*, Mexico D.F: Siglo Veintiuno.
Baumann, Peter (1975) *Menschen im Regenwald*, Dusseldorf: Droste Verlag.
Beals, Carleton (1932) *Banana Gold*, Philadelphia: J.P. Lippincott Co.
Bebbington, Peter C. (1962) 'The Summer Insitute of Linguistics', *Peruvian Times*, 12 January:10-13.
Beekman, John (1959) 'Minimizing religious syncretism among the Chols', *Practical Anthropology* (Pasadena, California), November/December, 6(6):241-50.
Beekman, John and Hefley, James C. (1974) *Peril by Choice* (1st edition 1968), Grand Rapids, Michigan: Zondervan.
Benson, Foley C. (1978) 'The introduction of new protein sources among Peruvian Amazon Indians', paper read to 'Amazonia: Extinction or Survival' conference, Department of Anthropology, University of Wisconsin, Madison, 20 April.
Blair, Betty (1982) 'Aftermath of a Martyrdom', *Charisma* (Winter Park, Florida), May. p.28-31.
Bledsoe, Jerry (1972) 'Saint', *Esquire* (New York), July:123-32, 145-54.
Blomberg, Rolf (1956) *The Naked Aucas* (Swedish edition c.1950), London. Allen and Unwin.
Bloom, John (1981) 'And Jesus said, "mai eeneno",' *Texas Monthly* (Austin), June:149-53, 252-73.
Bodley, John H. (1982) *Victims of Progress*, (2nd ed.) Menlo Park, California: Benjamin/Cummings.
Bonfil Batalla, Guillermo (1979a) 'Los pueblos indigenas: viejos problemas, nuevas demandas', *Sabado (Uno Mas Uno)*, 16 June:1-3.
————— (ed.) (1979b) *Indianidad y Descolonizacion en America Latina: Documentos de la Segunda Reuinion de Barbados*, Mexico, D.F: Nueva Imagen.
Bonilla, Victor Daniel (1970) 'Disecion de un etnocidio', *Flash*, 16 October (57):14-23.
————— (1972a) 'The destruction of the Colombian Indian groups', in Dostal:56-75.
————— (1972b) *Servants of God or Masters of Men?* Harmondsworth: Penguin.
Boutilier, James A. et al, (eds.) (1978) *Mission, Church and Sect in Oceania*, Ann Arbor: University of Michigan.
Bravo Ahuja, Gloria (1977) *Los materiales didacticos para la ensenanza del Espanol a los Indigenas Mexicanos*, Mexico: Colegio de Mexico.
Brichoux, Felicia S. (1970) *Gaspar Makil*, Grand Forks, North Dakota: SIL.
Brintnall, Douglas E. (1979a) *Revolt Against the Dead*, New York: Gordon and Breach.
————— (1979b) 'Race relations in the southeastern highlands of Mesoamerica', *American Ethnologist* (Washington, D.C.), November, 6(4):638-52.
Brinton, Daniel G. (1884) *A Grammar of the Cakchiquel Language of Guatemala*, Philadelphia: American Philosophical Society.
Broennimann, Peter (1981) *Auca on the Cononaco*, Basel: Birkhauser.
Browman, David L. and Schwarz, Ronald A. (1979) *Peasants, Primitives and*

Proletariats, The Hague: Mouton.

Buckingham, Jamie (1974) *Into the Glory,* Plainfield, New Jersey: Logos.

Bunzel, Ruth (1952) *Chichicastenango,* Publications of the American Ethnological Society, vol. 22, Locust Valley, New York: J.J. Agustin.

Burgess, Paul (1926) *Justo Rufino Barrios,* Philadelphia: Dorrance.

————— (1957) *Historia de la Obra Evangelica Presbiteriana en Guatemala,* Guatemala.

Burns, Donald H. (1971) 'Cinco anos de educacion bilingue en los Andes del Peru', mimeo, May, Lima.

Camino, Alejandro (1979) 'Sociocultural change in Upper Urubamba, Peru', in Browman and Schwarz:125-47.

Cano, Ginette et al (1979) *Die frohe Botschaft unserer Zivilisation: Evangelikale Indianermission in Lateinamerika,* Gottingen: Gesellschaft fur bedrohte Volker.

————— (1981) *Los Nuevos Conquistadores: El ILV en America Latina* (translation of Cano et al 1979), Quito: Centro de Estudios y Difusion Social.

Cardenas, Lazaro (1973) *Obras,* 2 vols., Mexico, D.F: Universidad Nacional Autonoma de Mexico.

Chirif, Alberto (1980) 'El despojo institucionalizado', *Amazonia Indigena* (Lima), July, 1(1):15-24.

Chomsky, Noam and Herman, Edward S. (1979) *The Washington Connection and Third World Fascism,* Boston: South End Press.

Chomsky, Noam and Zinn, Howard, (eds.) (1971) *The Pentagon Papers,* vol. 1, Boston: Beacon Press.

Cisneros, Carlos (1970) 'Donde el Auca no mata', *Vistazo* (Guayaquil):91-100.

Clastres, Pierre (1980) *Society Against the State,* New York: Urizen.

Colby, William (1978) *Honorable Men,* New York: Simon and Schuster.

College of Ethnologists and Social Anthropologists (1979) *El ILV en Mexico: Dominacion ideologica y ciencia social,* Mexico, D.F.: Nueva Lectura.

Correal, Gonzalo et al (1972) 'El ILV en Colombia', report to the National Council on Indian Policy, mimeo, 10 March, Bogota.

Corry, Stephen (1976) *Towards Indian Self-Determination in Colombia,* London: Survival International.

————— (1977a) 'Peru 1976', *Survival International Review,* Winter (17):9-10.

————— (1977b) 'Bilingual education in Peru', *Survival International Review,* Autumn, (20):9-11.

Cotter, George (1981) 'Spies, strings and missionaries', *Christian Century* (Chicago), 25 March:321-4.

Cowan, George M. (1979) *The Word that Kindles,* Chappaqua, New York: Christian Herald.

Cowan, Marion M. (1962) 'A Christian movement in Mexico', *Practical Anthropology,* September/October, 9(5):193-204.

Damboriena, Prudencio (1962) *El Protestantismo en America Latina: Etapas y metodos del Protestantismo Latino-Americano,* Bogota:FERES.

D'Ans, Andre-Marcel (1981) 'Encounter in Peru', in Aaby and Hvalkof:144-62.

Davis, Shelton H. (1977 *Victims of the Miracle: Development and the Indians of Brazil,* New York: Cambridge University Press.

Davis, Patricia M. (1979) 'Lo que nos ha ensenado la experiencia Peruana', in

Larson et al:223-90.

Deicat, Gerardo Wipio (1979) 'La educacion en el pueblo Aguaruna', in Larson et al:97-111.

Diener, Paul (1978) 'The tears of St. Anthony: Ritual and revolution in eastern Guatemala', *Latin American Perspectives* (Irvine, California), Summer, 5(3):92-116.

Diment, Eunice (1976) *Kidnapped!* Exeter; Paternoster.

Dale, James G. (1943) *Katherine Neel Dale,* Grand Rapids, Michigan: Eerdmans.

Dame, Lawrence (1941) *Yucatan,* New York: Random House.

————— (1968) *Maya Mission,* New York: Doubleday.

Daniels, Josephus (1947) *Shirt Sleeve Diplomat,* Chapel Hill: University of North Carolina.

Dostal, Walter (1972) *The Situation of the Indian in South America,* Geneva: World Council of Churches.

Eichenberger, Ralph (1965) 'Principios para programas de salubridad entre tribus indigenas', *V Congreso Indigenista Interamericano,* vol. 3:139-47, Quito.

Elliot, Elisabeth (1961) *The Savage My Kinsman,* New York : Harper.

————— (1966) *No Graven Image,* New York: Harper and Row.

————— (1970) *The Shadow of the Almighty: The life and testament of Jim Elliot* (1st edition 1958), Grand Rapids, Michigan: Zondervan.

————— (1974) *Through Gates of Splendor* (1st edition 1956), Old Tappan, New Jersey: Spire.

Elson, Benjamin, (ed.) (1960) *Mayan Studies I,* Norman: SIL of the University of Oklahoma.

Emery, Gennet Maxon (1970) *Protestantism in Guatemala,* Sondeos no. 65, Cuernavaca: Centro Intercultural de Documentacion.

Escribens, Augusto (1975) 'Himnos nacionales y techos de calaminas', *Suceso (El Correo,* Lima), 7 December (226):7.

Falla, Ricardo (1972) 'Evolucion politico-religiosa del indigena rural en Guatemala 1945-65', *Estudios Sociales Centroamericanos* (San Jose), January-April, 1(1):27-41.

————— (1978) *Quiche Rebelde: Estudio de un movimiento de conversion religiosa . . . en San Antonio Ilotenango, Quiche 1948-70,* Guatemala: Editorial Universitaria de Guatemala.

Fell, Doris (1979) *Lady of the Tboli,* Chappaqua, New York: Christian Herald.

Figueroa Ibarra, Carlos (1976) *El Proletariado Rural en al Agro Guatemalteca,* Guatemala: Universidad de San Carlos.

Fitzgerald, Frances (1972) *Fire in the Lake,* Boston: Little, Brown.

————— (1981) 'A disciplined, charging army', *New Yorker,* 18 May:53-141.

Floyd, Olive (1944) *Doctora in Mexico, The life of Dr. Katherine Neel Dale,* New York: G.P. Putnam's Sons.

Foundation Center (1976) *Foundation Center Source Book 1975/6,* vol. 2, New York: Columbia University.

Friede, Juan et al (1979) *Indigenas y represion en Colombia,* Bogota: Centro de Investigaciones y Educacion Popular.

Friedemann, Nina S. de (1975) 'Niveles contemporaneos de indigenismo en Colombia', *Indigenismo y Aniquilamiento de Indigenas en Colombia:* 15 37. Juan Friede et al, Bogota: Universidad Nacional.

Fuller, Daniel P. (1972) *Give the Winds a Mighty Voice: The story of Charles E. Fuller,* Waco, Texas: Word Books.

Galarza, Jaime (1974) *El Festin del Petroleo* (1st edition 1970), Quito: Editorial Universitaria.

Gall, Norman (1967) 'The legacy of Che Guevara', *Commentary* (New York), December: 31-44.

Garrard, Martha (1970) *More Glimpses of Bolivia,* Santa Ana, California: WBT.

Gartelmann, Karl Dieter (1977) *El Mundo Perdido de los Aucas,* Quito: Imprenta Mariscal.

Georg, Norbert (1979) 'Missionsgesellschaften und Kulturwandel in der peruanischen Selva: Am Beispiel der Shipibo-Conibo', in Cano et al 1979: 128-56.

Geyer, A.F. (1961) 'American Protestantism and World Politics', Ph.D dissertation, Boston University.

Goddard, Burton L. (1967) *Encyclopedia of Modern Christian Missions,* Camden, New Jersey: Thomas Nelson and Sons.

Goff, James E. (1968) *The Persecution of Protestant Christians in Colombia, 1948-1958,* Sondeos no. 23, Cuernavaca: Centro Intercultural de Documentacion.

Goldman, Irving (1981) 'The New Tribes Mission among Cubeo', in Wright 1981: 7-8.

Goody, Jack and Watt, Ian (1963) 'The consequences of literacy', *Comparative Studies in Society and History,* April, 5(3): 304-45.

Gossain, Juan (1970) 'Violencia en los Llanos: Fracaso cooperativo origino la rebelion', *El Espectador* (Bogota), 27 February: 5A.

Gott, Richard (1973) *Rural Guerrillas in Latin America,* Harmondsworth: Penguin.

Gray, Gloria (1953) 'Bolivar Odicio, el Cashibo civilizador', *Peru Indigena* (Lima), 4(9): 146-55.

Green, James R. (1978) *Grass Roots Socialism: Radical movements in the Southwest, 1895-1943,* Baton Rouge: Louisiana State University.

Greene, Graham, (1978) *The Lawless Roads* (1st edition 1939), London: William Heinemann.

Grimes, Barbara F., (ed.) (1978) *Ethnologue,* (9th edition) Huntington Beach, California: WBT.

Haas, Frances (1978) 'By the year 2000, a Bible for the world', *Dallas Morning News,* 7 May, section G.

Hall, Clarence W. (1959) 'Two thousand tongues to go', and 'Through gates o of splendor', *Adventurers for God:* 106-55 and 228-65. New York: Harper and Row.

——— (1980) *Miracle in Cannibal Country,* Costa Mesa, California: Gift Publications.

Hart, Laurie (1973) 'Pacifying the last frontiers: Story of the Wycliffe Translators', *Latin America & Empire Report* (New York: North American Congress on Latin America), December, 7(10): 15-31.

Heath, Shirley Brice (1972) *Telling Tongues,* New York: Teacher's College.

Hefley, James C. (1969) *By Life or By Death,* Grand Rapids, Michigan, Zondervan.

——— (1970) *Aaron Saenz, Mexico's Revolutionary Capitalist,* Maco, Texas: Word Books.

———————— (1978) *God's Freelancers,* Orange, California: Wycliffe Associates.

Hefley, James and Marti (1972) *Dawn Over Amazonia,* Waco, Texas: Word.

———————— (1974) *Uncle Cam,* Waco: Word

———————— (1976) *No Time for Tombstones* (1st edition 1974), Wheaton, Illinois: Tyndale.

———————— (1980) *The Secret File on John Birch,* Wheaton: Tyndale.

Hefley, James C. and Steven, Hugh (1972) *Miracles in Mexico,* Chicago: Moody Press.

Hernan Ramirez, Luis (1976) 'El ILV y su expansion en el Peru', June, mimeo, Lima: Departmento de Linguistica, Universidad de San Marcos.

Hitt, Russell T. (1973) *Jungle Pilot: The life and witness of Nate Saint* (1st edition 1959), Grand Rapids, Michigan: Zondervan.

Hoffman, Hans (1964) 'Money, ecology, and acculturation among the Shipibo of Peru', *Explorations in Cultural Anthropology*, (ed.) Ward H.: 259-76. Goodenough, New York: McGraw-Hill.

Hoke, Donald E., (ed.) (1975) *The Church in Asia,* Chicago: Moody Press.

Hostetter, Douglas 1973 'Religious agencies in Vietnam: An insider's story', *Latin America & Empire Report,* December, 7(10):3-14, 31.

Howard, Philip E. (1941) *Charles Gallaudet Trumbull, Apostle of the Victorious Life,* Philadelphia: Sunday School Times Co.

Huntington, Deborah and Kaplan, Ruth (1981) 'Whose gold is behind the altar? Corporate ties to evangelicals', *Press-on!* (Berkeley: World Student Christian Federation), 1(4) and 2(1):1-10.

Huxley, Matthew and Capa, Cornell (1964) *Farewell to Eden,* New York: Harper and Row.

Inter-American Indigenist Institute (1980) *Anuario Indigenista* (Mexico, D.F.).

International Linguistic Center, Inc. (1977) 'What one cause of international importance has brought us together?' pamphlet, Dallas.

Jackson, Jean E. (in press) *The Fish People: Linguistic Exogamy and Tukanoan Identity in the Northwest Amazon,* Cambridge: Cambridge University Press.

Jennings, Francis (1975) *The Invasion of America,* Chapel Hill: University of North Carolina.

Jonas, Susanne and Tobis, David (1974) *Guatemala,* Berkeley: North American Congress on Latin America.

Jordan, W.F. (1926) *Central American Indians and the Bible,* New York: Fleming H. Revell.

Kensinger, Kenneth M. (1967) 'Change and the Cashinahua', *Expedition* (Philadelphia: University of Pennsylvania), Winter, 9(2):4-7.

Kingsland, Rosemary (1980) *A Saint Among Savages,* Glasgow: William Collins Sons.

Kintner, William R. (1950) *The Front is Everywhere,* Norman, University of Oklahoma.

———————— (1962) *The New Frontier of War,* Chicago: Henry Regnery Co.

Klare, Michael T. (1970) *War Without End,* New York: Knopf.

Kung, Andres (1981) *Bruce Olson: Missionary or colonizer?* (Swedish edition, 1977), Chappaqua, New York: Christian Herald.

Landabaru, Jon (1979) 'The double-edged sword: The SIL in Colombia', *Survival International Review,* Autumn, (27):5-8. First appeared in *Alternativa* 28 August:30-1, 4 September:30-1 and 11 September:38-9, 1978.

Lansdale, Edward G. (1972) *In the Midst of Wars,* New York: Harper and Row.

Larson, Mildred (1974) 'Greater is He that is in you', *Translation* (WBT), September/October:4-6.

Larson, Mildred L. et al (1979) *Educacion Bilingue: Una experiencia en la Amazonia Peruana,* Lima: Ignacio Prado Pastor.

Latoree Cabal, Hugo (1978) *The Revolution of the Latin American Church,* Norman: University of Oklahoma.

Leite, Yonne et al (1981) 'Os missionarios da linguagem,' *Religiao e Sociedade* (Rio de Janeiro), July:59-73.

Lernoux, Penny (1980) *Cry of the People,* New York: Doubleday.

Le Tourneau, Richard (1976) *Success Without Succeeding,* Grand Rapids, Michigan: Zondervan.

Le Tourneau, Robert G. (1967) *Mover of Men and Mountains* (1st ed. 1960), Chicago: Moody Press.

Lewis, Norman (1978) 'Eastern Bolivia: The white promised land,' doc. 31, Copenhagen: International Work Group for Indigenous Affairs.

Lewy, Guenter (1974) *Religion and Revolution,* New York: Oxford University Press.

Lloret, Albert Julian (1976) 'The Mayan Evangelical Church in Guatemala', Th.D dissertation, Dallas Theological Seminary.

Long, Jerry (1970) *Amazonia Reborn,* Portland, Oregon: Multinomah Press.

Longacre, Robert E. (1976) *An Anatomy of Speech Notions,* Lisse, Netherlands: Peter de Ridder Press.

Loos, Eugene et al (1979) 'El cambio cultural y el desarrollo integral de la persona: Exposicion de la filosofia y los metodos del ILV en el Peru,' in Larson et al 1979:401-47.

MacNaught, A. Roy (1932) 'Horrors of Communism in Central America', *Central American Bulletin* (Paris and Dallas, Texas), 15 March (181):8-10, 25-27.

Mangin, William P. (1972) 'The Indians', in Sharp 206-36.

Marquina, Brigido (1981) *Las Neuvas Tribus,* Caracas: Comite Evangelico Venezolano por la Justicia.

Marsden, George M. (1980) *Fundamentalism and American Culture: The shaping of Twentieth Century Evangelicalism 1870-1925,* New York: Oxford University Press.

Matallana Bermudez, Jose Joaquin (1976) 'Ministerio de defensa nacional comision especial de reconocimiento y verificacion,' in University of Antioquia p.17-95.

Matthiessen, Peter (1961) *The Cloud Forest,* New York: Viking.

———— (1965) *At Play in the Fields of the Lord,* New York: Random.

Maullin, Richard L. (1968) 'The fall of Dumar Aljure, A Colombian guerrilla and bandit', RM-5750-ISA, Santa Monica, California: Rand.

Maxwell, Nicole (1961) *Witch Doctor's Apprentice,* Boston: Houghton, Mifflin.

McCoy, Alfred W. (1972) *The Politics of Heroin in Southeast Asia,* New York: Harper and Row.

McCurry, Dan C. (1972) 'U.S. church-financed missions in Peru', Sharp:379-415.

McKinlay, Archibald (1944) *Visits with Mexico's Indians,* Glendale, California:WBT.

329

McLoughlin, William G. (1959) *Modern Revivalism,* New York: Ronald Press.
———— (1978) *Revivals, Awakenings and Reform,* Chicago: University of Chicago.
McWilliams, Carey (1973) *Southern California: An island on the land* (1st edition 1946), Santa Barbara, California: Peregrine Smith.
Melville, Thomas and Margarita B. (1977) 'Oppression by any other name: Power in search of legitimacy in Guatemala', *Ideology and Social Change in Latin America,* (ed.) June Nash:267-94. New York: Gordon and Breach.
Mendelsohn, Jack (1965) *The Forest Calls Back,* Boston: Little, Brown.
Merrifield, William R. (1977) 'On the ethics of Christian mission', paper read to the 76th annual meeting of the American Anthropological Association, 29 November-3 December 1977, Houston, Texas.
Miles, Michael W. (1980) *The Odyssey of the American Right,* New York: Oxford University Press.
Miller, Carolyn Paine (1977) *Captured!* Chappaqua, New York: Christian Herald.
Ministry of War (1966) *Las guerrillas en el Peru y su represion,* Lima.
Moennich, Martha L. (1944) *That They May Hear,* Chicago: Chicago Gospel Tabernacle.
Mole, Robert L. (1970) *The Montagnards of South Vietnam: A study of nine tribes,* Rutland, Vermont: Tuttle.
Moore, Thomas R. (1981) 'SIL and a "new-found tribe": The Amarakaeri experience', in Aaby and Hvalkof:133-43.
Morillo Cajiao, Pablo (1978) 'El ILV y nuestras comunidades nativas', *El Tiempo* (Bogota), 2 December:15E.
Morote Best, Efrain (1957) 'Tres temas de la selva', *Tradicion* (Cuzco), 7 January:19-20.
———— (1961) 'Trabajo y escuela en la selva Peruana', in SIL-Mexico 1961:301-12.
Moser, Brian (1971) 'War of the Gods', Disappearing Worlds film series, London: Granada Television.
Muller, Sophie (1952) *Beyond Civilization,* Woodworth, Wisconsin: Brown Gold Publications.
———— (1960) *Jungle Methods,* Woodworth, Wisconsin: Brown Gold.
Muratorio, Blanca (1981) 'Protestantism, Ethnicity, and Class in Chimborazo', in Whitten 1981:506-34.
Najar, Jorge (1976) 'Confesiones de un Aguaruna', 28 February:10 and 'Confesiones de un Huitoto', 6 March *El Correo* (Lima):11.
Nelson, Michael (1973) *Development of Tropical Lands,* Baltimore: Johns Hopkins University.
Nida, Eugene A. (1954) *Customs and Cultures: Anthropology for Christian missions,* New York: Harper.
Niebuhr, H. Richard (1936) *The Kingdom of God in America,* New York: Harper & Bros.
Nimuendaju, Curt (1952) *The Tukuna,* Berkeley: University of California Publications in Archaeology and Ethnology.
Novo, Salvador (1933) *Jalisco Michoacan,* Mexico, D.F: Imprenta Mundial.
Ochoa Zazueta, Jesus Angel (1975) *El Instituto Linguistico de Verano, A.C.,* Cuadernos de Trabajo, DEAS, Estudios 11, Mexico, D.F: Instituto Nacional de Antropologia y Historia.

Oppenheimer, Evelyn and Porterfield, Bill, (eds.) (1976) *The Book of Dallas*, New York:Doubleday.

Ossio A., Juan M., (ed.) (1973) *Ideologia Mesianica del Mundo Andino*, Lima: Ignacio Prado Pastor.

Palau, Luis (1981) 'The Lord's Chessboard', *In Other Words:*15-11 (WBT)' Summer.

Palomino, Cebero, (ed.) (1980) *El ILV: Un fraude*, Lima: Ediciones Rupa Rupa.

Parreno Ruiz, Tito A. (1975) 'El censo de los Aucas: Encuentro de dos mundos', *Ejercito Nacional* (Quito: Ministerio de Defensa), February:38-42.

Patzelt, Erwin (1976) *Free as the Jaguar*, Quito: Editorial Las Casas.

Paulston, Christina Bratt (1970) 'Algunas notas sobre la ensenanza bilingue del idioma en el Peru', *America Indigena*, January, 30(1):99-106.

Paulston, Rolland G. (1970) 'Maestros como agentes del cambio comunal', *America Indigena*, October, 30(4):929-43.

Pereira F., Luis A. (1981) 'Go forth to every part of the world and make all nations my disciples', in Aaby and Hvalkof:108-19.

Perez Ramirez, Gustavo (1971) *Planas, Un Ano Despues*, Bogota: Editorial America Latina.

Peters, George W. (1975) *El Despertamiento en Indonesia*, Tarrasa, Spain: CLIE.

Phelan, John Leddy (1956) *The Millennial Kingdom of the Franciscans in the New World*, vol. 52, Berkeley: University of California Publications in History.

Pike, Eunice V. (1981) *Ken Pike, Scholars and Christian;* Dallas, SIL.

Pike, Frederick B. (1967) *The Modern History of Peru*, New York: Praeger.

Pike, Kenneth L. (1959) 'Our own tongue wherein we were born', *Bible Translator* (New York), April, 10(2):70-82.

———— (1960) 'Building sympathy', *Practical Anthropology*, November/December, 7(6):250-2.

———— (1961) 'Stimulating and resisting change', *Practical Anthropology*, November/December, 8(6):267-74.

———— (1962) *With Heart and Mind*, Grand Rapids, Michigan: Eerdmans.

———— (1967) *Stir, Change, Create*, Grand Rapids: Eerdmans.

Pike, Kenneth L. and Brend, Ruth M., (eds.) (1977) *The Summer Institute of Linguistics, Its Works and Contributions* (articles date to 1973-4), The Hague: Mouton.

Pittman, Richard (1969) *Elwood Jacobsen*, Grand Forks, North Dakota: SIL.

Quebedeaux, Richard (1979) *I Found It! The story of Bill Bright and the Campus Crusade*, New York: Harper and Row.

Raby, David L. (1974) *Educacion y revolucion social en Mexico*, Mexico, D.F: Sepsetentas.

Razon, Felix and Hensman, Richard (1976) 'The Oppression of the Indigenous Peoples of the Philippines', doc.25, Copenhagen: International Work Group for Indigenous Affairs.

Rembao, Alberto (1942) 'Outlook in Mexico', Outlook Pamphlets on Latin America, New York: Friendship Press.

Reina, Ruben E. (1966) *The Law of the Saints*, New York: Bobbs-Merrill.

Ribeiro, Darcy and Wise, Mary Ruth (1978) 'Los grupos etnicos de la Amazonia Peruana', *Comunidades y Culturas Peruanas* (Lima:ILV, Ministerio de

Educacion), no. 13.

Richardson, Don (1981) 'Who really killed Chet Bitterman?' *Mission Frontier* (Pasadena, California: U.S. Center for World Mission), April 3(4):1,4-7.

Riester, Jurgen (1975) 'Indians of eastern Bolivia: Aspects of their present situation,' doc. 18, Copenhagen: International Work Group for Indigenous Affairs.

Robbins, Christopher (1979) *The Invisible Air Force: The story of the CIA's secret airlines,* London: Macmillan.

Robinson, Scott S. (1975) 'La empresa transnacional misionera', *Suceso (El Correo,* Lima), 7 December (226):8-9.

————— (1981) 'Fulfilling the Mission: North American evangelism in Ecuador', in Aaby and Hvalkof:40-9.

Rossi, Sanna Barlow (1975) *God's City in the Jungle,* Huntington Beach, California: WBT.

Rus, Jan (n.d.) 'Managing Mexico's Indians: The historical context and consequences of *indigenismo*', unpublished paper.

Rus, Jan and Wasserstrom, Robert (1981) 'Evangelization and political control: The SIL in Mexico', in Aaby and Hvalkof:163-72.

Saenz, Moises (1936) *Carapan,* Lima: Imprenta Gil.

Saint, Rachel (1965) 'Ten years later', *The Dayuma Story,* Ethel Emily Wallis: 273-304. New York: Harper and Row (this edition only).

————— (1971) 'Epilogue', in Wallis 1971:214-23 (first appeared in 1960 edition).

Sandeen, Ernest, (1970) *The Roots of Fundamentalism: British and American Millenarianism 1800-1930,* Chicago: University of Chicago.

Santos, Fernando (1980) 'Belaunde y la colonizacion de la Amazonia', *Amazonia Indigena,* October, 1(2):7-18.

Santos Ortiz de Villalba, Juan (1980) *Los Ultimos Huaorani,* Pompeya, Rio Napo: Prefectura Apostolica de Aguarico.

Savage, Roberto C. and Andrade Crespo, Jose (1956) *El Drama del Curaray,* Quito: Editorial Artes Graficas.

Scofield, Cyrus Ingerson (1924) 'The signs of the times . . . . The future state', *Central American Bulletin* (these sermons were originally delivered c.1888), 15 January through 15 November: Nos. 132-7.

Shapiro, Judith R. (1981) 'Ideologies of Catholic missionary practice in a postcolonial era', *Comparative Studies in Society and History,* January, 23(1):130-49.

Sharp, Daniel A., (ed.) (1972) *U.S. Foreign Policy and Peru,* Austin: University of Texas.

Sharp, Nonie (1977) *The Rule of the Sword: The story of West Irian,* Victoria, Australia: Kibble Books.

Siverts, Henning (1969) *Oxchuc,* Mexico, D.F: Instituto Indigenista Interamericano.

————— (1972) 'Tribal survival in the Alto Maranon: The Aguaruna case', doc. 10, Copenhagen: International Work Group for Indigenous Affairs.

————— (1979) 'Jivaro headhunters in a headless time', in Browman and Schwarz:215-24.

Slocum, Marianna C. (1956) 'Cultural changes among the Oxchuc Tzeltals', *Estudios Antropologicos en Homenaje al Dr. Manuel Gamio:* 491-5. Mexico, D.F: Universidad Nacional Autonoma.

Smith, Joseph Burkholder (1976) *Portrait of a Cold Warrior*, New York: G.P. Putnam's Sons.

Smith, Richard Chase (1981) 'The SIL: Ethnocide disguised as a blessing', in Aaby and Hvalkof:120-32.

Sochurek, Howard (1965) 'Americans in action in Viet Nam', *National Geographic* (Washington, D.C.), January, 127(1):38-65.

————— (1968) 'Viet Nam's Montagnards', *National Geographic*, April, 133(4):443-87.

Solnit, Albert J. (1964) 'Bilingual education and community development in the Amazon', *Peruvian Times*, 7 February.

Spain, Mildred W. (1954) *And in Samaria*, Dallas: Banks, Upshaw.

Spann del Solar, Hans (1972) 'Un antiguo problema y un nuevo camino', *Educacion* (Lima), July, 3(9).

Spiller, Maximiliano (1974) *Historia de la Mision Josefina del Napo*, Tena, Ecuador: Mision Josefina.

St. Clair, David (1958) 'A jungle Tower of Babel', *Peruvian Times*, 6 June 6,8,10 and 13 June:6,8.

Steven, Hugh (1974) *It Takes Time to Love*, WBT.

————— (1976) *They Dared to be Different*, Irvine, California: Harvest House.

————— (1978) *To the Ends of the Earth*, Chappaqua, New York: Christian Herald.

————— (1980) *Never Touch a Tiger*, Nashville; Thomas Nelson.

Stipe, Claude E. (1980) 'Anthropologists versus missionaries: The influence of presuppositions' and comments, *Current Anthropology* (Chicago), April, 21(2):165-79.

Stott, John R.W. and Coote, Robert, (eds.) (1980) *Down to Earth: Studies in Christianity and culture*, Grand Rapids, Michigan: Eerdmans.

Suharno, Ignatious and Pike, Kenneth L., (eds.) (1976) *From Baudi to Indonesian: Studies in Linguistics*, Irian Jaya: Cenderawasih University, SIL.

Sullivan, James Lamkin (1970) 'The Impact of Education on Ticuna Indian Culture', Ph.D dissertation, North Texas State University.

SIL-Bolivia (1975) 'Forjando un manana mejor', ILV.

SIL-Brazil (1974) *Relatorio de atividades do Summer Institute of Linguistics*, April, Brasilia.

SIL-Ecuador (1969) 'Entre los Aucas', March, Quito.

————— (1980) *Informe de Actividades 1953-1980*, July, Quito.

SIL-Mexico (1960) *Veinticinco anos del Instituto Linguistico de Verano en Mexico*.

————— (1961) *A Wm. Cameron Townsend en el XXV aniversario del ILV*, January, Mexico, D.F.

SIL-Peru (1955) *Dos Lustros Entre Los Selvicolas*, Lima.

————— (1959) *Los Selvicolas en Marcha*, Lima: Ministerio de Educacion.

————— (1966) *Veinte Anos al Servico del Peru*, Lima: ILV, Universidad de Oklahoma, Ministerio de Educacion Publica.

————— (1975) *Informe General 1971-74*, May, Yarinacocha: ILV.

SIL/WBT (1961) *Reports from the Biennial Conference of WBT and the SIL*, September, Sulphur Springs, Arkansas.

————— (1963) *Who Brought the Word*, Santa Ana, California.

————— (1964) *Biennial Conference Reports of WBT and the SIL,* May 1963, Tahlequah, Oklahoma.

————— (1971) *Biennial Reports of the WBT and the SIL,* May, Mexico D.F.

————— (1972) *Language and Faith,* Santa Ana, California.

Swem, Greg (1979) 'Now you can visit a once-forbidden Auca village', *The Courier-Journal* (Louisville, Kentucky?), 11 November:H19.

Tanner, Louise Bentley (1957) 'The jungle Indians of Peru and the work of the SIL', *Peruvian Times,* 5 and 12 April.

Thompson, Phyllis (1974) *Matched With His Hour,* London. Word Books.

Tippett, A.R. (1972) 'Taking a hard look at the Barbados Declaration', *Evangelical Missions Quarterly* (Wheaton, Illinois), Summer, 8(4):202-3, 209-17.

Townsend, William Cameron (1920) 'The Guatemalan Indian and the San Antonio Mission Station', *Central American Bulletin,* 15 September (112):4-13.

————— (1921) 'One of Guatemala's Indians, his witch doctor and a torn tract', pamphlet, Paris, Texas: Central American Mission,

————— (1922) 'Among Guatemala's Indians', *Christian Herald,* 21 January.

————— (1924-5) 'A great Cakchiquel evangelist', serial, *Central American Bulletin,* 15 July through 15 January:135-8. Republished as 'Cakchiquel evangel evangelist Antonio Bac' in Wallis 1981:39-88.

————— (1925) 'Giving the Indian a chance', *Central American Bulletin,* 15 May (140):11-15.

————— (1928) 'Romish priesthood in Guatemala', *Central American Bulletin,* 15 January (156):8-10.

————— (1936) 'Tolo, the Volcano's Son', serial, *Revelation,* April through October.

————— (1940) *The Truth About Mexico's Oil,* Los Angeles: Inter-American Fellowship.

————— (1948) 'Overcoming barriers to reach Bibleless tribes', *Sunday School Times* (Philadelphia), 24 January:67-8, 31 January:87-8 and 7 February:108-9.

————— (1952) *Lazaro Cardenas, Mexican Democrat,* Ann Arbor: Wahr.

————— (1956) 'Notes on spiritual work for WBT field workers' (written 1948),in *Mexican Branch Handbook,* WBT.

————— (1972) *They Found a Common Language,* New York: Harper and Row.

————— (1981) *Tolo, the Volcano's Son,* (ed.) Hugh and Norma Steven, Huntington Beach, California: WBT.

————— and Pittman, Richard (1975) *Remember All the Way,* Huntington Beach, California; WBT.

Trujillo, Jorge (1981) *Los Obscuros Designios de Dios y del Imperio: El ILV en el Ecuador,* Quito: Centro de Investigaciones y Estudios Socioeconomicos.

Trumbull, Charles Gallaudet (1920) *Life Story of C.I. Scofield,* New York: Oxford University Press.

Turner, Paul R. (1972) *The Highland Chontal,* New York: Holt, Rhinehart & Winston.

————— (1979) 'Religious conversion and community development', *Journal for the Scientific Study of Religion* (Jamaica, New York), 18(3):252-60.

Tuveson, Ernest Lee (1968) *Redeemer Nation,* Chicago: University of Chicago.

U.S. Agency for International Development (1978) *Congressional Present-ation,* Fiscal Year 1979, Annex A, in American Statistics Index 78: 7204-16.

University of Antioquia (1976) 'El Instituto Linguistico de Verano', anthology, *Boletin de Antropologia* (Medellin), 4(15).

Uribe T., Carlos A. (1980) 'La antropologia en Colombia', *America Indigena,* April/June, 40(2):281-308.

Varese, Stefano (1972a) 'Inter-ethnic relations in the selva of Peru', in Dostal: 115-39.

———— (1972b) 'The forest Indians in the present political situation of Peru', doc. 8, Copenhagen: International Work Group for Indigenous Affairs.

———— (1975) 'Milenarismo, revolucion y conciencia de clase', *Educacion,* 6(13):45-48.

———— (1976a) 'Carta abierta al triunfalismo facil', 30 January:11 and 31 January:10, and 'Despues del ILV que?' 3 February *El Correo* (Lima):11.

———— (1976b) 'La conquista continua', *Postdata* (Lima), January/February.

Varese, Stefano, et al (1970) *Estudio sondeo de seis comunidades del Alto Maranon,* Serie de Estudios 1, Lima: Division de Comunidades Nativas de la Selva, Direccion de Comunidades Campesinas, Ministerio de Agricultura.

Vargas Llosa, Mario (1965) *La Casa Verde,* Barcelona: Seix Barral.

———— (1971) *Historia Secreta de Una Novela,* Lima: Cuadernos Marginales.

Vickers, William T. (1981) 'The Jesuits and SIL: External policies for Ecuador's Tucanoans through three centuries', in Aaby and Hvalkof:50-61.

Wallis, Ethel Emily (1956) *He Purposeth a Crop* (1st edition 1955), Glendale, California: WBT.

———— (1965) *Tariri: My Story,* New York: Harper and Row.

———— (1971) *The Dayuma Story* (1st edition 1960), Old Tappan, New Jersey: Spire.

———— (1973) *Aucas Downriver: Dayuma's story today,* New York: Harper and Row.

———— (ed.) (1981) *The Cakchiquel Album,* Costa Mesa, California: Gift Publications.

Wallis, Ethel E. and Bennett, Mary A. (1966) *Two Thousand Tongues to Go* (1st edition 1959), London: Hodder and Stoughton.

Wares, Alan C. (1974) *Bibliography of the SIL 1935-72,* (7th edition) Hunting-ton Beach, California: SIL.

———— (1979) *Bibliography of the SIL,* vol. 1:1935-75 (vol. 2 to begin with 1976), 8th edition.

Warren, Kay (1978) *The Symbolism of Subordination: Indian identity in a Guatemalan town,* Austin: University of Texas.

Wasserstrom, Robert (1975) 'Revolution in Guatemala: Peasants and politics under the Arbenz government', *Comparative Studies in Society and History,* October, 17(4):443-78.

Weber, Timothy P. (1979) *Living in the Shadow of the Second Coming: American Premillennialism 1875-1925,* New York: Oxford University Press.

Weyl, Nathaniel and Sylvia (1939) *The Reconquest of Mexico,* London:

Oxford University Press.

Whitten, Jr., Norman E. (1976) 'Ecuadorian ethnocide and indigenous ethno-genesis', doc. 23, Copenhagen: International Work Group for Indigenous Affairs.

————— (ed.) (1981) *Cultural Transformations and Ethnicity in Modern Ecuador* Urbana: University of Illinois.

Willoughby, William F. (1976) 'David Farah on CIA using missionaries', *Washington Star.News,* 8 January:A1, B8.

Wilson, Bryan (1970) *Religious Sects,* London: Weidenfeld and Nicolson.

————— (1975) *Magic and the Millennium,* St. Albans: Paladin.

Wilson, Samuel, (ed.) (1980) *Mission Handbook: North American Protestant ministries overseas,* (12th edition) Monrovia, California: Missions Advanced Research and Communication Center.

Wistrand, Lila (1968) 'Desorganizacion y revitalizavion de los Cashibo', *America Indigena,* July, 28(3):611-18.

—————(1970) 'Bilingual jungle school', *Americas* (Washington, D.C: Organization of American States), August, 22(8):2-8.

World Radio Missionary Fellowship (1976) 'The Auca Story: Friendship on Friday, glory on Sunday, praise forever', tape cassette, Opa Locka, Florida.

Wright, Robin Michael (1981a) 'History and Religion of the Baniwa Peoples of the Upper Rio Negro Valley', Ph.D dissertation, Stanford University.

————— (ed.) (1981b) 'The New Tribes Mission in Amazonia', *ARC Bulletin* (Boston: Anthropology Resource Center), December, (9).

Wycliffe Bible Translators (1978) *Prayer Directory,* Huntington Beach, California.

————— (1979) ibid.

————— (1981) ibid.

Yost, James A. (1979) 'El desarrollo comunitario y la supervivencia etnica: El caso de los Huaorani', Cuadernos Etnolinguisticos, (6), Quito: ILV.

————— (1981) 'Twenty years of contact': the mechanisms of change in Huao ('Auca') culture', in Whitten 1981:677-704.

Index

Acatenango, Guatemala 37, 39
acculturation 70, 161, 224–5
Africa 6, 22, 31, 108, 142, 198, 218, 237, 241, 243–8, 264
Aguacatec Maya 51, 53–5
alcoholism 26, 31–5, 39–41, 44, 52, 58, 125, 146, 148, 180, 212, 214, 218, 223, 299
alienation 15, 142–3, 203, 215, 229
Alliance for Progress 4, 8, 63, 82, 138, 144, 167
alliances 2–3, 10, 15, 75, 118, 133, 142, 202, 206
Amazon Jungle 4, 63, 73, 84, 98–138, 141–50, 152–62, 173–81, 202, 207–13, 216–23, 261, 269–72, 278–315
Andes Mountains 3, 99, 102, 144, 150, 166, 179, 198, 211, 213–5, 217–9, 221, 283, 292
anthropologists (anthropology) 3, 8, 11, 16–17, 70, 84, 120, 124, 127–9, 141, 145, 156–7, 159–60, 166, 169, 178, 182–3, 185, 199, 202, 212, 215–16, 218, 220–1, 224, 226, 228, 231–2, 255, 297–9, 302–6, 311, 314
anti-clericalism 4, 45, 62–3, 66–7, 69, 118
Antigua, Guatemala 32–3, 38–9
anti-imperialism (ists) 3, 11, 15, 17, 65, 70–1, 140–3, 147, 151–2, 165, 170, 173, 175, 178–85, 189, 198–200, 203, 207–8, 213–16, 222–4, 226–31, 240, 298, 313
Arajuno, Ecuador 284–5, 288
Argentina 248
Asia (ns) 6, 22, 29, 63, 80, 86–7, 241–2, 246, 248–9, 276
Auca, see Indians: Huaorani
Australia(ns) 5, 87, 245, 249
Ayacucho, Peru 151

Bagabag, Philippines 93

Bangladesh 247–8
Baptists 78, 132, 263
Barbados Declaration 141–2; II meeting 250
Bellavista, Peru 148–9
Beni Jungle 217–18
Bible institutes 27, 46, 107, 114, 125, 192, 208, 269, 309
Bible translation 4, 6, 12, 14, 22–3, 36, 42–3, 63–4, 66, 75–6, 86, 101, 121, 126, 129, 171, 177, 237–9, 249–50, 252–3, 258, 289
bilingual education 6, 37, 52, 54, 66, 68–9, 88, 99–102, 108–9, 112, 114–26, 128–30, 133, 144–8, 151–4, 158–61, 172, 175, 184, 190–1, 207–12, 214–21, 223, 225, 241, 245, 249, 251, 292; see also literacy work
Bitterman, Chester Allen III, 1–3, 83, 165, 191–4, 199, 216, 263, 273
Bolivia (n) 2, 99, 138, 140, 183, 185, 198, 217–19, 224, 230
Bolsheviks (ism) 19, 42, 48, 57, 63, 74–5
Borneo 245, 247
Brazil 2, 11, 99, 117, 132, 138, 140, 170–1, 174, 198, 201, 204, 219–22, 230, 248, 269
Britain 5, 7, 87, 102–3, 167, 237, 242–3, 247, 281, 283
Brown & Root Company 118, 261
Bukidnon people 92

Caballococha, Peru 131, 148
Cakchiquel Maya 10, 18, 32–43, 49–50, 53, 66, 69, 73, 126, 250, 256
California, U.S.A. 5, 28–9, 38–9, 46–7, 50, 64–5, 78, 80, 103, 107–8, 110, 112, 118, 240, 259–62
Cambodia 91, 198, 247
Camp Wycliffe 63, 67, 73–8, 80–1, 250
Canada (Canadians) 5, 19, 27, 53, 80, 87,

210; International Development Agency 215, 245

Candoshi 210; *see* Indians, Shapra

Cardenas, Lazaro 62–3, 65–71, 74–5, 77, 80, 87, 223, 230, 241

cargo systems 32–6, 48, 52–4

Catholic Church (clergy) 3, 4, 8, 10, 18, 31–2, 39–41, 53, 57, 62, 66–7, 74, 99, 103–4, 107, 109–20, 131, 140–4, 166–70, 172, 193, 201, 205–6, 213, 216–17, 228, 238; Catholicism (Catholics) 24, 27, 31–5, 40, 47, 52–5, 57, 63, 69, 152, 210, 241, 269–71; *see also* missionaries, Catholic

Catholic University of Ecuador 215, 298–9

cattle 2, 52, 56, 109, 114–15, 117, 124, 126, 148, 169, 171–2, 218, 302

Cauca, Colombia 172–3, 183

Central American Mission 19, 22, 26–7, 29, 31–42, 44–5, 49, 55

Central Intelligence Agency (CIA), *see* U.S. Government

Chamula, Mexico 52–3, 61

Charismatic Renewal 129, 240–1, 268–72

Charlotte, North Carolina 6, 167, 260

Chiapas, Mexico 51–3, 223–4

chicha beer 171, 174, 180, 232; see *masato*

Chile 230, 248

Chimaltenango, Guatemala 32, 37

Chimborazo, Ecuador 213–6

China (Chinese) 10, 27, 80, 90, 238, 247–9, 262, 283

Chol Maya 50–2

Chorti Maya 50

Christian and Missionary Alliance 88, 91, 108, 173, 213, 301

Christian businessmen 27, 29, 38, 46–7, 72, 77, 107–8, 112, 260–2

church-state separation 4–5, 75, 114, 223, 228–9

Coca, Ecuador 292–4, 309, 312

coca(ine) 128, 147, 165–6, 174, 176, 188, 192–3, 217–18, 232, 262

coffee 22, 27, 31, 35, 38, 52, 56, 101, 124

Cold War 7, 70, 83, 87, 89

Colombia(n) 1, 2, 8, 11, 81–4, 99, 138, 142–3, 165–94, 168–9, 172, 173, 177–9, 180–5, 188–9, 191–3, 198, 200–1, 203–4, 218, 220, 224, 231–2, 238, 241, 248, 251, 255, 262–3, 269, 271

colonists (colonization) 26, 40–1, 88, 92–4, 98–102, 108, 114–15, 117–18, 124, 126, 128–9, 138, 143–5, 153–4, 155–6, 160–1, 165–6, 169–73, 188–91, 207–13, 218, 220, 222, 246, 279, 293, 298

Colta, Ecuador 214

Comalapa, Guatemala 33–4, 57

communists (communism) 3, 8, 9, 19, 22, 24, 42–6, 48–51, 56, 62–3, 65, 75, 81–2, 86–92, 104, 108, 114, 131, 138, 140–1, 148, 151, 156, 158, 160, 162, 167, 169, 172–3, 191, 198–9, 201, 206–7, 216, 247, 262, 272; parties 19, 46, 216, 228, 245

community development 52, 100, 117, 124–5, 146–8, 161, 168, 177, 179, 212–13, 219

community labour 127, 146–8, 160

compadrazgo 305, 313–15

concientizacion 175–6, 180, 231

Cononaco River 292, 295, 311, 313

conspiracy theory 16, 165, 178, 181–3, 185, 189, 198–200, 206–7, 215, 220, 222–3, 226–7, 255, 293–4, 298

co-operatives 2, 8, 57, 116–17, 123, 146, 148, 170, 172, 190

corporations 2, 9, 14, 57, 81, 92–3, 98, 102–3, 107–8, 114–15, 117–18, 132, 143, 145, 152, 156, 211, 213, 261, 279, 281–2, 291–2, 297, 301

counter-insurgency 8, 14, 50, 57–8, 83, 86–93, 138, 144, 150–1, 154, 167, 169–70, 199, 225

Cowan, George 9, 12–13, 16, 18, 77, 121, 179, 239

criollos 31, 115, 146, 208

Cuba 3, 70, 82, 138, 140–1, 167, 193, 214

Cuiaba, Brazil 221

Cult of the Cross 131, 148, 150

Cushillococha, Peru 131–2, 146–50, 202, 271

Dallas, Texas 6, 26, 67, 229, 239, 260–1

Dani people 246, 261

Dawa 301, 305, 309

Dayuma 279, 281, 283–91, 293, 295, 297, 299, 302–5, 307–14

Dayuno, Ecuador 301–5, 313, 315

dependency 10, 15, 128, 131, 142, 145–6, 149, 155, 208, 218, 222, 228, 293, 304–5, 307–8, 313, 315; theory 140–1

drug trade 2, 14, 83–4, 165–6, 172, 174, 192–3, 217–18, 241, 247, 262

Dutch 174, 246, 263, 281

Easter Island, Chile 248

ecological issues 101, 114, 123–5, 131, 188, 210, 211, 212, 215–16, 287, 298–300, 302, 303, 311–12

Ecuador(ian) 2, 11, 82, 99, 138, 142, 145, 151, 159, 198–9, 201, 211–16, 262, 271, 273, 278–315

ecumenism 7–8, 111–13, 141–4, 168, 216, 271
elites 52, 120–4, 146–50, 160, 201, 212
Elliot, Elisabeth 279, 284–5, 288–91, 305, 315
El Salvador 19, 22, 24, 36, 42, 44–5, 48, 193, 199, 262
epidemic disease 16, 101, 156, 174, 218, 282, 290, 296–7, 314–15
ethnic identity 16, 37–8, 129, 149, 153, 156, 161, 174, 201, 214, 230–1, 281, 304, 315
ethnocide 3, 14, 37, 100, 115–16, 123, 127, 129, 141, 157, 202, 314
Europe(ans) 5, 7, 27, 40, 98, 131, 150, 237, 243, 301, 308

faith missions 12–13, 71–9, 102, 128, 130, 155, 211, 249–52, 259–73
Fascism(ists) 46, 66, 74, 103
fincas 39–45, 47–8, 53; *see also* plantations
First International Bancshares, Inc. 261
folk healers 32–5, 59, 130–1, 146, 174, 188, 189, 216, 255, *see also* shamans
Formosa 86
Fort Bragg, North Carolina 167
France (French) 87–8, 251
Free Papua Movement 246
French Polynesia 245
Friends of SIL committee 107–8, 117, 144
Fundamentalism (Fundamentalists) 3, 4, 16, 26–8, 46, 63–4, 69, 71–2, 78, 81, 113, 120, 129, 142, 147, 158, 160, 238, 251, 258, 262–3, 267, 309

Ganso Azul Petroleum Company 103, 109, 114
Germany (Germans) 40, 42, 103, 222, 298–300, 302–3, 314
Gikita 290, 305, 309
gold 93, 123, 156–7, 181, 220
Good Neighbour Policy 62–3, 70, 80, 132
Gospel Missionary Union 211, 213–14, 282
Graham, Billy 114, 260, 273, 287, 308
Great Commission 1, 64, 86, 142, 237, 240, 250, 293
Great Depression 41, 46, 72–3, 103, 260
Great Tribulation 25–6, 28–30, 56
Green Berets *see* U.S. Special Forces
gringos 14–15, 70, 172, 181, 189
Guatemala(n) 2, 3, 19, 22–4, 28–44, 47–51, 53–8, 73, 130, 138, 151, 217, 260, 262, 268
guerrillas 1, 2, 50, 57–8, 81, 83, 87–94, 99, 140, 144, 147, 150–1, 165–6, 169–70, 172–3, 182–3, 190–3, 199, 206, 225
Guyana 184

haciendas 11, 14, 144, 154, 211, 265, 279, 283, 286, 289, 303
Halliburton, Inc. 261
hallucinogens 174–5, 271
Halmahera, Indonesia 245
head-hunting 132–3, 262
Hefley, James and Marti 38–9, 42, 50, 62, 67–8, 70–1, 74–7, 89–90, 103, 108, 110, 112–13, 116, 133, 151, 238
Helio-Courier Aircraft Co. (Airplanes) 84–5, 150, 287, 292
hide trade 117, 133, 156, 212
Hinduism (Hindus) 242, 245, 247–8
Hmong Montagnards 10, 218
Honduras 2, 36, 49
Huanuco, Peru 125, 258

Igorot people 93
imperialism 9–10, 14–15, 17, 22, 70–1, 81, 140, 142–3, 166, 173, 183, 207–8, 212, 228–9, 262
India 237–8, 242, 247–8
Indians: Achual (Atshuar) 130, 282; Aguaruna 117–18, 130, 159–62, 207–8, 270; Amahuaca 123; Amarakaeri 123, 156–7; Amuesha 120, 128–9, 131, 157, 207, 209; Arhuaco 180, 188–91, 251; Aymara 218; Aztec 68; Baniwa 171, 174; Bayano Cuna 222; Bororo 222; Campa 101, 122–4, 131, 140, 150, 152–4, 158, 207; Camsa 179–80; Carapana 176; Carijona 192; Cashibo 126; Cashinahua 101; Catio 179; Chacobo 218; Cocoma 146; Cofan 212, 292; Cogui 188–9, 191; Comanche 73; Conibo 210; Coriguaje 83; Cuaquier 179; Cubeo 171, 174–7; Cuiva 171, 255; Curipaco 170–1; Desano 175, 177; Guahibo 142, 169–72, 256; Guambiano 173, 256; Guanano 175; Guayabero 171; Guaymi 222–3; Huaorani 142, 213, 272, 278–315; Huitoto 207; Inga 255; Jupda-Macu 175–6; Machiguenga 101, 131, 134, 145, 208; Malayo 188–9, 191; Mapuche 248; Mayoruna *see* Matses; Matlatzinca 229; Matses 155; Mazahua 229; Mixteco 237; Otomi 229; Paez 172–3, 256; Piapoco 171; Pipil 19, 24, 42, 44–5; Piratapuyo 175–6; Piro 100, 125–6, 131–2, 284; Puinave 171; Quechua 23–4, 99, 102, 140, 144,

150–2, 203, 207, 210, 218, 248, 258 *see* Quichua; Saliva 171; Secoya 212–13, 271, 292; Shapra 132–3, 284; Shipibo 126, 131, 137, 210; Shuar (Federation) 159, 211, 214, 216, 282, 298; Siona 180, 193, 212–13, 292; Sioux 73; Siriono 218; Ticuna 100, 123, 131–2, 146–50, 271; Tlahuica 229; Tucano 175–6; Tunebo 179; Tuyuca 175–6; Zapotec 299
indigenismo 63, 66, 68, 141, 167, 225, 229–30
indigenists 2, 10, 17, 63, 65–6, 68–71, 104, 107, 116, 118–20, 145, 166–7, 169, 178–9, 191, 201, 205, 218, 221, 223–31
indigenous civil rights organizing 2, 11, 15–17, 24, 52–5, 57, 92–3, 98, 102, 141, 153–4, 161, 166, 169, 180–1, 189–91, 201, 207, 211, 213–16, 218–22, 225–6, 228–32, 250
indigenous organizations 2, 24, 32, 37, 53–5, 57, 153–4, 161–2, 166, 169–73, 176–7, 180–1, 190–1, 201, 207, 211, 213–16, 220–2, 225–6, 230–2, 246, 250, 298
indigenous rebellions 3, 19, 24, 42–5, 50, 57–8, 62, 66, 88, 92–3, 131, 150, 159, 169–70, 172, 221, 225, 242, 246–7
individualism 8, 122, 160, 214
Indonesia 87, 91, 243, 245–6, 248, 261, 276
Institutional Revolutionary Party (PRI) 62, 223–5, 228
integration 15–16, 63, 99, 119, 140, 143, 146, 149, 167, 201, 215, 220–1
Inter-American(ism) 10, 64, 68, 70, 80–2, 84, 103–4, 109, 138, 167, 217, 219, 230–1
Interdenominational Foreign Missions Association (IFMA) 112, 114, 116
internal colonialism 10–11, 14–16, 141–2, 199, 208–9, 211–13, 276
International Congress of Americanists 6, 90, 103, 145, 152, 157, 239–40, 248, 254, 261–2
Iran 241, 248
Islam 199, 238, 243–8; Muslims 87, 92–3, 213
Ismarth de Araujo Oliveira, General 220
isolationism 16, 145, 171, 212, 299
Italians 103, 282–3, 286
Ixil Maya 58
Ixmiquilpan, Mexico 223

Japan(ese) 87, 103, 248
Jehovah's Witnesses 26, 213, 226
Juayua, El Salvador 19, 44
Judgement Day 23, 30, 56
Jungle Aviation and Radio Service (JAARS) 6, 81, 84–5, 92–3, 104, 107–9, 111–13, 115, 117, 132, 145–6, 150, 153, 155, 167, 170, 175, 199–200, 240, 258, 260, 265, 269, 272, 286, 294–6, 312
Jungle Camp 223, 227, 229, 248, 264

Kekchi Maya 42
Keswick sanctification 28, 72
kidnappings 93, 192
Korea (Translation Mission) 81, 240, 248–9

Lacandon Forest 52, 223, 227
ladinoization 37–8, 59; *Ladinos* 31–4, 36–41, 45, 48, 52–7
Lago Agrio, Ecuador 279, 292
land rights 2, 14, 25–6, 31, 34, 40–4, 51–2, 56–7, 66, 87–8, 92–3, 102, 117, 124, 126, 144, 146, 155, 157, 160–1, 165–6, 169–73, 188–9, 208–9, 213–15, 222, 224–5, 229, 232, 279, 291–300, 303–4, 313
language informants 6, 19, 43, 99–100, 120–2, 179–80, 188–9, 192, 239, 243, 250, 257, 265, 284–8
Laos 10, 88, 218, 247
Las Pacayas, Guatemala 58
Latacunga, Ecuador 213
Legters, Leonard Livingston 73, 76–8, 95, 98
Limoncocha, Ecuador 215, 279, 283, 292, 295, 302, 304, 307, 309, 312
linguistic approach 6, 10–11, 18, 36–9, 42, 63, 68–9, 99–100, 116, 120, 123, 126, 249–50, 263; – policies, national 182, 187, 215, 226–8, 249–50, 257
linguists 11, 68–70, 144–5, 166–9, 178, 182, 187, 205, 215, 221, 223, 228, 231, 249–58
literacy work 4, 10, 14, 36, 43, 50, 55, 57, 77, 174, 177, 190–1, 201, 214, 237, 254–7, 302–3, 305; *see also* bilingual education
llanos, Colombian 166, 168, 182, 184, 190, 192
Lomalinda, Colombia 83, 168–9, 177–83, 186–9, 192
lumber industry 92, 109, 114–15, 117, 126, 147, 154, 181, 210, 298
Lutherans (Bible Translators) 238, 240
Luzon, Philippines 93–4

M-19 guerrillas 192-3
McCarthyism 7, 208, 262
Maengamo 285, 287-8, 305
magic 32, 34-5, 129-31, 133, 170, 268,
   270-1, 297
Malaysia 192, 241, 247
malocas, see communal houses
Mam Maya 38, 43
Manaus, Brazil 221
Maniba, *see* Indians, Baniwa
Manu National Park, Peru 145
Maranao people 85
Maranon River 102, 117-18, 160, 203, 271
Marginal Jungle Highway 144
marijuana 83, 147, 165, 188, 192-3, 218
martyr(s)(dom) 1, 8, 22, 24, 45-6, 51-3,
   56, 89-91, 193-4, 263, 273, 278-85,
   287, 289-91, 297, 305-7, 310-11
Marxism(ists) 3, 11, 67, 86, 91, 140, 167,
   183, 199, 205-6, 225, 245
masato beer 128-9, 160, 212; see also
   chicha
Maya 19, 22, 24, 77, 250, 257; *see also*
   Aguacatec; Cakchiquel, Chol, Chorti,
   Ixil, Kekchi, Mam, Pocomam, Quiche,
   Tzeltal, Tzotzil, Tzutujil, Uspanteco
   and Protestants
medical work 6, 14-15, 99, 129-30, 133,
   150, 154-6, 161, 174, 177, 188-91,
   200, 216, 218-19, 221, 226, 304;
   medicine, Western 10, 38, 51, 101,
   130, 133, 159, 212-13, 315
Mendoza, Juan 109, 138, 140, 205
Meo, *see* Hmong
Metropolitana Tours of Quito 309, 312
Mexican Indian 22, 42, 47, 65, 67-9, 74,
   224-31
Mexic(o)(an) 2, 8, 11, 22, 42-4, 46-7,
   51-3, 56, 62-77, 80, 86, 92, 99, 107,
   109, 111, 127, 132, 140, 198, 200-1,
   223, 226, 228-31, 237-8, 240, 248,
   251, 255-7, 259, 265, 272-3; Mexico
   City 67-8, 103, 107, 223, 226, 241
military, the 2-4, 8-11, 14-15, 19, 41,
   43-5, 50, 53, 55, 57-8, 62, 67, 69,
   80-5, 87-93, 99, 103-9, 111, 116-19,
   124, 133, 138-40, 142-4, 150-5, 165-
   74, 181-3, 185, 188, 191-3, 198-200,
   203-7, 210-11, 216-22, 244-7, 278, 285,
   292-4, 297, 300-1, 308, 311-13
Millenarians(ism) 26-8, 46, 72, 91, 240
millennialism 1, 22-8, 30, 58, 91, 131-3,
   146-50, 160, 170-4, 195, 237-8, 240-1,
   273; pre- 26-30, 56, 147, 273; post-25-6
Mindanao, Philippines 92-4
minerals 14, 181-2, 199, 220, 227, 282

Mintaka 285, 287-8, 305
Miro Quesada, Francisco 151, 203, 205-6
missionaries, Catholic 1, 2, 7, 10-11, 18,
   35-6, 53-4, 57, 73, 99, 104, 109-13,
   115-20, 123, 131, 133-4, 141-2,
   156-7, 159-62, 168-81, 189-91, 208-
   11, 214, 219-21, 270-2, 282-3, 292,
   294-5, 311
Mitla, Oaxaca 223
Montagnards 10, 84, 88-91, 96, 218, 240,
   246
Montgomery, Lawrence J. 85, 104, 285,
   287
Moody Bible Institute and Memorial Church
   27, 38, 46, 107
Morales Bermudez, Francisco 203, 206-9
Mormons 7, 26, 213, 226
Moro National Liberation Front 92-3
Morote Best, Efrain 116-20, 146, 148, 151,
   157, 159, 161, 257
music 128, 174

Nahuala, Guatemala 40
Nahuizalco, El Salvador 45
Nampa 288, 305-7
Napo River 210, 282, 292-3, 295, 301-2,
   313
Nasuli, Philippines 92
nationalism(ists) 2-4, 10-11, 15, 17, 25,
   62-3, 80, 115, 118-19, 138, 140, 142,
   144-6, 149-50, 178, 182, 198, 211, 213,
   215-16, 218, 226-9, 238, 242;
   indigenous 3, 15, 201, 225, 257
nationalization 11, 62, 69-70, 115, 119-20,
   144, 178-9, 182-4, 187, 190, 205-9, 215-
   16, 228-9, 238-9, 242-6, 248-50
native writer workshops 213, 255, 257
Nazareth, Peru 161
Nepal 198, 238, 242-3, 247
New Caledonia 245
New Hebrides 245
New People's Army (NPA) 92-93
New Testament dedications 41-2, 94, 125,
   129, 132, 152-3, 210, 258
New Tribes Mission 16, 169-72, 174, 176,
   248
Nicaragua 9, 36, 248, 262
Nimonga 300, 306
North American Congress on Latin America
   (NACLA) 142, 170, 182, 194

Oaxaca, Mexico 224
oil (companies) 14, 30, 46, 62-3, 65, 70-1,
   75, 100, 102-3, 107-9, 114, 117-18,
   142, 145, 147, 155-7, 169, 179, 181,
   198, 203, 211-13, 218, 223, 225-7,

229, 244, 246, 260, 278-9, 281-2, 286, 291-3, 295-302, 305, 309-11, 313
Oncaye 294-6
Operation Auca 278-9, 282-5
Organization of American States (OAS) 166, 193, 230
Organization of Petroleum Exporting Countries (OPEC) 211, 279
Oxchuc, Mexico 52

pacification 24, 142, 285-9, 291-7
Padilla, Sam 281, 286, 293, 297-300, 306-7, 309-15
Pakistan 247
Palm Beach 278, 285-7, 290, 298-300, 305-7, 310-11
Panajachel, Guatemala 38, 43, 66
Panama 2, 11, 198-9, 201, 222-3
Papua New Guinea 87, 92, 223, 243-5, 269
patronage battles 3, 10-11, 15-16, 39, 98-101, 116-18, 126, 142, 145, 159, 170-81, 188-91, 201, 211-16, 224-7, 257, 308-14
patronatos 144, 223-4
patrones 10, 29-30, 48, 98-101, 116-18, 121, 123-5, 131-3, 146, 148, 150, 155-9, 174-5, 178, 202, 207-8, 282, 286-7
Patzelt, Erwin 298-301, 306, 308-9
Patzun, Guatemala 33-4, 38-9, 42-3, 49-50
peasant leagues 48-9, 55
Pentecostals 26, 28, 72, 78, 129, 149, 213, 238, 240, 243, 268-72
peonage 29-31, 33-4, 36, 39-42, 44, 55, 98-101, 218, 284, 286, 300, 303
Peru(vian) 2, 9-12, 15, 49, 70, 75, 78, 80-1, 84-5, 98-134, 137-8, 140, 143-62, 166-8, 198, 200-11, 217, 224, 241, 248, 250-2, 256-8, 264-5, 268-72, 281, 284
Philippines 49, 63, 85-7, 92-4, 97, 99, 198, 243, 245-6, 269
Pike, Kenneth 18, 77, 95, 97, 103, 127, 138, 219, 242, 248-9, 251-4, 256, 258, 287, 307
Pioneer Mission Agency 63, 67, 73-4, 76-8, 95, 240, 281, 290
plantations 19, 30-1, 33-4, 36, 51, 55-6, 59, 144, 148, 213; see also *fincas*
Planas, Colombia 142, 169-70, 173
Pocomam Maya 48
Point Four Program 63, 82, 104, 108
political socialization 6, 8, 99, 118-20, 144, 201
polygamy 93, 100, 120, 211-12, 291, 296

population, concentration of 98-102, 117, 122-5, 130-1, 141-3, 145-6, 148, 155-6, 158, 212, 291-305, 313, 315-16
prayer 5, 13, 72, 130, 133, 192, 194, 198, 228, 259, 266, 268
Presbyterians 24, 28, 37, 66, 72-3, 78, 103, 263, 269
protectionism 15, 219, 221, 281, 299, 303
Protectorate, Huao 298-301, 303-5, 311-13, 316
Protestant Ethic 34-5, 40-1, 52, 124-5, 211, 214
Protestants 1, 3, 7-9, 22, 24-30, 46-7, 56, 62, 66, 69, 71-2, 88, 100, 112-14, 120-4, 128-9, 131-3, 143, 146-52, 156, 159-61, 166, 168-9, 170-4, 176, 187, 191, 193, 212-14, 216, 221-2, 238-9, 250, 259-63, 271, 289-90
Pucallpa, Peru 99, 108-9, 115, 121, 124, 126, 137, 208, 269-70
Puerto Lleras, Colombia 168, 183, 187
Putumayo, Colombia 179-80

Quaker Oats Co. 46, 107
Quempiri, Peru 101, 122-3, 153
Quezaltenango, Guatemala 42, 44
Quiche Maya 30, 35, 37-8, 40, 43-4, 50, 59
Quichua: Highland 213-15; Lowland 211, 278-9, 282-6, 288-9, 292-3, 295-6, 300-5, 309-10, 313, 315
Quito, Ecuador 215, 287, 300, 302, 308-10, 312

racism 15-16, 36-9, 115, 121, 212, 238
Regional Indian Council of the Cauca (CRIC) 169, 172-3, 176, 180-1, 183, 232; Vaupes (CRIVA) 176-7
religious freedom 13, 40-1, 52, 62, 66, 86, 104, 178, 213, 216
reservations 26, 93, 155, 172-3, 212, 219, 221-2, 279, 292; see also Protectorate
revivals 25, 27-8, 88, 146, 149, 174, 214
Ridge Huaorani 297-300, 304, 308, 310-15
roads 31, 57, 98, 100, 114, 118, 129, 143-4, 153, 155, 159-60, 162, 173-4, 179, 212, 214, 219-20, 279, 282, 292, 298
Robinson Bible Institute 38, 44, 49, 66
rubber boom (industry) 98, 101-2, 117, 131, 155, 173, 175, 178, 208, 278, 281, 286
Russia(ns) 19, 24, 42-4, 48, 56, 75, 80

Sabah, Malaysia 247
Saint, Nate 282-5, 305-7; Rachel 134, 262, 279, 281, 283-312, 314; saints, Mayan 24, 32-5, 40

San Antonio Aguas Calientes, Guatemala
32–9, 43–4
San Pedro La Laguna, Guatemala 48–9
Santa Catarina Barahona, Guatemala 32–3,
36, 38
Santa Maria de Nieva, Peru 117–18
Satan(ization) 1, 3, 7, 9, 13, 24–5, 39,
42–4, 73, 83, 89, 111, 125, 129–31,
138, 142, 156, 174, 176, 181, 185–6,
190–1, 232, 240–1, 255, 267–8, 270,
272
Scofield, Cyrus Ingerson 26–9, 47, 56, 72,
91, 268
Second Coming of Christ 1, 22–3, 25–6,
91, 132, 273
sects 12, 14–15, 28, 184–5, 187, 203, 213,
257
sedentarization 98–102, 122–3, 160, 255;
see also population concentration
self-determination 16, 128, 141, 158, 161,
176
Sepa, Peru 107, 125
Seventh Day Adventists 26, 109, 126, 226
shamanism 34, 126, 128–31, 133, 156,
174, 181, 212; *see also* folk healers,
magic, witchcraft
Shandia, Ecuador 283, 285
Shell Mera, Ecuador 282–3, 294
Sierra Macarena, Colombia 181, 183
Sierra Nevada de Santa Marta, Colombia
184, 188–91, 251
Socialism 25–6, 28, 30, 66; Socialist
Education Movement 62, 67
Solomon Islands 245
Southeast Asia 65, 80, 84
Soviet Union 4, 7, 16, 48, 66, 80, 138,
214, 216, 229, 238, 241–2, 244–5,
248–9, 269
Spain (Spanish) 22, 24, 103, 110, 131,
273, 282
state expansion 6, 15–16, 98, 201, 208–9,
216
sterilization 14, 180, 189, 215, 223
Sulawesi, Indonesia 245–6
Sulu Islands 92–3
Summer Institute of Linguistics (SIL):
the 'alternative' 13, 16, 127, 157–8,
160, 188; attitude toward the state 4,
9–10, 13, 41, 63–4, 217; attitude toward
indigenous languages and cultures 16,
37, 52, 100, 115, 123, 125–30, 157–8,
160–1, 173, 185, 188, 216, 227, 252,
256, 258–9, 289, 299; bases 6, 99–100,
238, 258, 263–72 *see* Limoncocha,
Lomalinda, Yarinacocha; bibliographies
249–51; contracts, state and university

2, 4, 10–11, 13, 83, 85, 87–8, 92, 99,
103–4, 114, 144–5, 167–8, 179, 182–4,
203, 210, 215–16, 218–20, 222, 229,
241–4, 246–7, 272; dual identity 3–6,
11–14, 16–17, 62–79, 103–4, 107,
109–14, 116–20, 157, 167–9, 182, 186,
199–200, 227, 242–3, 249, 283;
evangelism, method of 6, 99–101,
120–2; founding 3–6, 62–78; non-
ecclesiastical claim 75–6, 111, 113–14,
125, 151, 156, 168; non-missionary
claim 4–5, 11, 78–9, 110–12, 168,
238, 283; non-political claim 4, 13, 75,
89, 92, 151; non-sectarian claim 75,
110–11, 238, 241, 263; statistics 1, 2,
5–6, 11, 98, 102, 194; summer schools
6, 78, 168, 192, 250–1, 264, 284
Survival International 15, 189, 210, 220

tagmemics 251–2, 256, 258
Tamazunchale, Mexico 73
Tboli people 93–4
Terminal City, Ecuador 284–5, 288
Tetelcingo, Mexico 66, 68–9, 74, 119
Thailand 247
theology of liberation 8, 141, 173, 175,
271–2
Tibet 80, 98, 249
Tigueno 288–305, 308–11, 313
Tlalpan, Mexico 223
Tona 297, 299, 302
tourism 16, 35, 188–90, 281, 301–2,
309–16
Tournavista, Peru 114–15, 125, 131
Townsend: Elaine Mielke 112, 241, 266,
269; Elvira Malmstrom 38, 241;
Institute of International Relations 210;
Paul, 38–40, 74, 103; William Cameron
3, 4, 9–10, 12–13, 18–19, 22–4, 26–48,
50–1, 53, 55–8, 62–82, 85–7, 95,
97–100, 103–4, 107–17, 119–20, 123,
125–6, 132–3, 138, 140, 143–4, 151,
153, 166–9, 184–6, 200–1, 208, 210–11,
217–19, 223, 226, 229–30, 238, 240–2,
249–53, 256, 259–60, 262, 266–7,
269, 272–3, 278, 283, 286–7, 290–1
trade (goods) 6, 10, 98, 100–1, 120,
123–5, 133, 141, 146, 155–7, 160–1,
174, 177, 189, 212–13, 281, 289, 293,
295–8, 301–5, 310, 315
Trans-Amazon highways 174, 219–20
Tucanoans, Eastern, 173–8; Western, 212
Tumi Chucua, Bolivia 218
Tzeltal Maya 50–1, 227
Tzotzil Maya 52–3
Tzutujil Maya 38, 43

Fishers of Men or Founders of Empire?
266.0237 S87S4

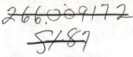

Uaupes, Brazil 220
Ubico, Jorge 41-2, 44, 48, 56
U.S.A.I.D. 7, 54-5, 57, 85, 88-90, 124,
   150, 205, 214-15, 218, 244-5
U.S: Air Force 85, 278; ambassadors,
   diplomats, embassies 8-10, 14, 30-1,
   48, 64, 68-71, 77, 80-1, 83-5, 94,
   103-4, 145, 151, 183-4, 200, 203-6,
   242, 292; Army 82-3; CIA 1, 3, 7, 10,
   14, 48, 50, 71, 81-8, 90, 151, 165-6,
   193, 198, 205, 213, 218, 223, 226,
   241-2, 245, 247, 264, 294; Congress
   70, 262; Department of State 80-2,
   103, 204, 220-1; Drug Enforcement
   Agency 165, 217; Government 4, 7-11,
   16, 24, 26-7, 48, 50, 63-4, 69-70,
   80-6, 103-4, 143, 165, 167, 192,
   199-201, 211, 218-19, 226, 229,
   242, 281; Marines 14, 19, 69, 89, 208;
   military advisors, aid, intervention,
   mission, veterans 3, 65, 69, 104, 150,
   154, 199, 244-5, 282; Panama Command 155, 278, 282, 285; Peace Corps
   54, 140, 151, 215, 218; Pentagon 88,
   108, 204, 242, 260; Rubber Development Corp. 102; Special Forces 10, 14,
   50, 88-90, 167
Universities 6, 12, 67, 77-8, 99, 104, 110,
   112, 118, 129, 132, 134, 138, 151, 166,
   168, 202-4, 206, 219, 221, 239, 252,
   254, 258, 287; *see also* International
   Linguistic Center
Urakusa, Peru 117, 161
uranium 174, 182
Uspanteco Maya 58

Vargas Llosa, Mario 117, 205
Varon Valencia, Abraham 182-3
Vasquez Benavides, Oscar 107-8, 117
Vaupes, Colombia 173-8, 184, 220
Velasco Alvarado, Juan 144, 202-3, 205,
   208
Venezuela 230, 248, 255
Victorious Life Testimony 72-3, 283
Vietnam War 7, 10, 50, 84, 86-93, 142,
   156, 198, 214, 240-1, 243, 246-7, 268

Wallis, Ethel 62, 67-8, 87, 133, 248, 285,
   290, 296, 302, 305
Wasserstrom, Robert 35, 51, 53, 94, 223
West Papua New Guinea 245-6, 261
Wheaton College 108, 114, 205, 282
Winaemi, Zoila 300-2, 306, 308, 310, 316
Witanocort, Leonardo 146-7, 149
witchcraft (doctors) 31-5, 43, 52, 123,
   130-1, 133, 146, 160, 170-1, 185, 198,

   212, 223, 268, 272, 297, 299, 305-6,
   313; *see also* shamanism
World Council of Churches (WCC) 1, 124,
   141-2, 193, 199, 213-14, 226
Wroughton, James 150, 168, 203-4
Wycliffe Bible Translators (WBT): 'Answers
   to Questions' 113; biennial conferences
   133, 178, 203, 237-8, 252, 265, 269;
   board of directors 78, 81, 104, 112, 114,
   192, 264-5; budget 5, 259-60; founding
   3-5, 62-78; fund-raising 5, 72, 77, 81,
   107-8, 111-12, 180, 187, 238, 259-63;
   furlough 266-7; membership 5,
   63-5, 74-9, 223, 237-40, 263-7;
   millennialism 1, 23, 58, 237-8, 240-1,
   273; policies of 5, 12-13, 63-5, 75-9,
   83-5; publicity 5, 72, 77-8, 80, 113,
   120, 132-3, 279, 281, 287, 294, 307-8;
   recruitment 192, 260, 263-4; social base
   in U.S. 3, 7, 22-30, 32, 46-7, 56, 259-63;
   Statement of Doctrine 5, 111, 158, 263;
   'Strategy for the Conclusion of Our Work
   in Peru' 113-14
Wycliffe, John 4

Xingu Park (Valley) 117, 219, 221

yaje 175, 177, 212
Yarinacocha, Peru 99, 109, 114, 116-21,
   124-6, 131, 133, 144, 146, 150-2,
   155-6, 204, 207, 209-10, 265, 268-72
Yucatan, Mexico 77

Zaparoans 315
zone of the generals 55, 57